T0178995

Enterprise Interoperability

Enterprise Interoperability

Interoperability for Agility, Resilience and Plasticity of Collaborations

I-ESA'14 Proceedings

Edited by

Matthieu Lauras
Martin Zelm
Bernard Archimède
Frédérick Bénaben
Guy Doumeingts

   WILEY

First published 2015 in Great Britain and the United States by ISTE Ltd and John Wiley & Sons, Inc.

ISTE Ltd
27-37 St George's Road
London SW19 4EU
UK

www.iste.co.uk

John Wiley & Sons, Inc.
111 River Street
Hoboken, NJ 07030
USA

www.wiley.com

British Library Cataloguing-in-Publication Data
A CIP record for this book is available from the British Library
ISBN 978-1-84821-799-7

Table of Contents

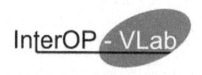

Preface

I-ESA 2014 Workshops on Enterprise Interoperability

Enterprises and organizations of any kind embedded in today's economic environment are deeply dependent on their ability to take part in collaborations. Consequently, it is strongly required for them to get actively involved for their own benefit in emerging, potentially opportunistic collaborative enterprise networks. The concept of "interoperability" has been defined by INTEROP-VLab as *"The ability of an enterprise system or application to interact with others at a low cost in a flexible approach"*. Consequently, interoperability of organizations appears as a major issue to succeed in building on the fly emerging enterprise networks.

The International Conference on Interoperability for Enterprise Systems and Applications (I-ESA 2014) was held under the motto *"interoperability for agility, resilience and plasticity of collaborations"* on March 26-28, 2014 and organized by the École des Mines d'Albi-Carmaux, France on behalf of the European Laboratory for Enterprise Interoperability (INTEROP-VLab).

On March 24-25, co-located with the conference, eight workshops and one doctoral symposium were held in four tracks complementing the program of the I-ESA'14 conference. The workshops and the doctoral symposium address areas of greatest current activity focusing on active discussions among the leading researchers in the area of Enterprise Interoperability. This part of the conference helps the community to operate effectively, building co-operative and supportive international links as well as providing new knowledge of on-going research to practitioners. The workshops and doctoral symposium aimed at exploiting new issues, challenges and solutions for Enterprise Interoperability (EI) and associated domains of innovation such as Smart Industry, Internet-Of-Things, Factories of the Future, EI Applications and Standardisation.

These proceedings include the short papers from the I-ESA'14 workshops and the doctoral symposium. The book is split up into 9 sections, one for each workshop and one for the doctoral symposium. All sections were organized following four tracks: (1) EI and Future Internet / Factory of the Future; (2) EI Application Domains and IT; (3) EI Standards; (4) EI Doctoral Symposium. For each section, a workshop report is provided summarizing the content and the issues discussed during the sessions.

The goal of the first track was to offer a discussion opportunity on interoperability issues regarding the use of Internet of Things on manufacturing environment (Workshops 1 and 3) on one hand, and regarding the potential of innovation derived from the use of digital methods, architectures and services such as Smart Networks (Workshops 2 and 4) on the other hand.

The second track focused on particular application domains that are looking for innovative solutions to support their strong collaborative needs. Thus, the track developed one workshop on the use of EI solution for Future City-Logistics (Workshop 5) and one on the use of EI solutions for Crisis / Disaster Management (Workshop 6).

The third track studied the recent developments in EI standardization. Two workshops were dedicated to this issue. The first one has proposed to focus on the management of standardization (Workshop 8) and the second one has chosen to work on the new knowledge on standardization developments in the manufacturing service domain (Workshop 9).

The last track, the doctoral symposium presented research results from selected dissertations. The session discussed EI knowledge issues, notably in terms of gathering through social networks or Internet of Things and of exploitation through innovative decision support systems.

Again, the I-ESA workshops and doctoral symposium have succeeded in providing active, rich and efficient discussions and debates between the attendees. Hence, a new research agenda on Enterprise Interoperability appeared and concrete industrial exploitations of current research works became visible.

Matthieu Lauras, Workshops Co-chair
Martin Zelm, Workshops Co-chair
Bernard Archimède, Doctoral Symposium Chair
Frédérick Bénaben, Conference Chair
Guy Doumeingts, INTEROP-VLab General Manager

Workshop 1

IoT Interoperability for Manufacturing:
Challenges and Experiences

Report

Domenico Rotondi

TXT e-solutions SPA
70010 Valenzano (BA), Italy
domenico.rotondi@txtgroup.com

The goal of I-ESA 2014 Workshop 1 titled IoT Interoperability for Manufacturing: challenges and experiences was to offer a discussion opportunity on interoperability issues when the Internet of Things is applied in the manufacturing environment.

Indeed the new industrial wave envisaged by the German Industry 4.0 programme and the General Electric promoted Industrial Internet, will see the development and deployment of intelligent devices, intelligent systems, and intelligent decision making to support a deeper integration of the physical world (machines, facilities, fleets, networks, etc.) with the digital world and virtual world.

As planned the workshop held on 24 March, 14:00-18:00 had two specific sub-sessions the 1st one addressing the technological and scientific challenges, while the 2nd one focused on the business aspects and test cases. Both sub-sessions had a short introduction and 3 specific presentations, followed by an open discussion.

Technological & scientific challenges session

1. *Smart Industry Services in times of Internet of Things and Cloud Computing – J. Martin Serrano (DERI)*

   The presentation discussed the issues related to the in-field deployment of Smart Industry Services there have high demands for information interoperability and Linked Data to enable automated services composition. It is challenging to make smart systems capable to deal with such automation and enable complex operations in the absence of high degree of interoperability, as main requirement a large number of open services are defined by diverse and heterogeneous systems.

2. *Designing and Executing Interoperable IoT Manufacturing Systems – Udo Kannengiesser (Metasonic)*

   This presentation proposed a conceptual framework for designing and executing sustainable, interoperable IoT-based manufacturing systems. It is motivated by the observation that manufacturing systems operate in a complex and dynamic environment, requiring constant evolution in order to be sustainable. It is based on a view of interoperable agent-based systems as the results of continuous re-design processes, addressing changing needs from the socio-technical, ecological or economic environment. The presentation introduced the Function-Behaviour-Structure (FBS) framework from design science to describe the fundamental processes involved in re-designing these systems.

3. *IoT Research position in interoperability to address manufacturing challenges – Philippe Cousin (eglobalmark)*

The presentation introduced discussion within the Internet of things research cluster (IERC) on interoperability challenges and in particular on semantic interoperability. It presented IoT challenges in technical and semantic interoperability also as defined in an EU position paper to be published in 2014. Business and manufacturing aspects were not been taken into account yet but there is an important need to include requirement and challenges from this area as there are a lot of common issues and additional values that experience in manufacturing can bring. In particular on semantic discovery and interoperability issues related to intangible assets and to products-services manufacturing ecosystems.

Business aspects & test cases session

I. *Manufacturing integration challenge: top-down Interoperability and bottom-up Visibility toward a global information backbone – Van Khai Nguyen (Cadcamation)*

This presentation was focused on introducing the drastic shift of the manufacturing paradigm from the mechanic-based system to the computer-assisted system driven by knowledge. The end-to-end process integration toward the virtual factory could be realized if only based on a fully digital factory model composed by Product, Process, Resource and Plant and their live data throughout their lifecycle. Can standards help solve this "big picture" integration issue? Knowing that the top-down integration depends on application interoperability while the bottom-up integration starts on big data analytics!

II. *An improved decision support system in factory shop-floor through an IoT approach – Pierluigi Petrali (Whirlpool)*

This presentation discussed how the deployment of low cost automation and pervasive computing, transformed modern shop-floor into a big data generation engine. This huge quantity of data and information are rarely used in an effective way, both in real time and analytical post-processing. The speech discussed how an IoT approach could be designed to leverage this potential and how factories of the future should transform to maximize its effect.

III.   *Leveraging IoT Interoperability for Enhanced Business Process in Smart, Digital and Virtual Factories – June Sola (Innovalia)*

This speech focused on quickly discussing how IoT technologies are enabling technologies for new Smart Manufacturing solutions. IoT Interopeability opens the opportunity to develop horizontal platforms that provide services and information that can be linked across multiple domains and collaborators. This new scenario with increased visibility, rich and abundant real-time information about many kinds of sensors and product information; are the perfect ground to build new business processes that contribute towards STEEP objectives of European re-industrialization. The presentation quickly discussed the new technical capabilities leveraged by IoT interoperability frameworks such as those developed as part of the ComVantage and FITMAN projects, as well as the new business models and business processes that can be implemented by manufacturing industries based on these new technical foundations.

The discussion focused some of the issues highlighted by the presentations, especially on the need to have supporting tools and methodologies that can help structuring and formalizing the evolution of the ICT manufacturing systems the deployment of IoT and the new business models request.

Smart Industry Services in Times of Internet of Things and Cloud Computing

Martin Serrano — Panos Dimitropoulos

Insight Centre for Data Analytics, NUI Galway, Galway City, Ireland
(Digital Enterprise Research Institute – DERI)
martin.serrano@deri.com

Sensap Microsystems, Athens City, Greece
pdimi@sensap.eu

ABSTRACT. This paper discusses about today's industry transformation process towards smarter industry, by means of semantic technologies, Internet of things and cloud computing enabling more intelligent services. In the field of smart industry services there are high demands for using information interoperability to, for example, enable automated services composition and provide to the systems with intelligence. It is challenging to make smart systems capable to deal with such automation and enable complex operations in the absence of high degree of interoperability, as main requirement a large number of open services that must be integrated are defined by diverse and heterogeneous systems. By using Internet of things, heterogeneity issues can be overcome and by means of cloud computing, the distributed storage and large-scale processing required capacity addressed. A specific scenario from the OpenIoT framework is briefly discussed as an exemplar approach to support the transformation towards smarter industries in times of Internet of Things and Cloud Computing.

KEYWORDS: Cloud Computing, Internet of Things, Service Openness, Service Composition, Smarter Industry, Manufacturing.

1. Introduction – Internet of Things in the Manufacturing Industry

The benefits of the Internet of things (IoT) technologies in the area of manufacturing have motivated enormous progress and potentially are generating big economic impact. Based on the advent and deployment of RFID solutions, the Internet of things is being consolidated as the progress engine in the manufacturing sector and smart industry in general [Johnson02], [Rockwell04]. RFID deployments have exposed benefits associated with the reduction of labour and inventory costs, as well as other techno-economic benefits [Lee04], [Toffaletti10]. These benefits stem from the use of unique identification (including the ability for serialization), item level track and trace and enhanced track and trace, automated genealogy, elimination of the need for line-of-sight for data readability and, finally, historical tracing. This gave rise to a number of RFID deployments for manufacturing, which however tend to be isolated and focused on specific companies and cases studies [Brintrup08].

In general, RFID deployments in manufacturing cover all the different stages of the production process. For example, in the area of product design the EU FP6 PROMISE project [Promise04] has validated the RFID based linking of field usage data with the product design stage, with a view to improving future designs of products. In terms of production planning, RFID has been used to optimize production rescheduling [Hozak08], as well as dynamic improvements in production planning [Li06].

Several case studies have also focused on the production stage, mainly based on tracking and tracing of the production processes/steps towards improving quality [Huang07], scheduling and production decision making. Other (validated) RFID applications in manufacturing include storage management of perishable materials [Mills-Harris05], Internet-based inventory control [Zhou07], automating outbound shipments of a product after manufacturing [Wessel06], as well as reconfiguring machines in response to changed product configurations [Huang07]. Most of the above RFID-based solutions are custom system integrated on the basis of the specific manufacturing requirements (for various industries), and implemented in a way that data silos have been created rather than solutions derived from general-purpose platforms using more large-deployed infrastructure (cloud).

IoT solutions for manufacturing have been gradually extended in order to include multiple sensors, actuators and devices of the shop floor in addition to RFID. Practical solutions have been developed as part of recent IoT projects (such as IoT@Work – see [Dürkop12] and [Gusmeroli12]), but also as part of IoT vendors' offering. Cisco, SAP and Bosch have undertaken prominent commercial efforts leading the market and opening a new vision towards how the Internet in general will look like in the future.

A prominent example is advertised by Ford Focus Electric, which has built its own Internet of Things that enables communication and data exchange across devices within its vehicles, but also between in-vehicle devices and the company that built it. Ford has built a cloud-based secure server enabling vehicle owners to access a wide range of information via an on-board wireless module and a smartphone app or through Ford's website. The vehicle information provided includes battery state of charge, overall efficiency, energy consumption, and braking regeneration. This infrastructure enables the issue of appropriate alerts in the case of problems. Furthermore, it provides the means for reporting the car's location when it's lost in a parking lot, being used by the owner's teenage drivers, or stolen[1].

Cisco emphasizes on the convergence of factory systems with IT networks, as part of its wider portfolio of IoT-related solutions. On the other hand, SAP and Bosch promote the communication and interconnection of the numerous devices that comprise a plant for tasks such as manufacturing performance monitoring and predictive maintenance. Recently, solutions that combine IoT with the cloud (i.e., as promoted by OpenIoT) have been also reported [Soldatos12][Serrano13].

In general, IoT Cloud solutions are expected to play significant role in the manufacturing industry, as also proclaimed by the initiative Industry 4.0[2], a term introduced by representatives of German industry leaders, researchers, industry association, and unions.

2. Smarter Services by Service Composition in Cloud Environments

Currently it is more than evident the business benefits of cloud systems, apart of the reduction in maintenance cost the capacity to run more robust processes, cloud significantly increase systems flexibility to react to user service demands efficiently and by replacing, in a best practice manner, a plethora of proprietary software platforms with generic solutions supporting standardised development and scalable stacks over the Internet. Thus Cloud is ideally the best ecosystem for service composition. Research initiatives addressing this cloud-based design trend and inspired mainly by software oriented architectures (SOA) requirements argue that the future rely in application layers above virtual infrastructures that can meet various requirements whilst keeping a very simplistic, almost unmanaged network. IP for the underlying Internet for example, GENI NSF-funded initiative to rebuild the Internet [GENI, online Feb 2011] is an example of this. Others argue that the importance of wireless access networks requires a more fundamental re-design of the core Internet Protocols themselves [Clean Slate, Online April 2011][AKARI, Online May 2011]. Whilst this debate races nothing is a clear outcome in terms of information interoperability or data models sharing.

The service composition is a complex process; it implies the identification of service features and elements, as well as it implies the possible evaluation of operation and functionality before the new service can be composed. Thus it can be regulated by semantic rules where if multiple operations are required, then these

---

1. Karen Wilhelm, "The Internet of Things in Manufacturing", *Manufacturing Pulse Feature Story*, May 13, 2013, available at: http://www.manufacturingpulse.com/.
2. Stefan Ferber, "Industry 4.0 – Germany takes first steps toward the next industrial revolution", available at: http://blog.bosch-si.com/industry-4-0-germany-takes-first-steps-toward-the-next-industrial-revolution/

operations are performed using the appropriate applications, as defined by service composition rules and/or polices defined by the data associations. Best practices in SOA suggest that a narrow focus on designing optimal networking protocols in isolation is too limited; instead a more abstracted view is required. This offers the advantage of non-dependency on physical infrastructures offering limited amount of services. In this view multiple services are now result of subservices, this method is commonly called composition. When meaning of various distributed protocols and delivering sub-services orchestrate multiple sub services, the operations (e.g., applications, computing processing, distribution of services, networking) can be done more efficiently. In other terms, a more realistic way of offering services is following mechanisms to organise operations according to changes in the parameters and based on users needs. However, realistically this new holistic view increasingly stops to become a matter of critical infrastructure, in this sense cloud computing infrastructures with virtualisation, as main driver is a promising alternative of solution to this stopping problem.

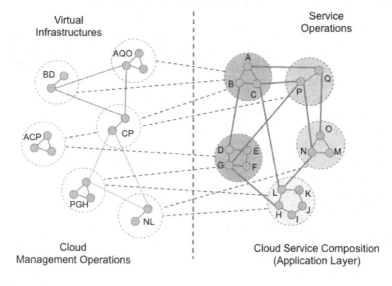

Figure 1. *Service Composition processes representation on Cloud Environments*

Figure 1 depicts the mentioned cloud service composition, its implementation relies on the inference plane [Serrano09], or knowledge layer where the exchange of information (Linked-Data structures) [Decker08] facilitates knowledge-driven support and generation of cloud composed services with operations by enabling interoperable information on networked connected objects [Hauswirth11]. From down to top and having cloud infrastructures representation as example, isolated components representations are depicted with no capacities of sharing information, linked data mechanisms are missing and "X" represented. In an upper Layer linked mechanism are represented and used to define virtual infrastructure operations and expose them externally. So the migrations towards composed services and networks increases providing solutions to a number of significant technical issues by using more standard information exchange and promoting sharing information. At the upper part of the linked data mechanisms are supported by ontology representations and ontology-based mapping allowing at the same time original services (e.g., ABC) can be managed effectively and most important offering open opportunities for a knowledge-based service-oriented support having a fundamental impact on cloud composition of services (e.g., BD, AQO, PGH, etc.) by a complete information sharing and sub-services representation (e.g., bd, cl, pnl, nl).

In this sense, there are some interesting approaches, some of them following linked-data principles some others SOA principles; the commonality in all of them is the nature of information sharing between the different components or subservices. [Chen09] introduces an approach where a matching algorithm SMA between cloud computing services of multiple input/output parameters is used. The algorithm considers the semantic similarity of concepts in specific lexical parameters. Particularly a service composition algorithm Fast-EP and the improved FastB+-EP were used as reference. Within this approach QoS information is utilized to rank the search results and it is shown based on experiment that this approach has better efficiency of service composition than other traditional approaches.

In other interesting approach [Gutierrez-Garcia10] concentrates on cloud service provider requirements and their mappings with the cloud infrastructure resources in order to automate the service composition process. Founded on agent-based applications their propose a three-layered multi-agent system which by using self-organizing principles the agents make use of contract net protocol to evolve and generate adaptive service compositions. This approach demonstrates how by composing the incomplete information and make a comparison with available information about resources operations for generating a new service can be to allocate.

Further activities have been proposed [Deloitte09] more in the sense of what cloud computing can offer for new services definition rather than for re-using of services that are suitable to host new enterprise services. But while these different approach concentrates on offerings new services, even if they provide clear benefit to particular corporations, it is limited the capacity of what offers they have for composing services. The fact that applications or service systems cannot post the information they can offer as a sub-service does not help to scale or generate new enterprise enriched services. From this point of view and as an inherent feature in cloud systems, service composition is restricted or limited. However this last has not to be understood as a weakness, it is a particular and specific service-goal orientation in how to cope with the service definition and their requirement. It is just meaning that in cloud systems, it simply means composition is limited for regulations or policies and not for computing resources. In this paper we just concentrate on describing the alternatives and not to compare one or other design approach.

3. Linked Data and Services Management

A current activity, attracting the attention of many research and industrial communities is the formalization of data models (ontology engineering). Enabling information for management of services and control of operations is an example where this formalization is used [Serrano07]. This process focuses in the semantic enrichment task where descriptive references about simple data entries are used to extend data meaning (semantic aggregation), to for example, provide an extensible, reusable, common and manageable linked data plane, also referenced as inference plane [Serrano09]. Thus management information described in both enterprise and infrastructure data models (physical or virtual) with ontological data can be used inherently in both domains

The semantic aggregation can be seen as a tool to integrate user data with the management service operations, to offers a more complete understanding of user's contents based on their operational relationships and hence, a more inclusive governance of the management of components in the infrastructure (resources, devices, networks, systems) and or services inclusive. The objective is sharing the integrated management information within different management systems (liked data). This approach is to use ontologies as the mechanism to generate a formal description, which represents the collection and formal representation for network management data models and endow such models with the necessary semantic richness and formalisms to represent different types of information needed to be integrated in network management operations. Using a formal methodology the user's contents represent values used in various service management operations, thus the knowledge-based approach over the inference plane [Strassner07] aims to be a solution that uses ontologies to support interoperability and extensibility required in the systems handling end-user contents for pervasive applications [Serrano09].

4. Smarter Services for Manufacturing Industry

In the manufacturing industry there is huge demand for making services more efficient; on-demand usage of computing resources and services seems as a viable alternative, but as the same time a restriction because of the limited control on aspects related with the services provisioning (privacy and security mainly) in order to provide scalability and other features by means of using cloud infrastructures. However, in the race for deploying cloud computing services, solutions enabling information interoperability between the different service applications or service stacks (information sharing) have emerged and as consequence the industry of services is every day getting more importance and evolving positively towards enabling smarter services.

The OpenIoT Cloud-based platform provides opportunities for integrating such solutions, while providing compelling features in terms of sensors and data streams integration, but also in terms of dynamic sensors and sensor data discovery and use between different manufactory environments as depicted in Figure 2.

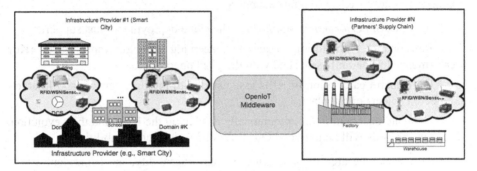

Figure 2. *OpenIoT manufacturing use case on Cloud Environments*

OpenIoT can act as a blueprint framework that will allow solution makers (notably SMEs) to provide and experiment with novel IoT cloud-based technologies for manufacturers, notably small or medium end users that do not have the equity capital to invest on the emerging solutions of the large vendors. OpenIoT's strong points relate to versatility and innovation, yet the prototypes to be developed in the scope of the project will not be able to compete in terms of maturity and robustness with the above-mentioned commercial solutions. However OpenIoT can be seen OpenIoT as a novel sensor cloud system, which allows users/integrators to select the most appropriate sensors for a given job/task, while also filtering their data. Currently existing solutions offer only primitive sensor discovery and virtually no sensor orchestration functionalities so far.

OpenIoT is perceived as a middleware solution for the Dynamic Integration and Discovery for the Internet of Things enabling Service Creation and Delivery by means of interoperable self-organizing management on cloud environments for sensors, sensor networks and smart devices along with semantic open-linked data techniques, utility computing, and including security and privacy schemes.

The OpenIoT manufacturing application showcase the ability of a cloud-based system platform to deploy and execute multiple on-demand utility-based services over a sensor and actuator infrastructure within a manufacturing plant. For the purposes of the use case, manufacturing tasks that maintains warehouses of source and second materials, as well as manufacturing plants is described. The basic setting considers that within each manufacturing plant, there are multiple production lines. Each of the production lines executes a production phase or a task of the production processes. Each production line involves certain machines, which feature a specific serial number. In the scope of the production process, different production resources (e.g., tools) are associated with the machines of the production lines for specific time intervals. This association concerns the production of specific numbers/units of finished products. While the manufacturing sector is wide, there are common features a cloud-based system must support.

In the area of *performance monitoring*, the cloud deployment must support:

– Performance monitoring requests concerning one or more KPIs (Key Performance Indicators) associated with the plant operation.

– On-demand calculation of KPIs associated with multiple sensors and Internet-connected objects of the plant.

– Generate dashboards for automatically displaying the KPIs and their evolution. These dashboards will be based on OpenIoT's HMI/mashup capabilities.

Likewise, in the area of production process traceability, the cloud deployment must support:

– Requests for tracing specific production orders, task or steps and report on their quality.

– Be able to trace production orders, steps or tasks (i.e., different granularities).

– Be able to connect to actionable logics including M2M interactions (e.g., tagging of a lot, configuration of a machine or tool).

– The process and its quality characteristics will be visualised (e.g., based on appropriate mashups).

A possible implementation of the OpenIoT middleware in the manufacturing domain could leverage readily available blueprint implementations of semantic infrastructures for other areas (such as IoT), which have been already realized by IERC projects (e.g., the OpenIoT open source cloud-based discovery infrastructure for IoT resources, which is available at: https://github.com/OpenIotOrg/openiot/).

5. Conclusions

In this paper research trends and main efforts for service composition have been discussed towards designing and building composed services in cloud environments for the Internet of Things in the framework of Smarter Industries as implementation main scenarios in Manufacturing is given as an application example in the framework of the OpenIoT project.

Information sharing is a crucial activity to satisfy the requirement in convergence service and particularly manufacturing systems. Implications for composing services and virtual infrastructures management are still under research (service composition in cloud).

In cloud environments high demands of information interoperability and of semantic annotation (linked data) are demanded to satisfy service discovering and services composition requirements being controlled by diverse, heterogeneous systems and thus make more dynamic the perform of cloud-based system.

Remaining research challenges regarding information model extensibility and information dissemination conduct our attention to continue our activity towards virtual infrastructure management, perform more cloud service control experiments and look for full linked data representations for service composition in cloud environments.

6. Acknowledgments

Part of this work has been carried out in the scope of the project ICT OpenIoT Project (Open source blueprint for large scale self-organizing cloud environments for IoT applications), which is co-funded by the European Commission under seventh framework program, contract number FP7-ICT-2011-7-287305-OpenIoT and by the GAMBAS Project (Generic Adaptive Middleware for Behaviour-driven Autonomous Services), contract number FP7-ICT-2011-7-287661-GAMBAS. Special acknowledge for all partners of the OpenIoT project.

7. References

[AKARI] Architecture Design Project for New Generation Network, http://akari-project.nict.go.jp/eng/index2.htm.

[Brintrup08] Alexandra Brintrup, Paul Roberts, Osama Ghwash, Mark Astle, "Definition of RFID Decision Support System for Manufacturing Applications", *BRIDGE Project White Paper*, June 2008.

[Clean Slate] Clean Slate Program, Stanford University, http://cleanslate.stanford.edu.

[Deloitte09] Deloitte Technical Report on Cloud Computing, "A collection of working papers Demystifying Clouds: Exploring Cloud and Service Grid Architectures" by Thomas B Winans and John Seely Brown, Deloitte, 2009.

[Decker 2008] Decker, Stefan, Hauswirth, Manfred, "Enabling Networked Knowledge", *Proceedings of the 12th International Workshop on Cooperative Information Agents XII* (CIA 2008), LNCS, 5180, Prague, Czech Republic, 2008.

[Dürkop12] Lars Dürkop, Henning Trsek, Jürgen Jasperneite, Lukasz Wisniewski, "Towards Autoconfiguration of Industrial Automation Systems: A Case Study Using PROFINET

IO", *17th IEEE International Conference on Emerging Technologies & Factory Automation* (ETFA 2012), Kraków, Poland, September 2012.

[Gusmeroli12] Sergio Gusmeroli, Salvatore Piccione, Domenico Rotondi. "IoT@Work Automation Middleware System Design and Architecture", *17th IEEE International Conference on Emerging Technologies & Factory Automation* (ETFA 2012), Kraków, Poland, September 2012.

[Hauswirth11] Hauswirth, Manfred, Pfisterer, Dennis, Decker, Stefan, "Making Internet-Connected Objects readily useful", *Interconnecting Smart Objects with the Internet Workshop*, Prague, 2011.

[Hozak08] Hozak K., Hill J. A., "Issues and opportunities regarding replanning and rescheduling frequencies", *International Journal of Production Research*. 99999(1):1-16, 2008.

[Huang07] Huang G.Q., Zhang Y.F., Jiang P.Y., "RFID-based wireless manufacturing for real-time management of job shop WIP inventories", *International Journal of Advanced Manufacturing Technology*, 2007.

[Johnson02] Johnson D., "RFID tags improve tracking, quality on Ford line in Mexico", *Control Engineering*, 11:16-16, 2002.

[Lee04] Lee Y M., Cheng F., Leung Y. T., "Exploring the Impact of RFID Supply Chain Dynamics", *Proceedings, Winter Simulation Conference*, pp.1145-1152, 2004.

[Li06] Li D., Kehoe D., Drake P., "Dynamic planning with a wireless product identification technology in food supply chains", *International Journal of Advanced Manufacturing Technology*, 30:938-944, 2006.

[Mills-Harris05] Mills-Harris M. D., Soylemezoglu A., Saygin C., RFID Data-based Inventory Management of Time-Sensitive Materials. *31st Annual Conference of the IEEE Industrial Electronics Society (IECON'05) Special Session: Integrated Manufacturing and Service Systems*, Raleigh, North Carolina, 6-10 Nov. 2005.

[Promise04] PROMISE: EU project FP6-IST-IP-507100, Product Lifecycle Management and Information Tracking using Smart Embedded Systems; http://www.promise.no

[Rockwell04] Rockwell Automation, "Global Manufacturing Solutions; RFID in manufacturing: A practical guide on extracting measurable value from RFID implementations in plant and warehousing operations", http://www.rockwellautomation.com, October 2004.

[Serrano13] Martin Serrano, Hoan Nguyen M. Quoc, Manfred Hauswirth, Wei Wang, Payam Barnaghi, Philippe Cousin, "Open Services for IoT Cloud Applications in the Future Internet", *IEEE proceedings of the 2nd IEEE WoWMoM 2013 workshop on the Internet of Things and Smart Objects*, IoT-SoS, http://www2.ing.unipi.it/iot-sos2013, Spain, 2013.

[Serrano09] Serrano, M. Strassner J. and ÓFoghlú, M., "A Formal Approach for the Inference Plane Supporting Integrated Management Tasks in the Future Internet", *1st IFIP/IEEE ManFI International Workshop*, 1-5 June 2009, Long Island, NY, USA.

[Soldatos12] John Soldatos, Martin Serrano, Manfred Hauswirth, "Convergence of Utility Computing with the Internet-of-Things", *IEEE 2012 Sixth International Conference on Innovative Mobile and Internet Services in Ubiquitous Computing* (IMIS 2012).

[Toffaletti10] Sebastiano Toffaletti and John Soldatos, "RFID-ROI-SME Project Promises Big Help for Small Business", *RFID Journal*, 14 June 2010.

[Zhou07] Zhou S., Ling W. Peng Z., An RFID-based remote monitoring system for enterprise internal production management, *Int J Adv Manuf Technol*, 2007.

Designing and Executing Interoperable IoT Manufacturing Systems

Udo Kannengiesser* — Georg Weichhart*'**

Metasonic AG, Pfaffenhofen, Germany
Udo.Kannengiesser@metasonic.de
Georg.Weichhart@metasonic.de

** *Johannes Kepler University, Linz*
Department of Communications Engineering, Business Informatics
Georg.Weichhart@jku.at

ABSTRACT. *This paper proposes a conceptual framework for designing and executing sustainable, interoperable IoT-based manufacturing systems. It is motivated by the observation that manufacturing systems operate in a complex and dynamic environment, requiring constant evolution in order to be sustainable. It is based on a view of interoperable agent-based systems as the results of continuous re-design processes, addressing changing needs from the socio-technical, ecological or economic environment. The paper uses the Function-Behaviour-Structure (FBS) framework from design science to describe the fundamental processes involved in re-designing these systems.*

KEYWORDS: *FBS Framework, S-BPM, Multi-Agent Manufacturing, Interoperability.*

1. Introduction

Modern enterprises are required to continuously evolve in a dynamic environment. At the same time the products and manufacturing processes are getting more and more complex (Weichhart 2014). From a systems theory perspective, enterprises can be viewed as systems combining multiple (sub-)systems (i.e., a single manufacturing enterprise or a supply network). Manufacturing systems that are interoperable are more resilient than integrated systems (one extreme) or non-compatible systems (other extreme) (Dassisti et al. 2013). The observed dynamics requires a design approach supporting the co-construction of (sub-)systems. In enterprise systems, these sub-systems consist of collaborating (human and artificial) agents.

The rest of the paper is organised as follows. Section 2 discusses interoperability solutions for dynamic enterprise environments. Section 3 introduces a generic design framework and specialises it for designing and re-designing agent-based manufacturing systems. Section 4 concludes the paper.

2. Interoperability of Enterprise Systems in Dynamic Environments

Research in Enterprise Interoperability provides a problem-space-solution cube which allows the classification of interoperability solutions (see Chen et al. 2008, Ducq et al. 2012). The interoperability solution dimension distinguishes three strategies for overcoming interoperability barriers with respect to different concerns (Chen et al. 2008, Ducq et al. 2012): Integrated approach, Unified approach, and Federated approach.

Dynamics in the environment parts to be adapted. By definition, changing one part of an integrated system affects the overall system, due to the strong coupling of the sub-systems. The underlying assumption does not allow an integrated approach.

On the one hand, a federated approach is inefficient, as changing a part requires to renegotiate the interfaces. On the other hand, this aspect provides an additional level of flexibility. Therefore we are building on an approach which attempts unification with respect to technological interoperability barriers and federation with respect to organisational and conceptual barriers.

Weichhart and Wachholder (2014) have shown that Subject-oriented Business Process Management (S-BPM) (Fleischmann et al 2012) can provide the basis of a unified approach for interoperable enterprise systems. S-BPM views enterprise systems as sets of active entities (representing "subjects") that communicate via messages. Subjects represent process-centric roles executed by human or artificial agents. Commercial tool support (www.metasonic.de) is available for executing processes in enterprise systems and unifying the interaction of legacy systems by wrapping these with subjects. Within an on-going FP7 Factories of the Future project (www.so-pc-pro.eu) this support is currently extended to include production machines as subjects within a process. S-BPM provides a language and management method for design and execution of a unified model of the manufacturing system. The overall objective of the S-BPM approach is to be simple, flexible and suitable for end-users to model processes, allowing them to participate in the system (re-)design making use of their work knowledge.

As manufacturing systems involve human agents, different views and mental models of the system may exist. System participants need to negotiate a common understanding of work processes (Oppl et al. 2014). Here the proposed approach moves towards the "federated approach" category in the interoperability framework.

3. Designing and Re-Designing Interoperable Systems

The Function-Behaviour-Structure (FBS) framework (Gero 1990) from design science provides a uniform representation to describe any type of system including agents and multi-agent systems (Gero et al. 2007). In this paper, we will use the generic term "agent system" to refer to single agents and multi-agent systems.

Function (F) represents the teleology or purpose of the agent system. *Behaviour (B)* represents the attributes that can be derived from the structure of the agent system and its interactions with the environment. These attributes comprise descriptions of how the agent system operates in terms of its actions in response to an input, and measures of performance associated with these actions. *Structure (S)* represents the components of the agent system and their relationships; i.e., "what the agent system consists of". It may be conceptualized in terms of the agent system's physical structure (hardware), virtual structure (software, or organizational structure) or cognitive structure (beliefs, desires, intentions, etc.).

These three ontological categories form the basis of the FBS framework, shown in Fig. 1. It has eight labelled processes that are seen fundamental for all designing. They may occur in any order (Gero 1990).

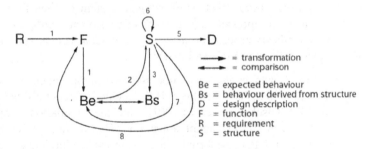

Figure 1. *The FBS framework*

3.1. *Specifying Expected System Behaviour*

Designing usually commences with formulating a set of functions and expected behaviours (process 1 in Figure 1), based on perceived or given needs stated as requirements (R). This process sets up a problem space guiding the search for design solutions.

Functions include overall system goals such as providing high quality products, flexible production, and a safe work environment. Some of these functions can be refined into subfunctions. S-BPM provides the notion of subjects as a representation of subfunctions that together produce operational system functions in terms of a process.

A set of expected behaviours (Be) are then formulated to achieve the functions (and subfunctions). We can generally distinguish three types of behaviours: (1) external (or black-box) behaviours that consist only of input-output descriptions, (2) internal behaviours that provide more details about the steps and decisions leading to the externally visible behaviour, and (3) performance measures associated with the external or internal behaviour, often referred to as Key Performance Indicators (KPIs). S-BPM provides representations for external and internal behaviours: Subject interaction diagrams (SIDs) describe external behaviours in terms of the messages exchanged between multiple subjects. Subject behaviour diagrams (SBDs) describe internal behaviours using sets of states connected by transitions (i.e., as state machines).

3.2. *Continuously Generating, Assessing and Deploying System Solutions*

Once the problem space is formulated, the solution space can be explored by means of synthesising (process 2), analysing (process 3), evaluating (process 4) and documenting (process 5) candidate agent systems that exhibit the formulated behaviour. This is often performed iteratively and may occur even after a design solution has been implemented and deployed.

Synthesising (process 2) the structure of an agent system is often facilitated by existing agents or agent components and tools to compose and configure them. S-BPM supports this synthesis process by assigning individual agents and groups of agents to the subjects defined in SIDs and SBDs.

Analysis (process 3) and evaluation (process 4) of human agent systems are supported by the validation phase of the S-BPM method. Recent extensions and tools such as jSIM (Fleischmann et al. 2012) include simulation support for computational agents with limited agent autonomy. This allows analysing agent systems by simulating their internal and external behaviours "offline". Kannengiesser (2014) shows how S-BPM models can be used as a basis for value stream analysis in lean manufacturing. Tool support for specifying KPIs associated with S-BPM diagrams is available (Fleischmann et al. 2012).

Documentation (process 5) of agent systems is often done for purposes of deployment. The formal underpinnings of S-BPM, based on abstract state machines and process grammars, provide a design description that is directly executable including in real-time production environments (Kannengiesser 2013).

3.3. *Reformulating Problem and Solution Spaces*

After a design for an agent system is found, it can be reformulated in terms of its structure (process 6), its expected behaviour (process 7) or its function (process 8).

This allows adapting the system to changed environments or novel opportunities (e.g., technological innovations) that cannot be incorporated using existing design concepts. These reformulations can be viewed as modifying the problem or solution space within which new design solutions can be found using the synthesis-analysis-evaluation cycles described above.

Reformulating the structure (process 6) of an agent system involves modifying the set of candidate agent systems to subjects, often by introducing new types of agents. For example, an existing manufacturing system may be reformulated by adding an intelligent sensor for detecting inflammable gases. This can be a response to new requirements related to human safety.

Reformulating the behaviour (process 7) of an agent system may concern internal behaviour, external behaviour, and KPIs. For example, one may leverage extended sensing capabilities of agents by including a new data analysis activity in an SBD (as new internal behaviour), new communication activities to inform other agents about the results of these analyses (as new external behaviour), and new KPIs such as sensor response time and accuracy.

Reformulating the functions (process 8) of an agent system includes modifying an existing set of subjects. This may occur in response to new needs from the environment (e.g., new business or manufacturing strategies, and changed competitive environments) or internally identified opportunities (e.g., enhanced safety features provided by a new sensing technology).

4. Conclusions

In this paper we show that an existing framework from design science captures the adaptation of interoperable IoT manufacturing systems to dynamic environments. The FBS framework provides an ontological description of these processes. It is able to capture the re-design of IoT manufacturing systems that are in many ways heterogeneous and dynamic. This opens up the potential for new knowledge-based support systems, based on existing applications of FBS in design science. This paper has also shown that the S-BPM approach supports most of the processes in the FBS framework. It aligns with recent work proposing S-BPM as a basis for representing interoperable systems.

5. Acknowledgements

Udo Kannengiesser has received funding from the European Union Seventh Framework Programme FP7-2013-NMP-ICT-FOF(RTD) under grant agreement n°609190: http://www.so-pc-pro.eu/. Georg Weichhart has received funding from the European Commission within the Marie Curie Industry and Academia

Partnerships and Pathways (IAPP) programme under grant agreement no 286083: http://www.ianes.eu.

6. References

Chen D, Vallespir B, Daclin N., "An Approach for Enterprise Interoperability Measurement". *MoDISE-EUS'08*, 2008.

Dassisti M, Jardim-Goncalves R, Molina A, Noran O, Panetto H, Zdravković MM, Demey Y, Panetto H., Sustainability and Interoperability: Two Facets of the Same Gold Medal. *On the Move to Meaningful Internet Systems: OTM 2013 Workshops*, Berlin: Springer; 2013.

Ducq Y, Chen D, Doumeingts G., "A contribution of system theory to sustainable enterprise interoperability science base". *Computers in Industry*. vol 63, 2012, pp.844-885.

Fleischmann A, Schmidt W, Stary C, Obermeier S, Börger E., *Subject-Oriented Business Process Management*. Springer, 2012.

Gero JS. "Design prototypes: A knowledge representation schema for design". *AI Magazine* 1990, vol. 11 no. 4, pp.26-36.

Gero JS, Kannengiesser U., "An ontology of situated design teams". *AIEDAM 2007*; vol. 21 no.3, pp.295-308.

Kannengiesser U., "Supporting Value Stream Design Using S-BPM". *Proceedings of S-BPM-ONE, Lecture Notes in Business Information Processing (LNBIP)*, Springer, 2014.

Kannengiesser U, Müller H., "Subject-Orientation for Human-Centred Production: A Research Agenda". *S-BPM ONE - Running Processes, Lecture Notes in Business Information Processing (LNBIP)*, Springer, 2013, pp.235-244.

Oppl S., Stary C., "Facilitating Shared Understanding of work situations using a Tangible Tabletop Interface". *Behaviour & Information Technology*, 2014, pp.1-17.

Weichhart G., "Requirements for Supporting Enterprise Interoperability in Dynamic Environments", *Enterprise Interoperability VI, Proceedings of the I-ESA Conferences 7*, March, Albi, France, pp.479-488.

Weichhart G, Wacholder D., "On the Interoperability Contributions of S-BPM", *Proceedings of S-BPM ONE, LNBIP*, Springer, 2014.

Internet of Things Research on Semantic Interoperability to Address Manufacturing Challenges

Philippe Cousin* — Martin Serrano** — John Soldatos***

* Easy Global Market
Sophia Antipolis, France
philippe.cousin@eglobalmark.com

** Insight-NUIG
Galway, Ireland
martin.serrano@deri.com

*** Athens Information Technology
Athens, Greece
jsol@ait.gr

ABSTRACT. *This paper gives an overview on interoperability challenges and in particular for semantic interoperability addressing manufacturing within the Internet of things research cluster (IERC). In the Internet of Things area, business and manufacturing aspects have not been clearly taken into account yet but there is an important need to include requirement and challenges from this area as there are a lot of common issues and additional values that current experience and deployments in manufacturing can be relevant. More specifically it is discussed semantic discovery and interoperability issues related to intangible assets and to products-services manufacturing ecosystems. The IoT challenges in semantic interoperability presented in this paper are also defined in an EU position paper to be published in 2014.*

KEYWORDS: *Internet of Things, Semantic Interoperability, Intelligent Manufacturing, Smart Industries.*

1. Introduction – IERC Activities

The European Research Cluster on the Internet of Things[1] (IERC) has created a number of activity chains to initiate close cooperation between the projects

---

1. http://www.internet-of-things-research.eu

addressing the IoT related topics and to form an arena for exchanging ideas, to have an open dialog on important research challenges and to disseminate the ideas and best practices in the areas around the IoT to other communities. The activity chains are defined as work streams that group together partners or specific participants from partners around well-defined technical activities that work on addressing the IERC objectives. Out of eight activities, there is the fourth one dedicated to Service Openness and Interoperability (IERC AC4) which is for about more than 2 years active in addressing Semantic Interoperability.

The design of the Internet and The Information and Communication Technology development relies on the convergence of Software Engineering and Technology (infrastructure). A common practice is required to think/design cross solutions between software and infrastructure in order to provide integrated solutions for some of the complex problems in the current and future Internet systems. In Information Technology and Communication (ITC) systems this convergence is evident, and the continuous evolution generates more and more devices or Internet connected objects (ICOs) that are becoming embedded with sensors and their respective associated services defined under the umbrella term: "Internet of Things" (IoT).

However, the conceptual realization of Internet of Things is far from achieving a full deployment of converged IoT services and technology. Current ITC research is focused on providing integrated solutions and primarily on the feature that enable convergence or what is called as "Interoperability". Interoperability can be generalized as the feature for providing seamless exchange of information to, for example, personalize services automatically or simply exchanging information in a way that other systems can use it for improving performance, enable and create services, control operations and information processing. This type of scenarios requires increased interoperability in service management operations.

The IERC AC4 in the Internet of Things Cluster is planning to release by mid 2014 a European position paper on semantic interoperability. In this document we review the recent trends and challenges on interoperability in IoT domain, discuss physical versus virtual sensors and while addressing technology interoperability challenges in parallel, discuss how, with the growing importance of data understanding and processing, semantic web technologies, frameworks and information models can support interoperability in the design of services in the Future Internet. The objective of this position paper is to identify relevant issues and challenges that need to be taken into account in the coming and future projects and H2020 and to identify synergies across the participating FP7 projects. This can be used to define an overall framework to address the interoperability challenges.

Interoperability is a global issue and semantics is a relevant approach that has emerged as a realistic approach for solving some of the issues for interoperability. Semantic interoperability is currently demonstrated and used in extensive Internet (Web) domains and with the use of the already deployed semantic technologies there is a lot of common challenges to share with manufacturing areas and therefore common actions might also be envisaged.

2. Internet of Things Research and Innovation on Semantic Interoperability

Internet of Things (IoT) is an emerging area that not only requires development of infrastructure but also deployment of new services capable of supporting multiple, scalable (cloud-based) and interoperable (multi-domain) applications. IoT has been considered as part of the Future Internet architecture and in the race of designing IoT, academia and Information and Communication Technology (ICT) industry communities have realized that a common IoT problem to be tackled is the interoperability of the information and services. In this paper we review the recent trends and challenges on interoperability, and discuss how semantic technologies, open service frameworks and information models can support data interoperability and particularly in the design of the Future Internet, taking the smart industries (manufacturing) as reference example of application domain.

IoT refers to objects ("things") and the virtual representations of these objects on the Internet. It defines how the things will be connected through the Internet and how those things "talk" amongst other things and communicate with other systems in order to expose their capabilities and functionalities "services".

IoT is not only linking connected devices by using the Internet; it is also web-enabled data exchange in order to enable systems with more capacities to become "smart". In other words, IoT aims to integrate the physical world with the virtual world by using the Internet as the medium to communicate and exchange information.

IoT is mainly supported by continuous progress in wireless sensor and actuator networks and by manufacturing low cost and energy efficient hardware for sensor and device communications. However, heterogeneity of underlying devices and communication technologies and interoperability in different layers, from communication and seamless integration of devices to interoperability of data generated by the IoT resources, is a challenge for expanding generic IoT solutions to a global scale.

In a coming position paper we present various parallel and inter-related interoperability challenges ensuring that technologies deliver information in a seamless manner while this information is understood whatever the context and can be efficiently processed to deliver the potential of innovative services that IoT is aiming for.

To provide seamless communication and interaction between and with the real world objects, at anytime and anywhere in future, we need to solve today's complex interoperability issues.

2.1. *Semantics and Technology*

IoT environments for Internet-connected objects facilitate the deployment and delivery of applications in different domains and will enable businesses and citizens to select appropriate data and service providers rather than having to deploy physical devices. At the same time, they will provide capabilities such as on-demand large scale sensing beyond what is nowadays possible.

It is important to highlight the origins of IoT are found in the area of Radio Frequency IDentification (RFID) domain where RFID tags are extensively used for data collection. The static information, a group of RFID tags, can generate the quick development of RFID middleware frameworks to the extent that nowadays RFID frameworks provides added functionality beyond the data collection, by means of filtering, event generation, as well as translation of tag streams into business semantics, etc.

At the Internet of Things, additional to the limits of physical devices (e.g., sensors) there is also a notion of "Virtual Sensor" that refers to virtualization of an element of the IoT platforms representing new data sources created from live data. These virtual sensors can filter, aggregate or transform the data. From an end-user perspective, both virtual and physical sensors are very closely related concepts since they both, simply speaking, measured data. In order to handle the measured data, an information model has to be used, thus the Semantic Sensor Network (SSN) ontology, provides the most important core vocabulary for sensing data: which defines the notion of sensor and physical devices in general, and therefore formally the concept of a virtual sensor as a subclass of the sensor concept are defined in the SSN ontology. Due to the rising popularity of IoT technologies and applications the emergence of a wide range of platforms that enable users to build and/or use IoT applications is unavoidable. In general there is a clear trend towards the convergence of physical worlds and virtual solutions by using IoT technologies.

In all cases either Physical or Virtual sensors, a middleware framework is the core element to be used for providing baseline sensor functionalities associated with registering and looking up internet-connected objects, exchanging messages between objects, as well as fusing and reasoning data from multiple-objects. Some features of these implementations are:

– Integrate ontologies and semantic structures, in order to enable semantic interactions and interoperability between the various objects, which will be a significant advancement over the existing syntactic interactions.

– Provide Open Linked Data interfaces (e.g., SPARQL (SPARQL Protocol and RDF Query Language) over ontologies for internet-connected objects within the physical world middleware to interact with virtual world).

– Define techniques for the automated data configuration of filtering, fusion and reasoning mechanisms, according to the problems/tasks at hand.

Taking a broader view of state-of-the-art and current developments in interoperability and in converging communications, many of the problems present in current Internet will remain in the Internet of Things systems and mainly generated by interoperability problems, thus there are three persistent problems:

– users are offered relatively small numbers of Internet services, which they cannot personalise to meet their evolving needs; communities of users cannot tailor services to help create, improve and sustain their social interactions;

– the Internet services that are offered are typically technology-driven and static, designed to maximise usage of capabilities of underlying network technologies and not to satisfy user requirements *per se*, and thus cannot be readily adapted to their changing operational context;

– network operators cannot configure their networks to operate effectively in the face of changing service usage patterns and rapid networking technology deployment; networks can only be optimised, on an individual basis, to meet specific low-level objectives, often resulting in sub-optimal operation in comparison to the more important business and service user objectives.

As the move towards Internet of Things, the convergence of communications and a more extended service-oriented architecture (SOA) design gains momentum, worldwide there is an increasingly focussing on how to evolve communications technologies to enable the "Internet of Things". The aim is directed mainly by pervasive deployment of Internet protocol suites and VoIP is a clear example of this.

By addressing evolution of networking technologies in isolation is not enough; instead, it is necessary to take a multi-domain adaptable holistic view of the evolution of communications services, their societal drivers and the requirements they will place on the heterogeneous communications infrastructure over which they are delivered.

By addressing information interoperability challenge issues, Internet of Things systems need to exchange information and customize their services. The Future Internet can reflect changing individual and societal preferences in network and services and can be effectively managed to ensure delivery of critical services in a services-aware design view with general infrastructure challenges.

3. IERC Challenges in Interoperability

In reference to the most common challenges for interoperability, and in reference to the manufacturing domain, (however in this respect and for having a more clear perspective it is recommended to read the full position paper) it is identified at first high level challenges as follow:

– *Integration of multiple data-sources*: This describes the necessity to be interoperable at the data/event level so that it becomes easier to combine/aggregate data/event coming from heterogeneous data sources. This raises also the challenge of being able to look up/discover data source and relevant data.

– *Unique ontological point of reference*: Semantic interoperability also means having a unique point of reference at the ontology level. This can be solved by third party responsible for translating between different schemes or via ontology merging/mapping. There could be also protocols for agreeing upon a specific ontology.

– *P2P Communication*: This describes the necessity for applications to communicate at a higher-level through exchange of "business" knowledge. Interoperability can be ignored at lower-levels and can be implemented at a higher-level.

Other main challenges in Semantic Interoperability and foreseen needed research:

– Data Modelling and Data Exchange;

– Ontology merging / Ontology matching & alignment;

– Data/Event Semantic Annotation (and dedicated ontologies);

– Knowledge Representation and related ontologies;

– Knowledge Sharing;

– Knowledge Revision & Consistency;

– Semantic Discovery of Data Sources, Data and Services;

– Semantic Publish/subscribe & Semantic Routing;

– Analysis & Reasoning.

4. IERC AC4 Position and Envisioned Solutions

The current position paper also in investigating the existing solutions has shown that:

– Often there is no general agreement on annotating the IoT data.

– There are several models, each having their own semantics and their own schema.

– In addition to the schema, it is also important to decide how the annotation will be done (according to the chosen schema).

– The models are often complex and express-ability vs. usability can be an issue in using complex and very detailed models (especially in large-scale deployments).

– Using different representation formats can also cause interoperability issues at the serialisation level.

The following summarises a set of recommendations to enhance the interoperability and to provide common solutions for semantic interoperability among various providers and users in the IoT domain. Some of the technical solutions that can be proposed to address the above issues are:

– Providing alignment between different and using ontology Mapping/Ontology Matching solutions.

– Using coordinated efforts to designing common specifications and core schema/reference models.

– Providing metrics, tools and interfaces for annotations, test and validation and integration.

Using linked-data can be also an effective solutions to link descriptions from different domain and models, to link resource descriptions to external metadata, and to use common vocabularies and taxonomies to describe different attributes of the data; e.g. Location (e.g., GeoNames), theme (e.g., DBpedia)

At the community level, setting up special taskforce among the projects can be considered to design a common (and minimum set) specifications that can be used for semantic descriptions of IoT data (i.e., observation and measurement data), resource descriptions (i.e., devices, network resources), command and interactions (i.e., actuation commands, publish, subscription, discovery and other similar messages), services (i.e., interfaces, application and higher-level services). The result of such an effort will be a set of basic models that can be used (and accepted) across different projects, tools for publishing and validating the descriptions according to the designed model and a set of best practices to annotate the legacy data according to these models.

5. IERC Semantic Interoperability and Manufacturing Challenges

Manufacturing (smart industries) is a privileged domain for applying the semantic interoperability technologies that are researched and produced in the scope of IERC. In particular, semantic technologies are key enablers for developing Virtual Factories (VFs), which allow the establishment and realization of complex and effective supply chains comprising several manufacturing plants around the world. The formulation of VF supply chains is a key enabler for realizing innovation driven transformations in the manufacturing domain, which is fully in-line with major trends associated with the future of manufacturing such as globalization, resource scarcity and the global knowledge society.

In particular,VF supply chains allow manufacturing stakeholders to monitor complex material flows in real-time, to optimize the use of manufacturing resources, to track (tangible and intangible) manufacturing assets, to deploy and operate advanced services (e.g., timely proactive maintenance), and overall to provide new and efficient ways for collaborating across the supply chain.

The importance of semantic web technologies for VFs (e.g., ontologies, RDF, LinkedData) stems from the fact that they can enable all stakeholders across the VFs supply chain to register and discover manufacturing assets and services in a uniform interoperable and web based way, which ensures semantic power, interoperability, versatility, flexibility and ease of use. In particular, a semantic web infrastructure for manufacturing assets and processes could empower the management of rich metadata, which facilitates the representation and management of (distributed) knowledge-intensive assets and processes.

At the same time, the use of common semantics for assets and services could facilitate the semantic interoperability of diverse enterprise systems (e.g., ERP (Enterprise Resource Planning), MRP (Manufacturing Resource Planning), MES (Manufacturing Execution Systems)) operated by different manufacturers across VF supply chains. Furthermore, semantic infrastructures can be distributed and are accessible over the web, which boosts collaborative processes involving geographically and administrative dispersed plants, factories and stakeholders.

The application of IERC semantic interoperability technologies in manufacturing is motivated from the fact that these technologies have been successfully applied in other segments of the Future Internet such as the internet-of-things (IoT) and the web-of-things (WoT). Indeed, several projects of the IERC cluster have selected and deployed semantic web infrastructures for the semantic interoperability of different IoT services, as well as for the dynamic discovery of sensors and ICO (Internet-Connected-Objects). Hence, the use of semantic infrastructures for the dynamic registration and discovery of sensors and IoT services is a successful paradigm, which could be replicated in the area of VFs and related manufacturing assets and processes. Under this prism, the IERC semantic web technologies could enable:

– Semantic discovery of assets for VFs, notably intangible assets such as people CVs, product catalogues, marketing plans and quality control processes. To this end, a semantic discovery infrastructure could be deployed in the cloud in order to facilitate on-demand access and management of assets from manufacturers engaging in VF business scenarios.

– Semantic interoperability for VFs with particular emphasis on the semantic interoperability of diverse enterprise systems (notably ERP (Enterprise Resource Planning), MRP (Manufacturing Resource Planning), CRM (Customer Relationship Management) and MES (Manufacturing Execution Systems)) with manufacturing assets and processes engaging in the supply chain and related collaborative processes.

The implementation of the above listed infrastructures for semantic discovery and interoperability can be realized based on the following steps:

– The semantic modeling of manufacturing assets and services in a way that can support the interoperability of enterprise systems (such as ERPs). This entails the development of models (i.e., ontologies), which will bring together the world of enterprise semantics / context modeling and Linked (Enterprise) Data with other relevant counterparts i.e. services, application and the Internet of Things (IoT) for optimizing manufacturing and Virtual Factories domain(s).

– The development of a semantic discovery infrastructure for manufacturing assets and services, which shall take into account existing semantic web discovery techniques successfully applied in the Internet of Things (IoT) domain.

– The integration of the semantic modeling and discovery infrastructure with tools and techniques for managing descriptions for manufacturing assets and services with Linked Unified Service Description Language (LinkedUSDL).

– The design and offering of APIs, which will allow VF applications and services to discover and manage resources, services and processes associated with VF applications.

The deployment of the discovery infrastructure in a cloud-based environment, where data about manufacturing assets and services used in VF scenarios will be stored and managed on demand. This will facilitate the establishment and validation of a Manufacturing-as-a-Service model across VF supply chains.

As already outlined, a possible implementation of the above technologies in the manufacturing domain could leverage readily available blueprint implementations of semantic infrastructures for other areas (such as IoT), which have been already realized by IERC projects (e.g., the OpenIoT open source cloud-based discovery infrastructure for IoT resources, which is available at: https://github.com/OpenIotOrg/openiot/).

6. Conclusions

In this paper we have introduced the research results and main efforts of the IERC cluster towards designing and building semantic interoperability systems for the Internet of Things in the framework of Smarter Industries as implementation main scenarios in Manufacturing.

The IERC cluster has been taking advantage of existing ontologies (such as the W3C SSN) and standards (e.g., RDF), but also of emerging technologies (such as Linked Data). On the basis of these technologies the IERC has produce a semantic interoperability manifesto [2], which includes/describes more detailed research challenges for semantic interoperability and additionally to that the main building blocks required in order to build semantically interoperable systems can be found in the manifesto. This manifesto is supported by a set of concrete blueprint semantic interoperability implementations for IoT and smart cities applications. At the manifesto we have illustrated how the building blocks could be used to support interoperability in manufacturing and related application domains (Virtual Factories and related supply chains).

The introduced semantic interoperability concepts for VFs could greatly boost collaborative and interoperable manufacturing in a globalized environment, where the exploitation and collaborative management of both tangible and intangible assets in becoming more important than ever before.

---

2 ERC-AC4-SemanticInteroperabilityManifesto http://www.probe-it.eu/wp-content/uploads/2013/10/IERC-AC4-SemanticInteroperabilityManifesto-V1_130830-Final1.pdf

Manufacturing Integration Challenges

Top-Down Interoperability and Bottom-Up Comprehensiveness Towards a Global Information Backbone for Smart Factory

Van Khai Nguyen

CADCAMation SA
1213 Onex-Geneva
Switzerland
vknguyen@cadcamation.ch

ABSTRACT. *The Manufacturing paradigm is envisioned to drastically evolve from the mechanic-based system to the computer-assisted system driven by knowledge. The end-to-end process integration towards the virtual factory could be realized if only based on a fully digital factory model composed by Product, Process, Resource and Plant and their live characterization throughout their lifecycle. Can standards help solve this "big picture" integration issue? Knowing that the top-down integration relies on applications interoperability while the bottom-up integration starts on unstructured data collection! The present paper refers on the work achieved within the FOFdation project (FP7-IP-FOF-ICT), which addressed the need for the Factory of the Future to be based on an "end-to-end Digital Manufacturing Foundation" for simultaneously tackling quality, productivity and sustainability through a unique and interoperable IT platform.*

1. The Importance of Information and Knowledge in Manufacturing

In the early nineteenth century, the industrial revolution which marked a major turning point in history, was the transition to new manufacturing processes going from hand production methods to mechanical systems. This led to the development of machine-tools that "help people to make things" by cutting and shaping metal parts. The first machine-tool was "free-handly" controlled by human who guided the tool-path manually, based on his knowledge of the part and the material he wanted to produce, but through a mechanical system that augmented his power and precision.

2. The Evolution

2.1. *From Automatic Machine...*

In the early 60's, machine-tool began to be numerically controlled and till today, the tool-paths are constrained by a NC program beforehand defined by a CAM software. Numerical control (NC) is the automation of machine tools that are operated by precisely programmed commands encoded on a storage medium, as opposed to controlled manually via hand wheels or levers, or mechanically automated via cams alone. Most NC today is computer numerical control (CNC), in which computers play an integral part of the control.

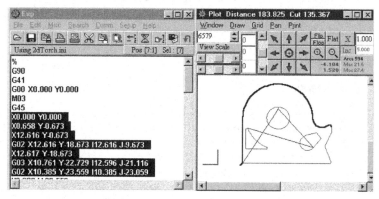

At present, machine-tool is still classified as an automatic machine: after once being set, it operates automatically and blindly follows the machining code provided and it is up to an operator to detect if a crash is about to occur, and for the operator to manually abort the cutting process. Indeed, any unforeseen condition cannot be met, and any hazard event may cause machine crash or failure, and harmful damage to the equipment and operator, despite collision detection through sensors or limiting switches that equip some modern machines.

2.2. ... *To Smart Machine*

In the Factory of the future, knowledge is essential and could or must be accessible everywhere, as the digital convergence will be also affecting manufacturing and allowing an interconnected web of information and production. Smart machines will collaborate with each other, with intelligent software, with tech-savvy workers, with customers, with managers all across the supply chain.

Machine-tool then can be augmented with new capabilities such as global awareness of human goals, perception of sensory and contextual information and decision for self-optimization capability.

3. The Technologies of Smart Factory Integration ...

Previously, the industrial value chain, including product design, production planning, production engineering, production execution and management-finance-business services were implemented separately and operated as isolated applications-islands such as PLM, MES, NC-controller and automation, ERP, CRM... By making these systems interoperable or able to communicate at the semantic level, industry can leverage them for supporting shorter innovation cycles, awareness and transparency in manufacturing operations, raising productivity through knowledge sharing and minimizing risk through predictability assessment.

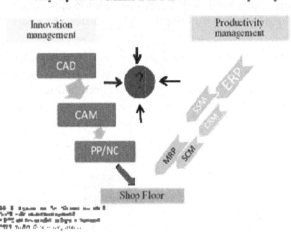

The key to making smart factory work is to create a dense mesh of technologies that are integrated and able to cooperating into a smarter and more efficient whole. Mobile Internet, Automation of knowledge work, the Internet of things and Cloud technology are the key disruptive technologies that sustain this new manufacturing paradigm.

4. But the Key Challenge is still the Semantic Meaning of Data...

4.1. ... *To Ensure Downstream Applications while Preserving Human's Design Intent to Machine*

Geometrical design is the first stage to represent the human's goal about the geometrical and physical aspects of the part he wants to produce and that can meet user's needs. Today digital CAD model has replaced "analog drawings", and the CAD model can be seamlessly transformed into a CAM model. But the interoperability is still not fully streamlined as the end-to-end integration of data is not yet achieved outside the integrated CAD-CAM software, and neither a machine-tool nor a simulation or monitoring software at the shop-floor level can fully understand the "as-desired" part requirements and its business context.

Despite the progress made by CAD-CAM and today's PLM software, the product design-engineering-production process and its different applications are still communicating through the data translation mechanism that might lose the semantic meaning and impoverish the data to the destined software due to its smaller focused input-output. The strategic issue is twofold and in both horizontal (between different CAD systems) and vertical dimensions (between CAD and manufacturing systems):

– Dynamic data structure for changing business environment: even when attempting to define data models that focus on specific application, the scope cannot be properly defined because of multiple needs in different sectors, and their change overtime.

– Thorough knowledge of the product design and the designer's intent, knowing that all stakeholders in manufacturing need a subset of the original model based design data which can be fortunately well structured and mathematically described with the addition of information such as process, resource, pricing, logistic and planning sequences etc.

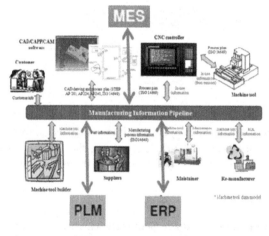

In FOFdation, the consortium proposes a Manufacturing Information Pipeline (MIP), based on STEP and STEP-NC to demonstrate a proof of concept of the manufacturing shift that consists of fully integrating the Design-Manufacturing process. The key proposition is the Smart Manufacturing Controller (SMC) tightly coupled with the Smart Manufacturing Optimizer (SMO): this combined SMC-SMO controller will exploit interoperability enabled by MIP, as a modern Master Model, between PLM-CAD systems and machine-tool while being able to optimize the cutting process in real-time, based on the closed loop assistance of the Smart Manufacturing Optimizer.

4.2. ... *To Comprehend Executive Operations: Bottom-Up Live Data, Resources Health and Work Context*

Many disruptive IT technologies are expected to help managers (and other knowledge workers) tackle overall management and planning tasks, by helping them aware of the manufacturing diagnosis through real-time information. The daily visibility of the factory shop floor health and the comprehensive awareness of the whole manufacturing eco-system (including customers and suppliers) are also primordial to the top management for taking the right decision at the right time within a global context, thus meeting the triple-bottom line objectives and requirements. Nevertheless, the bottom-up feedback process of data from the factory operational ground is still in the infancy stage today and many technologies are claimed to be the cornerstone for such innovating process like complex event processing, data pattern mining, or big data analytics... And at the data collection level, many commercial stand-alone solutions are existing on the market and can be classified into three categories:

– Dedicated data collection tools;

– MES based tools;

– Specialized systems for quality tracking or energy monitoring.

As a consequence of the analysis performed in FOFdation, our consortium has selected a MES system as a basis to our general monitoring solution and sustainability assessment. The data collection module (FoF-EMon) is proposed as a new feature of the extended MES (called Smart MES) which will be adapted to form a comprehensive approach for energy and resource monitoring, controlling and assessment. Such a combination leads to an improved awareness of the manufacturing operations performance through a configurable set of sustainability key performance indicators (KPIs).

The present approach is a pragmatic proposition to address a dedicated solution need: energy management or quality tracking. This might be not sufficient to address a general, real-time and permanent diagnosis in order to permanently watch after the manufacturing operations which generate huge data streams, but this could efficiently support engineering approaches towards product, process and resource characterizations that are needed to improve the optimization process reliability and correctness based on the fine-tuning of its validity scope.

5. Conclusions

This paper proposed a Manufacturing Information Pipeline framework built in a pragmatic way to support manufacturing interoperability towards global optimization. Nevertheless, many challenges are still ahead of us and the interoperability for optimization at the forefront of innovation, in the perspective of extending the model based design, thus providing manufacturing stakeholders with complete knowledge from-design-to-manufacturing linked to business requirements. In order to continuously improve the manufacturing process at the different time scale levels for decision making and closed-loop optimization, we need to map live data (output) and goal driven data (input) thus supporting the root cause analysis.

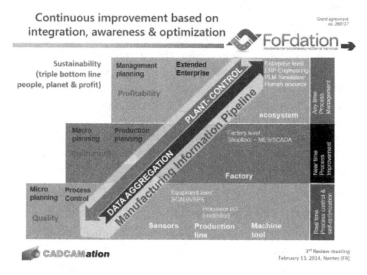

6. Acknowledgements

The work reported in this paper was partially supported by the EC / FP7 Programme under the project "FOFdation: the foundation for the Smart Factory of the Future" (FP7-2010-NMP-ICT-FoF-260137

7. References

[1] J.B. Hentz, V.K. Nguyen, W. Maeder, D. Panarese, J.W. Gunnink, A. Gontarz, P. Stavropoulos, K. Hamilton, J.Y. Hascoët, 2013, "An enabling digital foundation towards smart machining", 8th CIRP conference on Intelligent Computation in Manufacturing Engineering, Elsevier B.V.

[2] J. Larreina, A. Gontarz, C. Giannoulis, V.K. Nguyen, P. Stavropoulos, B. Sinceri, 2013, 11th Global Conference on Sustainable Manufacturing.

An Improved Decision Support System in Factory Shop-Floor Through an IoT Approach

Pierluigi Petrali

Whirlpool Europe
Biandronno (VA)
Italy
Pierluigi_petrali@whirlpool.com

ABSTRACT. *As a result of low cost automation and pervasive computing, modern shop-floor has become a big data generation engine. This huge quantity of data and information are rarely used in an effective way, both in real time and analytical post-processing. We demonstrate how an IoT approach could be designed to leverage this potential and how factories of the future should transform to maximize its effect.*

KEYWORDS: *Internet of Things, Mobile Device, Cloud.*

1. Context of White Good Manufacturing

Whirlpool business model is very similar to that of main other competitors which are acting all around the world. Large domestic appliance industry has been developed in the last 40 years in the form of loosely coupled integration model, i.e. factories are characterized mostly in assembly of components coming, the most, from external suppliers. In this context two of most important features of differentiation among competitors are cost and Quality and workers are becoming a crucial factor to control them. The uniformity of white good sector will be analyzed can be easily understood when analyzed along these perspectives:

– *Product Design*: both the overall design (in terms of shapes, dimension, line-up), architecture (i.e., how the sub-system are related one each other) and product technologies (i.e., which technical principles or solutions) are very uniform in European market among the main competitors. Products are differentiating in the marketplace mainly on brand equity. On the other hand market segmentation is very high, both vertically, in terms of different lifestyle or spending capacity, and horizontally, in terms of country related differentiation such as languages, habits, regulation etc. This lead to a very high complexity on both different models to be managed at each single production units, and number of different components to be handled.

– *Vertical Integration*: the level of integration (i.e., the number of manufacturing processes carried on internally versus those bought from third parties) decreased significantly in white good industries in the last 40 years. The majority of the people employed in a factory are dedicated to sequential assembly operations of components coming from the in-bound supply-chain.

– *Footprint*: all the white good industry in Europe has reached a balance between factories in western Europe, and those in low cost countries (east Europe: Poland, Czech Republic, Slovakia, Hungary, Russia; Middle east: Turkey; Far East: China, India). The reasons to spread the footprint to those counties are: low cost of labor and logistic optimization to serve emerging markets. On the other side, this enlargement of footprint is a challenge for manufacturing industries when they want to standardize the industrial culture and approaches.

– *Quality*: Product and post sales quality is becoming a major driver of differentiation between competitors. Humans are still the most important players both from Quality prevention (do the right thing) and control (check for deviations).

– *Lean manufacturing*: all the leading industries of large appliances did establish in the recent year their program of introduction of Lean Manufacturing, deriving it from Toyota Production System and declining it in own strategy. One of the basic and common principles shared among all the implementation of LM is its people centric approach, in which the worker is placed at the top of the model (reversed pyramid concept).

The economic situation of the sector is really challenging: the economic crisis caused major domestic appliance market to flatten in the last 5 years and raw material prices increases caused a contraction of the margins for all the players with consequences for both economic and social aspects.

2. Shop Floor Operating Model

A typical white good shop floor is organized in a combination of technical process essentially divided into capital intensive process, "fabrication" and human labor intensive process, "assembly". The first dedicated to transform raw material (polymer granules, steel) into parts; the latter dedicated to join the all the parts fabricated and, subsequently, all the part bought from the supply.

However, in the last 20 years evolution in ICT and automation technology allowed to shorten the gap between those process and many manual operations has been substituted by mechanical operation either assisted by simple automatism or more complex robots. This condition, along with a more and more integration of the data level to the ERP lead to a complex architecture shown in **Figure 1**.

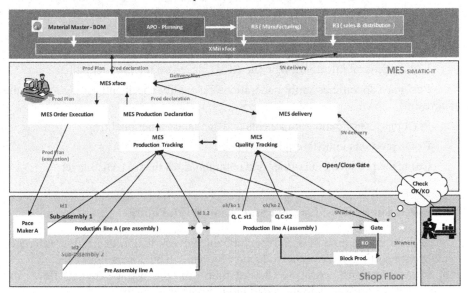

Figure 1. *Factory IS architecture*

The current architecture is characterized by an upper ERP level, based on SAP software, which main function is to manage the complete supply chain from the suppliers to the customers. Focusing on manufacturing area it is possible to identify:

– Material Master – contains a description of the product.

– APO – a finite scheduling module that calculates the production plan of the factory.

– R3 modules – calculates the requirement of materials, manages the order to the supplier and makes the production plan feasible.

– Xmii interface – is a module dedicated to manage the communication with MES

The second layer is constituted by MES: a set of modules based on SIMATIC-IT with the main function of coordinating the execution of the production plan received from SAP. Its main modules are:

– MES Xface – is a module dedicated to manage the communication with the corporate ERP system of Whirlpool based on SAP.

– MES Production order – is a module dedicated to manage the fulfillment of the production order (when, what, how many).

– MES Production order dispatching – is a module dedicated to send right information of what has to be produced to the workstations (directly connected to the assembly line).

The latter layer is the Shop floor: is constituted by a set of workstations directly connected with the assembly line and able to perform basic functions like:

– Update general information on the RFID placed on the product pallet.

– Perform a specific assembly operation or a quality check and saving locally the data results.

– Performs test of main components and appliance functionalities

– Route products in different branch lines.

– Count the produced quantities and communicates them to MES layer.

3. The Decision Process: Current Status and Weak Points

The help chain model is the operational process and organization reference structure supporting Whirlpool Production System which covers both execution and supporting functions, ensuring the stability of the value stream flow and sustainability of problem solving and continuous improvement.

Main element of WPS help chain models is the Problem solving and escalation system that ensures that problems are solved efficiently and completely, wherever they originate. The problem is escalated to the level that has the right skills to address the real root cause and eradicate the problem forever. This happens at different level:

– Help chain level 0: prompt intervention to support team members, provided by team leaders at Andon occurrence, for any deviation from the defined Standards.

– Help chain level 1: prompt intervention to support team leaders on issue management escalation, provided by functional group.

– Help chain level 2: structural process to support problem solving and continuous improvement at group level, value stream level and factory to definitively solve issues and update and consolidate operational standards, with factory resources.

– Help chain level 3: ad hoc project initiative to manage big issues, promoted by plant managers and staff, with local and central resources (cross functional teams).

Immediate reaction to support team members in case of deviation from pre-defined standards (Andon), ensures the continuity of the flow within a few Takt Times and basic problem solving. Of course a structure to support team leaders in case specific competencies or responsibilities is needed also, ensuring fast flow re-establishment and effective problem solving initiation. Resources are usually those within the shift and the value stream.

While the event and the decision process working at level 0 to 2 are pretty well managed, some problems arise when dealing with escalation process and the exception at level 3.

The challenges that the decision process has to deal with are:

1)   Improve the communication effectiveness along the help chain organization

As evident result of what has been described in the previous chapters, workers play a very important role in the manufacturing of large domestic appliances. Current Lean Manufacturing approaches are not leveraging enough the data integration that should be available from ICT technology to help the process. This trial is intended to demonstrate that using proper ICT technology to integrate Shop floor event to help chain can provide great benefit for all the manufacturing.

Having the worker organized in a help chain, able to react to event in a reliable a fast way could lead to improve the overall efficiency of the production lines: decrease of unavailability time (e.g. equipments can be reactivated faster by supervisor or maintenance); quality (e.g. an equipment which behavior is drifting from the average could be restored to its proper operation before producing defective parts)

2)   Improve the effectiveness of decision makers along their role in help chain

Workers role of making decision will not be replace by machine soon, so it's of a vital important that ICT be used to enhance their capacity in taking better decision. This can be achieved through enabling a more fact based and data based decision process. Obvious advantage of this are reflecting in very different level and can span from high level decision taken by managers to day-by-day decision taken by supervisors and workers, and could be translated easily in an improvement of the main business indicators: cost (reduction of wasted time); quality (reduction of defective parts and improvement of filtering capacity at factory level); people engagement (better decision lead to less workaround; problem fixed the first time etc; workers continuous learning process through a better knowledge of the parameters governing the production line)

4. The IoT Based Solution

The solution proposed along the FITMAN project is based on a simple concept, i.e. use mobile device to push events notification to decision makers, experimented within an innovative concept of Internet of Things, represented by FIWARE Generic

Enablers running on the cloud. Selected events are fed into GE DataHandling which has the capability to filter the events and in case of an important ones (i.e., faults, sequence of faults, process drifting) it will forward them to other services (BackEnd.ConfMan and BackEnd.IoTBroker) to deliver it to mobile devices associated to users.

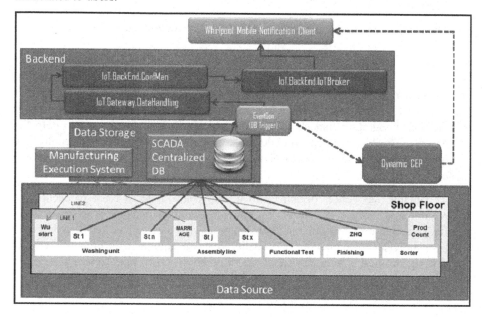

Figure 2. *FITMAN IoT based architecture*

This solution requires no additional hardware since all the GE are running in a private cloud, but in line of principle they can be deployed on a public cloud. The amount of additional software to be written is limited to the Specific Components: Event Generation, calls to GE to be placed when the event is recorded (either in DB or at sensor level) and the Mobile Client, which, for the demonstration time being will be a portable HTML page.

5. References

FIWARE homepage, http://www.fi-ware.eu/

FIWARE GE Catalogue, http://catalogue.fi-ware.org/

FITMAN homepage, http://www.fitman-fi.eu/

Leveraging IoT Interoperability for Enhanced Business Process in Smart, Digital and Virtual Factories

J. Sola — A. Gonzalez — O. Lazaro

Innovalia Association
Rodriguez Arias 6, 605, 48008 Bilbao (Spain)

ABSTRACT. IoT technologies are enabling technologies for new Smart Manufacturing solutions. IoT Interopeability opens the opportunity to the development of horizontal platforms that will provide services and information that will be linked across multiple domains and collaborators. This new scenario with increased visibility, rich and abundant real-time information about many kinds of sensors and product information; are the perfect ground to build new business processes that contribute towards STEEP objectives of European re-industrialization. This paper will presnets the new technical capabilities leveraged by IoT interoperability frameworks such as those developed as part of the ComVantage and FITMAN projects. The paper discusses the new business models and business processes that can be implemented by manufacturing industries based on these new technical foundations. The paper will share some insights into the impact that can be achieved with these new business processes and the Future Internet dimensions that are most valued by enterprises engaged in the development and definition of such innovative business processes.

KEYWORDS: IoT, Interoperability, Business Processes, Business Models.

1. Introduction

Over the last few years, an increasing effort has been put in place to enable enterprises to develop further business capabilties relying on Internet and IT enablers. Many projects in the area of Future Internet Networked Enterprise systems; e.g. FITMAN, ComVantage are dealing with the development of frameworks and software components (eneablers) that would allow IT developers to leverage the technical and service capabilites alllwing industry and manufacturing to deploy a new generation business process. This paper, deals with a very brief introduction to the interoperability capabilities that have been enabled by 3 reference platforms developed in the context of the FITMAN project and the collaboration framework delivered by the ComVantage project to capitalise on the industrial application of the linked data technology to developed mobile services. First the FITMAN innovative business process are presented with the expectations from the trials involved. Then the technical features that the platform will leverage are described based on business process expectations. Next a brief introduction to the ComVantage collaboration framework and the notion of Domain Access Server is provided.

2. FITMAN Bussiness Process Innovation and High Level Technical Features for Smart, Virtual and Digital Platforms

Regarding Smart Factory, the trials business processes aim to manage both tangible assets (energy, productivity, throughput, and wastes) and intangible assets (customer sentiments, workforce wellness, comfort and safety) to obtain more competitive and productive manufacturing environment. As a result, more efficient knowledge-management strategies will be implemented, achieving the intelligent and smart factory. Accordingly, the Smart Factory experimentation sites are mainly focused on the production activities located in concrete production lines or shopfloors; using sensors and monitoring systems deployed in the production lines and services/applications for sending messages or warnings.

Digital factory faces the challenge of improve the time-to product and time-to-market of products and services, managing more efficiently the product life-cycle information using intelligent knowledge flows and providing the services and tools to make easier the cooperation between the different systems, such as ERP, MRP II, social networks, testing system, etc. The digital factory experimentation sites will mainly be located into the different departments involved on the collaboration work, both people launching the information and customers/departments receiving them. For that purpose, web-services already deployed or applications and data servers for setting up new web platforms will be needed.

Virtual factory trials business processes aims to obtain collaboration models and platforms, in order to manage the activities that demand multi-partners interaction based on product-centric collaboration space. Accordingly, the virtual factory experimentation sites could be located in the collaborative private servers and networks where partners share information about their needs and tenders. A common component in most of virtual experimentation sites is SQL Server for enterprise-level data storage.

To meet the business innovation needs for each of the three domains some high level features have been identified to effectively support next generation business processes. In particular, smart factory processes are characterised by:

- Support of cyber-physical systems.
- Overcome data discontinuity.
- Facilitate production capacity as a service.

– Make start-up (ramp-up) production activities and operational routines much easier and more efficient.

– Support self-tuning, self-diagnosing and optimizing features of modern process control.

– Support advanced human-computer interaction.

– Support human-centric ergonomic manufacturing process implementation.

– Secure data handling.

On the other hand, the Digital Factory processes demand:

– Highly modular event-driven architecture.

– Interoperability with major PLM platforms.

– Quick, flexible, managed and intelligent integration of information.

– Real-time linking with shop floor (in-field) data.

– Secure (trusted) data management apps.

– Quick development of customised user-focused (engineer, customer, production manager, etc.) mobile and collaborative decision support apps.

– Effortless development of advanced data analytics and (mobile) data visualisation.

– Cost-effective service operation and maintenance.

And similarly for the Virtual Factory the following features have been identified:

– Virtuality.

– Usability.

– Flexibility.

– Collaboration.

– Security.

– Tangible and intangible asset management.

3. ComVantage Interoperability Framework for Business Collaboration

ComVantage envisions an inter-organisational collaboration space turning today's organisation-centric manufacturing approach into a product-centric one. Manufacturers will benefit from a flexible, efficient platform that helps them to operate as one virtual factory and thus gain competitive advantages in their markets. Based on best practises of Web 2.0 technologies the collaboration space will be an extension to existing business and engineering software. It will allow sharing, administrating and monitoring focused information throughout a product's life cycle in a de-centralised manner. The close collaboration on the B2B and B2C levels will foster existing trends such as Open Innovation or Crowd Sourcing.

The framework of the virtual factory will encompass a secure access control that is founded on dynamic workflow models and flexible user roles accounting for large enterprises, SMEs and for end-customers. It will enable temporary and de-centralised access management for ad-hoc collaboration between geographically distributed experts.

To adhere to changing working situations, to efficient communication, and to rich interaction technologies ComVantage will focus on mobile devices. Intuitive and trustful mobile apps shall support users in fast decision-making and problem solving. Information from different sources across the organisations is provided and maintained via Linked Data. The integration of sensor data allows for products to be members of the collaboration space.

The execution of business processes across organisational boundaries as well as cross-linking data sets of collaboration partners are key success factors and initiate the transformation of isolated individual companies towards an integrated, agile virtual enterprise.

The main challenges, from a semantic interoperability perspective to be faced by ComVantage are:

– Individual partners using specific workflows and local data sources need a uniform interface for applications to access these data sources and be integrated into the collaboration network.

– Applications in most cases need substantial modifications, even if only a new data source is added.

– All relevant entities and relations in the domain of the application partner should be described to generate a domain data model.

– Each partner has to understand the meaning of the data residing in the other partners' systems.

– Entities that occur in the systems of several partners, but are referenced by different names have to be identified and matched so that all information about this entity can be obtained upon request.

– Accessing this data must possible using just one access point, and all pieces of data returned in a common format, independent of the system they originate from.

– Different data sources have to be read, the underlying data models understood, the data matched and consolidated, before finally presented to the user.

The ComVantage (www.comvantage.eu) project has the goal to develop a reference architecture (see Figure 1) as well as a working prototype of a distributed collaboration infrastructure for virtual enterprises. In the following, the key high level features are described.

Even in a heterogeneous and distributed collaboration environment, companies want to continue running their legacy systems and want to keep full control of their valuable enterprise data. ComVantage fully decentralized approach proposes a separation into Domains where each domain is operated by one partner of the collaboration network. Within a domain, the partners are running their own collaboration infrastructure and their data sources.

Major *design-time activities* in setting up a domain are: First, definition of local access control policies in order to decide, which data should be shared with partners among the network. Second, ontologies (Domain Data Model) to describe the data model of each domain are needed to enable the semantic data harmonization. A specification of the used methodology and the developed meta-models can be found in the public deliverable D4.1.1 and D4.1.2 of the ComVantage project (see http://www.comvantage.eu/results-publications/publicderiverables/).

Major difficulties of *inter-organisational collaboration* consist in heterogeneous data models (structuring and naming of entities) and incompatible interfaces based on different technologies. In ComVantage we decided to use semantic data harmonization based on RDF, Linked Data and ontologies. RDF is used as uniform data format based on the Linked Data design principles. Within each domain of the collaboration network, a single point of access is provided by the Domain Access Server (Figure 1). It exposes a uniform interface for applications based on SPARQL and provides an interface for enforcing access control policies. The Data Integration Layer is responsible for distributing requests to the connected data sources of the domain and merges all results to a combined result set. The Domain Configuration Layer provides components for a domain specific configuration of the Domain Access Server.

Integration of *heterogeneous data sources* is crucial to data harmonization. The ComVantage approach is based on Linked Data adapters that will perform a mapping of syntactic data to RDF. The adapters are provided as generic components which will be configured with the Domain Data Model of the actual domain in order to connect to a specific data source. Using adapters offers the advantage of integrating legacy systems without modifications. Hence, the ComVantage approach can be used on top of an existing IT infrastructure and in parallel to already existing business applications. The adapters are provided for several technologies which are most common in micro-company environments. First, the Linked Data adapter for databases is based on the open source project D2RQ. The adapter translates SPARQL queries to SQL and returns results based on a domain-specific mapping. While the mapping is defined at design-time, the content is lifted to RDF on demand at run-time which avoids the problem of keeping redundant data in sync. Since the database doesn't contain the semantic information that is required for this transformation, it is provided in a mapping file. Second, an adapter for Excel spread sheets based on the project XLWrap is used. Third, an adapter for connecting to machine middleware solutions was developed within the project. In order to allow for inter-organisational interlinking of models and data sets, the tool chain of the Silk project will be leveraged in ComVantage.

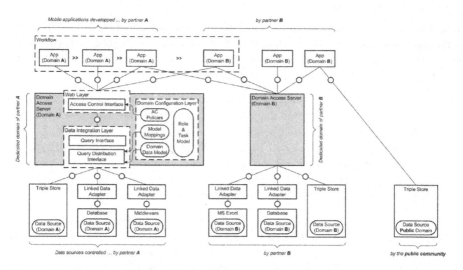

Figure 1. *Reference architecture for data- and process-interoperability in a virtual enterprise*

Inter-organisational collaboration relies on trust between partners and the fact that information from heterogeneous nature is accessible to authorized members only. An access control model is required that supports decentralized decision-making and that enables policy negotiation, establishment, management, monitoring and enforcement for a multi-domain access to Linked Data sources. We propose an authentication process based on SAML, identity federation and security credentials interchange. Afterwards, a multi-tiered authorization process takes place to provide multi-domain access control for Linked Data at two levels: (1) Rewriting of SPARQL queries by adding control checks related to the requesters user role. (2) Structuring of information in views for each data source to physically protect data that is not visible for a specific user role.

4. Acknowledgements

This work has been partly funded by the European Commission through the Project FITMAN: Future internet technologies for Manufacturing (Grant Agreement No. FP7 604674) and ComVantage: Collaborative Manufacturing Network for Competitive Advantage (Grant Agreement No FP7-284928). The authors wish to acknowledge the Commission for their support. We also wish to acknowledge our gratitude and appreciation to all the FITMAN and ComVantage Project partners for their contribution during the development of various ideas and concepts presented in this paper.

Workshop 2

Future Internet Methods, Architectures and Services for Digital Business Innovation in Manufacturing, Health and Logistics Enterprises

Report

Sergio Gusmeroli* — Guy Doumeingts**

*TXT e-solutions SPA
70010 Valenzano (BA), Italy
Sergio.Gusmeroli@txtgroup.com

**INTEROP VLab,
B1000 Brussels, Belgium
guy.doumeingts@interop-vlab.eu

The goal of this workshop is to study and analyse the Business Innovation potential of Methods, Architecture and Services developed in the frame of the EC FP7 FI/PPP (Future Internet/ Private Public Partnership) in the domains of Manufacturing, Health and Logistics

Four papers have been presented during this workshop, followed by a discussion between the attendees. This document is a summary of the discussion.

Three questions have been considered:

– *Cloud Strategy and Cloud Journey* for EU industries including pros and cons of centralization and decentralization of data and knowledge. Which are the requirements by Manufacturing, Logistics and Healthcare industries for a progressive and gradual migration of data and applications to the Cloud?

– *Combination and interoperability of generic software components for building new complex applications* by EU ICT industry. How to convince the SME (Small and Medium Enterprises) and LE (Large Enterprises) to build their own domain-specific value added applications on top of a set of Generic Enablers (GEs) and Specific Enablers (SEs)? How to interoperate existing systems with the new GE/SE based architectures?

– *Exploitation of FI PPP outcomes in commercial projects*. How to reconcile the pre-commercial nature of the FP7 FI PPP offer with the growing end-users' demand for reliable, stable and certified software solutions? How to bridge the gap between Research, Innovation and market in FI-based solutions?

1. Cloud Strategy and Cloud Journey

The discussion was quite animated on this point with diverse and sometimes divergent opinions. For some participants, the problem of the centralization comes from the infrastructure which must be elastic, secure, privacy-preserving and certified. For others, the main problem comes from the performances and the respect of Service Level Agreements, like the needed reactivity for real time applications.. And for others again, the problem is not the centralization but the interoperability of those data.

So when and where the cloudification of data and applications must start? There is the same question for the decentralization.

The centralization allows to save energy for data centers, but it increases the traffic in the network. On another point of view, the cloud middleware is able to implement data centres in a more efficient way. Anyway to solve the problem of interoperating real time decentralized computing and centralsied data storage and analysis is necessary.

2. Combination and Interoperability of Generic Software Components for Building New Complex Applications

The trials of the Phase II FI-PPP projects must be open in order to involve as many developers as possible. The problem is generally that the quality requirements expressed by the trials are much more demanding than the quality usually provided by GEs or SEs developed in R&D projects, due to their evolutionary and prototypal nature. The gaps identified in Phase I and Phase II of FI PPP between the requirements and implementation of GEs and SEs could be even more amplified by phase III, where consolidated and certified methods for software engineering, testing and validation will be less adopted.

Another point also mentioned was the difference between the projects FI-STAR and FITMAN in approaching Phase III developers. In the case of FI-STAR, the project is working with IT SMEs whose already have a good knowledge on the FI technologies developed and a good know how on their field of activity. On the other hand, the project FITMAN is dealing with ICT and manufacturing companies that have less knowledge in the domain of FI Technologies.

This scheme results in two complete different strategies in terms of SMEs and Web Entrepreneurs involvement.

It was a common understanding that more attention should have been paid in Phase I and Phase II on software testing and quality certification, in order to minimise the differences between the requirements and the implementation of the Enablers (Generic and Specific).

Among the possible solutions suggested during the meeting, there was the possibility to organize contests / hackathons for developers, in order to improve GEs SEs interoperability problems in concrete use cases.

3. Exploitation of FI PPP Outcomes in Commercial Projects

For the attendees of this workshop, the knowledge acquired from the Enablers is very important in term of specification, use case, open source, even if a re-implementation will be necessary for exploitation and commercial purposes. This is per se a success factor for the whole FI PPP: to have identified common and generic building blocks on top of which to develop very diverse applications.

Another aspects discussed was the trade-off between "Quantity Vs Quality" of such components: it seems that FI-PPP aimed to involve as many people as possible but on the other side it cannot be done with high quality. At the moment, the aim is to build a strong developer's community of FI technology. But the active and participative involvement of end users, SME and later-on certification authorities is also necessary and will come in time.

4. Open Questions

What beyond FI-PPP?

– What if new requirements for extensions are elicited in some GEs developed by FI-Ware? *"How does it work if future evolve?"*

– In the FI-PPP, the feedback loop from Phase I and Phase II end users was foreseen by FI-Ware with an iterative cycle of software releases. From a practical point of view it was not very effective, as there was not enough time by FI-Ware developers to accept and implement new requirements coming from the use cases.

– One other way to exploit the FI PPP in H2020 is to extensively use its results in other EC Units that could be complementary to FI-PPP (e.g., Internet of Things, Cloud Computing, Big Data or also other PPPs such as Factories of the Future or 5G). Some improvement could be found in the interconnection between units and could bring improvement to whole framework of the programme.

Future Internet Technologies and Platforms to Support Smart, Digital and Virtual and Business Processes for Manufacturing

J. Sola — A. Gonzalez — O. Lazaro

Innovalia Association
Rodriguez Arias, 6, 605, 48008, Bilbao (Spain)

ABSTRACT. *Future Internet technologies (BigData, Cloud Computing, Mobile Web Apps etc) offer manufacturing industries the possibility to engage in a digital transformation leveraging advanced business processes. The FITMAN project, Future Internet Technologies for Manufacturing is working on the development of Generic and Specific Enablers (GE, SE) that are the essential components of three reference platforms (smart, digital and virtual factory). The paper will discuss and present the drivers and methodology followed by enterprises for engaging in the definition of enhanced business processes based on Future Internet technologies. The paper will also present the high level features that are leveraged by the 3 FITMAN reference platforms and associated GEs/SEs to develop new business processes. The paper will discuss how these technical high level features represent a solid and flexible technical foundation for communities of developers and practitioners to develop both innovative services and business models in the digital economy facilitated by the Future Internet.*

KEYWORDS: *FI Drivers, FI for manufacturing, FI technology adoption.*

1. Introduction

Current factories are nowadays going through a transformation that should respond to major megatrends taking place worldwide. To address such challenges, future enterprises are developing new capabilities in their three dimensions smarter, digital and virtual factories. These advanced business capabilities can be achieved providing improved technologies for interoperability, connectivity, mobility and intelligence, which make enterprises smarter, more agile, mobile and collaborative. Future Internet technologies present enterprises with a new instrument to implement highly efficient business processes that leverage a competitive advantage for the enterprise.

The paper brings an insight into the business processes and business requirements that have been identified in the 10 trials defined by the Future Internet Phase 2 Use Case project FITMAN (Future Internet Manufacturing Technologies) to trigger the use of Future Internet technologies in the factories of the future, focusing on the production, engineering and technical support as the main departments within the enterprise that will provide the business requirements.

The paper provides a clear understanding of which are the business processes (and the value behind), use cases that are driven by Future Internet technology adoption and the business requirements that drive the adoption.

The document also presents the 5 drivers that should be in place for SME and industrial adoption of Future Internet technologies as a basis for the development of innovative business processes

2. Manufacturing Industry Drivers for Adoption of Future Internet Enablers and Smart, Virtual and Digital Platforms

The results presented in this Section have been obtained following an adaptation of the Wellington methodology [1], which is an iterative methodology based on 4 steps. FITMAN has defined 4 major phases to realise the analysis (1) Conceptual design. Approach discussion and agreement (2) Classifying and categorising the content (3) Creation of the template / interview (4) Template and Interview schedule. The complexity of the analysis (10 trials and up to 44 processes) demanded an agile and parallel approach. To address this issue, the FITMAN methodology has combined the use of a questionnaire, an interview process and the notion of trial handbook to perform two analysis iterations.

The results obtained provide a good reference in terms of motivational drivers for adoption of FI technologies by manufacturing industry and enterprises. While, the authors do not claim that the results are fully representative of the sector, they argue that they could be very useful in setting a good understanding on the rationale behind the adoption of innovative ICT solutions by manufacturing industries to support their innovative business processes. Please, also note that engineering and production departments have been mainly involved in the survey and therefore the results should be analysed with this perspective in mind.

The Section presents the results of the survey from different perspectives, comparisons between SF, DF, VF perspectives but also tries to make an analysis of the driving forces behind large and small enterprises while addressing the take up of innovative technologies.

Concerning the General Business Objectives for the adoption of FI technologies, although we see that the main objectives are quite well distributed among all trials, we could somewhat say that there are probably 5 objectives taking the lead over the rest:

- Improve communications/collaboration.
- Reduce production costs.
- Reduce time to market.
- Improve the usefulness of the information.
- Increase production capacity.

With respect to the *Business Impact* from the analysis we conclude that the expected impact is quite high, and that the two main impacts are linked to the reduction of costs and the improvement in efficiency.

Going into detail the Weaknesses and Bottlenecks the main problems detected are related to the inefficient data processing, the existence of rigid and static procedures and the challenging systems interoperability. All three weaknesses (mostly the first and third ones) can be addressed by the proper analysis, selection and implementation of the right IT tools.

Analysing the *Business Requirements* we conclude that the main business areas to which the requirements are related to, are IT and R&D, while management, production control, H&S and production are following behind. With respect to the type of requisites we can remark that most of the requisites are functional and user and technical-based.

The same indicators have been analysed from a Large Enterprises vs. SMEs perspective. The results in the survey reveal that Concerning the General Business Objectives most of them are similarly shared between LEs and SMEs, but we can detect the next divergences:

- As LEs' trials are more specific than SMEs' trials we see that LEs have a larger interest in increasing the production capacity and improving work safety and security, on the contrary LEs find it less significant than SMEs to improve communication and collaboration.
- On the other side, SMEs are much more interested in improving communication and collaboration. In fact, for SMEs this is the most important business objective, while the most important goal for LEs is increasing the production capacity.

With respect to the Business Impact we found that there are no meaningful variations if we take into account the size of the company.

Analysing the Weaknesses and Bottlenecks we conclude that there are not significant differences in the main weaknesses, while when studying the departments involved, we find out that the technical support department is more affected in the case of LEs than it is for SMEs.

Finally, analysing the results from Smart vs. Digital vs. Virtual Factories business process perspective with respect to the General Business Objectives we see that all three types of Factories are quite similar but there are a few points to be highlighted:

– Smart Factory's trials are less focused on reducing time to market and improving communications and collaboration than average. Their main objectives are reducing production costs, increasing production capacity and increasing the usefulness of information.

– Digital Factory's trials are likewise less focused on improving communications and collaboration than average, while reducing time to market is the most critical objective.

– Virtual Factory's trials are mostly centered on the improvement of communications/collaboration.

Such results are well in line with the main concept behind each of the Factories. Taken into account the Business Impact we see that all Smart, Digital and Virtual Factories coincide in identifying efficiency as the main improvement. With respect to the typology of the impact the Virtual Factory is more oriented to the user requirements followed by performance requisites, while both Smart and Digital Factories are mostly centered on technical requirements.

Concerning Weaknesses and Bottlenecks the main results are quite predictable, given that Digital Factory's trials have important bottlenecks related to the inefficient data processing, while human process dependency seems not to be a weakness for the Smart Factory's trials. Concerning the departments being affected by the weaknesses and bottlenecks we notice that for Virtual Factory's trials the most affected area is Technical support, while Management is the most affected area for the Digital Factory, and Manufacturing is the key one for the Smart Factory.

3. Drivers for SME Adoption of FI Technologies in Manufacturing

The previous Section has identified the main drivers business objectives and weaknesses-bottlenecks that maybe behind the successful adoption of FI GE, SE and platforms in a manufacturing context.

This Section briefly introduces the 5 drivers that are key to create the right techno-socio environment for the development of innovative business processes in SMEs. FITMAN has identified 5 drivers [2] shown below for SME engagement & open innovation ecosystem design for FI services for manufacturing.

As shown in the figure below, the main drivers for successful FI adoption lies on the right development of common visions between technology providers, consumers with the notion of minimum viable product-service as acore element in the interaction betwwen offer and demand. The MVP-S is therefore the central element in the development, assessment and communication of benefits laying behind the FI technologies.

The second key aspect is the co-creation of value propositions that are key elements in the development of sustainable business development for future operation of the processes in place.

1. Facilitate the means to discover, raise awareness and co-create a shared view on market needs-challenges and tech opportunities.

2. Facilitate mechanisms for continuous development and open interaction of potential customers in real environments with Minimum Viable Products-Services (MVP-S).

3. Facilitate the environment for co-creation ofa sustainable technological and business value proposition.

4. Support the definition of well founded business models, capitalising on FI assets, capable of capturing market value and financial resources.

5. Leverage the momentum for SMEs and WE through pro-effective (first of a kind) sectorial success story dissemination.

Figure 1. *5 FI-PPP drivers for SME engagement in open innovation ecosystems*

4. Conclusions

The previous sections have provided some discussions about the main findings obtained during the business requirements elicitation phase of the FITMAN project. The first conclusion is that drivers for digital business transformation through ICT in manufacturing differ from SMEs and LE. As highlighted by various studies and the results of this survey, cost remains the main decisive factor for SME adoption of innovative ICT solutions. It should also be noted that being engineering and production departments the majority of the departments taken active part in FITMAN, sales and marketing needs may not have been sufficiently highlighted by the results. After discussion with industry it became clear that enablers dealing with social media and customer-centric design are equally important and should be carefully addressed.

The second important conclusion is that the business value perceived from GEs, SEs and Trial Specific Components (TSC) will differ based on the category of application/service considered (Smart, Digital and Virtual). For instance, one GE could be perceived as enabler to cost reduction in a Smart Factory context and as a manufacturing flexibility enabler in a different context; e.g. Digital Factory. For this reason it is important that the GE is not perceived as an isolated module in the FITMAN context, but as a source of competitive advantage generation.

The third important conclusion lies on the fact that industry perceives FI enablers as a contributor in their business strategy implementation (particularly large enterprises). In this respect, GEs and SEs are an instrument, a means and not an end in the manufacturing innovation strategy. This observation reinforces the importance of presenting GEs as providers of business capabilities and not simply as technical functionality enablers. This entails a further complexity in the characterisation of the enablers developed.

The forth important conclusion lies in the fact that infrastructures for manufacturing innovation go beyond IT and connectivity infrastructures. FITMAN innovation demands that a suitable environment with the required data, equipment and IT infrastructure is available for experimentation. Failing to provide such complete infrastructure will impact on the value perception and innovation adoption of future FITMAN apps. The deployment of innovative apps and services over this types of infrastructures will accelerate the take up of the solutions.

5. Acknowledgements

This work has been partly funded by the European Commission through the Project FITMAN: Future internet technologies for Manufacturing (Grant Agreement No. FP7 604674). The authors wish to acknowledge the support of the EC and the project partners for their contribution during the development of various ideas and concepts presented in this paper.

6. References

[1] Wellington, Jerry, and Marcin Szczerbinski. *Research Methods for the Social Sciences*. London: Continuum International Publishing, 2007.

[2] O. Lazaro "Manufacturing Usage Area in the FI-PPP, Overview and Status Quo" *International FI-PPP Workshop – Status Quo and Outlook on Phase III*, 8 November 2013, Berlin.

Delivering Care in a Future Internet

Christoph Thuemmler* — Thomas Jell**

* School of Computing, Edinburgh Napier University, UK
Merchiston Campus, EH10 5DT
c.thuemmler@napier.ac.uk

** Siemens AG
Infrastructure & Cities Sector
IC MOL TI IMSP
Otto-Hahn-Ring 6
81739 Munich, Germany
thomas.jell@siemens.com

ABSTRACT. *In most European countries direct healthcare costs stand for around 10 percent of the GDP. Health spending is rising faster than GDP and it is estimated to reach 16% of GDP by 2020 in OECD countries. There is clear evidence that more and more health care will be delivered outside hospitals – in day clinics, surgeries, at patient's homes or – via the Internet. What service models will be applied to make the Future Internet serviceable and how may future business models look like?*

1. Introduction

The number of hospital beds in Europe has continuously declined over recent decades. This has in the first instance been due to socio-economic effects (demographic development, austerity) but also because of massive technological progress within the health domain, the area of nano-electronics and Information Communication Technology. As a matter of fact, more people than ever are being treated outside hospitals, in day clinics, day surgeries, GP practices, and lately over the Internet. Our societies have clearly moved from a hospital based, expert focused approach to a distributed, patient centric model, which also gives patients and medical professionals greater degrees of freedom and flexibility. However, in order to be more effective and efficient the distributed, patient cantered care model requires increased levels of mobility and seamless, safe and secure flow of information. In accordance with a recent study of the Oxford Internet Institute the Future Internet is in principle well suited to provide the backbone for seamless and fast safe and secure information access, anywhere, anyhow and at any time (Blackman et al., 2010).

2. Socio-Economic Context

In most European countries direct healthcare costs stand for around 10 percent of the GDP. Across OECD countries, health expenditure has grown by 5% annually between 2000 and 2009 but has seen a sharp decline in 2010 and 2011 due to sluggish government spending. Due to austerity measures the annual growth rates where down to 0.5 percent for both years. Many governments have also tried to contain the growth in hospital spending – one of the biggest ticket items in most countries – by cutting wages, reducing hospital staff and beds, and increasing co-payments for patients (OECD 2013). However Health spending is rising faster than GDP and it is estimated to reach 16% of GDP by 2020 in OECD countries (European Commission 2013).

3. Trends

There is clear evidence that more and more health care will be delivered outside hospitals – in day clinics, surgeries, at patient's homes or – via the Internet. Also there is a clear trend towards self-management and the involvement of more and more informal carers as a consequence of the general demographic development in Europe and recent spending cuts. Interestingly enough the pick up rate of e-health technology has been rather sluggish. A recent report on public consultations on e-health commissioned by the EC points out lack of large scale evidence for potential improvement of health care, budget constraints and the lack of political leadership as the top 3 constraints (European Commission 2011).

4. Requirements and Specification

A crucial part to any systemic effort to identify the most suitable service architecture for any industrial sector or domain is clearly the completion of a comprehensive requirements analysis. Requirements Engineering is well established in industrial domains such as automotive and manufacturing but is new to the health care, wellness and ambient assisted living domains. Although some methods require adjustments there can be no doubt that the general approach of Requirements Engineering is suitable and applicable in the health domain. Well structured and professionally guided requirements engineering workshops have been performed as integral part of FI-STAR for each of the seven use cases in order to model the human to human, human to machine and machine to machine interdependencies. Processes and workflows have been depicted by using standardized Unified Modeling Language (UML) in use case diagrams. The outcomes of the requirements analysis were used to confirm existing Key Performance Indicators (KPIs) and to establish further KPIs to have a clear set of defined, comparable parameters as the basis for evaluation and for future references. This also allowed the identification of a defined set of specifications as a basis for the evaluation of software modules, so called Generic Enablers, the validation of instances and the design of additional Specific Enablers.

5. Legal, Ethical and Technical Standards

One of the challenges of FI-STAR is the compliance with national regulations from at least seven European countries plus European and international regulations. An external ethical advisor has been appointed to watch over the compliance with European and national ethical norms. Data security and privacy are high priority requirements. The legal and ethical norms have a huge impact on the architectural specifications and subsequently on the corresponding business models. Existing technical standards such as ISO 80001, ISO 27000 and others have been considered during the FI-STAR development phase. An expert team is concerned with the validation of the FI-STAR technology and there are efforts towards certification, which have been identified as not only relevant to FI-STAR project but also to the entire FI-PPP program.

6. Architectures and Service Models in Health Care

Service oriented architectures (SoA) Principle advantage of any service oriented architecture or cloud is the ability to provide processing power in a flexible manner, which is also known under the technical term "load balancing". Clouds can operate more effective and efficient, safe energy and reduce the carbon footprint. Clouds have been used frequently in context with virtualization and the provision of services (Software as a Service – SaaS, Platform as a Service – PaaS and recently to express the omnipotence of cloud computing also the technical term of "everything as a Service" – XaaS has emerged). In principle 3 different kinds of Clouds can de distinguished: *Public clouds, Private clouds, Hybrid clouds.*

Public clouds have seen a big hype over recent years especially with regards to the healthcare, wellness and ambient assisted living domains. Although the Public Cloud concept seemed ideal for the health care domain with it's increasingly distributed provision of care and a growing demand for virtualization legal norms, governance issues and privacy concerns have led to a situation which have seen even the market leader to withdraw from the sector. *Private Clouds* are well accepted across the health care industry and in use in many organizations. This might be understood as evidence for the fact that the technological features of service oriented architectures are well accepted but that there are major concerns regarding the management of Quality of service and the establishment of coherent, end to end governance strategies across several organizations. A feasible solution seems to be the *hybrid cloud* concept.

Hybrid Clouds are SOAs typically consisting of interacting public and private clouds. Software, for example, can be provided by a public cloud while the private cloud is able to access data within a "secure zone". Healthcare IT architecture models frequently distinguish 3 different levels of security, the hot zone where no third party access is allowed (sometimes by law), the de-militarized zone where third party activities are allowed under certain conditions and the green zone, where third party activity is tolerated. There are very few reports about the use of hybrid clouds in real world environments available at this point in time. However, FI-STAR is considering a hybrid cloud approach as a feasible scenario, especially in conjunction with the "software to data paradigm" which is describing a reverse cloud approach whereby software is transported to the data rather than the far more common approach where data is transported to the cloud (Thuemmler et al., 2013). E-Health Grid E-Health grids have been discussed since the early 2000 but have never been assessed on a large scale (Keuchkerian et al., 2009). Recent research projects under FP7 and Artemis have revived the discussion regarding the use of grid technology to meet the requirements of an increasingly distributed, patient cantered care model where more and more care is taking place outside hospitals and the citizens are the stewards of their own information. While the Smart 4 All project investigated an innovative middleware platform for inter-working of smart embedded services in immersive and person-centric environments, through the use of composability and semantic techniques for dynamic service reconfiguration and by leveraging on P2P technologies, the CHOSeN Network was aiming to develop application-specifically adaptable communication technologies enabling the real deployment of smart wireless sensor networks in large-scale, performance-critical application fields (CHOSeN, 2008; SM4ALL, 2008). However, with additional outcome from different research domains grid technology might return into the spotlight with regards to safety, security and trustworthiness in order to bridge the cyber-physical gap in a highly distributed and heterogeneous environment.

7. Conclusion

While private clouds are well accepted in the healthcare industry the market has clearly rejected public clouds with their XaaS (everything as a service) approach. However, more dynamic structures seem to be required to fit the new trends in healthcare delivery such as self-management and mHealth platforms. Grid computing might undergo a revival after careful investigation of the new requirements. New business models will be required to depict the upcoming IT strategies.

8. References

Blackman C. et al. (2010), *Towards a Future Internet*, DG Information, Society and Media, European Commission.

CHOSeN (2008), *Cooperative Hybrid Objects Sensor Networks*, Research Project: Network Embedded and Control Systems. European Commision Online: ftp://ftp.cordis.europa.eu/pub/fp7/ict/docs/necs/fp7-fact-sheet-chosen_en.pdf.

European Commision (2013), e-Health : ICT solutions for patients, medical services and payment institutions. Online: http://ec.europa.eu/enterprise/policies/innovation/policy/lead-market-initiative/ehealth/

European Commission (2011), Report on the Public Consultation on eHealth Action Plan 2012–2020.

FI-WARE Lab (2013), *The Open Innovation Lab*. Online: http://www.fi-ware.eu/lab/.

FI-WARE Media Wiki (2013), Summary of FI-WARE Open Specifications. Online: http://forge.fi-ware.eu/plugins/mediawiki/wiki/fiware/index.php/Summary_of_FI-WARE _Open_Specifications

Keuchkerian S. et al. (2009), Grid Briefings: The future of healthcare : eHealth and Grid Computing. Grid Talk 2009. Online: http://www.gridtalk.org/Documents/ehealth.pdf

OECD (2013), *OECD Health Statistics 2013.*

SM4ALL (2008), *Smart hoMes for All; An Embedded MiddlewarePlatform for Pervasive and Immersive Environments for All*, Research Project: Network Embedded and Control Systems. European Commision. Online: ftp://ftp.cordis.europa.eu/pub/fp7/ict/docs/necs/fp7-fact-sheet-sm4all_en.pdf.

Thuemmler C. (2013), Norms and Standards in Modular Medical Architectures, *2013 IEEE Healthcom 15. International Conference.*

Thuemmler C., Magedanz T., Jell T., Covaci S., Panfilis S., Schneider A., Gavras A. (2013), Applying the Software-to-Data Paradigm in Next Generation E-Health Hybrid Clouds, New Generations IEEE (ITNG), 2013 *Tenth International Conference on Information Technology.*

FITMAN Verification and Validation Method

Business Performance Indicators and Technical Indicators

Guy Doumeingts* — Bruno Carsalade* — Michel Ravelomanantsoa*
Fenareti Lampathaki** — Panagiotis Kokkinakos** —
Dimitrios Panopoulos**

* INTEROP-VLab
21 rue Montoyer, 1000 Brussels, Belgium
www.interop-vlab.eu
guy.doumeingts@interop-vlab.eu

** National Technical University of Athens
Iroon Polytechniou str. 9, 15780 Zografou, Athens, Greece
www.epu.ntua.gr
{flamp, pkokkinakos, dpano}@epu.ntua.gr

ABSTRACT. *This paper describes the methods developed to determine the Technical Indicators and the Performance Indicators developed in the FITMAN project. This work is a part of the Validation and Verification methodology proposed by FITMAN project.*

KEYWORDS: *Technical Indicators, Performance Indicators, Future Internet, Validation and Verification.*

1. Introduction

The objective of this paper is to present the methods to determine *Technical Indicators* on one side and *Business Performance Indicators* on the other side for the *FITMAN project* (Future Internet MANufacturing: www.fitman-fi.eu/).

These methods are part of the Verification and Validation methodology developed by the Work Package 2 of the project.

Since the beginning of the project, it was obvious that the nature of the Performances was different to evaluate the technical performances of the Generic

Enablers, Specific Enablers or IT solutions and the performance on a Business point of view of the trial.

Based on these two methods a selection of Business Performance Indicators and Technical Indicators has been performed.

2. Business Performance Indicators

The objective of this chapter is to introduce the method used to determine Business Performance Indicators in the FITMAN project.

2.1. Definition of Business Performance Indicators

There are many definitions concerning Performance Indicators. Among them, the project has chosen the definition proposed in the ECOGRAI Method since 1990 by the laboratory IMS, Productics Group of University of Bordeaux.

BPI (Business Performance Indicator) is a quantified data which measures the efficiency of action variables or decision variables, in the frame of the achievement of an objectives defined for this system.

From these definitions, four elements are very important in order to define a BPI:

– *system* (Enterprise, workshop, department, Trials) in which the BPIs are defined: it is necessary to describe the components of the system and the links between these components in order to identify exactly the domain in which the performances are evaluated;

– *objective* assigned to this system;

– *action variable* or *decision variable*: the action performed or the decision taken to reach the objective;

– *performance indicators* (see the previous definition).

2.2. Determination of Business Performance Indicators Using ECOGRAI Method in FITMAN project

Numerous methods dedicated to Business Performance Indicators (BPIs) are around in the literature, promoted by scientist or practitioners. FITMAN has chosen ECOGRAI for several reasons:

– the support of a structured process to define and to implement the BPIs;

– the simplicity of the method and the logical approach;

– the good acceptance by the end-users (people working in the manufacturing unit);

– the participative approach: the end users are involved in the definition and the implementation of the BPIs;

– the competence of partners in the project on the method: University of Bordeaux and INTEROP-VLab.

2.2.1. *Strength and Originality*

The main advantage of ECOGRAI is to limit the number of BPIs. Usually the BPIs are defined directly from the objectives (arrow number 2). The result is a large number of BPIs because there are a lot of possibilities to determine the BPIs in such situation. The consequence is the difficulties to follow and to understand all the BPIs.

In ECOGRAI, the starting point to determine the BPI is the search of Decision Variable (DV) or Action Variable (AV) to reach the objectives (Arrow 1 between Objectives and DV/AV)). The PIs characterise the result of DV/ AV in reaching the objectives (arrow 1 between DV/AV and Objectives).

The consequence is a limited number of BPIs because usually there is a limited number DV/AV.

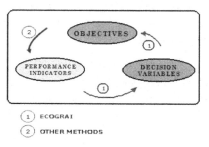

Figure 1. *ECOGRAI concept*

There is perhaps an inconvenience: it is impossible to determine directly the BPIs, it is necessary to use a reasoning which facilitates the understanding of the BPIs.

2.2.2. *The simplified ECOGRAI Method*

Usually, the complete ECOGRAI method has six phases. In the FITMAN project it was decided to use a simplified version of ECOGRAI with only three phases in order to facilitate the application in the trials:

– *First Phase:* Description of the system in which the performance indicators will be defined.

– *Second Phase:* According to the objective of the system the owner of the system determines the potential actions to reach these objectives (called Decision Variables (DV) or Action Variables (AV)).

– *Third Phase:* The performance indicators indicate or characterize the reaching of the objectives by using the DV/AV.

2.3. *Example of Business Performance Indicators resulting of ECOGRAI Application*

Table 1 is an example of one trial of the project.

Objective	DV/AV	PI
Reduction in the use of paper.	To use the trial platform	PI: Ratio: Average number of pages used in the test results recording, archival, after/before the DV/AV implementation during one concrete operation.
To reduce the time to perform, record and analyze the test results.	To use the trial platform	PI: Ratio: Average lead time needed to perform and record the test results after/before the DV/AV implementation during a period.

Table 1. *Business Indicators' Example*

3. Technical Indicators

As also mentioned earlier in the paper at hand, technical verification and validation constitutes the first part of the FITMAN integrated V&V methodology. In order to assess the (either developed or under development) software at all granularity levels and from as many technical perspectives as possible, a set of differentiated and compensated technical criteria have been identified. These criteria are accompanied by appropriate indicators in order to aid the measurement of the software. For each criterion, a set of associated technical indicators was proposed, as depicted in the following table:

– *Functionality* concerns the capability of the software to provide functions which meet the stated and implied needs of users under the specified conditions of usage.

– *Reliability* is the capability of the software product to maintain a specified level of performance when used under specified conditions.

– *Usability* concerns the capability of the software product to be understood learned, used and attractive to the user.

– *Efficiency* refers to the capability of the software product to provide appropriate performance, relative to the amount of resources used, under stated conditions.

SET OF CRITERIA	CRITERIA	INDICATORS
FITMAN GE/SE specific criteria	Openness	Openness Level
	Versatility	Generic Enablers Usage Index; Average Generic Enablers Usage per Trial
Usability	Understandability	Users' required IT background Level
	Ease of learning (learnability)	Learning time; Time to expertise
	Operability	Operation time
	Attractiveness	Users' attraction level; Users' engagement time; Users' satisfaction level regarding system's attractiveness
Functionality	Correctness	Fault Detection; Module fault density; Data integrity
	Interoperability	Interoperability Maturity Level
	Security	Authentication Mechanism Integrity
Reliability	Fault Tolerance	Failure Avoidance
	Recoverability	Availability
	Software maturity	Software Maturity Index (SMI); Failure density against test cases; Failure resolution
	Fault Tolerance	Incorrect Operation Avoidance; Breakdown avoidance; Failure avoidance level; Incorrect operation avoidance; Back up readiness on breakdown; Restorability; Mean recovery time; Restore effectiveness
Efficiency	Time Behaviour	Internal Response time; Internal Turnaround time; System Response time; Throughput; System Turnaround time; Waiting time
	Resource Behaviour	I/O utilization; I/O utilization message density; Memory utilization; Transmission utilization; I/O-related errors; User waiting time of I/O devices utilization
Portability	Adaptability	Adaptability of data structures; System software environmental adaptability; User environment adaptability (or Porting user friendliness)
	Installability	Installation time; Ease of setup retry; Installation effort; Installation flexibility; Ease of installation
	Coexistence	Internal coexistence; External coexistence
	Replaceability	Continued use of data; Function inclusiveness; User support functional consistency
	Hardware independence	Hardware Dependencies
Maintainability	Analysability	Activity recording; Diagnostic functions operability; Audit trail capability; Diagnostic function report
	Changeability	Change recordability; Modification complexity; Software change control capability
	Stability	Change impact; Change success ratio; Modification impact localization
	Testability	Built-in test functions; Autonomy of testability; Availability of built-in test function; Re-test efficiency
	Code Consistency	Cohesion ratio
	Modularity	Cohesion to Coupling

Table 2. *Technical Indicators' List*

– *Portability* concerns the capability of the software product to be transferred from one environment to another and incorporates the following criteria:

– *Maintainability* is interpreted as a set of attributes that undertake the effort needed to make the necessary updates and modifications to the software product and consists of six criteria.

- Finally, the *FITMAN-specific* set of criteria includes openness and versatility, two critical aspects to be considered when assessing the project's software solutions.

- In FITMAN, *versatility* as a criterion concerns the ability to deliver consistently high performance in a very broad set of application domains, from server workloads, to desktop computing and embedded systems and is measured by two indicators defined:

- *The Generic Enablers Usage Index Indicator* (Proportion of GEs that were used by any (at least one) trial) and

- *The Average Generic Enablers Usage per Trial Indicator* (Average number of GEs used in each trial).

- *Openness* in FITMAN is interpreted as the extent to which specific groups may access the software for free with specified rights. Openness is assessed with the help of the: *Openness Level indicator*, defining the four following levels:

- Level 0: Common understanding / open specifications
- Level 1: Provision / Enablers as a Service
- Level 2: Availability / Open-source code
- Level 3: Participation / Collaborative Implementation

4. Conclusion

We must consider the determination of the Technical Indicators (TIs) and of the Business Performance Indicators (BPIs) in the frame of the applications of the FITMAN V&V methodology. The V&V methodology supports also the reporting activity on TIs and BPIs and also the result of self-certification on SurveyMonkey forms. The analysis of the results for Technical Indicators gives for now five different TIs for trial solutions (Generics Enablers, Specific Enablers) and three different TIs for trial Components. Concerning Business Performance Indicators, there is a large variety of BPIs. This is the consequence of the dependence of the evaluation of the performance with the type of products or the type of processes. A generic classification will be produced.

5. Acknowledgements

The FITMAN project is supported by programme FI/PPP of the European Commission, Grant agreement FITMAN n° 604674 (http://www.fitman-fi.eu).

6. References

FITMAN Deliverable D2.1: FITMAN Verification & Validation, Method and Criteria.

FITMAN Deliverable D2.2: FITMAN Verification & Validation, Business and Technical Indicators Definition.

Validation and Quality in FI-PPP e-Health Use Case, FI-STAR Project

Philippe Cousin* — Samuel Fricker** — Dean Fehlmy*** — Franck Le Gall* — Markus Fiedler**

* Easy Global Market
Sophia Antipolis, France
philippe.cousin@eglobalmark.com
franck.le-gall@eglobalmark.com

** BTH
Karlskrona, Sweden
Samuel.fricker@bth.se
markus.fiedler@bth.se

*** Elvior
Tallin, Estonia
dean.felmy@elvior.com

ABSTRACT. The paper will introduce the work currently undertaken within FI-STAR, a FI-PPP Use Case in the e-Health domain. It will present the various issues and challenges faced by the developers in compliance to FI-PPP GE and SEs specifications. It will introduce the Quality indicators the project developed to help ensuring sustainability of the development as well as market acceptance. Quality of Experience as measured by end users as well as health impact are introduced so not only the project will develop interoperable products with high quality but should be accepted by users demonstrating high values of the deliveries.

KEYWORDS: FI-PPP Validation, Quality Indicators, Conformity to Enablers.

1. Introduction on FI-PPP and FI-STAR

With over a billion users worldwide, the Internet is one of history's great success stories. Its global, integrated communications infrastructures and service platforms underpin the fabric of the European economy and society. Yet today's Internet was designed in the 1970s, for purposes that bear little resemblance to current and future usage scenarios. Mismatches between the original design goals and how the Internet is being used are beginning to hamper its potential. Many challenges in the areas of technology, business, society and governance will have to be overcome if the future development of the Internet is to sustain the networked society of tomorrow. To answer these challenges, the European Commission has launched the Future Internet Public-Private Partnership Programme (FI-PPP; see more at www.fi-ppp.eu). The main goal is to advance a shared vision for harmonised European-scale technology platforms and their implementation, as well as the integration and harmonisation of the relevant policy, legal, political and regulatory frameworks. As set forth in the Digital Agenda for Europe, these are considered to be prerequisites for realizing a European online Digital Single Market (DSM) and, more broadly, an inclusive knowledge society.

Programme aims to:

− increase the effectiveness of business processes and infrastructures supporting applications in areas such as transport, health, and energy;

− derive innovative business models that strengthen the competitive position of European industry in sectors such as telecommunication, mobile devices, software and services, and content provision and media.

The FI-PPP follows an industry-driven, holistic approach encompassing R&D on network and communication infrastructures, devices, software, service and media technologies; In parallel, it promotes their experimentation and validation in real application contexts, bringing together demand and supply and involving users early in the research lifecycle. The new platform will thus be used by a range actors, in particular SMEs and Public Administrations, to validate the technologies in the context of smart applications and their ability to support "user driven" innovation schemes.

2. FI-STAR and its Involvement in Validation and Quality Towards Potential Certification

FI-STAR is one of the Future Internet projects aiming at trialling technology in live environments and testing in real-world healthcare, wellness and ambient assisted living situations with people as the grow older. FI-STAR will establish 7 early trials in the Health Care domain building on Future Internet (FI) technology leveraging on the outcomes of FI-PPP Phase 1. The participation of actors including SMEs and Public Administrations, to validate the technologies will lead to involve much more actors to use the platform components and therefore will raise a lot of new issues related to support these new stake holders in using the FI-PPP components. Confidence in the whole programme will be at stake and can be easily endanger if too much weaknesses would be detected. Information on difficulties to use the platform or weaknesses in technical elements uses to be quickly spread up by communities. To prepare such important taking up by larger communities, it is important to develop quality programme to reinforce the robustness of the technical elements while giving reasonable level of confidence to users.

This kind of activities is the basis for the establishment of certification or label scheme and such concept was raised at FI-PPP level in particular when FI-STAR made clear on its firm intention for its own project to ensure robustness of its development and to give confidence to end users by certification. In such new expectation from the FI-PPP programme, FI-STAR is invited to provide input to "certification" where good practices might be extended to the whole programme. As a part of FI-STAR, but not only, will be dedicated to check conformity of Generic Enablers (GEs) that embed common functionality and services for application developers and Specific Enablers (SEs) that embed health-care-specific functionality and services. It is likely feasible that FI-STAR tests and tools could be used for the FI-PPP programme. EC made also clear that, while FI-STAR is operating in the e-health domain, one of its important objectives is, through the e-health demonstrators and pilots, to support and validate the whole programme. Such statement made clear to FI-STAR partners that looking at certification requirements means paying a large attention to certification supporting the FI-PPP programme. Therefore high attention will be devoted to the possible use of certification approaches as part of the quality process. The work package 6 (WP6) "Quality and Validation" of FI-STAR aims at establishing quality monitoring processes within the FI-STAR project. It provides overall methodology, tools and indicators to the project as how to ensure conformity to project objectives and results. This activity defines a Quality Assessment framework leading to identification of Quality Indicators to be used for assessment the development, validation and deployment of the services. It also defines the various validation methods, which will be used within the projects.

3. Quality Assessment Framework and Quality Indicators

Developing a quality assessment framework requires to first clearly define its scope in terms of:

− *Stakeholders*: who are the groups of persons involved in the use of the quality assessment framework.

− *Subjects*: what are the subjects of which quality is to be evaluated.

− *Dimensions*: what are the topics to be considered in the quality evaluation and to which metrics can be associated? The framework associates indicators to the metrics thus allowing getting a measure of the quality level against the different considered dimensions.

It is worthwhile noting that the purpose of the quality assessment framework is not to evaluate everything in all dimensions but rather to focus on few points of interest expressed by the stakeholders and for which metrics can be collected. For that purpose, attention will be paid in selecting S.M.AR.T. (Specific, Measurable, Assignable, Realistic and Time bounded) indicators.

The quality and validation workpackage (WP6) works in close relation with other Workpackages in the project so fostering the use of a shared set of Key Performance Indicators (KPIs) among involved parties. The WP6 (and thus the present document) focuses on indicators being linked or of interest of third parties to the project. Any indicator solely related to the internal project performance is managed directly within the management activities of the project and is thus not considered in the present document. The distinction is then made between:

– *Quality Performance Indicators (QPI):* related to interaction with project third party (providers of generic enablers, users and beneficiaries of the FI-STAR applications, etc.).

– *Project Performance Indicators (PPI):* solely related to internal project performance.

3.1. *Quality Assessment Targets*

Quality expectations also depend on the subject evaluated using the quality assessment framework. The dimensions of interest may be different, the methods and tools to collect them may vary as well as the expected quality level targets. Categories of subjects have been identified at the levels of FI-PPP programme overall, at the FI-STAR project level and at the level of third parties:

– *At the FI-PPP level,* we find the *Generic Enablers* produced by the core platform and made available through the enablers catalogue (FI-WARE). Instances of these enablers can be run "As A Service" from *platforms* managed within the FI-PPP: Open Innovation Lab (OIL), (FI-WARE) and Xifi (federation of platforms).

– *At the FI-STAR project level,* which is the focus of the quality assessment, it starts from the *Specific Enablers* foreseen to be either built from Generic Enablers composition or completely developed depending on the correspondence between project requirements and functionalities offered by the GEs. Then these enablers are instantiated within *platforms* which are then linked through public or private cloud services. Project *application* is run from these *infrastructures*.

– *At third party level*: here are considered elements used in the deployment of FI-STAR solution but not under the project direct control. Examples of such elements include sensors and medical devices used as part of the applications as well as legacy systems of the involved organisations.

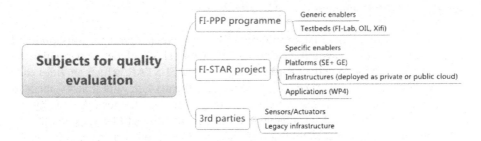

Figure 1. *Potential subjects to be evaluated within the quality assessment framework*

3.2. *Areas of Interest*

Four dimensions of interest have been retained as part of the quality assessment framework. These dimensions were then characterized into sub-dimensions and then indicators. These dimensions are:

– *E-Health:* this dimension includes aspects related to the specificities of the e-health sector and evaluates the value delivered according to the value cases defined by the project.

– *Software quality:* this part focuses on verification and validation of used (generic enablers) and produced (specific enablers and applications) software against its intended use but also analyse its reusability. Approaches proposed include in particular the integration and interoperability evaluation (enablers and 3rd-party systems/components/devices should interoperate according to predefined profiles), compliance (software should comply with the regulations and standards related to the health sector) and coverage (software that is put into use should be completely tested. Particular testing rigour is applied to critical parts of the system).

– *Quality of Experience (QoE):* quality of experience reflects the perception from a user of service. 'User' has to be understood in the wide sense: users include the end users has well as the medical teams intended to be the beneficiaries of the FI-STAR applications and services. In addition, software developers of the project are themselves users of pieces of software developed by other teams either from the FI-STAR project or from external stakeholders.

– *Quality of Service (QoS):* software services fulfil stated quality requirements that have been prioritized by considering the ISO/IEC 25010 Standard on Systems and Software Quality Requirements and Evaluation

Finally the sustainability of the FI-STAR, and more largely speaking FI-PPP, has been retained as a dimension of high interest but which corresponding indicators are already included in the other dimensions, in particular the one being sector specific (health impact) and the one related to reusability of the software.

4. Validation Methodologies Used by the Project

A study was first undertaken to define the requirements on standardisation and certification the project would have to comply with. This includes in particular the outlining of a validation and certification strategy for FI-STAR, which provides easy and simple proof of compliance to requirements to the market. This strategy needs to be pragmatic while complying with the existing regulatory framework, helping the issuing of high quality and sustainable outcomes by the project FI-STAR and the FI-PPP programme. Three different approaches are then proposed depending on the level of the considered requirements:

– *Regulatory requirements:* there is no other choice than ensuring the regulatory compliance of systems, devices and applications put on the market by the project FI-STAR. Nevertheless, this is usual business of the health IT providers being present in the project and thus does not require project specific attention.

– *External requirements:* these requirements come from third parties, external to the project and does not contain mandatory requirements of standardization or certification of IT products or IT-based services. Motivation for certification is thus mostly guided by interoperability interests (also here as also promoted as interchangeability and plugability): FI-STAR developers want to benefit from components (GEs) from the FI-PPP that are in-line with their specification while FI-STAR wishes to develop platforms that are re-useable by third parties (SEs) and which can connect and exchange data with medical systems. In that case, 2 options exist:

- *Validation of GEs/SEs:* this is not provided by any third party today and thus has to be conducted at the FI-STAR level and promoted at the FI-PPP level. This activity is being driven with WP6.

- *Interoperability with health systems:* many profiles based interoperability schemes and tools are already promoted by many EU projects and FI-STAR has to capitalize on this important existing offers. It should be conducted on a voluntary basis. For instance Projectathon organised in the framework of Connectathon is one of the most efficient way to expose FI-STAR outcome to the health market reality. Such activity has to be done by development teams within FI-STAR with the support of dissemination and exploitation teams. Other offers are developed within the e-Health thematic network Antilope.

– *Internal requirements:* while we need to communicate with the external world, we need to be sure what we deliver has high quality and is conform to the expectation (also from users' side). Quality improvement has to be sought to increase the acceptability of FI-STAR outcomes. The project thus has to set its own quality requirements and deploy its internal processes to monitor them.

To cover all the validation requirements we will use several methodologies such as:

– V&V White Box testing (e.g. using IEEE 1012) for addressing the Internal requirements;

– V&V Black-Box testing for conformity to GEs or SEs specifications;

– Quality of Experience (QoE) and Quality of Services (QoS);

– Model for ASsessment of Telemedicine (MAST) for evaluation of health impacts.

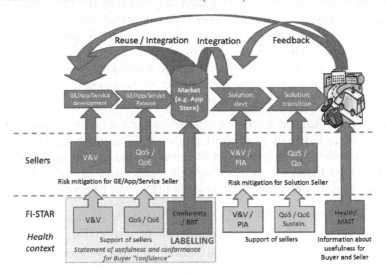

Figure 2. *Overview of FI-STAR validation tools*

We cannot present all the approaches but it is recommended to read the public FI-STAR deliverable D6.1 on Basic validation methodology and Quality control indicators. We can however present some specific approaches that FI-STAR will use such as Quality of Experience and Black Box testing using Model Based Testing.

4.1. *The Quality of Experience Methodology*

According to the newest working definition (Qualinet), Quality of Experience (QoE) is seen as "degree of delight or annoyance" of a user. Primarily, it is a subjective measure of user satisfaction. In fact, QoE problems are typically seen as triggers for user churn, i.e. a user may put a service aside because of bad experience, non-satisfaction, disappointment, etc. Depending on the business model, churn might entail direct or indirect loss of revenue, which explains the particular interest of service and network manufacturers, providers and operators in this matter.

QoE is the outcome of many underlying circumstances, ranging from technical parameters such as network-level Quality of Service (QoS) to content and context. Indeed, an important share of the research work on QoE focuses on quantifications of the relationships and inter-dependencies between QoE and underlying parameters, in particular QoS. For instance, discusses a generic relationship between QoE and QoS in form of exponential functions, which typically appear in the context of waiting times. Such an exponential relationship between the QoE (here: opinion score) and the QoS (here: response time) implies that each extra amount of waiting time leads to an extra reduction of user ratings by a certain percentage (typically 10.20% per second). The QoS "response time" can in turn be affected by other QoS parameters such as losses, link-level delays, bandwidth restrictions etc. Such relationships, which may include any number of parameters and which are not confined to QoS, are commonly denoted as QoE models.

QoE can be assessed directly by observing and/or asking users, e.g. using questionnaires, or indirectly by measuring relevant parameters within an application and/or network devices, under the condition that a valid QoE model can be used to translate QoS into QoE values. Such measurements might amongst others include usage of a feature in case a clear correlation with QoE can be derived.

In questionnaires, users are typically asked to provide:

– ratings in form of (typically numerical) opinion scores (OS);

– rationales in form of comments on QoE and/or explanations of their ratings.

Quantitative ratings and qualitative rationales represent two sides of the same coin. Through the latter, users can explain their perception and subsequent rating in their own words and in detail, while the numerical rating allows for deriving quantitative relationships between cause and consequence, such as trendlines/curves and correlation factors, etc.

In the FI-STAR context, different stakeholders are interested in different QoE aspects. In particular, we distinguish between the *user view* (as the addressee of FI-STAR solutions) and the *developer view* (who shall benefit from FI-PPP technology).

A nice study that demonstrates the strength of the coexistence of both ratings and rationales is [HP study 2000].

4.2. The Black Box V&V Testing Using MBT

Model-based Testing (MBT) is a generic term used to denote all testing approaches whereby model-design techniques are applied to enhance testing and affiliated activities quantitatively, qualitatively or both. This approach is used for developing Black box test and tools for the conformity to GEs or SEs.

As depicted in Figure 2, the MBT process mainly consists of two activities:

– Model-Based Test Design consists in using various sources of information describing the system or technology to be tested to design a so-called test model.

Among the information used for describing the system, one can name the requirements on it and a specification of the system, be it informal, formal (e.g. some formal model) or a combination of both. The test model resulting from this activity is a (semi-)formal representation of the system from a testing perspective. The testing perspective implies here that certain aspects may be highlighted in this model, that are only relevant from the point of view of testing, while others that play a less important role in that context may be hidden or encapsulated. One of the biggest challenges in MBT is finding the right balance between those various aspects in the test model to ensure that, while it would allow the derivation/ generation of test cases with the highest possible level of intended coverage, the model would still remain reasonably understandable to human readers thereof.

– Test Model Transformation consists of applying test generation algorithms or known test patterns to generate/derive executable test cases from the test model designed in the previous step. It's worth noting here that by executable test cases, one does not necessarily mean automatically executable test cases. In fact, the level of granularity for the generated test cases is highly dependent on the level of abstraction and the "completeness" of the designed test model. Therefore, automatically executable test cases or manually executable test procedures may be the output from this activity.

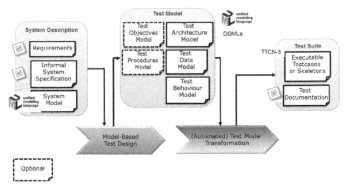

Figure 3. *The Model-Based Testing Process*
here with full chain tests development using TTCN-3

5. Conclusions

The FI-PPP programme is a very ambitious one and will face important challenges in validation in order to provide confidence in solutions to market stake holders including SMEs. FI-STAR is facing the same challenges although focussing in one area (i.e. e-health). It is however demonstrating that we can use cost-effective state of the art techniques to produce necessary tests and tools (e.g., MBT) while involving users in the validation process (e.g., QoE). Further proofs of concept have been developed in FI-STAR and several sets of tests will be developed until end of the project mid-2015. FI-STAR is also using generic methodologies, which would allow for the solutions to be applicable for the whole FI-PPP programme. FI-STAR expects therefore providing useful contribution to develop the market confidence in the FI-PPP solutions.

6. Reference

HP study 2000] A. Bouch, A. Kuchinsky, and N. Bhatti. *Quality is in the eye of the beholder: Meeting user's requirements for Internet quality of service.* Technical Report HPL-2000-4, HP Laboratories Palo Alto, January 2000.

Workshop 3

ICT Services and Interoperability for Manufacturing

Report

Keith Popplewell

Faculty of Engineering and Computing
Coventry University
k.popplewell@coventry. ac.uk

The purpose of Workshop on ICT Services and Interoperability for Manufacturing, Workshop 3 I-ESA 2014, were to review current research and developments in the delivery of ICT support to manufacturing enterprises and production networks, and to be a forum for discussion between researchers active in the related domains of enterprise interoperability, future internet enterprise systems and factories of the future. Although the call for papers was open to all, the workshop particularly targeted four EU FP7 projects: FLEXINET, ADVENTURE, IMAGINE and TELL-ME. The first three of these are all part of the Factories of the Future Public Private Partnership initiative whilst the last is a living lab funded by DG-CONNECT. We summarise here the presented papers, and the discussions which followed the presentations.

The first paper titled Holistic, Scalable and Semantic Approach at Interoperable Virtual Factories (Pavlov, G., Manafov, V., Pavlova, I., Manafov, A and emanating from the ADVENTURE project, examined an application of interoperable data provisioning and discovery (DPD) services to support collaboration in global virtual factories. A model of DPD was presented, which, building on earlier research, is holistic and extensible, and provides for industry interoperability. Software provides access to the DPD model through well-defined protocols exposing REST-orient service interfaces to encourage wide adoption. Future work is planned to prove viability through a real industrial case with hundreds of disparate organisations originating from a genuine supply chain ecosystem.

The second paper titled Predictive Industrial Maintenance: A Collaborative Approach by Ferreira, F., Shamsuzzoha, A., Azevedo, A., Helo P, again arising out of the ADVENTURE project, describes a loosely coupled virtual enterprise management tool supporting a collaborative approach to predictive maintenance, showing how a collaborative platform can help achieve predictive maintenance regarding on-the-fly collaboration between equipment suppliers and their customers. Hardware integrated with a process monitoring tool allows monitoring and management of collaborative maintenance processes through a user interface in the form of a dashboard showing the actual status of maintenance process instances using a holistic collaborative process live model. The dashboard will be part of a broader platform designed and developed within the ADVENTURE project.

The last paper from the ADVENTURE project titled On Optimizing Collaborative Manufacturing Processes in Virtual Factories (Schuller, D., Hans, R., Zöller, S., Steinmetz, R , presents an approach to optimisation of manufacturing processes in virtual factories (VF). In any VF there are potentially large numbers of alternative services and combinations of services available to meet any manufacturing requirement. This is modelled as a classical optimisation problem, and solved to present the optimal combination. The formulation of the problem is made more complex by the fact that alternative services are not necessarily equivalent, and subject to some constraints, may be applied in parallel or alternate sequences.

The first paper from the IMAGINE project titled Cloud-based Interoperability for Dynamic Manufacturing Networks by Stock, D. and Bildstein, A, showed how a cloud based integration platform for dynamic manufacturing networks (DMN) is able to support effectively the process of data exchange. One of the main challenges during in building up and managing a DMN is the exchange of required data between the partners. The authors show how a cloud-based integration platform for DMNs is able to effectively support the process of data exchange, and furthermore demosnstrates how a cloud-based integration platform allows. If production IT functionality is also provided on the platform in the form of services, even SMEs lacking proper IT systems are able to provide and exchange necessary current production data.

This IMAGINE project paper titled Modelling Interoperability-related, Economic and Efficiency Benefits in Dynamic Manufacturing Networks through Cognitive Mapping (Markaki, O., Koussouris S., Kokkinakos, P., Panopoulos, D., Askounis, D, proposes the use of the causal characteristics cognitive maps to create a network of interconnected performance DMN factors, attempting to cultivate an understanding around the benefits of DMN participation. Semi-structured interviews were used to elicit DMN concept variables and their correlation through concept maps. The derived map is generic to support application to the majority of DMN formations, but can still promote debate and further investigation, thus enhancing managerial decision making.

This paper, emanating from IMAGINE titled A smart Mediator to Integrate Dynamic Networked Enterprises by Diop, c., Kamoun, A., Mezghani, E., Zouari, M., Exposito, E, demonstrated how the IMAGINE integration platform can contribute through the addition of mechanisms for semantic reconciliation between partners. Future virtual ecosystems, where each SME involved exposes its systems and capabilities as services, will require a platform allowing management of a flexible and agile interpretation of available services. This paper shows the IMAGINE integration platform contributes by adding mechanisms for semantic reconciliation between partners as well as secure and scalable services collaboration within dynamic manufacturing networks. Current work addresses the implementation of the defined components that will be validated and integrated into the final release to the IMAGINE platform. Future work will be focused on the demonstration of the benefits of the proposed solutions to cope with the new generation of dynamic manufacturing networks for collaborative enterprises.

The paper from TELL-ME titled Binding Together Heterogeneous Future Internet Services in Manufacturing Workplaces by Sesana, M., Gusmeroli, S. and Sanguini, R., discussed the solution proposed by the project to bind together heterogeneous training services using a lightweight XML schemas. The living lab focuses on the remote training approach implying several challenges in the selection and blend of heterogeneous ICT learning services (for example a video lesson in YouTube, a pdf manual and an instruction list to some manual exercises to be done). The use of such heterogeneous training media and content is needed to meet differing needs imposed by the types of activity to be performed after training and the nature of the learning process.

The last paper of this workshop, from the recently started FLEXINET project, titled Intelligent Systems Configuration Services for Flexible Dynamic Global Production Networks by Young, R., Popplewell, K., Jaekel, F-W., Otto, B., Bhullar, G, elaborated on the vision of an ability to configure and re-configure global production networks to meet the ever-changing demands of product-service requirements. The research approach focuses on the provision of software services to support the need for rapid reconfiguration; services are underpinned by new enterprise modelling methods and a hierarchy of reference semantics that provide the core basis for knowledge sharing across the multiple factors that need to be addressed in effective production network configuration.

Following the presentations, discussion focused on the common interests of these projects, which clearly all address the issues of enterprise collaboration at some level. Commonalities include the need for system interoperability, which in turn requires considerable semantic alignment or, more commonly in the collaborative environment, semantic mapping. Whilst the broad problems addressed are common the projects approach from different perspectives, and overall we can probably conclude that there would be benefit to SMEs and larger enterprises if the services arising from all these projects could be available through coherent platforms, and might share common knowledge, information and data base infrastructures.

Intelligent Systems Configuration Services for Flexible Dynamic Global Production Networks

R.I.M. Young* — K. Popplewell** — F.-W. Jaekel*** — B. Otto**** — G. Bhullar*****

* Loughborough University
Loughborough, Leicestershire, UK
r.i.young@lboro.ac.uk

** Coventry University
Priory Street, Coventry, UK
k.popplewell@coventry.ac.uk

*** Fraunhofer Institute for Production Systems and Design Technology IPK
Pascalstraße 8-9, 10587 Berlin, Germany
frank-walter.jaekel@ipk.fraunhofer.de

**** Technische Universitaet Dortmund
August Schmidt Strasse, Dortmund, Germany
boris.otto@tu-dortmund.de

***** Control2K
Waterton Technology Centre, Waterton Industrial Estate, Bridgend, UK
gbhullar@control2k.co.uk

ABSTRACT. *The ability to re-configure effectively a global production network to meet the ever changing demands of business product-service requirements is a significant problem for manufacturing industry that raises issues for the dynamic sharing and reuse of information and knowledge between systems and across domains. The research approach discussed in this paper focuses on the provision of software services to support this need. These services are underpinned by new enterprise modelling methods and a hierarchy of reference semantics that provide the core basis for knowledge sharing across the multiple factors that need to be addressed in effective production network configuration.*

KEYWORDS: *Software as a Service, Ontology, Standards, Interoperability, Global Production Networks.*

1. Introduction

The FLEXINET project aims to provide services that support the design and provision of flexible interoperable networks of production systems that can be rapidly and accurately re-configured based on the implementation of new technologies. It applies advanced solution techniques to the provision of a set of Intelligent Production Network Configuration Services that can support the design of high quality manufacturing networks, understanding the costs and risks involved in network re-configuration, and then mitigating the impact of system incompatibilities as networks change over time. The FLEXINET end user partners are especially interested in understanding the impact of external demands, such as environmental regulations, on their business and most especially when related to the introduction of new product-service opportunities into their production network. Therefore, the availability, accessibility and usability of reliable data as well as the ability to use it for strategic and tactical decisions is of particular importance.

The provision of three key software services is under investigation, underpinned by a set of reference ontologies to ensure a consistent understanding of product-service production knowledge. The first is a strategic business model evaluator that will consider the strategic business interdependencies for product-service manufacture in order to provide cost comparisons and risk evaluations. The second is a production network configurator that can support the design and evaluation of the required organisational and process structures. The third is a compliance evaluator that will identify potential product versus service lifecycle compliance issues through the evaluation of proposed network changes. The underpinning reference ontologies will provide a standard foundation from which industry sector specific solutions can be adapted.

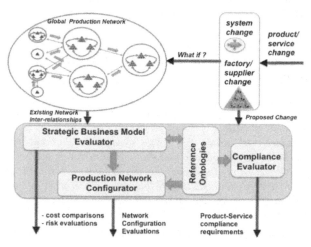

Figure 1. *The FLEXINET Concept: Intelligent Production Network Configuration Services*

The configuration of these service components is also aimed at improved integration between strategic and tactical business aspects to enhance the successful realisation of new business models. These configuration services, adaptable to suit multiple industrial sectors, will provide an understanding of the implications for the business of potential alternative production network configurations made necessary by product-service changes or new product-service requirements. The FLEXINET concept is illustrated in Figure 1.

2. Global Production Networks: The Need for FLEXINET Services

By employing a Global Production Network an organisation can become more adaptive to change, adopt technology at a faster pace, lower its costs and ultimately be more successful at fulfilling its customer and end user needs. Utilising a globally spread network introduces a broad range of factors that can potentially have significant effects on the design of product-service systems. Moreover the comprehension and utilisation of information between numerous and varied partners, suppliers and systems within such a network brings added complexity to the issue of interoperability. This leads to the need for flexible product-service design tools along with a set of underlying reference ontologies to provide a common semantic base that in combination can enable product-service design teams to undertake effective 'what-if' analysis on potential new GPN configurations.

Research has made some progress in understanding interoperability issues for enterprises and manufacturing, but less so upon interoperability for GPN (Young *et al.* 2007; Borgo and Leitão, 2007). A number of manufacturing models have been developed for the purposes of semantic interoperability and the consolidation of production centric standards (Chungoora *et al.* 2012; Chungoora *et al.* 2013a) which in combination provide the basis for the ontological approach being explored in FLEXINET.

The project is applying and extending this understanding to the co-evolution of product-service production network systems to provide compliance services that can evaluate the system compliance requirements of alternative product-service production network configurations. This new understanding is to be implemented and exploited through the use of emerging commercial ontology development and declarative KB tools tools, collaboration infrastructures and the systems integration tools of our IT industry partners.

3. The FLEXINET Approach

FLEXINET aims to support decision-making in the early design of global production network configurations, which are based on the implementation of new complex technologies, to support the realisation of new or adapted business models. FLEXINET is applying advanced solution techniques to the provision of a set of Intelligent Production Network Configuration Software Services that can support the design of high quality manufacturing networks. To do this it is targeting three areas of service as follows: (i) A strategic business model evaluator which supports the understanding of the costs and risks involved in network re-configuration (ii) a production network configurator that can support the design and evaluation of the required organisational and process structures and (iii) a product-service compliance evaluator that will identify compliance issues through the evaluations of proposed network changes against existing ontological models of the product-service-production systems.

These three key areas of service are underpinned by a set of reference ontologies to ensure a consistent understanding of product-service production knowledge. The reference ontologies will provide a standard foundation from which industry sector specific solutions can be adapted. The reference ontology will comprise concepts both internal (e.g., replenishment times, asset capacities) and external (e.g., raw material prices, labour market information) to the network in order to ensure all relevant information and data is considered during business model and production network design evaluation. The configuration of the service components is also aimed at improved integration between strategic and tactical business aspects to enhance the successful realisation of new business models. These configuration services, adaptable to suit multiple industrial sectors, will provide an understanding of the implications for the business of potential alternative production network configurations made necessary by product-service changes or new product-service requirements.

4. Development of Reference Ontologies for Global Production Networks

One of the main facets of the project will be to develop a set of reference ontologies on which to base the FLEXINET services. This will result in a clear understanding of the types of concepts involved in the reconfiguration of product-service globalised production networks and the constraints that must, or may, be considered when reconfiguring the network. The resulting knowledge formalisation, extended with a fact base, developed in Common Logic, will support network design by providing answers to "what if" queries that can be used to compare alternative potential network configurations. These comparisons will identify the extent to which interacting systems in the network comply with the conceptual interaction requirements inferred from the ontologies.

In FLEXINET we take the view that enterprise ontologies must be built from a common base for ease of construction, effective interoperability and flexible reuse, following the positive findings of the Interoperable Manufacturing Knowledge Systems project (Chungoora *et al.* 2012). Given we are focused on systems for the production of product-services, this leads to the view that we require multiple level ontologies, starting from a common 'systems' foundation ontology and building, through various layers, to enterprise specific ontologies that provide specialised concepts, but built layer upon layer so that a clear understanding of the concept relationships can be maintained. The initial systems foundation level ontology based on the work of Hastilow (Hastilow 2013).

Significantly, we anticipate that in order to maximise the industrial uptake of this approach that the lower level ontologies, from the systems foundation up to the product-service production ontology, should be ideal candidates for standardisation. In this way, ICT developers and industrial end users should be able to maximise the benefits of semantic consistency in their development and use of Software as a Service solutions.

5. Intelligent Platform and Configuration Services

FLEXINET is designing and developing the IT collaborative infrastructure and relevant services to implement the decision support systems for the representation, configuration and evaluation of global production networks. It will utilise existing Software as a Service technology as far as possible in order to develop its own Production Network Design configuration environment. This will be characterised by the three main service areas listed in section two above and detailed as follows:

1. An economic and risk assessment service which can be used to evaluate the impact of introducing innovations in an existing global production network. Innovations could be at the level of product (new materials, new design, new product line), at the level of production process (new production technologies, new supply chain, new logistic concepts) or at the level of service (e.g. diagnosis, maintenance, energy saving, environmental sustainability).

2. A product-service co-evolution management service with a specific focus on production phase in globalised product-service networks. This IT service will provide information compliance evaluation of production network options against product or service change requirements to help managers implementing the best production paradigm for product-service co-evolution.

3. A production networks evaluation service, which will evaluate and rank different possible alternatives of the product-service global production network, on the basis of a Social Technological Economic Environmental Political sustainability multi-criteria analysis. The service may also be extended with a maturity model and a change management facility that will help existing production networks improve their competitiveness in the various aspects of STEEP sustainability model.

In combination these three service areas are being developed to support the needs of our end user partners in three distinct areas of manufacturing industry; pumps, white goods and food and drink.

6. Conclusions

The FLEXINET project is in its early stages but is built upon a broad range of skill and experience in manufacture, in ICT support for manufacture and in related research. The ideas explained in this paper are currently under development against the on-going expansion of the understanding of the FLEXINET end user needs.

We anticipate producing exploitable results in three main areas: (i) new methods and models to help businesses understand the complexity of global production networks and the potential impacts of change (ii) software services that support decisions on the re-configuration of global production networks to meet product-service change requirements and (iii) reference ontologies and methods that can be standardised to support the multi-organisation interactions required in global production networks.

7. Acknowledgements

We wish to acknowledge the FLEXINET consortium and especially the financial support from the European Union Seventh Framework Programme FP7-2013-NMP-ICT-FOF (RTD) under grant agreement no 688627.

8. References

Borgo, S., and Leitão, P. 2007, Foundations for a core ontology of manufacturing. *Integrated Series in Information Systems*, Volume 14, pp.751-775.

Chungoora, N, Cutting-Decelle, A-F, Young, RIM, Gunendran, G, Usman, Z, Harding, JA, Case, K. 2013a. Towards the ontology-based consolidation of production-centric standards, *International Journal of Production Research*, 51(2), pp.327-345.

Chungoora, N., Gunendran, G.A., Young, R.I.M., Usman, Z., Anjum, N.A., Palmer, C., Harding, J.A., Case, K., Cutting-Decelle, A.F. 2012. Extending product lifecycle management for manufacturing knowledge sharing. *Proceedings of the Institution of Mechanical Engineers Part B - Journal of Engineering Manufacture*, 226 (A12), pp.2047-2063.

Hastilow, N. 2013. An Ontological Approach to Manufacturing Systems Interoperability in Dynamic Change Environments. PhD Thesis. School of Mechanical and Manufacturing Engineering, Loughborough University, UK.

Young, R.I., Gunendran, A.G., Cutting Decelle, A-F., Gruninger, M. (2007) Manufacturing knowledge sharing in PLM: a progression towards the use of heavy weight ontologies, *International Journal of Production Research*, 45(7), pp.1505-1519,

Binding Together Heterogeneous Future Internet Services in Manufacturing Workplaces

M. Sesana* — S. Gusmeroli* — R. Sanguini**

* TXT e-solutions
Via Frigia 27, 20126 Milano, Italy
michele.sesana@txtgtoup.com
Sergio.gusmeroli@txtgroup.com

** AgustaWestland Training and Helicopter Support System
Via Indipendenza 2, 20018 Sesto Calende (VA), Italy
roberto.sanguini@agustawestland.com

ABSTRACT. *Remote training approach in manufacturing workplaces implies several challenges in the selection and blend of heterogeneous ICT learning services. This paper will describe the approach followed in order to achieve Interoperability in mixing these Future internet Services. More in details the paper will discuss the solution proposed and under implementation created in order to bind together heterogeneous ICT training services by a loosely coupled integration based on the creation of a lightweight XML schema describing a Learning Path suggesting to the Blue Collar Worker (BCW) a set of actions to be done mixing different kind of training services and manual actions to learn the activity to be executed, and a technical architecture in which training services are mashed-up and run accordingly to the XML modelled.*

KEYWORDS: *Interoperability, Future Internet, Manufacturing, Training Services.*

The necessity to compete in the global market where emerging or survive is more and more difficult bring to European manufacturing companies the need to more and more assure to their customer the best quality level at the minimum price. For perceiving these objectives all the aspects of the company processes and environments should be taken into consideration and fostered to higher levels. In this scenario the training of Blue Collar Workers (BCW) should be seen more and more as an investment rather than a cost. A Computer Numerically Controlled (CNC) machine not correctly configured badly impact on the company in waste of material, waste of time to reset the production, etc. The consumption of training services by BCW at its workplace allows to widen the competence of manufacturing companies' blue-collar workers in the way they could execute a wider range of tasks, at mastery levels of performance; shortening the time to transform a poorly skilled worker (similar to a novice driver who is hesitant, error-prone and struggles with each element of driving) into a master (a skilled driver who drives safely and smoothly without thinking). The challenge is to empower all companies, but especially Small and Medium Enterprises (SMEs), to train with less effort, at less cost and in a shorter time raising their competitiveness to global levels.

The remote training approach implies several challenges in the selection and blend of heterogeneous ICT learning services (for example a video lesson in YouTube, a pdf manual and an instruction list to some manual exercises to be done). In training there are several standards to package different contents like SCORM but, unfortunately, every Learning Content Management System (LCMS) has adopted its own SCORM (Shareable Content Object Reference Model) customisation or proprietary extensions of standard making the interoperability difficult while not possible. In addition to that, more and more, learning contents are emerging from new disparate sources and are user-generated contents following the Web 2.0 approach that cannot be packaged in current LCMS in a short time. Has to be mentioned that all these approaches are content-based while, in manufacturing environment, the manual actions are essential part of the training and cannot be left out.

There are several research projects that are trying to achieve a smart way to combine different training services; in particular the FITMAN Digital and Smart factories is proposing solutions to simply blending together heterogeneous information source and TELL ME project has proposed a methodology to logically mix together different approaches depending on the activity to be carried out, the profile of the BCW and the context. Possible activities, instructional material, experience recording provided by training services are identified and sequenced and an initial schedule is devised, the simplest form of which is to linearly follow one step after the other. This paper wants to propose a solution to the technical problem of bound together different ICT training services and combine them together to overcome the interoperability among them implementing the methodology. The proposal focuses on the creation of a lightweight of an XML schema describing the mix of learning services, and a technical architecture in which training services are mashed-up and run accordingly to the XSD.

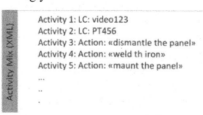

Figure 1. *Learning Path (simplified)*

The Learning Path binding together the heterogeneous services is defined as an XML schema in which a sequence of activities is reported. Activities can be the consumption of a learning contents or a manual activity. Learning Contents types can be very different starting from multimedia interactive lessons to tasks list, quiz or any other kind of document. Actions are described by a sentence.

The architecture running the XML is based on a set of training services running the Learning Contents accessible SaaS and composed by a back-end engine (typically a database/repository), and a front-end (usually a GUI in HTML5) providing access to the back-end engine/data source. While the back-end is hosted on every premises the front-end widgets of HTML5 components can be deployed in several containers depending of the kind of workplace addressed. For the first prototype three containers are supported: augmented reality, an HTML5 environment and a widget based container.

The CORE of the architecture is the *Activity Mashup Engine* that is a software composed by a multi-channel GUI providing the mash-ups of the different services access. The component goal is to read the training services needed in the XML file received in input, arrange the GUI mashing-up the single interfaces and composing the right sequence of steps to be done and communicate to each engine the Learning Content to be run and the modality by which it has to be executed.

Depending on the engine and the nature of the Learning contents to be played the run of the learning content as well as the communication of the right contents to play is done in different ways; it can be based on web-services (for example communicating the URL of the video to be played), or just relying on the mime-type by which the run is left to applications installed in the device (for example the PDF file is opened in the user browser if available on the container). Examples of supported engines under integration are: a streaming server that supports the video consumption; Precision Teaching engine providing the possibility to run Precision Teaching lessons; interactive job card reader, etc.

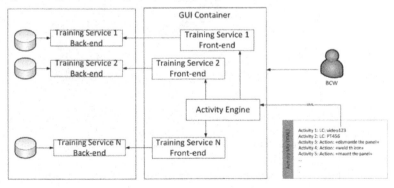

Figure 2. *Architecture (simplified)*

The AgustaWestland role is to trial and evaluates the solution in the aeronautical domain. In particular the final version of the application will be evaluated by AgustaWestland service stations (both internal and external) that are SMEs providing maintenance services to AgustaWestland helicopters.

The first trial in AW is related with the observation and correction, by ICT training services, of potentially dangerous behaviours that might be critical for the safety of the worker and the flight. Behaviours are linked to the so-called Foreign Object Damage (FOD). FOD is a crucial factor for the Aeronautic domain; anything that is where it doesn't belong can be FOD. Every item (tool, screw, sand, etc.) forget into the helicopter can be the cause of an accident during the flight and so it is critical to even avoid potential dangerous behaviours of technicians during maintenance.

Nowadays the training is done by a certified human-factor course and then the worker learn, at the workplace, to avoid potential dangerous behaviour from more experienced persons; for example learn how to discriminate in a very short time external item in the environment. With the remote training approach implemented binding together heterogeneous training services it is possible to approach the periodic refresh of human factor in a dynamic way where the methodology, based on the user profiles, created a customised course to the technician and the architecture presented mix together different learning contents. Typical examples of training services combined are: streaming of motivational videos, streaming of instructional videos, precision teaching lesson service, best practices pdf documents service, etc. At the time behaviour are detected the system mash-up training services to teach the user and to, hopefully reduce/eliminate potential dangerous behaviour.

Figure 3. *Activity Mashup (left) and PT lesson (right)*

The first version of the system described in this paper is currently implemented and under testing in end-users trials. First results of the evaluation are expected by end of July 2014.

Holistic, Scalable and Semantic Approach at Interoperable Virtual Factories

Georgi Pavlov — Velimir Manafov — Irena Pavlova — Atanas Manafov

I-SOFT OOD
Nadejda-3-334-D, 1229 Sofia, Bulgaria
irena.pavlova@isoft-technology.com

ABSTRACT. *In their attempts to support the collaboration between businesses in global context the Virtual Factories face interoperability challenges. The paper presents an approach to address the problem, applying advanced technologies and techniques for implementing interoperable Data Provisioning and Discovery services to support Virtual Factories lifecyle. This work is part of the FP7 EU project ADVENTURE (ADaptive Virtual ENterprise ManufacTURing Environment).*

KEYWORDS: *Adaptive and Distributed Virtual Factories, Interoperability, Manufacturing, Business collaboration.*

1. Introduction

In the current times of globalisation of markets, emergence of developing economies and resources and energy issues, factories are evolving much faster and are becoming more complex, expensive, and geographically distributed (ActPlT 13). Virtual Factories are now intensively being developed, in order to answer to the above challenges and foster the business competitiveness. They aim at widening the business visibility horizon that was for a long time being limited by the traditional isolated ERP and the like systems. Virtual Factories also come to speed up the business processes by facilitating the collaboration and interoperability between different enterprises.

The convergence between Enterprise Interoperability and Enterprise Collaboration is now taking place in the context of service developments within the momentum of the Future Internet movement (COIN 10). Now modern factories are eager to embrace the advanced capabilities of the Internet and shift their working models from centralized towards globalized and distributed business processes and real time streamlining workflows, where services are one piece in a much broader and wider global context and not just isolated offerings. Virtualization at all levels is a key modernization factor.

Nevertheless, Virtual Factories still face obstacles in their attempts to efficiently involve enterprises in cross-company distributed business processes and to support the collaboration between businesses in global context (Abbott et al, 13). One of the major issues is that widely used IT systems are neither interconnected nor interoperable, using a wide diversity of digital forms for information processing, which makes holistic representation, monitoring and management of the factories difficult. The task of overcoming this problem, known as "ensuring enterprise interoperability", appears to be an integral part of the development of the contemporary information services. Because of the need for intensive and at the same time highly precise information exchange, Virtual Factories are particularly sensitive concerning interoperability mechanisms that have to be capable to guarantee seamless global performance in connecting businesses.

The paper presents an approach to address the problem by involving advanced technologies and techniques in implementing interoperable Data Provisioning and Discovery services (DPD) for supporting adaptive and distributed Virtual Factories. This work is part of the FP7 EU project ADVENTURE (ADaptive Virtual ENterprise ManufacTURing Environment.

The paper is structured as follows: In Section 2, we provide an overview of the interoperability challenges of Virtual Factories in the context of the Future Internet. In Section 3, we present how DPD addresses the challenges in the Virtual Factory lifecycle; In Section 4 we outline future development directions and conclude.

2. Interoperability Challenges of Virtual Factories in the Context of the Future Internet

In its 2014 Roadmap (EFFRA 13), based on "The ActionPlanT Roadmap for Manufacturing 2.0" (ActPlT 13), has outlined a number of challenges that are relevant for the so called "Factories of the Future", where Virtual Factories that utilise Future Internet technologies are the main target. The roadmap outlines key ICT megatrends in collaboration, connectivity, mobility and intelligence, as game changers for European manufacturing. The vision embraces manufacturing enterprises and their collaborating stakeholders in a holistic supply chain that aims to be on-demand, optimal, innovative, green and human centred. Interoperability at different levels – technical, semantic and organisational is seen as one of the major concern for the fulfilment of this vision. Some of the challenges that are directly related to interoperability problem are listed below.

Integrated factory models for evolvable manufacturing systems – This challenge calls for development of integrated, holistic, scalable and semantic models for multi-level representation of factory assets, services, processes and resources from different perspectives. This includes multi-level access features, aggregation of data with different granularity, zoom in and out functionalities and support for fast and continuous plant reconfiguration avoiding obsolescence of machines, equipment and manufacturing services. The models should also allow for representation of all production functions and equipment in different industries, by utilizing cross-sector/cross-industry standards and open and interoperable protocols for data representation, communication and process modelling. A particular concern is to lower the barrier for adaptation and adoption of the models by SMEs.

Connected objects for assets and enterprises in the supply networks – Future Manufacturing enterprise assets and products are expected to leverage the concept of the Internet of Things (IoT), where objects carry information about themselves and communicate seamlessly with each other and the world around them, realizing the objective of interoperable, connected objects. Hence relevant abstractions of objects operating at the factory level, business-system and supply-network levels are needed, in order to realize the vision of 'Product-Centered Services'. Further, semantic modelling and description of IoT resources should be developed, such that they could be described and discovered through abstract specifications and partial service annotations.

ICT and market-based costing and manufacturability assessment – Searchable and popular ontologies should be exploited for mapping company experience, expertise and capability to deliver products and services.

Mobile maintenance and servicing cockpit for extended business offerings – Semantic search and linking (annotation) functionality should be developed, together with intuitive user interfaces for customers to visualize and browse the entire range of available service offerings for products.

3. The ADVENTURE Virtual Factory

There are a lot of different definitions of the term Virtual Factory, reflecting the different aspects of distributed manufacturing. In this paper, we will refer to the following definition:

ADVENTURE Virtual Factory (*Virtual Factory*) is a temporary alliance of factories from multiple organizations, managed by a distributed, integrated, computer-based system that interfaces with all systems (of the partnering organizations) necessary for the design, production and delivery of a product (ADV 11).

By this definition and put in the context of Future Internet, *Virtual Factory* faces all the challenges defined in the previous section. The *Virtual Factory* then requires efficient instruments for distributed and interoperable data management across factories and industries. The ADVENTURE technical component that addresses these requirements is called *Data Provisioning and Discovery* (DPD).

The *Virtual Factory* model defines phases of joining the ADVENTURE, searching for appropriate services, plugging in a manufacturing process and playing (executing) the *Virtual Factory* and DPD is actively involved in all of them.

At the *Join phase* factories can join ADVENTURE as *Members*. With the DPD service they can provision formal, structured, semantic-driven factory descriptions compliant with the domain model defined by DPD..

The domain model supported by DPD is very close to several existing distinct models with similar goal like (SEAMLESS 07) and (NEFFICS 12). This confirms its validity as generally applicable, *integrated* model that solves organizational interoperability concerns. Another relevant model is (VFF 12), but DPD is driven by the "Factory-as-a-Service" notion, considering holistically the key concepts of factory *assets*, *services*, *processes* and *resources*, from both business and operational perspective.

The model provides for drilling up and down and accessing data of different granularity. Further, the DPD domain model requires good extensibility capabilities from the modelling technologies that will be employed, in order to ensure effective and efficient tailoring to specific industries and needs.

The DPD model reuses existing and well established ontologies and classifications like Linked USDL, GoodRelations and Schema.org. The core model is further enriched by references to external established classifications like NACE or UNSPC. By employing these cross-sector and cross-industry standards DPD model enables multi industry collaborations. Where the existing standards do not sufficiently and holistically cover the ADVENTURE manufacturing domain model, new concepts are developed and contributed.

Virtual Factory leverages the concept of IoT, by describing through DPD model and then exploiting at runtime information coming from a number of smart objects. The objects are semantically modelled, described as services and are further made searchable through the respective annotations that realizes the vision of interoperable "Product-Centered Services".

DPD builds upon open and interoperable protocols for data representation, communication and process modelling. It relies on RDF (RDF) technology for data model representation, benefiting from its excellent, non-disruptive extensibility mechanism. The DPD model and services also leverage on the openness and the extensibility provided by the LinkedData (LOD) approach.

In an attempt to reach for maximum adoption DPD is designed to support dual service technology interface. The analysis of the state of the art and practice shows that the two most exploited service technologies are SPARQL and OData both building on the REST architecture paradigm and interoperable protocols. To implement this approach, the DPD model is realized as a relational model that is then mapped to RDF. The OData service consumes the relational model directly and presents it as a semi-structured JSON data model. The SPARQL 1.1 Query service works with the RDF representation of the relational model and presents results in one of its supported formats (standard XML search results, rdf, turtle, etc.).

In addition to its service interfaces, DPD also features a user interface that exemplifies how the services can be consumed, lowers the adoption barrier, especially with respect to SMEs, with a ready to use human-oriented interface and is designed according the common guidelines for lightweight, web citizenship.

At the second and the third phase (*Search and Plug)*, the factory descriptions can be correspondingly found and compared via DPD and eventually involved into manufacturing processes design by the interested parties. This is realized through the utilisation of the searchable and popular ontologies mentioned above, in order to find factories matching the required expertise and capabilities. Such searchable properties are provisioned by means of semantic annotations. DPD provides a simplified and intuitive user interface that allows exploring ontologies and choosing concepts from them.

During the Play phase when the process is executed step by step with the plugged services, a decision is taken at each step about the execution of the next one. Based on the current condition of the *Process*, the most suitable *Services* can be searched through DPD and selected for the next step.

4. Industrial Applicability, Future Work and Conclusions

Contemporary manufacturing processes are highly distributed, involving many different parties that provide various products, materials and services for assembling a single product. Often, a number of partners are integrated into manufacturing process, forming a Virtual Factory and utilising Future Internet technologies. In this context ensuring interoperability at all levels is of critical importance.

The paper presents an approach to address the problem by involving advanced technologies and techniques in implementing interoperable Data Provisioning and Discovery services for supporting Virtual Factories.

DPD model is holistic, extensible and provides for cross – industry interoperability, leveraging also IoT and realizing the vision of "Product-Centered Services". The DPD software is designed to provide access to the model via well-defined protocols and most of all with wide adoption in mind. It exposes a set of popular REST-oriented service interfaces that implement the most popular open protocols in the field.

As planned future work and in order to prove its viability and applicability the DPD solution is going to be validated through a real industrial case study in the automotive domain. The validation will occur with real data for hundreds of organizations of different magnitude and their operations, originating from a genuine supply chain ecosystem. Thus, the DPD solution will prove its effectiveness in ensuring interoperability in dynamic manufacturing processes in automotive virtual factories.

5. References

Abbott, P., Zheng, Y. and Du, R. "Innovation through collaborative partnerships: creating the MSN News for iPad app at VanceInfo Technologies", *Journal of Information Technology Teaching Cases*, Online publication 15 January 2013.

ActionPlanT EU FP7 Project, "ICT for Manufacturing The ActionPlanT Roadmap for Manufacturing 2.0", Available at: http://www.actionplant-project.eu/images/stories/vision.pdf.

ADVENTURE, EU FP7 Project "Vision Consensus Document", 2011, Available at http://www.fp7-adventure.eu/wp-content/uploads/2012/D2.1_Project_Vision_Consensus_Document_M3_Nov2011_v1.2.pdf.

COIN EU FP6 Project, "D6.2.1a Integrated EI Value Proposition – M24 issue", http://analytics.ijs.si/~mitja/Courses/Coin_deliverables/COIN_D6.2.1a_First_Integrated_EI_Value_Proposition.pdf.

EFFRA, "FACTORIES OF THE FUTURE, Multi-annual roadmap for the contractual PPP under Horizon 2020", Available at: http://www.effra.eu/attachments/article/129/Factories of the FutureRoadmap.pdf.

Linked Open Data, http://linkeddata.org/.

NEFFICS, FP7 EU Project, http://neffics.eu/.

RDF, http://www.w3.org/RDF/.

SEAMLESS: "Ontology and Multilingual Support Technical Specification", SEAMLESS Project FP6-2004-IST-4-026476, Deliverable D2.1.2, 2007.

VFF, FP7 EU Project, http://www.vff-project.eu.

Predictive Industrial Maintenance

A Collaborative Approach

Filipe Ferreira* — Ahm Shamsuzzoha** — Americo Azevedo* — Petri Helo**

* Manufacturing Systems Engineering Unit
INESC TEC (formerly INESC Porto), Porto, Portugal
filipe.ferreira@inescport.pt
ala@fe.up.pt

** Department of Production
University of Vaasa, PO BOX 700, Wolffintie 34, 65200 Vaasa, Finland
ahsh@uva.fi
petri.helo@uva.fi

ABSTRACT. *This paper focuses mechanisms that allow monitoring industrial equipment's and manage maintenance operations through collaborative business processes. At first, it highlights the concepts of predictive maintenance in industrial environments and how a collaborative platform can help achieve predictive maintenance regarding on-the-fly collaboration between equipment suppliers and their customers. Secondly, a hardware system to be applied to industrial equipment's is then focused. This hardware system is integrated with a process monitoring tool. This research also presents an interactive user interface layer in the form of dashboard with the objective to monitor the equipment status and notifications as well as monitor and manage the respective collaborative maintenance process. Overall research work presented in this paper is designed and developed within the scope of the European Commission NMP priority of the Seventh RTD Framework Programme for the ADVENTURE (ADaptive Virtual ENterprise ManufacTURing Environment) project.*

KEYWORDS: *Predictive Maintenance, Process Monitoring, Business Network, Virtual Enterprise Management Platform, Dashboard.*

1. Introduction

Today's uncertain and competitive business environment, manufacturing companies are not always capable to change with the times to adapt and thrive in.

SMEs are very much concern to sustain in such environment with respect to understand changes in the market, to recognize new business opportunities, to deliver new customer service and to adapt quickly their businesses to meet growing customers' requirements. In order to adapt such customer requirements efficiently and effectively manufacturing companies are moving towards business collaboration, where two or more likeminded companies cooperate with each other to establishing a mutually beneficial working environment. Growing concern of business collaboration inspires toady's manufacturing companies; especially SMEs to cooperate with each other instead of compete for mutual benefits. This cooperation can be formed and executed in several forms such as business community, industrial cluster, collaborative network organization (CNO) (Camarinha-Matos et al., 2008), virtual organization (VO) (Carneiro et al., 2010), virtual enterprise (VE) (Molina et al., 2007), etc. Taking into account this global scenario, there's no space for errors, rework or long periods of downtime in the shop floor and so the need for predictive maintenance that plays an important role. Typically, the manufacturing companies are SMEs, with dozens or hundreds of heterogeneous equipment's with no integration with the factory level i.e. each machine has its own isolated control system. Providing SMEs with tools to monitor and manage the equipment operation will help then to shift from a corrective to a predictive maintenance and thus decreasing the risk of failure and downtime of their production lines.

2. Theoretical Background

Predictive Maintenance attempts to evaluate the condition of equipment by performing periodic or continuous (online) equipment condition monitoring. The ultimate goal of predictive maintenance is to perform maintenance at a scheduled point in time when the maintenance activity is most cost-effective and before the equipment loses performance within a threshold. This is in contrast to time- and/or operation count-based maintenance, where a piece of equipment gets maintained whether it needs it or not. Time-based maintenance is labour intensive, ineffective in identifying problems that develop between scheduled inspections, and is not cost-effective. The "predictive" component of predictive maintenance stems from the goal of predicting the future trend of the equipment's condition. This approach uses principles of statistical process control to determine at what point in the future maintenance activities will be appropriate. Most inspections are performed while equipment is in service, thereby minimizing disruption of normal system operations. Adoption of predictive maintenance can result in substantial cost savings and higher system reliability.

Reliability centred maintenance (RCM) emphasizes the use of predictive maintenance techniques in addition to traditional preventive measures. When properly implemented, RCM provides companies with a tool for achieving lowest asset Net Present Costs for a given level of performance and risk (Zhou et al., 2007).

3. VE Predictive Maintenance Through Integration Black

In order to integrate the equipment, an integration "black box" as well as the software integration tool was developed. The raw data for predictive maintenance is collected by the black box from programmable logic controllers, Industrial PCs and Sensors. It has several interfaces such as Ethernet, 802.1x, RS482, RS232, USB as well as direct digital and analog IO which is helpful for old equipment's where there's to communication ports.

The Black Box as shown in Figure 1 Runs Linux Operating System and a webserver with make possible the integration with the overall platform via a Gateway Service. It connects to the internet via Ethernet or 802.1x protocol.

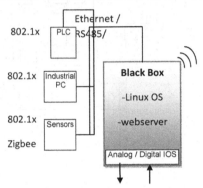

Figure 1. *Integration Black Box*

3.1. *Shop Floor Integration Black Box*

In order to integrate the equipment, an integration "black box" as well as the respective Gateway was developed. The Raw data for predictive maintenance is collected by the black box from programmable logic controllers, Industrial PCs, DCSs, Sensors from different vendors using different communication protocols and physical layers as it counts with several interfaces such as Ethernet, 802.1x, RS482, RS232, USB as well as direct digital and analog IO which is helpful for old equipment's where there's no communication at all and all is based on relays and discrete controllers (temperature, pressure, flow, timers, counters, encoders, etc.).

The Black Box Runs an OPC Server on top of Linux OS, enabling the integration with the overall virtual enterprise platform via a Gateway implemented Services. Moreover the black box counts with an intuitive User interface allowing the definition of alarm trigger rules. Events are exposed through the gateway to the workflow engine with retrieves and update the information to the process monitoring.

3.2. *Process Monitoring*

The monitoring component in the platform is the component that provides the real time monitoring of ongoing process, historical data relating to finished processes and instances and business analytics relating to process and activities types. The Process Monitoring component provides real time, log and performance data relating the virtual factory processes.

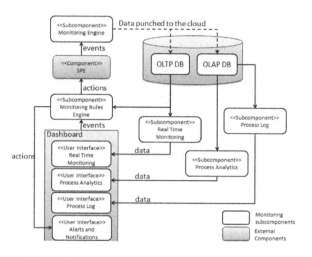

Figure 2. *Process Monitoring Subcomponents*

As represented in Figure 2, process monitoring component contains five main sub-components:

- – Monitoring Engine.
- – Real-time Monitoring.
- – Process Log.
- – Process Analytics.
- – Monitoring Rules Engine.

The Monitoring Engine captures the events produced by the Smart Process Engine and stores the relevant event data in the cloud. The Real-time Monitoring component provides a live view of the ongoing processes using the process editor interface, so that virtual factories brokers may decide to undertake flow adjustments and efficient decisions in order to improve the performance of the manufacturing processes.

The Process log component allows users to search for finished process instances and visualize its data in a graphical interface. The Process Analytics component provides the key performance indicators relating to the manufacturing processes and partners. Finally, the alerts and notifications component allows the definition of rules based on process execution delays (e.g., if a process has 5 days to execute and it is now day 6) that are evaluated by the Rules Engine. This component throws alerts to the Dashboard, as well as performs action upon the Smart Process Engine.

4. ADVENTURE Dashboard: Tool to VE Process Monitoring

The dashboard user interface as designed and developed within the contexts of ADVENTURE project (ADVENTURE, 2011) acts as a visual interface of VE business processes. This component displays the real-time status information of the VE processes. This status information can be displayed in the form of graphical representations (e.g. texts, tables, graphs) along with notifications and alerts. This status update of the processes with accompanying notifications and alerts helps VE broker and partners in decision making process. It would consequently support to avoid abnormal situations and managing risks. This kind of status information can also be used as predictive maintenance during VE operations.

Figure 3 (below) displays a snap shot of ADVENTURE dashboard prototype, where different widgets such as resources, process instances lists, my smart objects, etc., are displayed. These widgets are designed based on the requirements of the specific process information. For instance, 'Resources' widget visualizes the information associated with specific resource status such as CO_2 footprint, energy consumption, steps finished per day, resource shortage, resource failure, etc., during the VE execution.

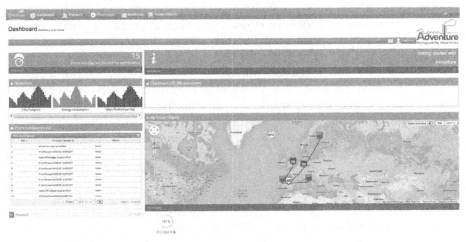

Figure 3. *Overview of the ADVENTURE Dashboard Homepage*

All such resource information can be obtained from the smart objects as attached to the specific resources in interest. For instance, the 'black box' integration tool as designed and developed within the scope of this research can be attached with specific equipment or resource to get its status information. This black box which also acts as a smart object collects equipment or resource data such as equipment temperature, humidity, CO_2 level, etc., and transmits such valuable information which is eventually displayed over the dashboard user interface. This information update is processed periodically following some kind of schedule. Such periodic information update of the specific equipment or resource contributes to forecast its condition. This information forecasting can be used as the major source of predictive maintenance of the equipment.

5. Conclusions

This research highlights a loosely coupled virtual enterprise management tool applied to the Predictive Industrial Maintenance Processes. The Real Time Monitoring will show the actual status of maintenance process instances using a holistic collaborative process live model. This way, it will be easy for the user to identify and track the process instances. The Business Activity Monitoring will be an independent service that will rely on the data stored by the Events Receiver in the Cloud Storage. The purpose is to allow the user to configure KPIs related to the maintenance processes and then provide a graphical display in the Dashboard in order to track the KPIs. The Rules Engine will allow the user to define rules and associated actions. For that purpose, a graphical rules editor should be developed.

This research also presents a holistic dashboard user interface which comprises of a set of advanced technologies in order to gather, aggregate and thus visualize real-time information update of the virtual enterprise business processes at the operational level. This dashboard used as a monitoring tool as part of a broader platform designed and developed within the scope of ADVENTURE European project. Through this dashboard, the VE broker as well the partners would be able to monitor and manage their processes in an effective and efficient way, which consequently contributes to avoid or minimize the overall risks levels within the VE business environment.

6. References

ADVENTURE (Adaptive Virtual Enterprise Manufacturing Environment) (2011), European RTD project, Grant agreement no: 285220, Duration 01.9.2011-31.08.2014.

Camarinha-Matos, L.M., Afsarmanesh, H,, Galeano, N. & Molina, A. (2008) "Collaborative Networked Organizations – Concepts and practice in manufacturing enterprise", *Computers & Industrial Engineering*.

Carneiro, L., et al. (2010), "An innovative framework supporting SME networks for complex product manufacturing". *Collaborative networks for a sustainable world*, Volume 336, pp.204-211.

Grefen, P. (2006), "Towards Dynamic Interorganizational Business Process Management (keynote speech)", *Proceedings 15th IEEE International Workshops on Enabling Technologies: Infrastructures for Collaborative Enterprises*; Manchester, UK, pp.13-18.

Molina, A., Velandia, M. & Galeano, N. (2007), "Virtual Enterprise Brokerage: A Structure-driven Strategy to Achieve Build to Order Supply Chains", *International Journal of Production Research*, Vol. 45, No. 17, pp.3853-3880.

On Optimizing Collaborative Manufacturing Processes in Virtual Factories

Dieter Schuller — Ronny Hans — Sebastian Zöller — Ralf Steinmetz

Technische Universität Darmstadt
Multimedia Communications Lab
Rundeturmstr. 10, 64283 Darmstadt, Germany
firstname.lastname@kom.tu-darmstadt.de

ABSTRACT. *In today's global manufacturing markets, manufacturing processes need be flexibly adaptable and efficient due to changing business demands and tough cost pressure. To cope with this situation, concepts such as Virtual Factories can be beneficially applied to facilitate the collaboration between enterprises, especially small and medium-sized ones, and therewith to achieve higher degrees of flexibility. In this paper, we propose an approach for optimizing manufacturing processes in Virtual Factories, which are realized by our research project ADVENTURE. This way, we achieve interoperability among the collaborating enterprises as well as flexibly adaptable and efficient manufacturing processes.*

KEYWORDS: *Process Optimization, Virtual Factory, Collaboration, Interoperability.*

1. Introduction

In today's global manufacturing markets, enterprises and factories, respectively, especially small and medium-sized ones, are facing various challenges such as short product lifecycles, changing business environments, and tough cost pressure. In order to cope with these challenges and to stay competitive in such global markets, manufacturing processes need to be flexibly adaptable and efficient. For supporting flexible process adaptations, concepts such as *Virtual Factories* aiming at enhancing and facilitating the collaboration between factories can beneficially be implemented and realized. In Virtual Factories, multiple *real* factories work closely together for collaboratively producing and providing goods and services. Achieving interoperability among the collaborating partner factories thereby is key. Making use of the concept of Virtual Factories, (collaborative) manufacturing processes need to be optimized for achieving efficiency. In this respect, we propose an approach for optimizing the structure of manufacturing processes and the selection of partner factories such that predefined constraints on non-functional aspects – as, e.g., production and delivery time or Carbon Footprint (CO2) levels – are satisfied and production cost are minimized.

The rest of this work is organized as follows: in Section 2 we briefly present our research project *ADVENTURE* for achieving Virtual Factories. Our approach for optimizing collaborative processes in Virtual Factories is described in Section 3. Section 4 finally concludes the paper.

2. The Research Project ADVENTURE

ADVENTURE – ADaptive Virtual ENterprise manufacTURing Environment – focuses on creating a framework that aims at supporting and enhancing the collaboration especially of Small and Medium-sized enterprises (SME). This is primarily realized by integrating the Information and Communication (ICT) systems of the collaborating SMEs for achieving interoperability among them and by providing enhanced monitoring facilities for monitoring the whole (collaborative) supply chain. Building on concepts from the field of Service-oriented Computing, ADVENTURE enables the creation of manufacturing processes in a modular way. Steps and activities of such processes can be modelled based on required skills and technical requirements. They are further enriched with semantic annotations such that a matchmaking can be carried out automatedly to find matching partner factories that have previously provided semantically enriched descriptions of their manufacturing capabilities and services to the ADVENTURE platform. This way, the process of finding (from a functional perspective) *fitting* partners is significantly facilitated by ADVENTURE. If, for instance, an SME requires quickly adapting its manufacturing processes due to dynamically changing customer requirements, it can use ADVENTURE to model the adapted processes along with a specification of the needed skills and manufacturing capabilities that it cannot provide itself. Conducting the aforementioned matchmaking, ADVENTURE shows and proposes appropriate partner factories. For achieving interoperability with the identified partner factories, ADVENTURE offers means for integrating their ICT systems, as previously stated. If multiple factories come into question for realizing certain steps of the manufacturing process, the SME can select between them according to its needs on non-functional aspects. A corresponding optimization approach is presented in Section 3.

3. Optimization Approach

Having briefly introduced the project ADVENTURE in the previous section, this section focuses on the optimization approach proposed in the work at hand. It thereby consists of two parts. The first part addresses optimizing the selection of partner factories and their offered manufacturing services, respectively, whereas the second part focuses on optimizing the structure of the modelled manufacturing processes.

3.1. *Optimizing Service Selection*

As previously stated, it will be possible to select between partner factories and services, respectively, based on non-functional aspects such as delivery time, $CO2$, cost, etc., if multiple services exist that are equally appropriate to perform the different activities and accomplish corresponding tasks of a process. In fact, the problem of selecting services based on non-functional aspects is commonly known and referred to in the literature as *Service Selection Problem[1]* (SSP) (Strunk 10). Related work in this field can be mainly distinguished by the workflow patterns (Aalst et al, 2003) and structure elements, the corresponding approaches consider, and by the type of optimization, i.e., whether the approaches aim at computing an optimal, e.g., (Ardagna et al., 2007), or a heuristic solution, e.g., (Canfora et al, 2005).

For optimizing service selection, our proposed approach aims at finding an optimal solution to the SSP. It differs from and extends related work in this field by considering OR-blocks, i.e., OR-splits with corresponding OR-joins, in addition to sequences, XOR-/AND-blocks, and by accounting for interlaced as well as unstructured workflows, which as yet have not been considered by related approaches.

For modelling the SSP as optimization problem, aggregation functions for aggregating values of non-functional service aspects according to aforementioned workflow patterns and structures have been developed. Due to space restrictions, the interested reader is referred to our former work in (Schuller et al., 2011), (Schuller et al., 2012) for further details. Exemplarily, we provide corresponding aggregation functions in Table 1.

	Cost (c)	*Delivery Time (d)*	*Production Rate (r)*
Sequ-ence	$\sum_{i \in I_s} \sum_{j \in J_i} c_{ij} x_{ij}$	$\sum_{i \in I_s} \sum_{j \in J_i} d_{ij} x_{ij}$	$\min_{i \in I_s} (\sum_{j \in J_i} r_{ij} x_{ij})$
AND-block	$\sum_{l \in L} \sum_{i \in I_l} \sum_{j \in J_i} c_{ij} x_{ij}$	$\max_{l \in L} \left(\sum_{i \in I_l} \sum_{j \in J_i} d_{ij} x_{ij} \right)$	$\min_{l \in L} \left(\min_{i \in I_l} \left(\sum_{j \in J_i} r_{ij} x_{ij} \right) \right)$
XOR-block	$\sum_{l \in L} p_l \sum_{i \in I_l} \sum_{j \in J_i} c_{ij} x_{ij}$	$\sum_{l \in L} p_l \sum_{i \in I_l} \sum_{j \in J_i} d_{ij} x_{ij}$	$\sum_{l \in L} p_l \cdot \min_{i \in I_l} \left(\sum_{j \in J_i} r_{ij} x_{ij} \right)$
OR-block	$\sum_{h \in H} p_h \sum_{l \in L^h} \sum_{i \in I_l} \sum_{j \in J_i} c_{ij} x_{ij}$	$\sum_{h \in H} p_h \max_{l \in L^h} \left(\sum_{i \in I_l} \sum_{j \in J_i} d_{ij} x_{ij} \right)$	$\sum_{h \in H} p_h \min_{l \in L^h} \left(\min_{i \in I_l} \left(\sum_{j \in J_i} r_{ij} x_{ij} \right) \right)$

Table 1. *Aggregation functions*

---

1. The Service Selection Problem is also referred to as Service Composition Problem.

While the parameters c, d, and r refer to non-functional services aspects as indicated in Table 1, the variables x constitute decisions variables indicating whether a service j for process step i is selected or not. Recursively applying the mentioned aggregation functions according to the considered manufacturing process enables specifying the optimization problem. If necessary, appropriate linearization techniques see Schuller et al., 2011) will be applied for obtaining a *linear* optimization problem that can be solved optimally by applying (Mixed) Integer Linear Programming (ILP) (Beasley 96). This way, an optimal service selection can be achieved.

3.2. *Optimizing Process Structure*

In addition to optimizing the selection of matching partner factories and their offered manufacturing services, the optimization approach presented in the work at hand also includes an optimization of the process structure. Optimizing the process structure in addition to optimizing the service selection is not addressed at all by related work. Thus, the work at hand extends related work to this degree.

In order to enable process structure optimization, the *space* for possible structure optimizations has to be explicitly indicated and provided. In ADVENTURE, we use the *Complex gateway* to indicate alternative process structures. For instance, in the example workflow in Figure 1, the process steps (PS) one, two, and three, i.e., PS_1 PS_2, and PS_3, are arranged in different structural orderings at the three different branches within the Complex-split and -join (forming a Complex-block). The three branches thereby indicate different execution possibilities assuming that it is not allowed in this example to execute all process steps PS_1, PS_2, and PS_3 in parallel. Thus, either the first, or the second, or the third branch, constituting allowed structures, is the optimal one. These three possibilities form the *space* for process structure optimization.

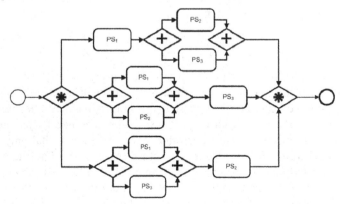

Figure 1. *Example workflow containing alternative structures*

In order to optimize the process structure, a selection of services has to be conducted since the optimal process structure depends on and is interwoven with the services selected for the corresponding tasks. As a first intuitive approach for optimizing the process structure in conjunction with selecting services, we propose to compute the optimal solution by considering each alternative branch separately for performing an optimal service selection step. For this, we adapt the aggregation functions by integrating a decision variable y indicating whether a certain branch k is considered as optimal regarding the process structure optimization or not. According to the example workflow in Figure 1, which contains a sequence and an AND-block within the Complex-block, the aggregation function for cost c is indicated in [1] – applying corresponding aggregation functions from Table 1.

$$\sum_{k \in K} y_k \left(\sum_{i \in I_{s_k}} \sum_{j \in J_i} c_{ij} x_{ij} + \sum_{l \in L_k} \sum_{i \in I_l} \sum_{j \in J_i} c_{ij} x_{ij} \right) \qquad [1]$$

The aggregation functions for the other considered non-functional service aspects can be developed analogously. Accounting for the example workflow in Figure 1, the optimization problem is indicated in Model 1.

Model 1. *Optimization problem for example workflow*

$$\text{minimize} \quad \sum_{k \in K} y_k \left(\sum_{i \in I_{s_k}} \sum_{j \in J_i} c_{ij} x_{ij} + \sum_{l \in L_k} \sum_{i \in I_l} \sum_{j \in J_i} c_{ij} x_{ij} \right) \qquad [2]$$

$$\sum_{k \in K} y_k \left(\sum_{i \in I_s} \sum_{j \in J_i} d_{ij} x_{ij} + \max_{l \in L} \left(\sum_{i \in I_l} \sum_{j \in J_i} d_{ij} x_{ij} \right) \right) \le b_d \qquad [3]$$

$$\sum_{k \in K} y_k \left(\min_{i \in I_s} (\sum_{j \in J_i} r_{ij} x_{ij}) + \min_{l \in L} \left(\min_{i \in I_l} \left(\sum_{j \in J_i} r_{ij} x_{ij} \right) \right) \right) \ge b_r \qquad [4]$$

$$\sum_{k \in K} y_k = 1 \qquad [5]$$

$$y_k \in \{0,1\} \quad \forall k \in K \qquad [6]$$

In [2], the objective function is provided, aiming at minimizing cost. The constraint in [3] restricts the delivery time to be lower or equal to a certain upper bound b_d while the constraint in [4] restricts the production rate to be larger or equal to a certain lower bound b_r. Both bounds need to be specified by the entity that is conducting the optimization. The constraint in [5] makes sure that only one of the possible process structures is selected, whereas [6] ensures that either a process structure is selected or not. Applying ILP, an optimal solution to the optimization problem in Model 1 can be computed. This way, both the process structure as well as the selection of services for the example workflow in Figure 1 may be optimized.

Having described the proposed optimization approach for optimizing manufacturing processes in this section, the subsequent Section 4 concludes the paper.

4. Conclusions

In order to cope with the challenges in today's global manufacturing markets such as changing demands and tough cost pressure, we proposed an approach for optimizing manufacturing processes in Virtual Factories, which are realized by our research project ADVENTURE. This way, we achieve interoperability among the collaborating partners as well as flexibly adaptable and efficient manufacturing processes that are needed to survive in such global markets. In this respect, we extend related work by additionally accounting for process structure optimizations.

Due to space restrictions, no detailed evaluation results have been presented in this paper. However, since the number of potential process structures increases exponentially with the number of (non-parallel) Complex-blocks, the number of individual optimization problems to be solved – and therewith the computational effort – also increases exponentially. Thus, we will improve the concept for considering process structure optimizations in our future work and develop corresponding heuristics. Nevertheless, being able to compute the optimal solution as enabled by our approach is indispensable since the optimal solution constitutes the *benchmark* against which heuristic solution approaches need to measure themselves.

5. Acknowledgements

This work is supported in part by the Commission of the European Union within the ADVENTURE FP7-ICT project (Grant agreement no. 285220), and by E-Finance Lab e. V., Frankfurt am Main, Germany (http://www.efinancelab.com).

6. References

Ardagna D., Pernici, B., "Adaptive Service Composition in Flexible Processes", *Transactions on Software Engineering*, vol. 33 no. 6, 2007, pp.369-384.

Beasley, J., *Advances in Linear and Integer Programming. Oxford Lecture Series in Mathematics and Its Applications*, Gloucestershire, Clarendon Press, 1996.

Canfora, G., Di Penta, M., Esposito, R., Villani, M., "An Approach for QoS-aware Service Composition Based on Genetic Algorithms", *Genetic and Evolutionary Computation Conference GECCO'05*, 2005, pp.1069-1075.

Schuller, D., Polyvyanyy, A., García-Bañuelos, L., Schulte. S., "Optimization of Complex QoS-Aware Service Compositions", *International Conference on Service Oriented Computing ICSOC'11*, 2011, pp.452-466.

Schuller, D., Lampe, U., Eckert, J., Steinmetz, R., Schulte, S., "Cost-driven Optimization of Complex Service-based Workflows for Stochastic QoS Parameters", *International Conference on Web Services ICWS'12*, 2012, pp.66-74.

Strunk, A., "QoS-Aware Service Composition: A Survey", *European Conference on Web Services ECOWS'10*, 2010, pp.67-74.

van der Aalst, W., ter Hofstede, A., Kiepuszewski, B., Barros, A., "Workflow Patterns", *Distributed and Parallel Databases,* vol. 14 no. 1, 2003, pp.5-51.

Modelling Interoperability-Related, Economic and Efficiency Benefits in Dynamic Manufacturing Networks through Cognitive Mapping

O.I. Markaki — S. Koussouris — P. Kokkinakos — D. Panopoulos — D. Askounis

Greek Interoperability Centre,
Decision Support Systems Lab, School of Electrical and Computer Engineering
National Technical University of Athens, Greece
omarkaki@epu.ntua.gr
skous@epu.ntua.gr
pkok@epu.ntua.gr
dpano@epu.ntua.gr
askous@epu.ntua.gr

ABSTRACT. *The decision of joining a Dynamic Manufacturing Network is quite important for any enterprise, since it is related to many changes in the way it operates; however its outcomes in terms of economic and efficiency benefits are only visible once a manufacturing project is completed. This paper attempts to cultivate an understanding around the benefits of DMN participation, utilizing the causal characteristics of Cognitive Maps to create a network of interconnected DMN performance factors.*

KEYWORDS: *Dynamic Manufacturing Networks, DMNs, Benefits, Cognitive Maps, CMs, Interoperability, Causal Relationships.*

1. Introduction

With increasing competition in the global market, manufacturing enterprises are seeking ways to improve their core capabilities, establish strategic alliances and position themselves for survival in the future [1]. One of the most promising solutions in their pursuit seems to be the emergence of Dynamic Manufacturing Networks (DMNs), i.e. dynamic alliances of manufacturing entities, collaborating for gaining mutual benefits. A DMN is a coalition, either permanent or temporal, comprising production systems of geographically dispersed Small and Medium

Enterprises (SMEs) and/or Original Equipment Manufacturers (OEM) that collaborate in a shared value-chain to conduct joint manufacturing [2].

For an enterprise, participating in a DMN can be considered as a systematic way for cultivating extended co-operation with other members of its supply chain, and calls for modifications in its modus operandi, so as to enable real-time communication and active collaboration among the different network nodes [3]. In this respect, it also creates the need for stimulating and supporting communication concerning the impact of the change and thereby for measuring performance [4].

This paper proposes an approach for reasoning on the drivers of participating in a DMN based on Cognitive Maps (CMs). Cognitive Maps hold the advantage of portraying information about a system more succinctly than the corresponding textual description [5], and suggest themselves as a means of bringing forth the way of thinking and making visible the perceptions of individuals. The proposed approach utilizes the causal characteristics of CMs as a modelling technique for generating a network of interconnected DMN performance factors.

2. Cognitive Maps

Cognitive maps were first introduced by political scientist Robert Axelrod [6] in the 1970s as a means of representing social scientific knowledge. A CM is a network diagram depicting causes and effects [7], and it is represented by a labelled, directed graph of nodes and edges. Nodes represent domain concepts and edges causal relationships between the nodes. The direction of an edge reveals the direction of a causal relationship, which is also called a feedback. A positive (negative) feedback from node A to node B means that an increase in variable A causally increases (decreases) variable B.

CMs are acknowledged as cognitive due to the fact that they use concepts to elicit and represent perceptions. They have been used in a variety of contexts, most prominently in operations management [8] as a means of facilitating brainstorming and communication. Thanks to their characteristics, CMs suggest themselves as a suitable method for capturing the complex interactions among concept variables in the DMN environment.

3. Causal Mapping of Benefits in DMNs

The proposed framework for modelling DMN benefits through CMs has been developed as the result of a benefits and risks study carried out within the IMAGINE project as a means of identifying business drivers for attracting enterprises into joining DMNs. Data gathering was done through semi-structured interviews with industry stakeholders and information collected was analyzed using a grounded theory approach [9] that served to qualitatively identify all factors bringing about positive impacts on the operation of both the single enterprise and the network as a whole. It is noted that the factors identified as well as their correlaptions are generic enough and can be applied to any DMN related scenario. The list of concept variables elicited by the stakeholders observations includes the following factors, provided thereafter along with a short explanation:

– *Information Validity*, indicating the level of completeness and up-to-datedness of partner information shared within the network.

– *Information Visibility*, expressing the degree at which information is accessible by different DMN members.

– *Information Availability*, indicating the degree at which uninterrupted and automated information exchange takes place among DMN members.

– *Suitability of Partner Selection*, denoting the appropriateness of long/short listed and thereby finally selected partners in terms of their capabilities, financial bid and quality offered.

– *Adequacy of Network Configuration*, referring to the level of aptness of the baseline network configuration, probably including a preliminary high level production schedule.

– *Adequacy of Network Design*, including the final production schedule.

– *Adequacy of Network Execution, Monitoring & Management*, pertaining to the effectiveness of operating and troubleshooting the network.

– *Application of Modifications & Corrective Actions*, pertaining to the need of taking appropriate measures to correct any deviations in the network's operation.

– *Automation of Manufacturing Processes*, denoting the degree at which manufacturing processes are executed in an automated manner.

– *Synchronization & Alignment of Manufacturing Processes*, relating to the extent at which the such processes are executed in parallel.

– *Partner Collaboration*, pointing to the extent at which collaborative practices are foreseen and applied in the context of new products' design and development.

– *Inventory Level*, indicating the amount of resources kept by a DMN member in stock to accommodate the manufacturing process.

– *Time for Contractual Formalization*, as a KPI pertaining to the time required for carrying out negotiations among potential partners and reaching agreement by means of establishing a legal contract.

– *Product Development Lead Time*, as metric of the time needed for defining the product specifications and developing accordingly a product prototype.

– *Manufacturing Lead Time*, expressing the time spent for a product.

– *Time-to-Market*, referring to the time interval covering all stages from the conceptualization of a new product to its actual launch in the market.

– *Product Development & Manufacturing Cost*, covering all costs related to the design, development and actual production of a product.

– *Inventory Cost*, corresponding to the costs of purchasing and warehousing.

– *Operational Cost*, involving all categories of fixed costs of the enterprise.

– *Maintenance Cost*, corresponding to the expenses carried out for infrastructure and equipment repairing and maintenance.

– *Marketing expenses*, pertaining to the resources consumed for advertising.

– *Cost due to Poor Quality*, relating to the costs imposed by the deficiencies of the manufacturing process in terms of quality assurance procedures.

– *Total Product Cost*, integrating all types of cost relating to a product.

– *Profitability*, a KPI referring to the net income of the enterprise after deducing the total expenses.

– *Product/Service Quality*, pertaining to the product or service features that enhance the former's value.

– *Competitive Advantage*, a qualitative indicator corresponding to the set or combination of attributes that allow a company to outperform its competitors.

What is noticeable with this list is that some concept variables clearly constitute Key Performance Indicators (KPIs), as in the case of "Time-to-market" and "Profitability", while others even though not pointing directly to positive outcomes, are mostly prerequisites for and contribute to the smoother and unhampered operation of the DMN, thus being identified as benefit-related factors. What is required is the identification of cause and effect relationships between the benefit-related factors and the KPIs. Below, the authors present some of the highlights of the raw correlations pointed out by the stakeholders interviewed:

– Availability of valid partner information enhances the chances for identifing the most appropriate set of partners, the selection of which in turn reduces the product development and manufacturing cost.

– Adequate planning of the network at the early stages of its creation and operation minimizes the need for applying modifications and taking corrective measures afterwards.

– Enhanced collaboration among cooperating DMN partners holds the potential to decrease product design and development time, and product development and manufacturing cost, while in parallel improving product or service quality.

– Information and data availability across the network fosters the synchronization and alignment of manufacturing operations which in turn allow the reduction of manufacturing lead-time and inventory levels.

– Time-to market, total product cost and product quality constitute factors upon which the networks' competitive advantage is highly dependent.

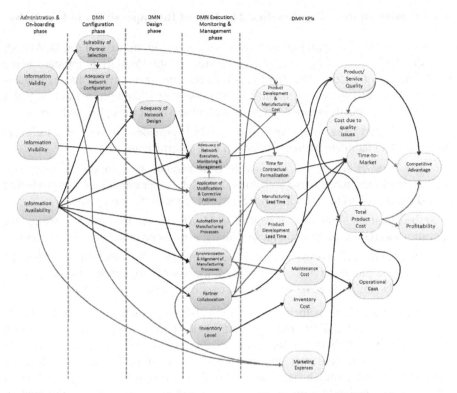

Figure 1. *Cognitive Map of concept variables relating to DMN benefits*

It can be seen from the above list of correlations that a positive outcome may be linked to several benefit-related factors. For instance, product development and manufacturing cost may be reduced as a result of both the selection of appropriate suppliers as well as the enhanced collaboration among partners. In other cases, the positive outcome generated by a concept variable becomes a factor that leads to some other. For example, synchronization and alignment of manufacturing processes is identified as a positive outcome of information availability across the network, while in parallel leading to cutting off manufacturing lead-time and inventory levels.

The relationships between the factors that advocate in favor of the DMN concept seem therefore to be more complex than what the above simple list of cause and effect relationships implies. In this context, the authors leverage the instrument of CMs to create a richer picture on the benefits involved in the novel and promising approach of DMNs. In the map of Figure 1, positive relationships among concept variables are marked in black, while negative ones in red.

4. Reasoning on the DMN Benefits: The Role of Interoperability in IMAGINE

With the view of applying the CM of section 1.3 in the case of the IMAGINE project, one has to highlight that the cornerstone of the IMAGINE approach is the DMN Blueprint Model. The former is a declarative meta-model that aggregates and modularizes production, manufacturing operations management and logistics information by specifying four types of inter-related blueprints [10], as follows:

– the *Partner Blueprint (Partner BP)*, which provides business and technical information to facilitate partners' selection by a specific contractor;

– the *Product Blueprint (Product BP)*, containing all components necessary, such as machines, tools, personnel skills, materials, other equipment, for producing a product, as well as other entities necessary for the manufacturing work;

– the *Quality Assurance Blueprint (QA BP)*, used to capture metrics for operations analytics, associating these with the end-to-end manufacturing processes,

– the *end-to-end Process Blueprint (E2E Process BP)*, which ties together the many discrete processes associated with all aspects of product development, while providing the ability to adapt to changing conditions and environments.

The latter, along with the IMAGINE platform which incarnates the DMN lifecycle and IMAGINE management methodology, are used to support interoperability and thereby information sharing, collaboration and enterprise-wide visibility. In this sense, leveraging the CM above, it can be deduced that all DMN economic and efficiency benefits are reduced to ensuring interoperability through the BP Model, which in turns guarantees the unhampered exchange of information and extensive collaboration across the network, covering also the aspects of information validity and visibility, depending on the BP data updating frequency and the access rights granted to different partners through the latter. This fact does not diminish the importance of the benefits identified, but raises instead the value of interoperability which appears eventually as their common denominator.

5. Discussion and Conclusions

This paper presented an approach to model performance-related factors and benefits in DMNs leveraging the causal characteristics of CMs. The approach has included the elicitation of DMN concept variables through semi-structured interviews and their correlation through CMs. The use of CMs in this process has been observed to facilitate communication, as well as to bring forth interoperability as the indisputable factor generating DMN benefits in the IMAGINE case. While the derived map is quite generic to cover the majority of DMN formations and is thus open to modifications depending on the particular case, it can promote debate and further investigation. This can in turn improve managerial decision-making.

6. Acknowledgements

The research leading to these results has been supported by the EC FP7 under the project "IMAGINE – Innovative end-to-end management of Dynamic Manufacturing Networks" Grant Agreement No. 285132.

7. References

[1] Mc Clellan M. *Manufacturing Enterprise 3.0: The New Information Management Paradigm Built On Processes*. Vancouver: Collaboration Synergies Inc; 2009.

[2] IMAGINE Project: Innovative End-to-end Management of Dynamic Manufacturing Networks. Description of Work www.imagine-futurefactory.eu.

[3] Camarinha-Matos L.M., Afsarmanesh H., Galeano N., Molina A. "Collaborative networked organizations – Concepts and practice in manufacturing enterprises". *Computers & Industrial Engineering*, August 2009; 57(1): 46-60.

[4] Chalmeta R., Grangel R. "Performance measurement systems for virtual enterprise integration". *Int. J. Computer Integrated manufacturing*, February 2005; 18(1):73-84.

[5] Huff A.S. *Mapping Strategic Thought*. USA: Wiley and Sons; 1990.

[6] Axelrod R. *Structure of Decision - The Cognitive Maps of Political Elites*. Princeton, NJ: Princeton University Press; 1976.

[7] Bryson M, Ackermann F, Finn C. *Visible Thinking: Unlocking causal mapping for practical business results*. John Wiley & Sons, Ltd; 2004.

[8] Scavarda AJ, Chameeva TB, "Goldstein SM, Hays JM, Hill AV. Review of the Causal Mapping Practice and Research Literature". *Proceedings of the 2nd World Conference on POM and 15th Annual POM Conference*, Cancun, Mexico; 2004.

[9] Martin PY, Turner BA. "Grounded Theory and Organizational Research". *Journal of Applied Behavioral Science*, April 1986; 22(2): 141-157.

[10] Markaki O, Panopoulos D, Kokkinakos P, Koussouris S, Askounis D. "Towards Adopting Dynamic Manufacturing Networks for Future Manufacturing: Benefits and Risks of the IMAGINE DMN End-to-End Management Methodology". *Proceedings of the 22nd IEEE International Workshop on Enabling Technologies: Infrastructure for Collaborative Enterprises (WETICE)*. Hammamet, Tunisia; 2013.

Cloud-based Interoperability for Dynamic Manufacturing Networks

Daniel Stock — Andreas Bildstein

Fraunhofer Institute for Manufacturing Engineering and Automation IPA
Nobelstraße 12, 70569 Stuttgart, Germany
daniel.stock@ipa.fraunhofer.de
andreas.bildstein@ipa.fraunhofer.de

ABSTRACT. Due to market pressures, manufacturing companies are forced to find new ways to remain competitive. Dynamic manufacturing networks (DMNs) could be a solution for this task. One of the main challenges during the process of building up and managing a DMN is the exchange of required data between the partners of such a DMN. However, the efficient exchange of relevant data between the partners within a DMN is a hard endeavour. Within this paper the authors show how a cloud-based integration platform for DMNs is able to effectively support the process of data exchange within a DMN. The major components of this platform and their functions are also discussed. Furthermore this paper presents how a cloud-based integration platform allows SMEs, even if they lack in proper production IT, to be part of a DMN that heavily relies on current production data.

KEYWORDS: Dynamic Manufacturing Networks, Interoperability, Data Exchange, Cloud-Based Platform, Production IT, Production Data.

1. Introduction

Due to market pressures, manufacturing companies all over Europe are forced to find new ways to remain competitive. One solution for this task are so called dynamic manufacturing networks (DMNs) where companies align with other manufacturing companies to be able to deliver a requested product order collectively. One of the main challenges during the process of setting up and managing a DMN is the exchange of required information between the partners of such a DMN. The required data for this is ranging from information about manufacturing capabilities and capacity rates for the partner selection process up to current production data from a partner's shop floor to effectively monitor a specific production process or the status of the overall production progress within the DMN. Syntactical and semantic heterogeneities have to be overcome to be able to exchange the required information between the partners in a DMN.

2. State-of-the-Art in End-to-End Management of DMNs and Interoperability Issues

A DMN lifecycle can be divided into three main phases, namely the configuration phase, the design phase, and the execution and monitoring phase (Markaki et al., 2013). Each of those phases requires a proper exchange of relevant production related data between the participating manufacturers within a DMN.

2.1. Configuration Phase

After a production order from the customer came to the attention of a DMN manager, the production order is analysed and mapped to production requirements, for which proper suppliers have to be found that are able to produce the identified parts of the overall product. Within this partner search process the requirements of the product on the one side have to be matched with the capabilities of the suppliers on the other side, whereby the supplier manufacturing capabilities can be described, for example, based on their tooling and skills. For this matching procedure an alignment between the product specification description and the supplier capabilities description with respect to a specific product has to be established, whereby both descriptions are representing a different domain of interest. The result of this alignment process will be a long list that shows all possible partners from the supplier's repository that arc able to produce a specific part or component of the requested product or that are able to do a specific process that is needed within the overall production process.

2.2. Design Phase

Once a long list with possible suppliers for specific parts, components or processes for the overall product is available, the final design of the envisaged DMN has to be defined. Within this design phase the high-level production processes from the configuration phase will be further fragmented, orchestrated and finally transformed to the final production schedule that takes into account not only the production capabilities from the suppliers in the long list, but also the current production capacities of those suppliers as well as key performance indicators (KPIs), like prices, place of location, CO_2 footprint or alike, that may be requested for the production of the product. The result of the matching of the final production schedule with the suppliers from the long list and with the requested KPIs is a so called short list. This short list provides for each production process the best fitting partner for the DMN with respect to the overall order specifications including the KPIs. For being able to define this short list, the data that describe the suppliers' current capacities and the KPIs have to be provided in a manner that supports at least a semi-automatic matching procedure between the production schedule and the description of the supplier capacities as well as the description of the KPIs. For this matching procedure, a semantic alignment between the different information sources and the differing knowledge representations has to be established.

2.3. *Execution and Monitoring Phase*

After the final production schedule has been filled with the best fitting partners for each of the processes, the DMN will be deployed and the production of the requested products can be started. For being able to govern the production process and to react on appearing issues in time it is necessary that all relevant production data are shown to the DMN manager, who is in charge of the timely delivery of the ordered products. Therefore the DMN manager does not only need all the relevant production data at his hands, but he needs this data also in a timely and automated manner for being able to have a holistic view on the current production progress at any time. The relevant production data comes from different IT systems with differing data models and has to be matched between the different information sources.

2.4. *Interoperability Issues*

As it can be seen from the preceding sections, within each of the DMN phases a proper exchange of data is needed for being able to match between demand and supply or production schedule and KPIs or alike. Additionally, within the execution and monitoring phase current production data from the shop floor are needed that describe the current progress within the overall production process. A major challenge within this process of the end-to-end management of DMNs is the fact that all this data comes from different information sources and has to be aligned on a semantic level to get meaningful answers on questions like "who is able to do which job within the DMN." Besides this semantic interoperability issue, another major problem is the situation that a huge number of SMEs lacks in proper production IT that is able to deliver the needed production data. A cloud-based interoperability architecture that also provides production IT functionalities for SMEs for being able to participate in DMNs that heavily rely on current production data will be presented in the following sections.

3. Cloud-Based Interoperability Platform for DMN-Management

Figure 1 shows a high level architecture of the proposed platform. The platform comprises the IMAGINE (http://www.imagine-futurefactory.eu) platform core components for DMN management and an mapping adapter component, which is specifically configured according to the specific business cases and needs to integrate legacy IT production systems. It is embedded into the Virtual Fort Knox (VFK – http://www.virtualfortknox.de/en.html) platform to ensure extended scalability, data security, information integrity and operational reliability.

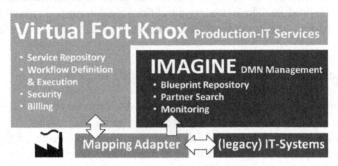

Figure 1. *Overall platform architecture*

The VFK platform provides production IT services in the form of software as a service (SaaS) as well as the required infrastructure. These services can range from simple mobile applications for specific production oriented tasks to full-fledged cloud-based MES and ERP systems. The following sections will give a brief description of the necessary core components of the overall solution.

3.1. *Blueprint Repository, Partner Search and Matching*

The Blueprint repository is a core component of the IMAGINE platform. It contains information profiles, mostly static data, which is formulated in a RDF based and standardized exchange format, namely Blueprints (Ferreira *et al.*, 2013). The search component allows querying of the Blueprint repository, to match partner profiles to the production requirements as described in detail in section 2.1 and 2.2. Blueprints can principally be classified into the following categories:

– Partner Profile Blueprints contain basic information about a platform participant. A platform participant is a company, which may offer production services or may supply parts and components of the product.

– Product Blueprints are used to describe products, respectively their production requirements. This contains a bill of material, the necessary production processes and required skills, standards and equipment.

– Quality Assurance (QA) Blueprints contain additional information regarding relevant production and process information and data. This comprises tolerance values for production processes or key performance indicators (KPIs), which can be used to assess process operations.

– End2end Blueprints describe the overall organised production process of a product and its sub products. It interconnects the requirements of a product and the capable platform participants, who have been selected to manufacture a specific product or sub product. The boundary conditions are determined in conjunction with the QA Blueprints, which allows the monitoring of a DMN based on defined KPIs.

3.2. Service Repository, Workflow Definition and Execution

Additionally to the more static information which can be found in the Blueprints, the service repository of the VFK platform contains the services offered on the platform and their description, which represents a virtual image of the resources. This enables services to be found using the discovery function so that they can be orchestrated and implemented. This means that information regarding materials, production capacities, and equipment is being offered in almost real time. It is expected that this information is being constantly updated by the partners' IT systems, either by automated periodic information updates or by manual triggers executed by an authorized person. The addition of a service repository additionally to the Blueprint repository allows the deployment of production or manufacturing services, which can be orchestrated to define an individual workflow. This workflow then can be executed in order to combine the features of several different services and allows the creation of more complex features and aggregated services of higher value, which in the end form the DMN. The workflow is being defined via BPMN and executed through a workflow engine, which is running on an enterprise service bus (ESB). To achieve this, a workflow is defined that logically links the VFK platform's basic services, such as monitoring and billing, integration services, integrated cyber-physical systems (CPS) or equipment with one another and enables them to be executed.

3.3. Integration Service Bus and Capability Mapping

The integration service bus (ISB) is used to connect the required IT equipment, which is needed to transfer and collect all necessary data regarding the services, profiles and the monitoring of an active DMN. Care must be taken here to ensure that the description of the service is both efficient and flexible, so that it is possible to directly map this information to the Blueprint repository's partner profile, which allows for automated capability publishing for an improved partner search. The mapping adapter component is responsible for the correct information mapping on a semantic level and also acts as a filter, which can be set up to define which information is being shared and forwarded to the service and Blueprint repository.

3.4. *Monitoring and Security*

To ensure best possible transparency and process security, all information collected by the components as described before have to be centrally aggregated and analysed. The monitoring component is receiving information and process data in real time and is constantly checking for deviations from the defined tolerance values, which are defined in the QA Blueprints. If a (potential) transgression of a set value regarding a quality parameter or of a service level agreement is being detected, required measures can be immediately induced. The measures can range from simple notifications to the responsible persons, who then can proceed to perform the necessary adjustments, up to automated control adaptions executed via the production IT services, for example emergency shutdowns. Security plays a major role throughout all levels of the platform architecture, i.e. from the factory level with CPS, equipment, etc. right up to the IT services offered to the user via the cloud platform.

4. Conclusion

The proposed approach shows that using a unified exchange format, which is being provided via a cloud-based platform, enables various IT systems of multiple production sites to be interconnected and to exchange information, even on a semantic level, that is needed for proper end-to-end management of DMNs. If production IT functionality is also provided on the platform in the form of services, even SMEs lacking in proper IT systems are able to provide and exchange necessary current production data.

5. References

Ferreira J., Beca, M., Agostinho C., Nunez, M.J., Jardim-Goncalves R., "Standard Blueprints for Interoperability in Factories of the Future (FoF)", *Manufacturing Modelling, Management, and Control*, vol. 7 no. 1, 2013, pp.1322-1327.

Markaki O., Panopoulos D., Kokkinakos P., Koussouris S., Askounis D., "Towards Adopting Dynamic Manufacturing Networks for Future Manufacturing: Benefits and Risks of the IMAGINE DMN End-to-End Management Methodology", *2012 IEEE 21st International Workshop on Enabling Technologies: Infrastructure for Collaborative Enterprises*, Hammamet Tunisia, 17-20 June 2012, pp.305-310.

A smart Mediator to Integrate Dynamic Networked Enterprises

Codé Diop — Aymen Kamoun — Emna Mezghani — Mohamed Zouari — Ernesto Exposito

CNRS LAAS
7 avenue du Colonel Roche, F-31400 Toulouse, France
Université de Toulouse UPS, INSA, INP, ISAE, UT1, UTM, LAAS
31400 Toulouse, France
cdiop@laas.fr
akamoun@laas.fr
emezghan@laas.fr
mzouari@laas.fr
eexposit@laas.fr

ABSTRACT. Current economical and industrial worldwide context requires an agile and efficient development of collaborating networked enterprises. More and more future organizations will involve a large number of Small and Medium Enterprises SMEs in order to create new products, activities, businesses, etc. These future organizations will be virtual ecosystems in which each involved SME exposes its systems and capabilities as services. In this context, a platform that allows managing a flexible and agile integration and collaboration of these services is required. Several research works and projects as the IMAGINE project propose approaches and tools to offer this kind of platform. The main goal of this paper is to show how we contribute in the IMAGINE integration platform by adding mechanisms that allow a semantic reconciliation between partners but also secure and scalable services collaboration within dynamic manufacturing networks.

KEYWORDS: Distributed Systems, Collaboration, Access Control, Interoperability.

1. Introduction

New business models based on collaborating enterprises need agile and efficient methods and tools in order to facilitate the composition, configuration and management of dynamic and heterogeneous enterprise networks. Manufacturing organizations may rely on digital ecosystems for aspects related to collaboration between diverse Small and Medium Enterprises SMEs.

For that, enterprises may expose business functionalities as services available through the network and that can be invoked and exploited by different partners. These collaborations may involve highly distributed and pervasive systems that are more and more designed following a service-oriented approach. In such case, the Enterprise Service Bus (ESB) represents an important building block within a service-oriented platform (Chappell, 2004). In fact, it implements standard-based and distributed integration and mediation strategies allowing various collaborating enterprises to share services and resources. Some platforms have been proposed to support Dynamic Manufacturing Networks DMNs (e.g. IMAGINE platform). These platforms have to meet several needs of involved enterprises, in particular:

– *A secure access to resources according to a set of roles.* Managing authorizations is a crucial issue in collaborative manufacturing networks, especially when roles, partners and tasks change dynamically during the production process (Tolone *et al.*, 2005). As well, members may have different roles during the collaboration, such as a coordinator in a project and a reviewer in another one, while also being the project leader of his organization.

– *A high performance.* The collaboration may result a high volume of communications and make complex the management of various and dynamic resources. A service bus could enable to support a high number of users that consume the different services provided by the enterprise partners. However, the scalability can become an issue (Chappel, 2004).

– *A semantic interoperability and reconciliation.* Each enterprise follows their own laws in organizing their business process, services and data. The formalization and representation of these concerns is the main challenge to integrate the different enterprise services and information systems. The diversity of enterprise information systems and models creates a high requirement for integrated methods to allow collaboration among the enterprises.

Our work tackles these problems by offering new mechanisms for smart management of non-functional aspects related to the communication performance, the heterogeneous data integration and the access control to multi-organization resources. We propose a semantic-based smart mediator that aims at facilitating enterprises collaboration, relying on decentralized control and self-configuration capabilities.

The paper is organized as follows. Section 2 introduces our case study related to the IMAGINE project. Section 3 details our approach. Finally, Section 4 gives concluding remarks.

2. Case Study

IMAGINE research project is an European project that targets the development and delivery of a novel comprehensive methodology and the platform for effective end-to-end management of dynamic manufacturing networks (DMN). It is aimed at supporting the emergence of a powerful and new production model, based on community, collaboration, self-organization and openness (IMAGINE Project, 2014). The main project's contributions are the IMAGINE DMN lifecycle management methodology and DMN ICT Platform that supports the proposed methodology (see Figure 1).

The methodology allows managing efficiently a networked supply chain in three phases: Network Configuration, Network Design, Monitoring and Governance. The Network Configuration phase aims at identifying and selecting partners for collaboration. During Network Design phase, the production systems of selected partners are interconnected and the end-to-end supply chains network processes put in place. The Monitoring and Governance phase aims at managing and controlling in a continuous way the operations of the network. The ICT platform gives the technical solutions that effectively enable the management of networked manufacturing supply chains. It is based on a set of blueprint repositories that introduce the data format models to describe the product, the partner's capacity, the end-to-end process and the required quality. An Enterprise Service Bus integrates the systems of collaborating partners and allows the access to the blueprint.

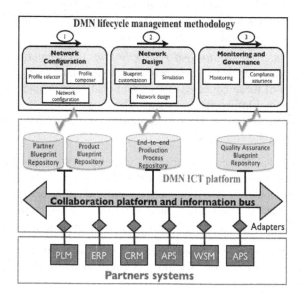

Figure 1. *IMAGINE Methodology and Platform*

The ICT Platform has to be able to support five living labs (LL), each one with a specific market and business context: (1) Aerospace and Defense domain *EADS LL,*

(2) Multi-site single factory domain *IPA LL*, (3) Furniture Manufacturing domain *AIDIMA LL*, (4) Car Manufacturing domain *FIAT LL*, and (5) Engineering domain *UoW/WMCCM LL*. In this context, it is possible to have issues related to access control, data heterogeneity and performance.

3. Overview of the Smart Mediator

The proposed Smart Mediator includes a set of distributed software modules that run based on a SOA oriented distributed execution platform. Figure 2 shows the functional architecture that consists in several interconnected components that deal with issues related to access control, data heterogeneity and performance. The next sections present these components.

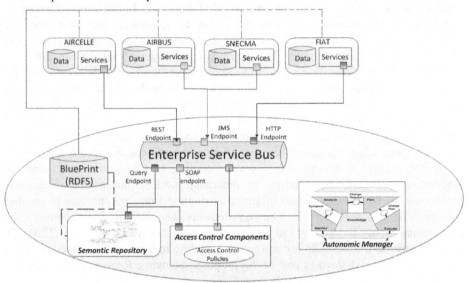

Figure 2. *The Smart Mediator for Collaborative Enterprise Network*

3.1. RBAC Based Model for Access Control Management

The access control component analyzes the user query for managing authorizations based on external policies that follow the RBAC model (Di *et al.*, 2005). In order to make decisions, it may refer to an LDAP server, which contains information about users and resources. The LDAP server (called IMAGINE LDAP) may need to contact another server of a specific DMN participant in order to fulfill the request. It is also possible that the IMAGINE LDAP contacts other servers on behalf of the client application and returns the combined results after completing the operation. The communication between the different LDAP servers is possible through the chaining mode of LDAP. In our work, we define also a semantic model based on ontologies in order to enable checking the consistency when defining or modifying the policies. The component detects inconsistencies based on this access control ontology.

3.2. *Autonomic Service Bus for Performance and Scalability Management*

An ESB runs in general on preconfigured infrastructure with a set of limited resources (CPU, memory, threads, etc.). When a situation with a big throughput and a lot of mediation processes inside the ESB arises, the ESB response time as well the ESB CPU and ESB memory usage increase. The maximum performance of the ESB is achieved when it uses all the resources of the host machine. It may become a bottleneck due to a lack of physical or virtual IT resources. In this context, we apply dynamically the vertical elasticity paradigm to guarantee the scalability by monitoring the state of the ESB context and tuning in an autonomic way the allocated resources if needed. The autonomic manager (Nami *et al.*, 2005) is responsible for implementing a control loop that reacts to events from managed ESB and may, as a result, change its behaviour. When tuning the IT infrastructure is not possible (for instance, there is no more resources to be allocated to the JVM), distributed and multi-instances deployment modes need to be done. A cluster-based deployment is configured and load will be balanced between the different nodes. The horizontal elasticity paradigm is applied, and instances are added or removed from the cluster in an autonomic way according to the global load. Another interesting approach is also applied by federating the ESB instances. Services and processes can be distributed and migrated at runtime from one instance to another one according to their performance requirements. The actions that implement the self-management functions and the autonomic behaviour of the ESB IT infrastructure and topologies are triggered according to a set of predefined policies. Those policies are defined as part of the proposed Semantic Repository presented in the next section.

3.3. *Semantic Repository for Semantic Interoperability*

Owing to the heterogeneity of the enterprises' services and processes, the collaboration remains a challenge. For that reason, we provide a semantic repository, which integrates an unified multi-level model that describes and formalizes services and resources based on the application context (Vujasinovic *et al.*, 2010). Each enterprise exposes its services to be consumed by other enterprises. A service is characterized by functional properties (what they offer) and non-functional properties (its quality of service such as capacity and response time). From one hand, this semantic description is stored in a repository, which is the basis of dynamic binding and discovery of services used by the ESB to match the consumer's requirements with the appropriate services. From the other hand, the role of the ESB is also to meet the contract established between consumers and providers expressing the QoS and the access control criteria. Thus, the semantic repository includes specific rules following the Service Level Agreement (SLA). The process of service selection based on semantics is the following. When the ESB receives requests, it consults the semantic repository, to select the appropriate services meeting the consumer requirements. Then, the ESB refers to the access control service, which in turns refers to the semantic repository that implements an ontology access control describing profiles and groups where the services are subscribed. Moreover, each ESB can represent a different configuration and resources naming. The semantic repository provides a unified and detailed view to the ESB about the resources and their consumption in order to select the best configuration and allow the smooth deployment of components with a minimal human intervention (developers, administrators or users) based on inferred rules.

4. Conclusion

In this paper, we have introduced a new generation integration architecture well suited to satisfy the challenges of dynamic manufacturing enterprises collaborations. Some problems related to interoperability, scalability and access controls when creating and dynamically reconfiguring complex networks of IT infrastructures have been presented. They have been illustrated by the business cases targeted by the IMAGINE European project. We have proposed an extension coping with the additional non-functional properties related to semantics, scalability and access control. Currently we are working on the implementation of the defined components that will be validated and integrated to the final release to the IMAGINE platform. Future work will be focused on the demonstration of the benefits of the proposed solutions to cope with the new generation of dynamic manufacturing networks for collaborative enterprises.

5. References

Chappell, D. A., *Enterprise Service Bus*, O'Reilly Media, 2004.

Di, W., Jian, L., Yabo, D., Miaoliang, Z., "Using Semantic Web Technologies to Specify Constraints of RBAC". In *Proceedings of the Sixth International Conference on Parallel and Distributed Computing Applications and Technologies (PDCAT '05)* 2005, pp.543-545.

IMAGINE Project, http://www.imagine-futurefactory.eu/index.dlg, 2014.

Nami M.R., Bertels K., "A survey of autonomic computing systems" *Proceedings of ICAS07*, 2007.

Tolone, W., Ahn,G., Pai, T., Hong, S., "Access control in collaborative systems", *ACM Comput. Surv. 37*, 2005, pp.29-41.

Vujasinovic M., Ivezic N., Kulvatunyou B., Barkmeyer E., Missikoff M., Taglino F., Marjanovic Z., Miletic I., "Semantic Mediation for Standard-Based B2B Interoperability", *IEEE Internet Computing*, 2010, pp.52-63.

Workshop 4

SmartNets – Collaborative Development and Production of Knowledge-Intensive Products and Services

Report

Armin Lau

DITF Denkendorf
73770 Denkendorf, Germany
armin.lau@ditf-mr-denkendorf.de

The Innovative knowledge-intensive products, processes and services are the basis for increasing the competiveness of European industry. Cross-sectoral collaboration in dynamic networks is beyond controversy one of the most powerful approaches to deal with the growing complexity and limited timeframe for the realization of such innovations. This workshop has followed the idea of Smart Networks which is especially suited for collaborative innovation due to its conscious handling of organisational, ICT and knowledge aspects of such collaboration.

The goal of the workshop was to get the participants acquainted with the idea of Smart Networking and to present most recent research and practical applications in this field. The contributions of the speakers served as input for vivid discussions and an open exchange of experiences between speakers and attendees. Below you will find a short summary of the workshop contributions and about issues covered during related discussions.

After introducing the topic of the workshop in general, the first paper titled The industrial model of Smart Networks for SME collaboration – Implementation and success stories presented by A. Lau focused on how companies, in particular SMEs, can be actively supported in introducing the concept of Smart Networking in their daily work. The presented paper provides an overview on results that have been achieved in the European research project SmartNets. To help dynamic SME networks all along the product life-cycle, throughout the network life-cycle and in particular in the transformation from development to production, ten methodological and technological means have been developed that are shortly described and explained with some practical examples from the project.

In the ensuing discussion, particular attention was given to the specific requirements that SMEs have towards such methods and tools. It was concluded that the provided methods and tools can really have a significant impact on improving collaboration of SMEs and enabling them to act in co-creation networks. According to the participants, the general applicability of the approach will favor the use even across industry sectors. The long-term effect of these results however still has to be confirmed.

This paper titled Towards a conceptual model of the resource base for hyperlinking in innovation networks focuses on the resource base that SMEs require in order to participate to enterprise innovation networks. The related research identifies five resource types and related competences that have significant impact for "hyperlinking" of assets which is considered a basis for Smart Networking. Based on this reference framework, it is possible to assess companies' competences and to guide them towards a more focused development and extension of their networking capabilities.

T.J. Marlowe presented the paper titled Technology Incubators: Building an Effective Collaborative SMART NET for Learning, Growth and Innovation. Technology incubators in the United States are successfully supporting s in their first steps. However, this paper argues that continuous support in growing "from childhood to adolescence" is required to encounter recurring problems of young companies e.g. regarding capital, human resources, knowledge acquisition, marketing and management. Incubators already have infrastructures in place that could be used in facilitation, but observed challenges and organizational inertia seem to prevent the next steps.

Workshop participants confirmed similar observations in Europe, even though few incubators and business angels have started to offer support for selected aspects of company growth. Results of SmartNets, e.g. supporting network coordination, were considered to be a good basis for such kind of support.

The paper titled Application of the SmartNets Methodology in Manufacturing Service Ecosystems was presented by M. Hirsch. Servitization, i.e. the transformation of product-centric manufacturers into service-oriented businesses, is a huge challenge that many companies are facing at the moment. The authors demonstrate that the SmartNets methodology can be successfully used to support the process of servitization. In particular, aspects of ecosystem modelling, knowledge-orientation and semantics as well as IT interoperability are illustrated in a use case from a small traditional company. Focusing on its own resources and the market demand, it has evolved from a textile producer to a provider of multiple services, including IT services.

In the context of this presentation, interoperability aspects have been addressed in the following discussion. Interoperability has to be supported on a top level, between actors in an ecosystem and between IT systems, but also on detail level, where processes and material flows, IT services and information flows have to be aligned. The approaches take that in consideration and try to provide easy-to-use methods and tools for SMEs to implement that in practice.

Within the final contribution of the workshop, the authors of the paper titled Application of a Domain-Specific Language to support the User-Oriented Definition of Visualizations in the Context of Collaborative Product Development by T. Reschenhofer, presented a hybrid wiki platform that enables domain experts to develop and implement their own knowledge structures and business rules on a collaboration platform without the help of IT experts. For that, the wiki provides a model-based expression language (MxL). The paper shows exemplarily the practical application of MxL and its continuous improvement on the SmartNet Navigator, a tool that is capable of extracting project status information from distributed knowledge items.

Enabling domain experts to configure the collaboration platform on their own strongly enhances the flexibility of the underlying IT system as well as the business-related services provided. That makes it well-suited for supporting dynamic networks. Furthermore it also facilitates the evolution of new knowledge structures arising in the context of collaborative development projects. Discussions were raised about the applicability of this approach in practice. Practical experience of the developer showed that domain experts are indeed willing – sometimes even eager – to take over this role in IT design phases. However, it is only possible to manage that if the underlying technological complexity is well-hidden and usability is given utmost importance.

Two other issues emerged in the discussion. The first concerned knowledge and its management: the tension between knowledge sharing and intellectual property protection, plus the handling of knowledge developed via integration of participant knowledge or from collaboration or collaborative products, as well as process knowledge and insight into conceptual/cognitive approaches. The second was the difference between product-intensive enterprises in which facilities and materials are significant, and the marginal cost of producing more of a given item is a consideration, and knowledge-intensive enterprises, in particular software application development, in which the primary resource is personnel, and the marginal cost of copies is negligible.

The Industrial Model of Smart Networks for SME Collaboration

Implementation and Success Stories

Armin Lau* — Meike Tilebein* — Thomas Fischer**

DITF Denkendorf, Centre for Management Research
Koerschtalstr. 26, 73770 Denkendorf, Germany
armin.lau@ditf-mr-denkendorf.de
meike.tilebein@ditf-mr-denkendorf.de

** *WHU, Otto Beisheim School of Management*
Chair of Business Information Science and Information Management
Burgplatz 2, 56179 Vallendar, Germany
thomas.fischer@whu.edu

ABSTRACT. *Small and medium-sized entreprises (SMEs) are drivers of the European economy. They develop and produce highly innovative products, processes and services in key markets. In many cases, SMEs need to involve partners to tap the potential of new technologies, to open up market opportunities or to extend production capabilities. Thus, efficient networking and interoperability with other organisations has become tremendously important. Concepts like extended enterprise, virtual enterprise and other forms of dynamic networks describe the mechanisms of such collaboration. However, support for implementing the concepts into industrial practice is still not completely covered. Within this paper, the industrial model of Smart Networks will be introduced and ways for its implementation in practice will be shown. Success stories from various industry sectors will affirm the proposed methods and tools.*

KEYWORDS: *dynamic networks, SME support, development and production, Smart Network.*

1. Smart Networks – Industrial Model for SME Collaboration

While the globalized market is often perceived as big risk for companies due to increased competition, it actually presents a huge opportunity to collaborate with suppliers, customers and complementors which are exactly fitting the very specific business needs of a company (Chesbrough 03). In particular SMEs require strong and trustworthy partners to extend own competences and resource capacities and to spread costs and risks inherent to the development of innovative, knowledge intensive products and services. They need to quickly build up network structures to respond to market needs, have to efficiently operate and finally also reliably terminate such networks. Thus, the competence of networking itself becomes one key success factor regarding sustainable and efficient development and production.

Many concepts have been developed in research and practice to understand how to support such collaboration. While support through information and communication technologies (ICT) has been intensively covered (Camarinha-Matos et al., 2005), the human factor is not always fully attended to. To account for that, the idea of the "Smart Organisation" regards virtual teaming, ICT support and knowledge hyperlinking as equally important factors (Filos 06). Applying this concept in practice in a large sample of SME innovation networks demonstrated the high practical relevance. It became also apparent that in particular regarding generalization and with respect to application along the whole life-cycle, further methodological and technological support would be required (Lau et al., 2011).

Within the European research project SmartNets, the objective was to develop and to evaluate concepts, methods and tools that enable the implementation of Smart Networking in the day-to-day business of SMEs as an industrial model for collaboration which is dedicated to SME needs, applicable along the whole product and service life-cycle and transferrable across industry sectors. Beneath the overall concept, ten interrelated methodologies and tools were developed which can be used independent of each other or in conjunction to improve networking capabilities of SMEs. In the following, these methods and tools will be shortly presented. Their practical usability is exemplarily illustrated in the success story from three networks which evaluated the project results in three different industry sectors.

2. Implementation of the Industrial Model into SME Partnerships

For the implementation of the industrial model in industrial practice, five methodologies and five tools have been provided. The methodologies have been developed, compiled and adapted with a clear focus on SME suitability, providing a clear and easy-to-follow process and several examples from practical applications.

While basically the methods can be implemented on many kinds of technological platforms, within SmartNets they have been realized prototypically on the hybrid Wiki system Tricia which is provided by one of the project partners. The original system is capable of handling both unstructured Wiki pages and structured information. SmartNets results use and extend these functionalities.

The frame of the industrial model is constituted by the *Smart Net Collaboration Model* that provides generally applicable structures, as shown in the centre of Figure

1. It is highlighting activities that have to be carried out, actors that can be involved and methods that can be applied and thus answers recurring key questions like "What to do next?", "Who can do it?", "Which method could help me?". To apply the SmartNet Collaboration Model in day-to-day business, there exists a simple step-by-step instruction which helps to adapt the model to specific projects to make most effective use of it (Lau et al., 2012).

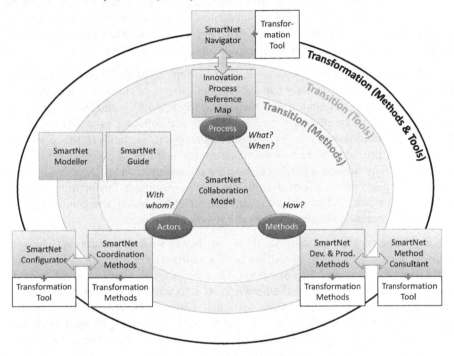

Figure 1. *SmartNet Industrial Model – Results for transition and transformation*

The complex value adding process basically follows the *Innovation Process Reference Map* (Lau 12) which forms the backbone for the *SmartNet Navigator*. The Navigator is a toolset to cope with the complexity of collaborative development. It assists in identifying the current status of development and production projects on basis of existing project documentation. Resulting status information can be used for choosing the next steps and selecting the best methods and partners, thus guiding enterprises and networks through the development and production process of products and services (Matheis et al., 2013).

To systematically support all the tasks associated with this process, *SmartNet Development and Production Methods* provide descriptions and step-by-step instructions for numerous SME-suitable methods and help SMEs with the selection and implementation of appropriate methods in their development project. The *SmartNets Method Consultant* represents the implementation of these method recommendations based on the particular project status on the project's collaboration platform (Matheis et al., 2013). How-to's and executable templates support the user in the application of the methods.

From the perspective of a single company, four main types of actors can be involved in collaboration. Suppliers, customers, complementors, in particular so-called Knowledge Intensive Service Providers, and sometimes even competitors may have significant impact on development and production (Chesbrough 03).

SMEs require support in organizing the involvement of such partners. *SmartNet Network Coordination Methods* support all four aspects of network management – selection, allocation, regulation and evaluation (Sydow 06) – and in particular the management of complementary and (potentially) conflicting issues (Lau et al., 2013b). The implementation of the methodology in a toolset, the *SmartNet Configurator*, provides basic project management features like collaborative task management with ad-hoc workflows, meeting organization and a flexible push/pull approach for distributing information in a secure environment. Furthermore, it gives suggestions for potential actors within the SmartNet Navigator and comprises a set of executable methods to actively support network coordination.

Key to successful coordination is to have a clear, common view of responsibilities, as well as available and missing resources, competences and processes in the network. The *SmartNet Modeller* is an easy-to-use tool that helps partners to conjointly describe the network, its actors and its ecosystem in order to understand roles and contributions of each partner as well as material and information flows (SmartNets 13a). The models can for example be used to identify concrete companies matching the actor recommendations given by the Configurator.

To make sure that partners actually have the capabilities to act in such networks, the *SmartNet Guide* can be used to identify, to assess and to improve capabilities of SMEs regarding organizational, knowledge and ICT networking and hyperlinking. A set of questions is used to conduct interviews in which available resources and competences of a company are assessed regarding their impact on networking. Improvement potential will be shown up and a regular re-evaluation will ensure that the networking capabilities of SMEs will be steadily ameliorated (SmartNets 13b).

For an efficient development, the early identification and consideration of production conditions and requirements is essential. *SmartNet Transformation Methods*, as shown in Fig. 1, are a set of easily applicable methods that complement the presented results in terms of contributing to a smooth and efficient system transformation from development network to robust production network. The transformation comprises changing the partner constellation, establishing reliable processes, evolving knowledge structures and integrating ICT tools (Lau et al.,

2013a). The *SmartNet Transformation Manager* implements the methodology by providing executable methods and by further connecting the previously introduced tools. It assists the operative planning, execution and control of the transformation towards reliable and robust production.

3. Success Stories from the SmartNets Project

Within the SmartNets project, the presented concepts, methods and tools have been extensively applied and evaluated by three networks acting in three different industry sectors. The first network has been established by three SMEs from Italy and United Kingdom to apply a new type of material in the development of an innovative motorcycle helmet. Starting from a basic idea about the final product and some preliminary promising tests, SmartNets methods and tools supported them in solving several technical problems, developing marketing ideas and tackling issues about required changes in the production process. SmartNets results also motivated the successful use of the material in other applications and other industry sectors.

The development of interior textiles has been in the focus of a network of two SMEs and a researcher from Belgium. After quickly bringing a coating for improved abrasion resistance to the market, they continued the evaluation with a new customer request. Starting from scratch in the innovation process, SmartNets methods and tools assisted them in quickly taking up the requirements and efficiently developing another innovative product. In a third collaboration, four companies and two research organisations from Germany and Czech Republic in the fields of medical devices and textile industry followed up a development for which already first prototypes were available. SmartNets results supported in particular the coordination of the complex development including several sub and side projects. Results also encouraged early development documentation with respect to an eventual product certification process and sparked several new product ideas.

4. Conclusions

The evaluation process of the three project networks showed that the results of the SmartNets project, even if used independent of each other, can significantly boost effectivity and efficiency in a collaborative development process. They not only accelerate regular development but also show up support, shortcuts and if necessary also steps back to quickly improve the development. Furthermore, a good interoperability of the results has been perceived.

In a generalization step, the overall industrial model has been checked for general applicability in SME networks in Europe. Feedback from project externals and own studies suggest that the industrial model and its single results are fully applicable for other industry sectors, differing company sizes, cross-sectoral work, different cultures and multi-lingual projects. Slight adaptations to the underlying models can be made quickly, if necessary. These findings have to be continuously evaluated in practice, e.g. with members of the SmartNets community.

5. Acknowledgements

This work has been partly funded by the European Commission through the Project SmartNets: Transformation from Collaborative Knowledge Exploration Networks into Cross Sectoral and Service Oriented Integrated Value Systems (Grant Agreement No. 262806, www.smart-nets.eu). The authors wish to acknowledge the Commission for their support. We also wish to acknowledge our gratitude and appreciation to all the SmartNets Project partners for their contribution during the development of various ideas and concepts presented in this paper.

6. References

Camarinha-Matos L.M., Afsarmanesh H., "Collaborative networks: a new scientific discipline". *Journal of Intelligent Manufacturing*. vol. 16, no. 4, 2005, pp.439–452.

Chesbrough H. W., *Open Innovation: The New Imperative for Creating and Profiting from Technology*, Boston, Harvard Business Press, 2003.

Filos E., "Smart Organizations in the Digital Age", in: Mezgar, I., *Integration of ICT in Smart Organizations*, Hershey, Idea Group Publishing, 2006, pp.1–37.

Lau A., *Methodisch-technologische Unterstützung kollaborativer Innovationsprozesse in Smart Networks*, München, Verlag Dr. Hut, 2012.

Lau A., Fischer T., "Cross-sectoral innovation networks for knowledge-intensive products and services", in: Spath D., Ilg R., Krause T. (eds.), *Innovation in Product and Production. Proceedings of the 21st International Conference on Production Research (ICPR21)*, Stuttgart, 31 July–4 August 2011, Stuttgart, Fraunhofer-Verlag.

Lau A., Fischer T., Hirsch M., Matheis H., "SmartNet Collaboration Model - A framework for collaborative development and production, in: Katzy B., Holzmann T., Sailer K., Thoben K.-D. (eds.), *18th International Conference on Engineering, Technology and Innovation, ICE 2012*, 18-20 June 2012, Munich.

Lau A., Hirsch M., Matheis H., "From Collaborative Development to Manufacturing in Production Networks: The SmartNets Approach", in: Windt K. (ed.), *Robust Manufacturing Control*, Berlin, Heidelberg, Springer, 2013a, pp.287-299.

Lau A., Tilebein M., "Kompetenz des Netzwerks durch Kompetenz des Netzwerkens - Förderung der Netzwerkfähigkeit kleiner und mittlerer Unternehmen", in: Biedermann H., (ed.), *Corporate Capability Management - Wie wird kollektive Intelligenz im Unternehmen genutzt?*, Berlin, GITO, 2013b, pp.351–376.

Matheis H., Lau A., Hirsch M., "Technological support for managing collaborative innovation projects in SME networks", in: Cunningham S. W., Salimi N., Ortt R., Rezaei J., Katzy B. R. (eds.), *Conference Proceedings of the IEEE Technology Management Conference & 19th ICE Conference.* 24-26 June 2013, The Hague.

SmartNets, D01.2 SmartNets Modeller and application guidelines. https://www.smart-nets.eu/main/file/hheuhqmfolct/SmartNets/Downloads/Public-Deliverables/D01.2 SmartNets Modeller and application guidelines.pdf (accessed 18 Dec 2013a).

SmartNets. D02.4 SmartNet Guide. https://www.smart-nets.eu/main/file/clat5h4grrtz/ SmartNets/Downloads/Public-Deliverables/D02.4 SmartNet Guide.pdf (accessed 18 Dec 2013b).

Sydow, J., "Management von Netzwerkorganisationen – Zum Stand der Forschung", in: Sydow J. (ed.), *Management von Netzwerkorganisationen: Beiträge aus der "Managementforschung".* Wiesbaden, Gabler Verlag, 2006, p. 387-472.

Towards a Conceptual Model of the Resource Base for Hyperlinking in Innovation Networks

Sven-Volker Rehm — Sven Gross

WHU, Otto Beisheim School of Management
Burgplatz 2, 56179 Vallendar, Germany
sven-volker.rehm@whu.edu
sven.gross@whu.edu

ABSTRACT. *Achieving competitive advantage requires capabilities for leveraging or developing unique features of a firm's resources. This is in particular relevant to small and medium enterprises (SMEs) when they target at innovation. SMEs need to connect their limited resource base to those of third partners. The hyperlinking concept has been proposed in this respect to assure business interoperability in networks. We develop a conceptual model linked to firm resources, for creating interoperability in innovation networks. The preliminary model comprises five types of firm resources which need to be prepared for hyperlinking, in addition to developing capabilities for networking towards collaborative innovation. We propose an audit method for improving the development of these types of resources which is intended to be applied by SMEs. The model and the method have been tested in three innovation network case studies.*

KEYWORDS: *Innovation Network, Conceptual Model, Hyperlinking, Resource Base.*

1. Introduction

Innovation has been identified as a main driver for developing competitive advantage (Chesbrough 2003). In particular for small and medium enterprises (SMEs) the objective to innovate creates the challenge to connect to innovation partners (Davenport et al., 2006). Such innovation is often taking place within innovation ecosystems (Adner et al., 2010). From ecosystems, innovation networks of various partners form (Cowan et al., 2007) in order to develop distinct new products, processes and services within cooperative New Product Development (NPD) projects. While they intend to create competitive products and services, SMEs involved into innovation networks need to adapt, develop or extend their resource base in order to assume a pro-active position in such projects. Previous literature proposes that through such endeavors, unique resource bases can be created that allow generating sustained competitive advantage (Barney 1991; Wernerfelt 1984).

Although this way to innovate in networks is a broadening trend in practice, there is a gap in literature about how to achieve an effective connection of a firm's resource base to that of innovation partners, and in particular, how SMEs can efficiently leverage these connections in order to broaden their resource base and to engage in multiple innovation networks.

We want to address this gap by developing a conceptual model of an SME's resource base, and by proposing ways to connect it to the resource bases of innovation partners. To do so, we follow a design science approach for developing our conceptual model which comprises five types of resources, human resources and knowledge, internal organizational structure, relationships, information systems, and physical resources. The model is intended to serve practice as a reference framework guiding SMEs in their efforts to connect their resource base to that of innovation partners. The model has been tested in three case studies, involving three European innovation networks of different industrial sectors.

We contribute to research by proposing a conceptual model which can be a basis for future studies on SME collaboration for innovation. We contribute to practice by offering a tested reference framework to SMEs which supports creating awareness of their resource base and guiding the subsequent development of connected competences. In the following paragraphs we give a short account of existing literature, state our research question and method, and outline the conceptual model. We close with a short summary including some implications for practice.

2. Literature on Integrating the Resource Base of Innovation Networks

Previous research has emphasized the significance of managing integration for the success of innovation networks (Word 2009; Schilling et al., 2007). This notion of integration involves factors such as trust, commitment, dependency, and compatibility, in particular for networks of SMEs (Rese et al., 2011). Several areas of learning have been identified as crucial for developing increased competence in collaboration, among them project selection, partner selection, and aspects covering management of collaborations (Dickson et al., 1997).

However, research literature providing approaches for *methodologically* guiding SMEs in their efforts for building and managing innovation networks is scarce. European research policy has targeted this gap within its European RTD programs, and several approaches have been proposed such as the "smart organization" (Filos et al., 2001a) or "enterprise interoperability" (Chen et al., 2008). Those are focused on providing methodological support to the development of firm's competences for engaging in networks.

The "smart networking" concept (Filos et al., 2001a, 2001b) highlights the need for SMEs to adapt to different organizational forms and types of cooperation. It uses the term "hyperlinking" in order to illustrate that organizations involved into cooperative NPD within innovation networks constitute from different but interconnected contexts. It denotes that a firm's resources and competences need to be prepared for networking (i.e., hyperlinked), in order to reach a "smart" behaviour of the resulting networked enterprise. "Smart" behaviour entails that businesses are seen as communities, and communities as sets of relationships where "connectivity breeds relationships"; embracing the notion of hyperlinking that this connectivity allows leveraging organizational knowledge to generate innovations.

This concept of hyperlinking highlights the need to connect assets in order to reach particular goals of cooperation within a network of firms. The role of managing assets is to assure balancing of patents, brands, market position, trust, commitment, and further factors such as human (knowledge), or structural and customer capital, in a way that goals such as resource optimization, synergy creation, achievement of a critical mass of partners, and an increase of benefits can be reached (Filos et al., 2001a). Three dimensions are proposed for providing a viable networking structure, organizational networking (hyperlinking), information and communication technology (ICT) networking, and knowledge networking (Filos et al., 2001b). Extant literature however fails in providing concrete hints about the *resources* which are to be hyperlinked, or aligned, within networked relationships, and which NPD functional *competences* are required in this context.

3. Research Design

Our research question asks which *types of resources* need to be linked by networking efforts within innovation networks. Explicating these resource types builds the basis to identify required *competences* for aligning a firm's organization and relationships to network partners. We adopt a Design Science approach (Hevner et al., 2004). The definition of resource types and related competences provides a basic *conceptual model of the resource base for hyperlinking in innovation networks*, as resulting artefact of our research. For evaluating the design of our artefact we chose to use case studies. We have worked with three innovation networks over a three year period. They consisted of three to five partners each (as core partners, and including further partners such as research institutes and consultancy agencies as periphery), and targeted innovations in the sectors of automotive, textile finishing and medical devices respectively. We started with an analysis of the intended NPD projects, and each firm's existing preconditions regarding their organizational structures, technological, ICT and knowledge aspects, partnerships, as well as networking issues and problems. Guided interviews and conversations along the progressing NPD projects allowed us to study the developments within the firms including knowledge exchanges, resource reconfigurations and in particular the development of related competences.

Resource types	Competences	Hyperlinking objectives
Human Resources and Knowledge	• Goal orientation, transparency, alignment • Team working competence • Problem solving competence	Conjoint orientation of common goals; clear understanding of responsibilities and an open and efficient exchange of requirements and boundary conditions
Internal Organizational Structure	• Team leadership competence • Process management competence • Knowledge management competence	Complete and thorough understanding of the NPD process; documentation of explicable knowledge in an appropriate form for manufacturing and certification
Relationships	• Supplier and customer integration competence • Service provider integration competence • Trust building competence	Clear communication of requirements and boundary conditions; reducing communication and alignment efforts; building up and maintaining trust
Information Systems	• Information management competence • Competence to provide or use collaborative work environments	Using modern ICT; knowing information domains of partners; identifying which information needs to be exchanged and protected; determining clear information flows; using virtual environments
Physical Resources	• Material processing competence • Material storage competence	(we have not considered physical resources in our case studies)

Table 1. *Resource types and competences for hyperlinking in innovation networks*

4. Conceptual Model of the Resource Base for Hyperlinking in Innovation Networks

The conceptual model developed by us comprises five types of resources as distinct elements (see Table 1). When engaging into cooperative NPD in innovation networks, each of these resource types needs to be hyperlinked between the partnering firms in order to achieve a balanced (efficient) and effective use of resources. Each firm brings into a network its own set of resources, and also individual competences to manage these resources. Through our investigations, we could identify a preliminary set of core *competences* that are connected to resource types in their use for hyperlinking. Table 1 highlights the objectives related to hyperlinking resources. We have used this conceptual model to identify and to evaluate firm resources and competences in our case studies. Applying the model can trigger awareness of available – or missing – competences and offers a possibility to systematically improve these with the help of dedicated instruments and procedures for innovation.

5. Summary

We propose a conceptual model that identifies five distinct resource types as a basis of hyperlinking the resource base in innovation networks. Part of the model are relevant competences that need to be developed by SMEs in order to achieve successful reconfigurations of these resources. Through our testing of the proposed conceptual model in three innovation networks as case studies, we have iteratively positioned the model as reference framework, which has proven suitable to guide the firms' efforts in networking. For the evaluation of competences we developed an audit scheme with 27 statements as basis for an initial audit and 27 corresponding statements for consecutive 'performance audits' during a running project. The statements help to gain comprehensive insight into relevant areas and to qualitatively evaluate the resource base. The audit approach intends to primarily identify (i) pre-existing competences, instruments and methodical knowledge, as well as (ii) existing strategies, including assets, resources, and goals. For each NPD project, consequently appropriate measures can be taken for internally developing required competences. Also, adequate efforts can be taken for providing internal resources to external partners or for hyperlinking to external resources. Such measures can be complemented through development of shared strategies with the innovation network partners. As we have recognized from our three case studies, orientation at the proposed framework and repeated engagement into resource reconfigurations can lead to an improved capacity of a firm for adapting to new resource and partnership constellations.

6. Acknowledgements

This work has been partly funded by the European Commission through the Project SmartNets: The Transformation from Collaborative Knowledge Exploration Networks into Cross Sectoral and Service Oriented Integrated Value Systems (Grant Agreement No. 262806). The authors wish to acknowledge the Commission and all the SmartNets Project partners for their support.

7. References

Adner R., Kapoor R., "Value creation in innovation ecosystems: how the structure of technological interdependence affects firm performance in new technology generations". *Strategic Management Journal* 31: 306-333 (2010).

Barney J., "Firm Resources and Sustained Competitive Advantage". *Journal of Management* 17: 99-120 (1991).

Chen D., Doumeingts G., Vernadat F., "Architectures for enterprise integration and interoperability: Past, present and future". *Computers in Industry: Enterprise Integration and Interoperability in Manufacturing Systems* 59: 647-659 (2008).

Chesbrough H.W., "The Era of Open Innovation". *MIT Sloan Management Review* 44: 35-41 (2003).

Cowan R., Jonard N., Zimmermann J., "Bilateral collaboration and the emergence of innovation networks: Bilateral collaboration and the emergence of innovation networks". *Management Science* 53: 1051-1067 (2007).

Davenport T.H., Leibold M., Voelpel S., *Strategic Management in the Innovation Economy: Strategy Approaches and Tools for Dynamic Innovation Capabilities*. Erlangen: Publicis, 2006.

Dickson K.E., Coles A.M., Lawton Smith H., "Learning issues in successful, long-term, inter-firm research collaboration". *Strategic Change* 6: 273-282 (1997).

Filos E., Banahan E., "Towards the smart organization: An emerging organizational paradigm and the contribution of the European RTD programs. *Journal of Intelligent Manufacturing* 12: 101–119 (2001a).

Filos E., Banahan E., "Will the organisation disappear? The challenges of the new economy and future perspectives". In: *E-business and Virtual Enterprises: Managing Business-to-Business Cooperation* (eds. Camarinha-Matos LM, Afsarmanesh H and Rabelo RJ), pp.3-20. Boston, Dordrecht, London: Kluwer Academic (2001b).

Hevner A.R., March S.T., Park J., Ram S., "Design Science in Information Systems Research". *MIS Quarterly* 2004; 28: 75-105 (2004).

Rese A., Baier D., "Success factors for innovation management in networks of small and medium enterprises". *R&D Management* 41: 138-155 (2011).

Schilling M.A., Phelps C.C., "Interfirm collaboration networks: The impact of large-scale network structure on firm innovation". *Management Science* 53: 1113-1126 (2007).

Wernerfelt B. "A Resource-based View of the Firm". *Strategic Management Journal* 5: 171-180 (1984).

Word J. (ed.), *Business Network Transformation: Strategies to Reconfigure your Business Relationships for Competitive Advantage*. 1st ed. San Francisco, CA: Jossey-Bass, 2009.

Enhanced Incubators

Fostering Collaboration, Growth and Innovation

Thomas J. Marlowe* — Vassilka Kirova** — Mojgan Mohtashami***

* Department of Mathematics and Computer Science
Seton Hall University
South Orange NJ 07079 USA
thomas.marlowe@shu.edu

** New Jersey Institute of Technology
Newark NJ 07102 USA
vassilka.kirova@alcatel-lucent.com

*** Advanced Infrastructure Design
Hightstown NJ 08520 USA
mojgan@aidpe.com

ABSTRACT. Technology incubators have been reasonably successful in creating new ventures and driving innovation, through provision of low-cost shared physical and electronic infrastructure, technical and management advice, interaction with faculty and students, and exposure to new processes and ideas. In many incubators, however, this emphasis on initiation leaves key problems unaddressed, particularly broadening enterprise focus and expertise and the transition from a "one-room" shop to a larger functioning and self-sustaining business. We present a summary of interviews with entrepreneurs and small business leaders, classifying common challenges and identifying possible solutions. We examine different forms of extended collaboration, education and knowledge sharing as tools for addressing the identified deficiencies and enhancing the role of incubators. Finally, we examine resulting opportunities and the benefits to participants, and discuss future directions for this work.

KEYWORDS: Incubator, Entrepreneur, Small-To-Medium Enterprise (SME), Collaboration, Growth.

1. Introduction

University, government and non-profit-sponsored technology incubators in the USA have met with varying success in creating new ventures and driving innovation. They offer many benefits: easy access to academic research, minimal overhead at the start, shared infrastructure, easy access to business expertise, marketing opportunities and some established business relations and communication channels. The academic-enterprise collaboration also offers benefits to academics and students: opportunities to apply and test new ideas, early feedback, and extending research directions. Too often, however, emphasis is on providing a low-cost shared infrastructure and technical and management advice, leaving key problems, such as the transition from "one-room" shop to a larger functioning business, out of the picture.

Here we analyze data gathered from selected interviews with entrepreneurs and small business leaders, classify common challenges in establishing and growing the business and identify possible solutions. We present an approach for enhancing the incubator, and addressing collaboration, analysis and transition to a larger venture. Finally, we evaluate challenges and benefits in this approach, for the enterprise, for academics and the professional community, and for students.

Section 2 summarizes the difficulties enterprises face in growth transitions, and Section 3 suggests enhancements to incubators to respond to these difficulties. Section 4 evaluates the challenges and potential benefits of this approach, and Section 5 presents brief conclusions and future directions.

2. Identifying the Problem

If the technical concept of an enterprise is valid and the entrepreneurs are business savvy, an incubator can succeed in creating a "garage-size" business, run internally with perhaps a few trusted outsiders. But past that scale, many small enterprises find common problems; four arose repeatedly in recent interviews (Mohtashami et al., 2014):

– Obtaining capital,

– Finding and retaining technical talent, with opportunities for professional growth and development of increased flexibility,

– Developing an improved knowledge base and better marketing, to remain competitive with more mature and often larger organizations, while addressing the differences imposed by smaller size, narrower focus, and specialized identity,

– Most significantly, enabling entrepreneurs to manage the increasing mix of business, technical and entrepreneurial tasks while remaining sufficiently current in each, and/or developing a management infrastructure of individuals who can contribute to each of these task areas as the need arises,

For technically-oriented firms, these issues refine standard concerns in establishing and growing a small business (Goelz 2012). Although enterprises may have started in incubators, and may make use of workshops and other support offered by academic and professional organizations, incubators and the support system seem not to be oriented to providing support for continued growth, with post-incubator support often perceived as superficial and not very practical, and not geared to the challenges of growth.

Small businesses are an engine for productivity and innovation. But the founders of small technology firms also have challenges. With few to no managers, they are faced with a dilemma: focus on technology, innovation and commercialization, or divide their attention and also leverage new management approaches while carrying out everyday responsibilities of effectively managing personnel. Introducing lean, agile management approaches, such as self-organizing teams, and effective management styles to boost morale and encourage innovation, is a promising direction, but to maintain a distinctive, innovative niche also requires good business and people management.

3. The solution – Extending the Incubator

In (Mohtashami *et al.*, 2014), we propose collaborations between small enterprises – in related fields but not directly competing – in an ongoing "loose" joint venture to enhance a firm's knowledge base of technical, management, and other capabilities, with the possibility of additional collaboration (Nousala *et al.*, 2008). However, small enterprises may not be prepared, in terms of processes, knowledge, resources or inclination, to participate in such activities, and without a structuring framework, the chance for success is limited. In our view, the incubator must be enhanced to assist with a transition to a larger-scale enterprise, and to inculcate structures and habits of mind to support healthy growth and future collaboration. In particular, we suggest the following changes in structure, activities and emphases:

– Encourage networking and interaction among incubator enterprises, and survey models and case studies of successful collaboration, providing an understanding of and roadmaps for relationships, including collaboration and joint ventures;

– Establish academic/non-profit collaboration with developing SMEs, driven not just by perceived immediate needs, but by fostering relationships and continued innovation;

– Communicate and practice (through exercises, simulations, role-playing, etc.) principles and practices for business and process evolution (Teichmann et al., 2011), and for adapting for collaboration. In addition, explore models for collaboration and guidelines for establishing relationships and selecting appropriate modes;

– Explore marketing, management, infrastructure and support challenges that arise from growth, to expand expertise, form relationships and collaborations, and seek capital (while current incubators typically support an initial IT infrastructure, with little emphasis on other eventual infrastructure or IT needs);

– Provide principles, structures and education for requirements, software architecture, interoperability (Koussouris et al., 2011, Marlowe et al., 2012), and assessment/metrics (Kolfschoten et al., 2007), and foster critical thinking through activities such as workshops and role-playing; in addition, emphasize the need for reflection and re-evaluation of processes, projects, and products, while continuing to improve the efficiency and focus of management and technical efforts;

– Offer discussion forums and provide examples of the changing focus of knowledge management/risk management (Flynn et al., 2008; Jastroch et al., 2011; Mohtashami et al., 2011) with enterprise and project scale, and with collaboration, through external presentations, case studies and workshops;

– Clarify the changing roles of innovators, managers and technical leaders with scale and with involvement with government and large corporation projects, and in particular the tension among extended responsibilities, greater specialization, and formalization of work and technical processes and provide focused workshops and training;

– Serve as a sponsor and host for focused multi-disciplinary advisory committees drawn from retired executives, technical specialists and academics, emphasizing technical and domain areas common to groups of past and present incubator enterprises, but also common problems for growing enterprises – fundraising, recruiting, retention and morale, business and technical processes, and infrastructure expansion; and maintain continued contact with incubator graduates, encouraging their interaction with current participants as mentors, experts or collaborative partners.

Achieving this vision requires three primary ingredients: (1) participation by current and past participants, by university faculty, post-docs and students, and by external experts; (2) willingness to share knowledge and expertise, to interact and collaborate, and to enter into relationships by these parties, with long-term benefits for all, and (3) focus on long-term and growth-oriented best practices, processes and structures in technical, management, marketing, infrastructure and support areas, by both participants and sponsors, with a concomitant focus on innovation in each areas.

4. Challenges and Benefits of this Approach

Challenges come from two sources: the longer-term horizon and the uncertainty with regard to best practices, which raise buy-in problems for all participants – academic institutions (and governments for public institutions), faculty and students, enterprises, managers, and technical staff – in terms not only of initial and continuing involvement, but also with respect to demonstrating program value and program assessment.

Benefits are clearer. For enterprises, employees benefit from a more secure enterprise and a better work environment. The incubator and its sponsor benefit in reputation, financially through patents, and possibly from contributions from past participants. Researchers benefit from presenting and testing ideas, and from improved gathering and analysis of data, and students by obtaining material for case studies and possible theses, real-world experience, résumé credentials, and possible internships or jobs.

Nonetheless, any proposed solution cannot be deemed satisfactory unless it addresses most or all of the four major issues discussed in Section 2.

– Difficulties in raising capital may be ameliorated by use of business and technical best practices, and by formation of solid relationships and potential collaborations.

– Relationships with universities and professional societies can aid in recruitment, and use of business and technical best practices, with improvements in infrastructure, knowledge management and marketing, should assist with retention and morale. Moreover, with the new focus, the incubator (with ongoing relationships and collaborations), will be a strong plus in continuing education and growth.

– An improved, richer and more flexible knowledge base will result from the long-term and transition-oriented focus of the incubator, emphasis on knowledge, requirements and risk, plus continuing interaction with previous clients, and ongoing relationships including knowledge sharing, and from related activities.

– Finally, the major focus of the incubator enhancements is to support exactly this transition from an incubator-supported business in a larger, standalone enterprise.

5. Conclusions

Incubators have been reasonably successful at creating seed businesses, but have not in general supported the transition of such enterprises to a larger scale. We have suggested changes and enhancements addressing these key deficiencies, but will need to monitor the acceptance and adoption of the new areas of focus and how successful they will be in helping individual participants. In our future work we will weigh the successes against the issues and goals identified in our earlier interviews. Further surveys, interaction and interviews will also be needed to refine the problems and identify additional assistance and support.

6. References

Flynn, D., Brown, E., Krieg, R., "A Method for Knowledge Management and Communication within and across Multidisciplinary Teams", *2008 Workshop on Knowledge Generation, Communication and Management (KGCM 2008)*, Orlando, FL, USA, June 2008.

Goelz, J., "Why Small Businesses Fail to Grow", *New York Times* Online Edition, 12 April 2012, http://www.boss.blogs.nytimes.com/2012/04/10/why-small-businesses-fail-to-grow/?_r=0, accessed December 19 2013.

Jastroch, N., Kirova, V., Ku, C.S., Marlowe, T.J., Mohtashami, M., Nousala, S., "Inter-organizational Collaboration: Product, Knowledge and Risk", *Journal of Systemics, Cybernetics, and Informatics*, Vol. 9 (5), 30-35, December 2011.

Kolfschoten, G.L., Lowry, P.B., Dean, D.L., Kamal, M., "A Measurement Framework for Patterns of Collaboration". HICCS Working paper, May 2007. http://www.hicss.hawaii.edu/Reports/41CEWorkshop.pdf, accessed January 2012.

Koussouris, F., Lampathaki, F., Mouzakitis, S., Charalabidis, Y., Psarras, J., "Digging into Real-life Enterprise Interoperability Areas – Definition and Overview of the Main Research Areas", *Collaborative Enterprise (CENT) 2011*, Orlando FL, July 2011.

Marlowe, T.J., Jastroch, N., Nousala, S., Kirova, V., "Collaboration, Knowledge and Interoperability—Implications for Software Engineering", *Collaborative Enterprise (CENT 2012), Proceedings of the 16th World Multi-Conference on Systemics, Cybernetics and Informatics (WMSCI 2012)*, Orlando FL, July 2012.

Mohtashami, M., Marlowe, T.J., Kirova, V., "A Collaborative Approach to Fostering Management Talent Strength for Small Technology and Technical Enterprises", *Northeastern Decision Sciences Institute Conference*, Philadelphia PA, March 2014.

Mohtashami, M., Marlowe, T.J., Kirova, V., Deek, F., "Risk-Driven Management Contingency Policies in Collaborative Software Development", *International Journal of Information Technology and Management*, Volume 10 (2-4), 247-271, 2011.

Nousala, S., Jamsai-Whyte, S., "The value of sustainable knowledge transfer methods for SMEs, utilizing socio-technical networks and complex systems", *Journal of Systemics, Cybernetics and Informatics*, Vol. 8(6), 40-45, 2010.

Teichmann, G., Schwartz, E.M., Dittes, F.M., "Collaborative Engineering of Inter-Enterprise Business Processes", *Journal of Systemics, Cybernetics, and Informatics*, Vol. 9 (5), 57-64, December 2011.

Application of the SmartNets Methodology in Manufacturing Service Ecosystems

M. Hirsch* — D. Opresnik** — H. Matheis*

DITF Denkendorf – Centre for Management Research
Koerschtalstr. 26, 73770 Denkendorf, Germany
manuel.hirsch@ditf-mr-denkendorf.de
heiko.matheis@ditf-mr-denkendorf.de

***Department of Management, Economics and Industrial Engineering*
Politecnico di Milano, Piazza Leonardo Da Vinci 32, 20133 Milano, Italy
david.opresnik@polimi.it

ABSTRACT: *In dynamic and globalized markets, manufacturers join forces to create, manage, and offer new industrial Product-Services. Thereby, technological competences and knowledge about materials as well as production capabilities are collaboratively merged and further elaborated in order to cope with rapidly changing demands of existing and new customer segments. In this paper, findings of two European Projects are integrated in order to demonstrate how members of Manufacturing Ecosystems can profit from conceptual, methodological, and technological Smart Networking principles for collaborative innovation. By providing knowledge- and ICT-driven, procedural as well as organisational support, product-centric industrial networks are empowered to transform into service-oriented consortia that provide highly innovative product-services to emerging markets. An industrial use case from the textile domain shows how long term collaboration might also imply a transformation of core competencies of network members.*

KEYWORDS: *Collaborative Innovation, Servitization, Industrial Ecosystems.*

1. Collaborative Innovation in Manufacturing Industry

Facing globalized and dynamic markets, manufacturing industries are forced to increase competitiveness by fostering sustainable innovation, continuous collaboration, and concurrent engineering capabilities. In this context, the European Project MSEE draws on the cultivation of a service-oriented industrial paradigm, so called Manufacturing Service Ecosystems (MSE). MSE contrast the strategy of isolated enterprises by combining their technological competences and knowledge about materials as well as production capability in order to build up "non-hierarchical form of collaboration where various different organizations and individuals work together with common or complementary objectives on new value added combinations of manufactured products and product-services" (Wiesner *et al.*, 2012).

Product-Services are defined based on their value proposition that relies on a dedicated mix of in- and tangible assets being designed and combined such that complex customer needs are addressed (Freitag *et al.*, 2013). Consequently, the main idea of MSEs is to build up temporary consortia, so called Virtual Manufacturing Enterprises (VME), that allow for combining complementary cross-sectoral core competencies in order to provide highly innovative product-services.

Traditional manufacturers that rely on proven (tangible) products, robust processes, and long term investments usually struggle with operational implications that derive from service-orientation principles comprised by the MSE concept. Their objections are strongly related to the fact that MSE recommends to apply Servitization principles ((Wiesner *et al.*, 2013), (Vandermerwe et al., 1988)), aiming at complementing, differentiating, and even substituting classic products by means of new service within the manufacturing domain.

This is where the findings of the European Project SmartNets comes in, identifying Servitization as a specific path within its Innovation Process Reference Map ([7]) that helps to transform (classic, tangible) products into highly innovative (product-)services. According to the Smart Networking approach, collaborative innovation means to transform knowledge-related, organisational, and procedural as well as information-technology related assets within a VME – from idea to final Product-Services. In order to foster smart innovation, SmartNets provides conceptual, methodological, and IT means that shall be applied in the following in order to enable Servitization within a dedicated MSE, led by a textile shirt manufacturing company.

In contrast to widely adopted assumptions, this use case will demonstrate that "joining complementary core competences" is only a first step towards a prudent extension of individual core competences of single members within collaborative innovation networks. The findings presented show that there are mutual dependencies between a company's internal core competences and the product(-service) it is providing on Ecosystem level. Consequently, the textile company in our use case will be empowered to comprise both, core competences of a textile producer as well as of an IT-service provider.

2. Systematic Support of Servitization

As mentioned above, Servitization is considered to be a dedicated path for innovation, implying the shift from product-centricity to service-orientation. In

SmartNets, concepts, methods, and tools are provided to adequately support respective innovation acitivities. The following figure depicts how SmartNets findings are exemplarily applied along the generic innovation process (Figure 1).

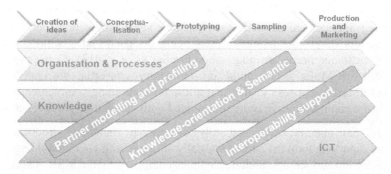

Figure 1. *Innovation support by means of Smart Networking concepts, methods, and tools*

Even though a huge selection of principles, methods, and technologies were analysed, contextualized, and described in course of the SmartNets project, only a small but powerful selection of them shall be outlined and applied within a textile use case. The following innovation-related principles are discussed in context of collaborative Servitization within a textile Manufacturing Service Ecosystem:

– The organisational perspective on innovation is tackled by a dedicated partner *modelling, profiling, and teambuilding methodology* that helps traditional manufacturing companies to join forces with IT-experts, consultancy agencies, and research institutes in order to implement a mature service-perspective.

– Knowledge orientation and transformation is addressed by introducing the *concept of semantics as well as modelling principles* that help to capture and optimize inter-organisational structures, information flows, and processes.

– In order to enable Ecosystem members to seamlessly interoperate also in IT level, dedicated *mapping, communication, and navigation features* are proposed along the product-service innovation process.

To prove positive impact on the given Ecosystem, the artefacts applied are evaluated against comprehensive criteria for measuring the maturity of innovation capabilities: a) degree of flexibility and adaptability of innovation process, b) openness and re-structuring possibilities within organisational networks, c) application of systematic methodologies for innovation, d) ability to manage and further develop inter-organisational knowledge-bases and e) integration of customers as well as f) implementation and usability of ICT support.

3. Success Story – A Textile Producer as (IT-)Service Provider

In the use case presented, a traditional shirt manufacturer – founded as a Belgian clothing manufacturer in 1954 – takes on the challenges imposed by the idea of Servitization in textile industry. The company's smart transformation from a resource-based and low added value manufacturer to a knowledge-based and high added-value service provider is outlined with regard to the above mentioned Smart Networking methodology.

The starting points for the company's evolution were new technological possibilities like Digital Textile Printing (DTP) or Rapid Manufacturing (RM). As a result, the textile company is now able to create and provide customized garments at a comparable price. Even though the newly developed Product-Services (such as Configuration as a Service, Manufacturing as a Service, Sizing as a Service) are provided as part of an interdisciplinary and cross-sectoral VME, the company's success story is not only about joining forces from manufacturing and ICT on Ecosystem level but to further extend individual core competences e. g. from textile production to (IT-) service provision.

After two years of anthropometric research, the company launched its patented biometric sizing technology for mass-customized shirts. Taking on this technology, a 3D shirt design platform was implemented, an early version of its so called configurable configurator. By further elaborating on this idea, an IT-service division was founded, aiming at providing dedicated services to commercial partners in the garments supply chain. To master this transformation, the following MSEE and Smart Networking ideas were applied:

– Partner modelling and profiling

Considering that agility and interoperability are esteemed to outpace traditional business characteristics like efficiency and robustness, appropriate modelling and evaluation methods are needed for pragmatic decision support as well as means for handling innovation networks setup and evolution (Figure 2).

SmartNets Models   Grai   Service Governance

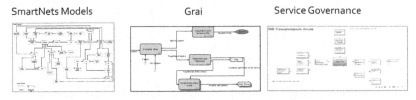

Figure 2. *Ecosystem partner modelling for collaborative product-service generation*

– Knowledge orientation and Semantics

When Ecosystem members collaborate across sectoral borders, functional, communicational as well as technical interoperability within networks becomes tremendously important. In the given textile Ecosystem, a domain specific ontology was developed and applied, providing knowledge workers from manufacturing and IT with context-specific information and advanced querying as well as reasoning functionalities for structuring, processing, assessing, and managing distributed knowledge.

By applying domain specific semantics, dispersed real-world Ecosystem assets got transformed into their virtual representation, namely Assets-as-a-Service. The resulting services could be easily shared and (re-)composed on Ecosystem level in order to derive innovative product services (Figure 3).

Asset	New Service Service "MaaS"	Service "Shirt-as-a-Service"	Service "Configuration-as-a-Service"	Service "Shirt Manufacturing as a Service" ...
Sewing Machine	✓			✓
Printer	✓			✓
Cutting Machine	✓			✓
Fabrics, Parts		✓		✓
Washing Machine		tbd		

Figure 3. *Assets-as-a-Service re-combined in innovative product-services*

– Interoperability support

As it is well known, that dynamic networking as well as concurrent engineering for sustainable innovation can be facilitated by Future Internet (FI) architectures as well as information and communication technologies (ICT) (Camarinha-Matos *et al.*, 2005), IT tools were provided to capture and guide the evolution of asset-related kowledge structures in the textile Ecosystem (Figure 4).

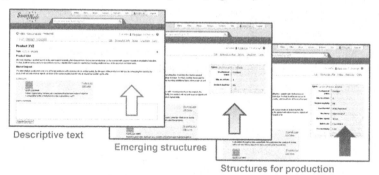

Figure 4. *Evolution of knowledge containers – from un- to structured*

4. Conclusions

As outlined above, industrial companies are able to provide new Product-Services on Ecosystem level as well as they are able to further extend their internal core competences by tacking on Smart Networking concepts, methods, and tools in context of Manufacturing Service Ecosystems. As for the presented use case, the following success indicators were gathered:

– Asset-as-a-Service allow for agile re-combination of assets for innovation.

– Profiling mechanisms foster partner acquisition and network extensions.

– Systematic Smart Networking methods provide guidelines for innovation.

– Flexible thus formalized structures enable consistent knowledge handling.

– Business model changed from product to service provision at the customers.

– ICT is used for collaboration and also to provide new product-(IT-)services.

5. Acknowledgements

This work has been partly funded by the European Commission through the Projects SmartNets: Transformation from Collaborative Knowledge Exploration Networks into Cross Sectoral and Service Oriented Integrated Value Systems (Grant Agreement No. 262806) and MSEE: Manufacturing Service Ecosystems (Grant Agreement No. 284860). We also wish to thank all the project partners for their contribution during the application of the concepts presented in this paper.

6. References

Camarinha-Matos L. M., Afsarmanesh H., "Collaborative networks: a new scientific discipline", *J. Intell. Manuf.*, vol. 16 no. 4–5, 2005, pp.439-452.

Freitag M., Kremer D., Hirsch M., Zelm M., "An Approach to standardize a Service Life Cycle Management", *5th International IFIP Working Conference, IWEI 2013*, Enschede The Netherlands, 2013.

SmartNets, "D1.3 SmartNet Collaboration Model. Public deliverable." Obtained through the internet: https://www.smart-nets.eu/main/file/k64yyecdxyk0/SmartNets/Downloads/Public-Deliverables/D01.3%20SmartNet%20Collaboration%20Model.pdf, 2012.

Vandermerwe S., Rada J., "Servitization of business: adding value by adding services," *Eur. Manag. J.*, vol. 6 no. 4, 1988, pp.314-324.

Wiesner S., Westphal I., Hirsch M., Thoben K.-D., "Manufacturing Service Ecosystems - Towards a new model to support service innovation based on Extended Products," *Advances in Production Management Systems. Competitive Manufacturing for Innovative Products and Services. IFIP WG 5.7 International Conference, APMS 2012*, Rhodes, Greece, September 24-26, 2012, Revised Selected Papers, Part II, 2012, vol. 398, pp.305-312.

Wiesner S., Winkler M., Eschenbächer J., Thoben K.-D., "Strategies for Extended Product Business Models in Manufacturing Service Ecosystems," *Product-Service Integration for Sustainable Solutions*, Berlin, Heidelberg, Springer, 2013, pp.239-250.

Application of a Domain-Specific Language to Support the User-Oriented Definition of Visualizations in the Context of Collaborative Product Development

Thomas Reschenhofer — Ivan Monahov — Florian Matthes

Chair for Informatics 19 (sebis)
Technische Universität München
Boltzmannstr. 3, 85748 Garching bei München, Germany
reschenh@in.tum.de
ivan.monahov@in.tum.de
matthes@in.tum.de

ABSTRACT. In the domain of Enterprise Architecture Management (EAM), multiple stakeholders with different responsibilities and backgrounds have to collaborate to achieve different predefined enterprise-related goals. To enable the definition of stakeholder-specific views onto the overall Enterprise Architecture (EA), we developed and prototypically implemented a domain-specific language (DSL) for defining model-based metrics and visualizations as management decision support in a commercial EAM tool. Since the domain of Collaborative Product Development (CPD) seemed to be similar to EAM with respect to the involvement of a diversity of stakeholders and the need for collaboration, we applied our prototype in the CPD domain by implementing an automated project status analysis and visualization called SmartNet Navigator as part of the EU research project SmartNets. However, since we faced several limitations and shortcomings (e.g., missing type checking and insufficient DSL syntax) during the evaluation of our prototype in the field of EAM, we redesigned the DSL and improved the prototype to solve the problems. This paper firstly provides an overview of the problems and improvements of our solution. Afterwards we present the application of our improved prototype in the domain of CPD by reimplementing the SmartNet Navigator and compare it to its initial prototype. Finally, we discuss possible benefits by the application of the improved DSL in the field of CPD and outline the need of further evaluation with experts from the SmartNet project according to the design science research method.

KEYWORDS: Domain-Specific Language, Enterprise Architecture Management, Collaborative Product Development, Metric, End-User Development.

1. Introduction

To cope with the continuous evolution of an enterprise's environment, it has to align its IT perpetually to the ever-changing business requirements to ensure effective and efficient IT support for the business. In this context, the Enterprise Architecture (EA) is defined as "the fundamental and holistic organization of an enterprise embodied in its components, relations and its environment" (ISO/IEC 42010:2007). Hence, to facilitate this alignment, enterprise architects have to manage the flexibility, efficiency and transparency of the EA. The corresponding management discipline is named Enterprise Architecture Management (EAM) and includes the development, implementation and control of the EA's evolution, i.e., the evolution of its components, attributes, and relations (Ahlemann et al. 2012).

However, due to the increasing complexity and the dynamics of today's enterprise architectures, qualitative models (e.g., visualizations) are not sufficient for efficient decision support (Kaisler et al. 2005). Therefore, quantitative models (e.g., metrics and performance indicators) are used to provide a meaningful and reliable assessment of an EA. Furthermore, the increasing size and complexity of EAs also implies an increasing need for adequate tool-support (Handler, Wilson 2012; Buckl et al. 2008), which also includes support for quantitative models by the EAM tool. Moreover, to cope with the need for a flexible EA model due to the changing environment and the need for collaboration support due to a plethora of involved stakeholders (Lucke et al. 2010), the *Wiki4EAM* approach (Matthes, Neubert 2011) makes use of the model-based and collaborative EAM tool *Tricia*. In order to enable the definition of metrics and thus to equip this EAM tool with quantitative modelling capabilities, we developed a domain-specific language (DSL) named model-based expression language 1.0 (MxL 1.0) for the user-oriented definition of metrics at runtime and integrated it in Tricia (Monahov et al. 2013).

	I Creation of ideas	II Concept development	III Prototyping	IV Sampling	V Production and Marketing
Planning	Innovation culture	Framework def. (Concept)	Framework def. (Prototype)	Framework def. (Sample)	Planning of market introduction and marketing
	Innovation strategy and objectives	IPR protection planning	Project planning (Prototype)	Planning of sourcing	Planning of production and life-cycle handling
	Identification of opportunities	Project planning (Concept)		Project planning for sample development	
Execution	Idea generation	Concept elaboration	Prototype elaboration	Sourcing for sampling	Market introduction
	Idea formulation	Functional description	Prototype test (α-test)	Process implementation	Continuous marketing
		Tech. feasibility		Production of samples	Continuous production and life-cycle handling
		Market study		Sample test (β-test)	
		Business plan			
		Marketing plan			
		Protection of IPR			
Control	Screening and first evaluation	Assessment of concept	Technical evaluation	Evaluation of test results	Evaluation of market response
	Evaluation of IPR situation	Evaluation of studies	Market-oriented evaluation	Evaluation of process reliability	Financial success control
	Recommendation of project	Financial assessment (Concept)	Financial assessment (Prototype)	Financial assessment (Sample)	
		Launch prototyping	Launch for sampling	Launch for production	

Figure 1. *A sketch of the SmartNet Navigator*

In addition to the DSL's application in EAM we also applied MxL 1.0 in the domain of Collaborative Product Development (CPD), since most of the general conditions of EAM (e.g., involvement of a plethora of stakeholders and collaborative tasks) also hold for CPD (Hauder et al. 2013). In this context, MxL 1.0 was employed in the EU project *SmartNets* by implementing the so-called *SmartNet Navigator* – a visualization of the aggregated status of a certain development project (Matheis 2013). The SmartNet Navigator aggregates the status of individual tasks and meetings to the status of corresponding activity types, development phases, and in the end to an overall project status and visualizes it by a certain color-coding.

Figure 1 shows a sketch of the SmartNet Navigator for an exemplary project. The Navigator's columns represent development phases, the rows represent management activity types, and the cells consist of multiple activity types, which in turn are related to the project's tasks and meetings. In the concrete example in Figure 1, the first development phase of the project is finalized (green), the second phase is in progress (orange), and the remaining phases are still open (grey).

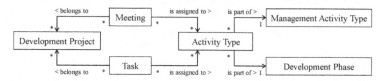

Figure 2. *The SmartNet Navigator's underlying meta-model*

We implemented the SmartNet Navigator in MxL 1.0 based on the meta-model shown in Figure 2. Hence, users are able to adjust the SmartNet Navigator's implementation at runtime, which makes it possible for the users to respond immediately to certain changes of the environment, e.g., a change of the rule for aggregating the status of multiple tasks. Figure 3 shows an excerpt of the SmartNet Navigator's implementation. However, the implementation of the SmartNet Navigator in MxL 1.0 suffers from several drawbacks, which we describe in the next Section.

Custom MxL Function Development Phase::smartnetNavigatorHeaderCell

```
Parameters    dp

Method Stub   "<td class='".concat(this.smartnetStatusOfProcessPhase(dp)).concat("'>")

                  /* Display the phase's order as a roman number, followed by
                     the phase's name */
                  .concat(this["Order"].first().roman()).concat("<br/>").concat(this["Name"].first())

              .concat("</td>")
```

Figure 3. *An MxL 1.0 function (Monahov et al. 2013) for the generation of HTML mark-up as part of the SmartNet Navigator's implementation. This function generates an HTML cell whose style is determined by the status of the corresponding process phase. The content of the cell is defined as the number of the process phase (in roman number format) followed by a line break and the name of the process phase.*

2. Redesign of MxL and Reimplementation of the SmartNet Navigator

While we have done the implementation of the SmartNet Navigator with MxL 1.0 (Hauder et al. 2013), the evaluation of MxL 1.0 in the domain of EAM revealed some weaknesses of the DSL and its implementation in Tricia. The most relevant to our understanding are:

W1 One of the goals of MxL 1.0 was to keep it minimal regarding its expressiveness and syntax. Consequently, we waived common language constructs (e.g., infix-notation for algebraic operators) and implemented them by function calls. However, this purely functional approach yields to incomprehensible expressions.

W2 Although the syntactic correctness of MxL 1.0 expressions (e.g., bracket matching) is checked at compile-time, the validation of an MxL 1.0 expression's static semantics (Voelter et al. 2013) is not performed at compile-time, but at runtime.

W3 Due to the lack of validation of the static semantics of an MxL 1.0 expression, these expressions are not analyzable at compile-time. Hence, the dependencies to MxL functions, attributes, types, etc. are not automatically observable.

W4 Changes of the underlying meta-model (e.g., renaming of attributes) affect the semantic consistency of all MxL 1.0 expressions referring to the changed elements.

Due to these shortcomings identified in the EAM domain, we redesigned the DSL and developed an improved version called MxL 2.0 (Reschenhofer 2013). To assess the added value of MxL 2.0 in the field of CPD, we reimplemented the SmartNet Navigator with MxL 2.0 to compare it to the initial prototype. Figure 4 shows an excerpt of the implementation of the SmartNet Navigator in MxL 2.0, while in the next Section we outline the benefits of the new prototype of the SmartNet Navigator.

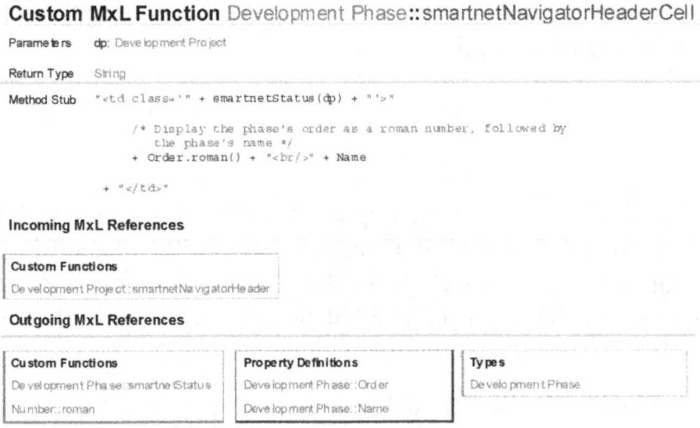

Figure 4. *Reimplementation of the SmartNet Navigator in MxL 2.0 (compare to Figure 3)*

3. Improvements and Evaluation of the Reimplemented SmartNet Navigator

In this paper, we elucidate the improvements by comparing an excerpt of the SmartNet Navigator's initial prototype (see Figure 3) with a corresponding excerpt of the reimplemented prototype using MxL 2.0 (see Figure 4). The main features of MxL 2.0 are an improved syntax as well as a type checker component as part of the MxL compiler (Reschenhofer 2013), leading to the following improvements, whereas each improvement Ix addresses the corresponding weakness Wx from Section 2:

I1 In MxL 2.0, we introduced infix-operators (e.g., plus operator for the string concatenation) as well as semantic enhancements (e.g., implicit *this*), so that the implementation of the improved prototype is more readable.

I2 The MxL 2.0 type checker validates the static semantics (Voelter et al. 2013) of MxL 2.0 expressions and therefore ensures semantic consistency at compile-time. For example, based on the expression in Figure 4 this means that the type checker ensures the existence of the attributes *Order* and *Name*. Moreover, the type checker determines the return type of the expression (e.g., *String*).

I3 The type checker enables the analysis of expressions, which means the observation of an MxL 2.0 expression's dependencies to MxL functions, attributes, types, etc. We use this expression analysis for generating and maintaining a computation graph. The nodes of the computation graph are MxL 2.0 expressions as well as objects these expressions refer to (e.g., attributes and types). Its edges represent the dependencies between them. For example, Figure 4 shows the *Incoming MxL References* (Expressions, which are referring to the current one) as well as the *Outgoing MxL References* (Objects, the current expression refers to).

I4 By using the computation graph, a tool implementing MxL 2.0 (e.g., Tricia) is able to propagate changes to those expressions, which are depending on the changing object. For example, if a user renames the attribute *Name* to *Title*, the reference in the expression of Figure 4 will be updated accordingly and therefore keeps consistency regarding its static semantics.

4. Conclusion

Since MxL 2.0 leads to significant improvements in the domain of EAM, we expect also benefits for the field of CPD, because most of the general conditions of EAM also hold for the domain of CPD. In this paper, we outlined these possible benefits by comparing the MxL 1.0 implementation of the SmartNet Navigator with a corresponding MxL 2.0 implementation.

However, to support the claim of achieving significant improvements in CPD, we still have to conduct further evaluation with experts of the field according to the design science research method (Hevner et al. 2004) in our future research activities.

5. References

Ahlemann, Frederik; Stettiner, Eric; Messerschmidt, Marcus; Legner, Christine (2012): *Strategic Enterprise Architecture Management*: Springer-Verlag.

Buckl, Sabine; Ernst, Alexander M.; Lankes, Josef; Matthes, Florian (2008): *Enterprise Architecture Management Pattern Catalog* (Version 1.0, February 2008). Chair for Informatics 19 (sebis), Technische Universität München. Munich, Germany. Available online at http://eampc-wiki.systemcartography.info/.

Handler, Robert A.; Wilson, Chris (2012): *Magic Quadrant for Enterprise Architecture Tools*.

Hauder, Matheus; Roth, Sascha; Matthes, Florian; Lau, Armin; Matheis, Heiko (2013): Supporting collaborative product development through automated interpretation of artifacts. In *3rd International Symposium on Business Modeling and Software Design*.

Hevner, Alan R.; March, Salvatore T.; Park, Jinsoo; Ram, Sudha (2004): Design science in information systems research. In *MIS quarterly* 28 (1), pp.75-105.

ISO/IEC 42010:2007 Systems and software engineering – Recommended practice for architectural description of software-intensive systems.

Kaisler, Stephen H.; Armour, Frank; Valivullah, Michael (2005): Enterprise Architecting: Critical Problems. In *Proceedings of the 38th Annual Hawaii International Conference on System Sciences*.

Lucke, C.; Krell, S.; Lechner, U. (2010): Critical Issues in Enterprise Architecting - A Literature Review. In *Proceedings of the Sixteenth Americas Conference on Information Systems*.

Matheis, Heiko (2013): SmartNet Navigator and application guidelines. In *Sehenth Framework Programme*.

Matthes, Florian; Neubert, Christian (2011): Wiki4EAM - Using Hybrid Wikis for Enterprise Architecture Management. In *7th International Symposium on Wikis and Open Collaboration (WikiSym)*.

Monahov, Ivan; Reschenhofer, Thomas; Matthes, Florian (2013): Design and prototypical implementation of a language empowering business users to define Key Performance Indicators for Enterprise Architecture Management. In *Trends in Enterprise Architecture Research Workshop*.

Reschenhofer, Thomas (2013): Design and prototypical implementation of a model-based structure for the definition and calculation of Enterprise Architecture Key Performance Indicators. Master's Thesis. Technische Universität München.

Voelter, Markus; Benz, Sebastian; Dietrich, Christian; Engelmann, Birgit; Helander, Mats; Kats, Lennart C. L. et al. (2013): DSL Engineering-Designing, Implementing and Using Domain-Specific Languages: dslbook. org.

Workshop 5

Collaboration Issues for City-Logistics

Report

G. Macé-Ramète* — J. Gonzalez-Feliu**

* École de Mines, Albi-Carmaux
81000 Albi, France
maceramete@mines-albi.f r

** Centre National de la Recherche Scientifique
69363 Lyon, France
jesus.gonzalez-feliu@cnrs.fr

This Workshop targeted to exchange, to share, and to disseminate new knowledge on city logistics, and more precisely on collaboration issues in logistics organization while dealing with urban deliveries. The particularity of this Workshop is that it addresses the question of collaboration from a private company perspective, as well as from that of interoperability. Three main issues were discussed in the workshop. The first regarded how collaboration would be achieved in urban logistics. The second concerned the information systems for stakeholder business processes. The third was related to sustainable performance, more precisely in which way these issues meet the sustainability requirements. We summarise the content of the presented papers and report the issues brought up during the discussion in the workshop and add comments generated in the peer reviews of the papers.

In the first paper titled Simulation-based analysis of urban freight transport with stochastic features, presented by J.R. Montoya-Torres, the authors propose a VRP method combined with simulation to estimate impacts of an urban consolidation centre. The novelty of the approach is that demand, of stochastic nature, is simulated in time. The VRP algorithm is based on Ant Colonies optimization. Authors propose an algorithm that first defines a suitable set of routes then it tests its robustness using simulation.

During the discussion, the main applicability issues were addressed. The tests presented are based on scientific literature instances, where in real world data is presented differently. Authors showed the interests of applying the proposed method to real data, and assured that the method is easily adaptable to real urban contexts.

The second paper titled Impacts of Urban Logistics on Traffic Flow Dynamics presented by N. Chiabaut, addressed a question that has not been studied in-depth in literature: that of impacts of urban logistics on traffic flow dynamics. Authors proposed a method to relate traffic fluidity (to travel speed) on a network's edge to traffic flow (the quantity of vehicles per hour), defined by simulation. This method was applied to a simplified network where the impacts of trucks stopping in double line to deliver were assessed.

In the discussion it was stated that, even using strong simplifications of the network, such methods can estimate the impacts of double lines in traffic, completing existing works on the interests of intelligent delivery bays. Moreover, simulation can be a valid alternative to traffic counts for such assessment issues.

The third paper titled A conceptualization of one collaborative basic city logistics' solution: the Urban Consolidation Centre presented by L. Faure, focused on defining collaboration via the "physical internet theory". To do this, a model of city was defined, from where the main types of flows where characterised. Then, the main changes in organization related to the implementation of an UCC were identified. The configuration of the "standard" city was compared to real urban contexts, showing the main similitudes and strengths of the approach.

The presentation showed how an established theory can be applied to city logistics, and put the urban consolidation centre at the middle of the discussion. It seems from the different exchanges that such conceptualization can help further simulations like those proposed in presentations 1, 2 and 4.

The fourth paper titled VRP algorithms for decision support systems to evaluate collaborative urban freight transport systems transport systems presented by J. Gonzalez-Feliu concerned the vehicle routing problem for urban consolidation, but from another point of view than for presentation 1. Indeed, authors propose to include both inbound and outbound flows in assessing the suitability of UCCs. Authors compared a semi-greedy and a genetic algorithms, on the basis of several test cases for the city of Lyon.

Although the methods were standard, results shown the interests of using UCCs in some contexts, and the discussion showed that both presentations 1 and 4 are complementary. A further work of coordination and synergy between both approaches should be suitable.

The fifth paper titled City logistics for perishable products. The case of Parma's Food Hub presented by E. Morganti , addressed the issues of food distribution in urban areas. Two new concepts were presented, the food hub and the last food mile, to explain the particularity of perishable products logistics in urban distribution. An analysis framework was presented and applied to the experiences of Padova and Parma UCCs in Italy.

During the discussion, questions of public policy and economic continuity raised. Indeed, UCCs for perishable products are difficult to deploy and maintain, and they need both a solid organization and a support of public authorities. This support, as is shown with the example of Parma, does not need to be only financial:

public authorities can promote UCCs by favouring policies or make them stop by political decisions.

The sixth paper titled Supporting decision for road crisis management through an agile and collaborative Information System presented by G. Macé-Ramète, addressed a particular question: that of road crisis management. More precisely, authors proposed a method to support decisions in terms of fleet deployment to act when snowfalls are expected (or effective) in middle-sized cities. An optimization algorithm was proposed and tested on realistic cases.

This research shows the importance of non-delivery flows in urban logistics, like road maintenance, electric, water and communications maintenance, or waste management. More precisely, the paper showed that urban management flows are as important as deliveries since they can, on specific moments, have strong impacts on traffic and congestion.

Simulation-Based Analysis of Urban Freight Transport with Stochastic Features

N. Herazo-Padilla*·** — J.R. Montoya-Torres* — S. Nieto-Isaza**·*** — L. Ramirez Polo** — L. Castro** — D. Ramírez** — C.L. Quintero-Araújo*

* Escuela Internacional de Ciencias Económicas y Administrativas
Universidad de La Sabana
km 7 autopista norte de Bogotá, D.C., Chía (Cundinamarca), Colombia

** Fundación Centro de modelación Empresarial del Caribe (FCIMEC)
Carrera 53 # 74-86 Oficina 402, Barranquilla, Colombia

*** Departamento de Ingeniería Industrial
Universidad de la Costa
Calle 58 # 55-66, Barranquilla, Colombia

ABSTRACT. Transport infrastructure investments have been of the highest importance in cities all around the world in order to facilitate people and freight mobility within congested urban areas. This paper studies the problems of freight delivery in congested cities and the location of urban distribution centres. The problem is modelled using the stochastic version of the Location-Routing Problem in which vehicle velocity and delivery costs are probabilistic parameters. A discrete-event computer simulation model is proposed in which a vehicle routing optimisation engine is incorporated. The approach is tested using random-generated datasets and numerical results show its effectiveness when tracking with different data structures. Hence, the approach shows to be promising for real-life application.
KEYWORDS: City Logistics, Freight Delivery, Stochastic Location-Routing, Simulation.

1. Introduction

According to the United Nations' Report on Planning and design for sustainable urban mobility (UN Habitat 2013), "most countries have experienced rapid urban growth and increased use of motor vehicles". Hence, transport infrastructure is a prerequisite for, and somehow a guarantee of, economic development (Adler 1987). As pointed out by Moore and Pulidindi (2013), economically vibrant urban areas cannot exist without a system for moving people, goods and services. The health of cities, and their ability to generate income and wealth for their inhabitants, is improved if the transportation system is efficient. When addressing the problem of goods transport in urban areas, the literature refers to the concept of "city logistics". Depending on the circumstances, some 20% to 25% of truck-kilometres in urban areas are outgoing freight, 40% to 50% are incoming freight, and the rest both originates from and is delivered within the city (Dablanc 2009).

Urban freight distribution concerns a vast range of activities insuring an adequate level of service for a variety of urban supply chains. To solve goods distribution problems in urban areas, the idea of implementing consolidation platforms has gained a lot of interest from the different actors involved: policy-makers, transporters and practitioners, academics and transport researchers, as well as from the general public. These platforms are also called as Urban Distribution Centres (UDC) (Taniguchi *et al.* 1999). The general goal is to solve – or at least to reduce – traffic problems and pollution impact within urban areas. In addition, shopping areas, restaurants, and other social attraction poles influence mobility and commercial activities and impose restrictions in flows of freight deliveries (Ligocki and Zonn 1984).

In such a context, the problem of locating UDC and its operations becomes of high relevance when seeking for more efficient freight delivery systems in congested urban areas. In the Operational Research literature, this problem has very often been modelled as a Location-Routing Problem (LRP). The final decision to be made corresponds to find the optimal location of the distribution centre(s) and the routing of vehicles to deliver goods from the UDC to a set of geographically dispersed customers or clients (restaurants, shops, stores, etc.). Majority of works in the academic literature has focused on studying the deterministic version of this problem (Muñoz-Villamizar *et al.* 2013, Herazo-Padilla *et al.* 2013). However, because of the congested traffic within cities, the most appropriate model is the Stochastic Location-Routing Problem (SLRP).

This paper aims at presenting a computational approach based on discrete-event simulation that allows the evaluation of different system configurations (i.e., distribution centre location and vehicle routes). We first evaluate a cost-based objective function. The main difference between our approach and those from the literature is at least twofold. Firstly, we consider a system in which the stochastic component of the model is the travel velocity of vehicles, which impact the actual travel cost (that hence becomes stochastic as well). Secondly, the proposed approach also includes an optimisation engine that allows the finding of effective delivery routes.

2. Simulation-Based Solution Approach

The SLRP has been relatively little studied in the Operations Research literature. A two-step hierarchical approach coupling optimisation and discrete-event simulation is presented here. The objective is to determine the strategic location of distribution centres, as well as the allocation and sizing of the vehicle fleet needed to meet customer demand. Although the stochastic nature of this problem, to the best of our knowledge, none of previous works has implemented discrete event simulation (DES) to deal with probabilistic parameters. Our work intends to fill this gap in the literature. Our aim is to propose more accurate methods that meet needs of transportation companies. The general structure of the proposed solution approach is presented in Figure 1.

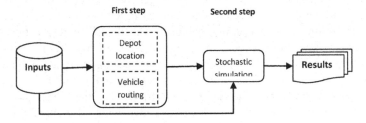

Figure 1. *Schematic representation of the proposed approach*

Input data consist on possible locations of depot(s), actual location of customers, distance matrix, vehicle capacities, etc. In the first step, a random selection strategy is applied to find initial solutions to the depot location problem. In parallel, a solution to the sequencing problem is obtained and hence the order in which customers are going to be visited from each depot location is constructed. This problem is modelled using the well-known structure of the capacitated vehicle routing problems (CVRP). For the case of small distribution networks (5 to 10 clients), the problem is solved using mathematical programming. However, because of its NP-hardness, bigger datasets (with 20 and 50 clients) have to be solved using alternative procedures. An Ant Colony Optimisation (ACO) procedure is hence implemented. A detailed description of these two approaches can be found in the work of Herazo-Padilla *et al.* (2013).

These two solutions (depot location and customer service sequences) are introduced as inputs into a discrete-event computer simulation model in order to compute the expected total cost of freight distribution. Simulation of a series of routing problems starting from each depot considering stochastic parameters is carried out. Probabilistic velocities have a direct impact in travel times and hence in the cost of the operation. Every time that an expected routing time is violated, a penalty is charged considering that a delay in the process of delivery of goods to customers locations generate complains that increase the operational cost. For this reason travel costs are also uncertain parameters included in the simulation model. After all replications are run a feedback process is carried out in order to find optimal solutions for the location decision.

3. Numerical Evaluation and Opportunities for Collaborative Transportation

The approach was validated using random data sets generated as those proposed by Laporte *et al.* (1989) and employed by Herazo-Padilla *et al.* (2013). The set of nodes representing customers were obtained generating points within a square area $(0, 100) \times (0, 100)$ according to a uniform probability distribution with coordinates (X_i, Y_i). Euclidian distances are obtained. Instances of 5 to up to 50 nodes were considered, each one with 5 possible depot locations. Demand of clients are generated from a uniform distribution $U(1,50)$ and homogeneous vehicles are considered with maximum load capacity of 100 units. For each dataset, we run a number of replications for the vehicle routing problem given the different location of UDC. System performance is measured using the final expected cost. In order to guarantee a 95% confidence level when computing the objective function, a sample size of 10 replications with a relative error of 1% was calculated. In our simulation experiment, we observed that the higher the size of the network (i.e., the higher the number of clients to be served), the higher the difference between the different solutions among the possible UDC locations: gaps between 10% and 45% for the final value of the objective function were observed. These results put in evidence the relevance of considering stochastic issues when addressing the design and operation of urban goods distribution problems. Table 1 presents the final best average cost over all replications and the corresponding best location of the distribution centre for each dataset considered in our numerical experiment.

	5 clients		10 clients		20 clients		50 clients	
	Cost	UDC	Cost	UDC	Cost	UDC	Cost	UDC
I1	368.913	D4	626.374	D5	988.541	D5	2.765.943	D4
I2	293.368	D1	481.293	D1	1.161.436	D1	2.503.846	D1
I3	367.000	D5	749.474	D2	1.422.496	D4	1.966.563	D2
I4	271.695	D2	666.615	D4	1.039.961	D3	2.427.844	D1
I5	410.081	D2	681.683	D1	1.120.941	D5	2.635.377	D4
I6	489.400	D2	747.896	D5	1.313.411	D1	2.570.861	D3
I7	346.556	D3	657.953	D5	978.877	D2	2.403.209	D1
I8	465.824	D4	661.158	D1	923.442	D1	2.503.152	D3
I9	474.752	D1	628.183	D1	870.793	D4	2.639.117	D4
I10	273.390	D1	593.461	D2	928.089	D1	2.975.972	D5

Table 1. *Final expected cost for the stochastic goods distribution problem*

Urban transport for people and goods is rapidly becoming one of the major challenges for politicians at city, regional and even national levels (Gonzalez-Feliu and Salanova 2012). In some countries (i.e., Colombia and other developing countries), it is most likely observed that urban transportation system have encountered difficulties given the lack of infrastructure and technology making the system critical and thus requiring collaborative structures. Collaborative transportation seems to be a good alternative to improve the operation of urban consolidation centres, but it is still in a development stage (Hagson and Lindholm 2011), although the extraordinary recent advances in information technology and transportation science. Some researchers and practitioners worldwide have seen the concepts of Cooperative Game Theory and the Shapley value as one solution to these cooperative games in urban freight transport. Some applications have shown that a collaborative environment between stakeholders is necessary in order to reduce the negative operational impacts and at the end stakeholders will have no incentive to leave the coalition.

4. Conclusions

This paper studied the problem of freight distribution in congested urban areas by considering stochastic issues regarding both travel speeds and delivery costs. A Stochastic Location Routing Problem (SLRP) model was employed and an analysis using discrete-event simulation was carried out. The approach also included an optimisation engine to determine vehicle delivery routes. In future works, the approach has to be tested using real-life data. This may imply to take into account additional constraints that may include producer-related or customer-related distribution issues, depending on the city under study. Also, the approach could be adapted according to the type of distribution under study (e.g., independent retailing, chain retailing, food deliveries, parcel and home deliveries, waste collection, etc.). Another line for further research could consider the inclusion of social and/or environmental related objective functions.

5. Acknowledgements

This work has been partly funded by the Colombian Department of Science, Technology and Innovation (Colciencias) under Grant No. 731-2011 (project code: 333-502-27900). The work of the first author was also funded by a postgraduate research scholarship awarded by the School of Economics and Management Sciences at Universidad de La Sabana, Chía, Colombia. Part of this work was also done within the context of research project ANNONA funded by the French National Research Agency (ANR)

6. References

Adler H.A., *Economic Appraisal of Transportation Projects: A Manual with Case Studies*. Economic Development Institute of the World Bank, Baltimore (Published for the World Bank by Johns Hopkins University Press), 1987.

Dablanc L., *Freight Transport for Development Toolkit: Urban Freight – Freight Transport, a Key for the New Urban Economy*, World Bank, Washington, D.C., USA, 2009.

Gonzalez-Feliu J., Salanova J., "Defining and Evaluating Collaborative Urban Freight Transportation Systems", *Procedia - Social and Behavioral Sciences*, vol. 39, 2012, pp.172-183.

Hagson A., Lindholm M., "Collaborative Urban Transport Solution (CUTS) State of the Art report", Report Göteborg: Chalmers University of Technology, 2011. 39p.

Herazo-Padilla N., Nieto Isaza S., Montoya-Torres J.R., Ramirez Polo L., Muñoz-Villamizar A., "Coupling ant colony optimisation and discrete-event simulation to solve a stochastic location-routing problem", *Proceedings of the 2013 Winter Simulation Conference*, R. Pasupathy, S.-H. Kim, A. Tolk, R. Hill, M. E. Kuhl (eds.), 2013, pp.3352-3362.

Laporte G., Louveaux F., Mercure H., "Models and exact solutions for a class of stochastic location-routing problems", *European Journal of Operational Research*, 39, 1989, pp.71-78.

Ligocki C., Zonn L.E., "Parking Problems in Central Business Districts", *Cities*, 1, 1984, pp.350–355.

Moore T., Pulidindi J., "Understanding Urban Transportation Systems: An Action Guide for City Leaders". National League of Cities. http://www.nlc.org. (accessed 31 July 2013).

Muñoz-Villamizar A., Montoya-Torres J.R., Juan A.A., Cáceres-Cruz J., "A simulation-based algorithm for the integrated location and routing problem in urban logistics", *Proceedings of the 2013 Winter Simulation Conference*, R. Pasupathy, S.-H. Kim, A. Tolk, R. Hill, M. E. Kuhl (eds.), 2013, pp.2032-2041.

Taniguchi E., Noritake M., Yamada T., Izumitani T., "Optimal Size and Location Planning of Public Logistics Terminals", *Transportation Research Part E*, 35, 1999, pp.207-222.

UN Habitat, 2013, United Nations Human Settlements Programme UN Habitat. Planning and design for sustainable urban mobility – Global Report on Human Settlements 2013.

Impacts of Urban Logistics on Traffic Flow Dynamics

Nicolas Chiabaut* — Jean-Michel Sigaud* — Guillaume Marques**
Jesus Gonzalez-Feliu***

* LICIT, ENTPE / IFSTTAR
Université de Lyon, France

** FAYOL-EMSE
CNRS-UMR5600, EVS,
École Nationale Supérieure des Mines, F-42023, Saint-Etienne, France

*** Laboratoire d'Économie des Transports
Lyon, France

ABSTRACT. Even if urban logistic has been extensively investigated in the literature, its effects on traffic flow dynamic remain unknown. This paper aims to assess the impact of pickup-delivery trucks on traffic conditions. Among city freight collaborative solutions, dedicated delivery/pickup areas may be implemented by city administrators. These public areas have to be shared by independent carriers. Currently used, it is today difficult to anticipate their impact on the traffic flow. To this end, we resort to a theoretical but realistic urban arterial where deliveries can be completed in double-park or in dedicated area. Both solutions are investigated using a microscopic traffic simulator. Comparisons can be carried out using an aggregated and parsimonious indicator: the macroscopic fundamental diagram. It turns out that capacity and delays are less reduced when delivery areas are used.
KEYWORDS: Urban Logistic, Traffic Flow, Simulation, Pickup-Delivery Manoeuvres.

1. Introduction

In urban environments, there are now many challenging problems concerning freight transport. As cities around the world grow rapidly, there is an increase in pickup-delivery truck traffic in urban areas. It turns out that commercial traffic is now a major source of externalities in metro areas, including congestion, noise, air pollution and traffic incidents [1]. To overcome these issues, many interesting and innovative strategies have been developed in the world. Some researchers have proposed the idea of city logistics to solve these difficult problems [2-3]. The idea of this concept is to rationalize the freight activities in cities by optimizing operations considering the traffic conditions and the congestion issues. It turns out that a key point in predicting the impacts of city logistics is the influence of freight on traffic dynamics. Especially, pickup-delivery trucks manoeuvres generate road capacity reduction and lead to delay for individual drivers. Although this is a crucial topic, the literature rarely addresses this issue.

The main goal of this paper is to assess the effects of double-park pickup and delivery maneuvers on traffic conditions. To this end, the study focuses on a theoretical but realistic urban arterial. Using a micro-simulation software, the capacity reductions and the ensuing delays generated by urban freight can be determined. Moreover, in order to understand dynamics of the system and to quantify its performance, we seek to estimate equivalent mean states for various traffic conditions. An equivalent mean state is needed. One way to obtain it is to estimate the Macroscopic Fundamental Diagram (MFD) that is an aggregated model for urban arterial that account for effects of traffic signal and urban freight. Finally, this permits to analytically compare the efficiency of different city logistics solutions such as parking regulations [4].

2. Background on Traffic Flow Theory

In this paper, we resort to Newell's car-following model [5]. This model is the Lagrangian formulation of the kinematic wave model inspired by fluid dynamics. It has been implemented in the SymuVia software package. Moreover, the model has been refined to take into account bounded acceleration, lane-changing phenomenon, relaxation after lane-changing phenomenon signalized intersections, heavy trucks, etc. [6-7]. Thus, the simulation software is able to accurately reproduce the impacts of pickup-delivery maneuvers on the remaining of the traffic in the arterial.

Various theories have been proposed to reproduce traffic stream on an aggregate level. Among this existing body of works, models that are adapted to characterize traffic in arterials have to account for (i) traffic signal and (ii) transit systems. Many of these papers are based on the key idea that it exists a macroscopic fundamental diagram (MFD) able to reproduce both free-flow and congested traffic conditions. Evidences of existence of MFD have been exhibited only very recently [8,9]. On their seminal works, the authors pointed out a major insight: the MFD is an intrinsic property of the network itself and remain invariant when demand changes. MFD is thus a reliable tool for traffic agency to manage and evaluate solutions for improving mobility. [7] furnished a very good example of how MFD can be used to dynamically control signals to prevent congestion. It is thus appealing to estimate an accurate MFD for various urban sites and traffic. MFD can be directly estimated with the simulated results. We used the trajectories-based approach proposed by [10]. The authors resort to Edie's definitions [11] to calculate flow and density. [11]

computes density K and flow Q based on the observation of vehicles across a space-time window A:

$$K = \sum_j \frac{t_j}{A_j} \quad (2)$$

$$Q = \sum_j \frac{l_j}{|A|} \quad (3)$$

where l_j and t_j are respectively the length traveled and the time spent in the area by vehicle j and $|A|$ the area of A. It turns out that such measurements perfectly match MFD definition [11]. In the case of a single pipe, the estimated measurements perfectly match the theoretical MFD. Thus, simulations can be performed for any value of demand. We also add an exit bottleneck to generate congested states. Thereby, the congested part of the MFD will also be appraised.

3. Evaluation of an Urban Arterial with Double-Park Deliveries

3.1. Case Study

In this paper, we consider here a hypothetic urban arterial (see Figure 1) composed of 11 successive links (l_j=200m) with traffic signal and 3 lanes. In this urban arterial, we assumed that pickup-delivery maneuvers occur with a time frequency fi and can be located anywhere on the urban arterial xi. Each maneuver lasts δ_i. To quantify the effect of double-park pickup-delivery on traffic flow, we will estimate MFD using simulated vehicles trajectories. To this end, many simulations have to be performed to reproduce the whole range of traffic condition. Therefore, various values of inflow are tested to mimic the free-flow condition. Then, outflow is reduced to reproduce to generate congested waves that travel upstream. We perform a one-hour simulation that ensures six measurements of flow and density, i.e. A is equal to 10 minutes multiplied by the length of the arterial.

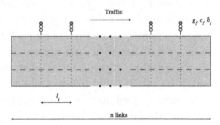

Figure 1. *Theoretical case study*

3.2. Estimation of MFD

It is now possible to estimate MFD from simulated vehicles trajectories. In order to compare the different logistic policies, we first estimate the MFD when no delivery occurs. Figure 2 proposes this reference. It clearly highlights the existence of a well-defined MFD for an urban arterial. Notice that the estimated MFD match the MFD that can be analytically calculated from the case study parameters. The small discrepancies comes from the fact that lane-changing are not accounted for in the analytical approach. Consequently, the simulated flows are always smaller.

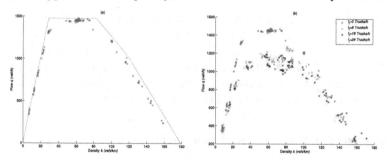

Figure 2. (a)MFD for the reference case; (b) MFDs for different values of f_i

Then, Figure 2 shows the MFD estimated for different frequency f_i of pickup and delivery. It turns out that higher the frequency is, lower the capacity is. It is not surprising because the right lane is no more available for individual cars when the frequency increases. It is also worth noticing that the slope of the right part of the MFD, i.e. free-flow situations, corresponds to the free-flow speed of individual vehicles. It appears that the pickup-delivery maneuvers reduce this speed. The reduction is about 25 % for f_i=15 trucks/h. Consequently, urban logistic leads to an increase of individual travel times by generating delays.

It is thus appealing to relate these modifications of MFD shapes to urban logistic parameters, i.e. frequency fi. Indeed, obtaining a MFD in simulation is a tedious task because several runs have to be performed to reproduce the whole range of traffic conditions. Therefore, we aim to approximate the estimated MFDs with a function to determine a general formulation that can hold for any case study. To this end, MFDs are fitted by quadratic functions that depend on delivery frequency f_i. Figure 3 depicts the associated results. It is interesting to notice that the maximal capacity is well estimated by the quadratic function on the contrary of the free-flow observation. Indeed, it turns out that it is very difficult to find a simple formulation that accurately matches the measurement for the whole range of traffic conditions. It is thus appealing to resort to analytical model to precisely determine the shape of the MFD. However, this work gives a first hint to a general formulation of MFD that accounts for logistic.

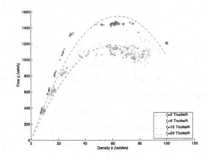

Figure 3. *Quadratic approximations of MFDs*

3.3. Comparison with Delivery Areas

Since MFD makes it possible to assess effects of pickup-delivery trucks on traffic dynamics, it also permit to compare in simulation the efficiency of different city logistics solutions such as parking regulation, off-hour deliveries or consolidation programs. In this paper, we only focus on an urban arterial case study. Consequently, we now aim to compare the double-park deliveries with a solution where delivery areas are available. In such as situation, pickup-delivery manoeuvers no more constrain the traffic flow because they happen outside the road. However, trucks may still have an influence because they travel slower than individual cars. Delivery areas can be easily implemented in the simulator Symuvia. Consequently, MFD can be estimated based on the simulated trajectories. Figure 4 shows the associated results: variations of the free-flow and mean speeds, and evolution of the maximal capacity with fi. It turns out that the capacity is less reduced in the case of delivery areas such as the free-flow speed of the vehicles. It ensures that cars will experience fewer delays. This policy is very promising to limit the effect of urban logistic on traffic flow dynamics on condition that areas are available and that truck drivers use them.

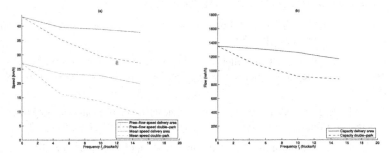

Figure 4. *Comparison with delivery ares a. free-flow and mean speeds ; b. capacities*

4. Conclusions

In this paper, we further study the effects of urban logistics on traffic flow dynamics under different traffic conditions. In order to cross-compare logistic policies, we resort to a microscopic traffic simulator to reproduce traffic of an hypothetic but realistic urban arterial where pickup-delivery manoeuvers occur. To assess effects of such operation on traffic dynamics, we resort to an aggregated and parsimonious relationship: the Macroscopic Fundamental Diagram (MFD). It makes possible to encompass in a unique function dynamics of traffic flow and effects of urban logistic for different traffic conditions.

Based on the estimates of MFD, it turns out that the higher the frequency of pickup-delivery manoeuvers is, the smaller the capacity is. This is not a surprising result but we furnished a general formulation to assess traffic dynamics that account for pickup-delivery manoeuvers. It thus makes possible to compare these situations with the case where delivery areas exist. Results clearly show that the traffic flow is no more constrained by pickup-delivery trucks.

5. References

[1] Dablanc, L. "Best Practices in Urban Freight Management: Lessons from an International Survey". *Transportation Research Record - Journal of the Transportation Research Board* 2014.

[2] Taniguchi, E., and Thompson, R.G. "Modeling City Logistics", *Transportation Research Record - Journal of the Transportation Research Board* 2002; 1790: 45-51.

[3] Dablanc, L. City Logistics, In: Rodrigue, J-P., Notteboom, T. and Shaw, J. (eds.). *The Sage Handbook of Transport Studies* 2012, London: Sage.

[4] Holguin-Veras, J., Ozbay, K., Kornhauser, A., Brom, M.A, Iyer, S., Yushimito, W.F., Ukkusuri, S., Allen, B., and Silas, M.A. "Overall Impacts of Off-Hour Delivery Programs in the New-York City Metropolitan Area". *Transportation Research Record - Journal of the Transportation Research Board* 2011; 2238: 68-76.

[5] Newell, G.F. "A simplified car-following model: a lower order model", *Transportation Research Part B* 2002; 36: 195-205.

[6] Leclercq, L., Laval, J. A., Chevallier, E. "The lagrangian coordinates and what it means for first order traffic flow models", *Transportation and Traffic Theory 2007 (ISTTT17)*, Elsevier, 735-754.

[7] Laval, J. A., Leclercq, L. "Microscopic modeling of the relaxation phenomenon using a macroscopic lane-changing model", *Transportation Research Part B* 2008; 42(6): 511-522.

[8] Daganzo, C. F., Geroliminis, N., "An analytical approximation for the macroscopic fundamental diagram of urban traffic", *Transportation Research Part B: Methodological* 2008; 42(9): 771-781.

[9] Buisson, C., Ladier, C. "Exploring the Impact of Homogeneity of Traffic Measurements on the Existence of Macroscopic Fundamental Diagrams", *Transportation Research Record: Journal of the Transportation Research Board* 2009; 2124: 127-136.

[10] Courbon, T., Leclercq, L. "Cross-comparison of macroscopic fundamental diagram estimation methods", in *Proceeding of the 14th European Working Group on Transportation Meeting* 2011.

[11] Edie, L. C., "Discussion of traffic stream measurements and definitions2, in OECD, ed., *Proceedings of the 2nd International Symposium on the Theory of Traffic Flows* 1963; 139-154.

A Basic Collaborative City Logistics' Solution

The Urban Consolidation Centre

L. Faure* — B. Montreuil** — G. Marquès* — P. Burlat*

* Institut Fayol-EMSE, CNRS-UMR5600, EVS,
École Nationale Supérieure des Mines de Saint-Etienne
158 cours Fauriel, CS 62362, 42023 Saint-Etienne Cedex2 (France)
lfaure@emse.fr

** Canada Research Chair in Enterprise Engineering, CIRRELT Interuniversity
Research Centre on Enterprise Networks, Logistics and Transportation,
Faculty of Administration Sciences, Laval University
Pavillon Palasis-Prince, 2325, rue de la Terrasse, G1V 0A6 Québec (Québec)
Benoit.Montreuil@cirrelt.ca

ABSTRACT. *This paper proposes one solution to conceptualize a specific collaborative city logistics' solution: the Urban Consolidation Centre (UCC). We first give a quick literature review about UCC, then we present our conceptualization approach, and finally we apply this method to an illustrative example. Our aim is to elaborate a methodology to support model helping a "What if" decision. This study is the first step to establish a realistic and precise model.*

KEYWORDS: *City Logistics, Collaborative Network.*

1. Introduction

City logistics are the last link of complex supply chains which involve numerous stakeholders: carriers, shopkeepers, e-customers, inhabitants, public administration, etc. It is a small part of the total travelled distance, nevertheless it can represent until 28% of the total transport cost (Roca-Riu et al., 2012). Moreover air pollution emissions related to urban freight transport is estimated between 16% and 50% of the global pollution made by transport activities in a city (Albergel et al., 2006). On the top of that public decision-makers do not have, most of time, enough knowledge to take adapting local public policy to face these stakes (Dablanc, 2007). Finally they disinterest of this topic to concentrate their effort on a subject with more direct repercussion on inhabitant life: the transport of persons. Yet a good integration of urban goods movements in the urban policy of cities can be a way to create attraction in the city by helping the implantation of proximity shops for example (Taniguchi et al., 2013). That is why, it is necessary to help public decision-makers to think about solutions to relieve the traffic congestion on the city centre and reduce the environmental impact of urban freight transport.

Lots of city logistics' solutions are available in the literature (Allen et al., 2007; Boudouin, 2006). It appears that those are always based on the use, by combination or not, of two principles: the multi-modal and the pooling. Two research questions emerge from this observation. The first one is: how the use of multi-modal facilities can be a solution to city logistics issues? The second is the purpose of this paper: which impact can have the use of pooling concept on the logistics in the city?

It appears a lack of tools to check the efficiency of city logistics measures in a given context. Indeed, there is a need to establish models which allow ex ante assessment (Russo et al., 2011; Taniguchi et al., 2003).

Moreover, in a carrier point of view, delivery trucks are often full and round are optimized. Carriers find a local optimum. This behaviour is individualist and often bad in a global point of view. For example, streets are congested because of the overexploitation of the road (e.g. two carriers can deliver the same shop). Our aim is to introduce collaboration to reach a global optimum.

In this paper, a quick background will be given. After that, a methodological approach to characterize city logistics schemes will be exposed. We will then apply this model to an illustrative example based on the use of Urban Consolidation Centre which is the most popular solution in European cities to face city logistics issues (Chwesiuk et al., 2010). Any generality will be done from results of this application. We will need further research to generalize the results presented in this paper. Nevertheless, it will be the opportunity to enlighten what it could be done by using this kind of collaborative network. This work is one try to conceptualize one type of city logistics' solutions.

2. Background

Urban Consolidation Centre has been extensively described in the literature. The most popular definition is given by Browne (Browne et al., 2005). It is known that it should have a lot of benefices as noise and pollution emission reduction, congestion limitation, etc. (Browne et al., 2011; Chwesiuk et al., 2010). The principle of consolidation himself seems to be a good opportunity to improve urban freight transportation (Verlinde et al., 2012). Nevertheless, the resulting flow disruption makes difficult to obtaining a high productivity level. UCC is economically based on basic and variable costs. Variable costs come from two points which manage the time delay. The first one is the time due to flow disruption. It could be decrease with a technological contribution. The second one is the transportation time which could be decrease by making shorter rounds. In this paper, we suggest an approach by conceptualization. We will try to basically define what an UCC is and if it really allows an improvement of, e.g., transportation time.

3. The Proposed Approach

3.1. *Multi-Sources and Multi-Destination Logistics*

The first step of our approach is to characterize the system under study. The aim is to define a situation closer as possible than what happens in a middle size city. So it was important to take into account the density of flow and actors in the city. That is why we choose studying multi-sources multi-destinations logistics which means: more than one carrier can deliver the city, one delivery point can receive freight from more than one carrier and a carrier delivers more than one delivery point.

City's constraints like street size, acute curve, etc. require the use of small truck. The definition of vehicle's type is primordial to take into account the quantity of freight to deliver. That is why we made an assumption about the type of vehicle that can be used it will be developed in the application case. The second step of the method is the definition of key performance indicators (KPIs) that we choose to evaluate the performance of the system. Those are detailed in the next section.

3.2. *One Way to Quantify the Performance*

This section presents the chosen KPIs. Indeed, our aim is to evaluate the impact of a collaborative network in comparison with a traditional one. To do so, it is necessary to define a scale of measure. It is what we have done by selecting KPIs. The first one is the accumulated travelled distance. It is formed by the addition of the travelled distance by each truck. This kind of indicator is current in the literature (De Assis Correia et al., 2012; Henriot et al., 2008; Patier et al., 2010; Van Rooijen et al., 2010). This choice is based on the fact that distance is a synonym of cost for carrier. This indicator is taken into account when carriers determine the total transport cost. The distance is also a way to quantify the mobility in the city.

$$D_{Total} = \sum_{i=1}^{n} D_{Truck}^{i} \qquad [1]$$

The second KPI is the total time. This value is obtained by adding delivery times (driven and loading/unloading times) of each vehicle. It represent a cost (time is money) but also a sign of service quality for the customer who could be the receiver or the sender (Roca-Riu et al., 2012; Patier et al., 2010; Henriot et al., 2008; De Assis Correia et al., 2012).

$$T_{Total} = \sum_{i=1}^{n} T_{Truck}^{i} \qquad [2]$$

Finally, the last chosen KPI is the CO_2 emissions quantity, as in (Patier et al., 2010; Henriot et al., 2008), which is the first source of greenhouse gas (Albergel et al., 2006). In the equation i represent the different types of vehicle and EF_i is the Emission Factor for the vehicle i.

These three KPIs give us an opportunity to evaluate city logistics solutions under the scope of sustainability.

$$E_{CO_2} = \sum_{i}^{\text{For each vehicle type}} D_{Total}^{i} \times EF_i \qquad [3]$$

4. An Application of the Methodology to One City Logistics Solution: Urban Consolidation Centre

4.1. Presentation of the Illustrative Case

We will then present an example based on a schematic conception of a city. Although this representation of the city is conceptual, it is close to the configuration of many real cities all over the world. Indeed, our choice is to describe the city as an ellipse full of demand points (delivery points) which can be a shop, a factory, an inhabitant, etc. As explain in section 1.3.1, the study is about multi-sources multi-destinations logistics (see Figure 1).

In this example, we consider 7 different carriers, who are represented by different colours, who go into the city. Each carrier can enter the city by a preferential and unique access point close to his platform. Each round is made by considering two parameters: the rationality of delivery order and the quantity of freight which has to be delivering in different points. Firstly, our approach is not based on the construction of optimal round but feasible round. Any optimization algorithm is used but delivery points are group together with logic of proximity: that is our definition of rationality. Secondly, the load of truck is checked. It is the insurance that freight can be transported in the vehicle. We used trucks adapted for city which have a 40m³ volume. One truck contains 16 parcels whereas a semi contains 34 parcels in a 94m³. In the following parts, we distinguish truck (40m³ vehicle) and semi (94m³ vehicle). In the aim of optimizing deliveries, we also use vans which are utility vehicles with a 20m³ volume containing 8 parcels. In the case where the freight quantity is too high to get into one truck, round is recalculated. We made the assumption that one delivery point receives its freight from one carrier in one time. It is not possible to share a delivery in several parts.

By exploiting this way to do we obtained values for each KPI. These values will be the base of comparison to evaluate offered opportunities by the collaborative network presented in the next section. So, the total travelled distance is 347km, the total time is 14,5h and emissions of CO_2 are equal to 334kg.

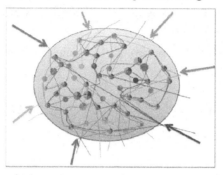

Figure 1. *A multi-sources and multi-destinations logistics*

4.2. Establishment of One UCC

This section exposes the detail of the test of establish one Urban Consolidation Center in the south of our conceptual city (see Figure 2).

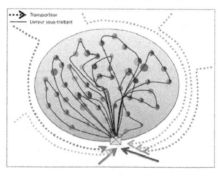

Figure 2. *The described city with the implantation of one UCC*

The same method as in section 1.4.1 has been used to generate rounds distribution. Some relevant observations can be made before calculated KPIs values. First of all, we observe that some carriers have to make a detour to deliver their freight to the UCC. In one hand it implies a higher distance to travel. On the other hand the average speed in the ring around the city is higher than inside the city. Secondly, in a visual point of view, it is obvious that flows are less jumbled as in the initial situation. Thirdly, maximum 10 trucks enter the city vs 12 in the initial system. It can be reduce to 2 (vs 10) if a good coordination is made. These two last observations seem to show a gain of the collaboration.

The next section is dedicated to the analysis of each KPI's value. We will see if our first intuition is validated or not.

4.3. *Results*

The first studied KPI is the total distance. Even if carriers make a detour, we observe a reduction of 33% of total travelled kilometers. It is due to the fact that UCC allows the construction of pool of delivery points very close the one from each other. The detour makes by each carrier is lower as the gain obtained by the pooling. So, the total distance is shorter. The total time is logically lower (-52%) because of the total distance but also because a part of this travel is made faster by using the ring. Finally, the CO_2 emissions are lower (-32%) because we use less trucks than in the initial solution. Also, these trucks go in a lower distance so it is less pollutant. Of course, regarding the art to calculate those indicators we are aware that numbers are not arguments but it can give a trend and enlighten what we expect to do in a collaborative perspective.

5. Conclusions

The obtained results are very relevant because it give an approximation of the potential gain of collaborative solution. This work quantifies for the first time the difference between two configurations in one particular case (an elliptical city, etc.). The calculation model should be improved to getting closer to a realistic case. It can be interpreted as a step in the aim to obtain better ex ante assessment of city logistics measures impacts.

This paper gives a proposition of conceptualization and modeling of city logistics. The exposed example produces an illustrative case about the opportunity of collaboration in supply chain, even in the city scale. Indeed, we show that the collaboration could be adapted to solve some mentioned issues of urban freight transport. It also allows highlighting the role of interoperability in the split between prevision and reality. Actually, the collaboration implies the interoperability and this notion is not yet describe in our model.

This study is a part of an ANR project (French Agency for the Research) and so could be improved and deal with in depth. In future work, it would be, of course, necessary to simulate other urban contexts. An interesting work could be to introduce other UCCs around the city and also other city logistics measures. It could be a way to create a powerful collaborative network. Of course, the interoperability will be more and more important and problematical. Finally, it could be relevant to couple the pooling approach with a multi-modal approach.

6. References

Albergel. A, Ségalou. E, Routhier. J-L, De Rham. C, 'Mise en place d'une méthodologie pour un bilan environnemental physique du transport de marchandises en ville', 2006.

Allen. J, Thorne. G, Browne. M, 'BESTUFS good practice guide on urban freight transport', Monograph, 2007.

De Assis Correia. V, De Oliveira. LK, Leite Guerra. A, 'Economical and Environmental Analysis of an Urban Consolidation Center for Belo Horizonte City (Brazil)', *Procedia - Social and Behavioral Sciences*, vol. 39, 2012, pp.770–782.

Boudouin. D, *Guide méthodologique: Les espaces logistiques urbains*, La Documentation française, Paris, 2006.

Browne. M, Allen. J, Leonardi. J, 'Evaluating the use of an urban consolidation centre and electric vehicles in central London', *IATSS Research*, vol. 35, no. 1, 2011, pp.1–6.

Browne. M, Sweet. M, Woodburn. AG, Allen. J, 'Urban freight consolidation centres: final report', Monograph, 2005.

Chwesiuk. K, Kijewska. K, Iwan. S, 'Urban consolidation centres for medium-size touristic cities in the Westpomeranian Region of Poland', *Procedia - Social and Behavioral Sciences*, vol. 2, no. 3, 2010, pp.6264–6273.

Dablanc. L, 'Goods transport in large European cities: Difficult to organize, difficult to modernize', *Transportation Research Part A: Policy and Practice*, vol. 41, no. 3, 2007, pp.280–285.

Henriot. F, Patier. D, Bossin. P, Gérardin. B, *Méthodologie d'évaluation des innovations en matière de logistique urbaine*, PREDIT, 2008.

Patier. D, Browne. M, 'A methodology for the evaluation of urban logistics innovations', *Procedia - Social and Behavioral Sciences*, vol. 2, no. 3, 2010, pp.6229–6241.

Roca-Riu. M, Estrada. M, 'An Evaluation of Urban Consolidation Centers Through Logistics Systems Analysis in Circumstances Where Companies have Equal Market Shares', *Procedia - Social and Behavioral Sciences*, vol. 39, 2012, pp.796–806.

Van Rooijen. T, Quak. H, 'Local impacts of a new urban consolidation centre – the case of Binnenstadservice.nl', *Procedia - Social and Behavioral Sciences*, vol. 2, no. 3, 2010, pp.5967–5979.

Russo. F, Comi. A, 'A model system for the ex-ante assessment of city logistics measures', *Research in Transportation Economics*, vol. 31, no. 1, 2011, pp.81–87.

Taniguchi. E, Thompson. GR, Yamada. T, 'Recent trends and innovation in modelling city logistics', *Proceedings The 8th International Conference In City Logistics*, Bali, Indonesia, 2013.

Taniguchi. E, Thompson. R, Yamada. T, 'Predicting the effects of city logistics schemes', *Transport Reviews*, vol. 23, no. 4, 2003, pp.489–515.

Verlinde. S, Macharis. C, Witlox. F, 'How to Consolidate Urban Flows of Goods Without Setting up an Urban Consolidation Centre?', *Procedia - Social and Behavioral Sciences*, vol. 39, no. 0, 2012, pp.687–701.

VRP Algorithms for Decision Support Systems to Evaluate Collaborative Urban Freight Transport Systems

Jesus Gonzalez-Feliu* — Josep-Maria Salanova Grau**

* *Centre National de la Recherche Scientifique*
ISH 14 Avenue Berthelot, 69363 Lyon Cedex 07, France
jesus.gonzalez-feliu@cnrs.fr

** *Hellenic Institute of Transport, CERTH*
6 km Charilaou, Thermi Rd., P.O. Box: 60361, 57001, Thermi, Thessaloniki, Greece
jose@certh.gr

ABSTRACT. *This paper proposes a comparison between genetic and semi-greedy algorithms for a collaborative VRP in city logistics. In order to compare the performance of both algorithms on real-size test cases, we develop a cluster-first route second algorithm. The clustering phase is made by a seep algorithm, which defines the number of used vehicles and assigns a set of customers to it. Then, for each vehicle, we build a min-cost route by two methods. The first is a semi-greedy algorithm. The second is a genetic algorithm. We test both approaches on real-size instances Computational results are presented and discussed.*

KEYWORDS: *City Logistics Systems, Two-Echelon Vehicle Routing, Cross-Docking, Simulation, Collaboration.*

1. Introduction

Vehicle routing (VRP) optimization is a popular research subject, where several soft computing-based meta-heuristic methods have been proposed (Golden et al., 2008). One of the main application fields is city logistics, as we observe three main categories of problems: (1) vehicle routing with time windows, related to accessing city centers, (2) dynamic vehicle routing problems, which take into account variable travel times, and (3) two-echelon vehicle routing, that takes into account ruptures of charge. Although very advanced techniques and algorithms are often proposed in literature, they remain still used in academic cases not always related to real practices. On the other hand, collaborative transport is being a main issue for researchers and practitioners, but no simulation and optimization tools are available

(Gonzalez-Feliu and Morana, 2011). Furthermore, the existing heuristics do not allow to analyse collaborative transport route optimization, since they are related to a single carrier. Collaboration in transport can take several forms (Gonzalez-et al., 2013). Moreover, if we observe the algorithms developed for multi-echelon vehicle routing optimization in city logistics (see Mancini et al., 2014 for a detailed review), we observe that only few of them are applicable to real-life cases, most of which have been developed in the 70's-80's and are fast constructive heuristics.

When two companies want to collaborate, each of them having its two-echelon distribution schema, they will find a common cross-docking point. Then we can state that in partial collaboration a part of the freight to be delivered will be shared then some customers will be visited once (each company will deliver a part of the other company's customers which have in common) and others twice (each company will visit them once). Finally, in a total collaborative approach, each customer is visited once by a company, because they will optimize their transport schemes to divide the geographical area into zones where only one of them will deliver. In this case, the optimization problem presents three main issues:

   – Allocate customers to companies for the last-mile distribution (allocation problem).

   – Locate the most suitable cross-docking points (location-allocation problem).

   – Construct the second-echelon routes (vehicle routing problem).

   – Construct the first-echelon routes (vehicle routing problem) transshipping the freight at the cross-docking facilities in order to load the second-echelon vehicles (matching problem).

This paper aims to propose and compare two fast algorithms for real-life collaborative urban logistics. First, we propose the two algorithms, that follow a sequential structure (cluster-first route-second procedure plus a post-optimization algorithm, the first a semi-greedy and the second a genetic algorithm). Second, we test both algorithms on a set of real-life instances and compare them, highlighting the advantages and limits of each procedure.

2. Proposed Algorithms

In order to compare both algorithms, we propose two clustering-first-route second algorithms which start from the same clustering phase. After that, the route construction and the post-optimization heuristics of each algorithm are different. The common clustering procedure is derived from the well-known sweep algorithm (Golden, 1988) and allows us to feed each algorithm with the same inputs.

2.1. Semi-Greedy Algorithm

Given the satellite clusters defined in the first phase, we build routes using a semi-greedy algorithm (Toth and Vigo, 2002). This procedure constructs routes following an iterative procedure that adds each customer to a route. Given iteration i and an uncompleted route, a list of candidates is defined by taking the n closest customers to the last point of the route. This is made by defining a distance threshold δ. Customers whom distance to the last point of the route is less than δ are included into the so-called Restricted Candidate List (RCL). Then, the customer inserted on the route is chosen at random from the RCL customers. Finally, the first echelon routes are built following the same principle, knowing the load that will transit on each satellite from the second-echelon routes.

2.2. Genetic Algorithm

The genetic algorithm is applied to build a near-optimal route from the clustering results. We choose to use a mutation algorithm on single routes because the complexity of the chosen problem applied to real applications needs fast and robust algorithms (Larranaga et al., 1999). The first generation of solutions (tours) is generated randomly to avoid very time-costly procedures. The ith generation is obtained mutating groups of solutions of the $(i-1)^{th}$ generation. The possible mutations are the following: flip (reversing the order of the nodes in a sub-route of the solution), swap (interchanging two nodes within the route), and slide (a sub-route of the solution goes).

E	F	G	H	I	J	K	L	M	N	O	P
E	F	G	N	M	L	K	J	I	H	O	P

E	F	G	H	I	J	K	L	M	N	O	P
E	F	G	N	I	J	K	L	M	H	O	P

E	F	G	H	I	J	K	L	M	N	O	P
E	F	G	I	J	K	L	M	N	H	O	P

Figure 1. *Proposed mutations for the Genetic Algorithm*

We initialize the algorithm as follows. The initial number of solutions is set to 60. The number of iterations depends on the number of nodes, with a lower bound of 1000 for small problems, and a higher bound of 10000 for larger problems.

Both algorithms have been programmed in MATLAB 7.9.0 and run in an Intel Duo Core 2 T9300, 2,5GHz and 4 GB RAM.

3. Computational Results

First, and to assess the suitability of the methods, we applied them to classical 2E-VRP instances (Gonzalez-Feliu, 2008) comparing it to best solutions found

(Baldacci et al., 2013). We are aware that those algorithms are not the best for this problem, since they have been adapted to a more complex case and aim to find a suitable solution quickly. The aim of the proposed methods is not to solve an optimization problem but to provide a quick indicator. Moreover, routes obtained with this algorithm follow behavioral patterns that are close to the reality, as it is observed when comparing results of single routes with the route database, in terms of length and travelled distances.

Group of instances	Literature distance	Algorithm distance	Gap	Computational time
20 customers	5.59	5.17	7.60%	0.08
31 customers	8.98	7.89	12.19%	0.12
50 customers	46.91	41.86	10.77%	0.11

Table 1. *Summary of computational results on Gonzalez-Feliu's (2008) instances*

After that, we apply both algorithms to specific instances in urban context. Those instances are based on scenarios proposed in Gonzalez-Feliu and Salanova (2012). The first scenario considers no collaboration, so a single VRP (one stage) is defined. Scenarios 2 and 3 propose a first level of collaboration, but based on infrastructures (no freight transport pooling is allowed but all transport carriers use 2E-VRP approaches). Then, scenarios 4 and 5 propose a real transport pooling approach.

Test	Vehicles	Semi-greedy	Genetic	Gap	Vehicles	Semi-greedy	Genetic	Gap	Semi-greedy	Genetic
1.1	1	88 720	80 477	9%	0	0	0	0%		
1.2	2	119 013	101 903	14%	0	0	0	0%		
1.3	2	189 732	177 316	7%	0	0	0	0%	0,06	95,18
1.4	2	124 321	116 321	6%	0	0	0	0%		
1.5	2	210 067	203 896	3%	0	0	0	0%		
2.1	2	31 550	31 550	0%	8	143 631	136 466	5%		
2.2	3	34 560	34 560	0%	11	224 191	215 530	4%		
2.3	3	95 593	95 593	0%	4	112 867	97 761	13%	0,08	330,26
2.4	2	40 829	40 829	0%	7	170 426	162 786	4%		
2.5	2	73 787	73 787	0%	6	162 388	154 993	5%		
3.1	1	60 975	60 975	0%	8	166 858	154 070	8%		
3.2	2	87 760	85 495	3%	11	237 304	219 030	8%		
3.3	3	234 348	234 348	0%	5	116 336	104 120	11%	0,15	454,09
3.4	2	106 665	106 665	0%	7	142 476	128 300	10%		
3.5	2	205 976	200 108	3%	8	140 424	133 850	5%		
4.1	3	34 560	34 560	0%	11	224 191	215 530	4%		
4.2	2	40 829	40 829	0%	7	170 426	162 786	4%	0,09	355,91
4.3	2	73 787	73 787	0%	6	162 388	154 993	5%		
4.4	3	121 694	121 694	0%	12	207 464	194 274	6%		
5.0	9	960 847	650 186	32%	39	1 015 965	518 594	49%	0,00	437,93

Table 2. *Computational results of both algorithms on proposed realistic instances*

The route lengths obtained by the semi-greedy algorithm are in average 5.5% higher than the routes obtained by the GA. From Table 2 we can see that the average difference of distances in relation to the number of nodes. Due to the low capacity of the smaller trucks, most of the routes (55%) have less than 10 nodes, with an average overestimation of 2%. For longer routes, the average overestimation is 10%. In terms of computation time, the semi-greedy algorithm has an average time of 0.001 seconds, while the GA needs 5.25 seconds. The computation time grows exponentially with the number of nodes for both algorithms, but the GA has a fix quantity of time of 5 seconds.

Figure 2 shows the solutions of both algorithms for 2 of the routes. We observe that the semi-greedy algorithm overestimates the route distance, but it is much faster than the GA. However, the differences of distances are small even for big routes, so both algorithms are suitable in strategic planning decision support methods.

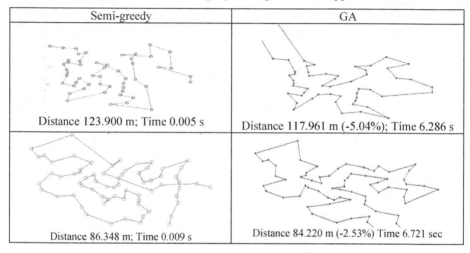

Semi-greedy	GA
Distance 123.900 m; Time 0.005 s	Distance 117.961 m (-5.04%); Time 6.286 s
Distance 86.348 m; Time 0.009 s	Distance 84.220 m (-2.53%) Time 6.721 sec

Figure 2. *Routes comparison in terms of length and computation time*

4. Conclusions

The algorithm presented compares the route obtained by a semi-greedy Algorithm with the route obtained by a Genetic Algorithm for the same set of customers. The routes obtained by the genetic algorithms are shorter than the routes obtained by the Greedy Algorithm (from 2% to 14%), but the computation time of the Genetic Algorithm is much higher than the computation time of the semi-greedy Algorithm. When solving real-life problems with an important number of customers, Genetic Algorithms need a big quantity of time.

Faster algorithms must be developed for complex problems such the problem presented above in realistic conditions, where is more important to analyse many configurations with suboptimal routes and clusters than less configurations with optimal routes and clustering, Genetic Algorithms can be used after the first set of iterations done by faster algorithms, when the most important variables have been decided (who is collaborating and the way they are collaborating) for optimizing the results obtained by the first group of algorithms in the clustering and routing phases.

Further developments are the following. Genetic algorithm should be programmed also for the clustering phase and for the whole problem solution, merging nodes from different clusters in the routes. When using genetic algorithms for both phases the complexity of the problem will increase, and the computation time needed for convergence will increase importantly. If the new genetic algorithm runs in reasonable times, the final step will be to use it for the collaborative 2E-VRP decision support, deciding the groups of operators that will collaborate and the way they will do it.

5. References

Baldacci, R., Mingozzi, A., Roberti, R., & Calvo, R. W. (2013). 'An exact algorithm for the two-echelon capacitated vehicle routing problem'. *Operations Research*, 61(2), 298-314.

Golden, B.L. (1988), *Vehicle routing: methods and studies*. Elsevier, Amsterdam, Studies in management science and systems, vol. 16.

Golden, B.L., Raghavan, S., Wasil, E.A. (2008). *Vehicle routing: Latest advances and challenges*, Kluwer, Boston, USA.

Gonzalez-Feliu, J. (2008), 'Models and Methods for the City Logistics – The Two-echelon Capacitated Vehicle Routing Problem'. PhD Thesis. Politecnico di Torino, Turin, Italy.

Gonzalez-Feliu, J., Morana, J. (2011). Collaborative transportation sharing: from theory to practice via a case study from France. In Yearwood, J.L. and Stranieri, A. (eds.). *Technologies for Supporting Reasoning Communities and Collaborative Decision Making: Cooperative Approaches*, Information Science Reference, pp.252-271.

Gonzalez-Feliu, J., Salanova Grau, J.M., Morana, J. Ma, T.Y. (2013), 'Design and scenario assessment for collaborative logistics and freight transport systems', *International Journal of Transport Economics*, vol. 40, n. 2, pp.207-240.

Gonzalez-Feliu, J., Salanova, J. (2012), 'Defining and evaluating collaborative urban freight distribution systems', *Procedia Social and Behavioral Science*, vol. 39, pp.172-183.

Larranaga, P., Kuijpers, C. M. H., Murga, R. H., Inza, I., Dizdarevic, S. (1999). 'Genetic algorithms for the travelling salesman problem: A review of representations and operators'. *Artificial Intelligence Review*, 13(2), 129-170.

Mancini, S., Gonzalez-Feliu, J., Crainic, T.G. (2014), 'Planning and Optimization Methods for Advanced Urban Logistics Systems at Tactical Level'. In Gonzalez-Feliu J., Semet, F., Routhier, J.L. (eds), *Sustainable Urban Logistics: Concepts, Methods and Information Systems*, Springer, Heidelberg, pp.145-164.

Toth, P., Vigo, D. (2002). *The Vehicle Routing Problem*. SIAM Society for Industrial and Applied Mathematics, Philadelphia, USA.

The Last Food Mile Concept as a City Logistics Solution for Perishable Products

The Case of Parma's Food Urban Distribution Center

Eleonora Morganti* — Jesus Gonzalez-Feliu**

* SPLOTT, IFSTTAR
Cité Descartes, 14-20 Boulevard Newton, 77447 Marne-la-Vallée cedex 02, France
eleonora.morganti@ifsttar.fr

** LET, CNRS
ISH, 14 Avenue Berthelot, 69363 Lyon Cedex 07, France
jesus.gonzalez-feliu@cnrs.fr

ABSTRACT. *This paper analyzes last mile logistics for fresh food products and the food deliveries schemes to urban food outlets, i.e. corporate retail chains, independent retailers and hotel, restaurants and catering (Ho.Re.Ca.) sector. We present two concepts: that of food hub and that of last food mils, as well as an analysis framework to understand food last mile distribution. To illustrate it, two experiences of urban food distribution are compared to a reference situation using the proposed framework.*

KEYWORDS: *Food Hub, Last Food Mile, Urban Distribution Center (UDC), City Logistics, Profession Knowledge.*

1. Introduction

City logistics incorporates the "last mile" or "final mile" of the freight delivery journey, identified as the small scale distribution of goods in urban environment. This part of the freight transport system is often the most expensive because of a high diversity of stakeholders, each with specifics aims, the scarcity of space, and a multiplication and constraints that make difficult to have economies of scale so have an impact on both delivery costs and environmental nuisances. Indeed, the resulting scenario is a variety of vehicles circulating within the city without co-ordination.

This paper aims to present the concept of last food miles, mainly in the case of city logistics, as well as an analysis framework to compare urban distribution centers

(UDC) for fresh foods deliveries. First we propose an overview on food hubs and present the main concepts of last food mile logistics. Second, we propose an analysis framework based on a set of indicators, referred to a standard initial situation. Finally, we illustrate the framework by comparing two cases of food deliveries systems, that of Parma and that of Padua, both in Italy.

2. Last Food Mile Logistics and Food Hubs in City Logistics

A renovation in the traditional wholesale produce market is observed around Europe. New organizational concepts are now discussed by researchers under the model known as regional and/or alternative food hubs (FH), defined as "partnership based arrangements that coordinate the distribution of a range of food products from producers of a uniform provenance to conventional or hybrid markets" (Morley et al., 2009). They can be developed at existing supply chain infrastructures playing a new or renewed role as alternative intermediaries, at wholesalers' level, at retailers' level, or can take the forms of public sector initiative, producer cooperatives or producer-entrepreneur partnerships. At a logistics level, the FH core components are: (1) Aggregation/ Distribution – Wholesale, (2) Active coordination and (3) Permanent facilities.

Moreover, successful wholesaling requires a good balance between small-scale and large-scale suppliers and a diverse mix of customers to provide the best marketing option for each product (Morganti, 2011a). As the supply base continues to consolidate, alliances must be built with large national and regional supply organizations while at the same time, relationships must be maintained with small, high quality producers. Among the WPM customers, there is a growing number of retail chains. Servicing the supermarkets requires a high level of quality assurance, supply planning, transport, logistics and business management. By contrast, servicing the independent stores requires attention to detail and developing good personal relationships, and logistics service too.

There are crucial components such as marketing, organizational and technical elements which determine the performance of the wholesale market at both commercial and logistics levels. Going further in this double function perspective, the FH should be able to integrate logistic urban networks and to provide services to achieve a high degree of collection in the goods flows, in order to supply efficient transport from the market area to the city centre. By doing so, the FH can play the logistics role of *urban distribution center* for food products (it can be only fruit and vegetables, potentially, for other food and non-food products), having as principal advantage the alleviation of local environmental and traffic concerns in urban areas by increasing in the load factors of commercial vehicles dedicated to food deliveries.

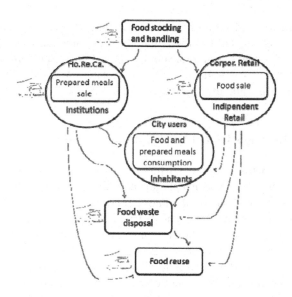

Figure 1. *The urban food flow – Focus on transport activities (Morganti, 2011b)*

At different phases of the urban distribution system, logistics and transport implement and control the forward flows of food products and related information between the point of origin and the point of destination. Figure 1 shows the main processes of the urban food chain and the related transport functions operated by commercial vehicles: from local warehouses, wholesalers and suppliers facilities foodstuffs are transported to urban food retailing and catering operators (corporate and independent retailers, Ho.Re.Ca., institutional food services and business canteens), so-called "last mile" logistics. Then, additional transport operations are needed from food outlets to the landfill and to the food reuse site.

Within a *food miles* analysis (Pirog et al. 2001; Pirog, 2004), we investigate only the final part of the food supply chain delivery and we identify the environmental impact caused by urban food transport, in terms of air pollutants. For this purpose, we adopt the concept of "last food mile" (Morganti, 2011), being an expression combines the *last mile* and *food miles* concepts, and we use it in the study to facilitate the comprehension of the research. Last food mile logistics refers them to *"the physical distribution of food occurring in the last part of food supply chain"*. (Morganti, 2011). It concerns then the final delivery of perishable goods to urban food outlets. This concept includes logistics criteria related to the efficient and effective distribution schemes, related to the economic, environmental and social sustainability of urban communities. It usually consists in small deliveries managed by transport operators and suppliers, wholesalers and distributors, and also, as self-provisioning operation, by shop owners and food retailers.

3. The Proposed Analysis Framework

The urban food distribution scheme is different according to the type of supply chain it relates with. In this study, we focus on the "last mile" logistics, notably for retailing, often consists of light goods vehicles (LCV) deliveries taking place over short distances, reconciling many customers and a variety of shipments. The "last mile" is one of the most important yet problematic parts of the supply chain due to two facts: (1) the small scale distribution of goods in urban environment is the least efficient part of the supply chain due to the high atomization of receivers and to their increasing requirements, and (2) the high degree of "empty running" implies extra costs. As LCVs perform a greater proportion of their vehicle trips and vehicle kilometers in urban areas than HGVs, they make a greater contribution to urban congestion than HGVs. Operations involving de-consolidation from a few HGVs to many LCVs at urban distribution centers (UDCs) because of traffic restriction on HGVs may result in worsening urban congestion.

To describe this complex scenario related to urban food transport, we focus on selected components characterizing city logistics and perishable goods logistics processes, on the basis of the technical guidelines issued by the Regione Emilia Romagna, Mobility and Transport Department (Rosini, 2005). According to them, there are logistics, technological, organizational variables characterizing the performance of city logistics, as described in table 1.

Categories	Variables	Details
Logistics variables	Frequency	delivery frequency
	Load unit	shape in which the goods are usually grouped and loaded on vehicles (pallet, roll, box, etc.)
	Delivery features	number of deliveries /trip, weight of each delivery
Technological and organizational variables	Typology of vehicles	dimensions and technical features of the vehicles
	Delivery period	period of the day in which the delivery of the goods is usually carried out
	Level of logistics optimization	capacity utilization of the vehicle (in weight and/or volume)
	Carriers typology	on own account, self provisioning, third party logistics

Table 1. *City logistics variables set (Morganti 2011)*

4. Results

To make a comparison among urban food hubs, we propose to compare the two main examples of fresh food urban distribution systems to a reference. The reference is obtained from Morganti and Gonzalez-Feliu's (2014) results, by agregating the main characteristics of routes for last food mile deliveries (including all types of carriers on the same category). Data from Parma's UDC is adapted from Morganti's

(2011a,b) analyses. For Padua's UDC, which is part of a global service involving food and non-food deliveries, data has been obtained from Gonzalez-Feliu and Morana (2010), Morana and Gonzalez-Feliu (2011) and Vaghi and Percoco (2011) with data for fresh food obtained by a phone interview with the manager of the system. We present in Table 2 the different variables for each case:

Categories	Variables	Reference	Parma's UDC	Padova's UDC
Logistics variables	Frequency	1.8 times/day	Once/day	Once/day
	Load unit	Pallet, parcel	Pallet/parcel	Parcel
	Num. deliveries/trip	1,6 hypermarkets 4 other stores	1 hypermarkets 18 other stores	12 (no hypermarket deliveries
	Weight/delivery	150 kg	160 kg	100 kg
Technological and organizational variables	Types of vehicles	Diesel, different sizes	Gas, 3.5T	Gas, 3.5T
	Delivery period	Morning (peak hour: 6 a.m.)	6 a.m.-1 p.m.	9 a.m.-1 p.m. 2 p.m.-6 p.m.
	Loading rate	Under 50%	More than 80%	About 70%
	Carriers typology	Mainly own account	Third party	Third party

Table 2. *City logistics variables for the three considered cases*

We observe that Parma's UDC, which has been developed at a food hub and targeting both grocery distribution and Ho.Re.Ca. stakeholders, has characteristics closer to the reference, in terms of logistics variables. However, we observe a high level of optimization, due to the flow rationalisation. Indeed, Parma's UDC delivers near 20 customers in a route, where reference routes serve in average about 4 customers per route. This is due to the dominance of own account, which is one of the main targets of Parma's UDC (not only Ho.Re.Ca. but also supermarkets, which present important parts of own account in Italy). Padua's platform is not a food hub, but a classical logistics facility operational since 2004 that has included food delivery services since 2010. Their market is restricted and their main customers are small shops and Ho.Re.Ca., so their performance is lower than that of Parma or that of non-fresh products but remains higher than that of classical food distribution.

Note that similar systems can also be found in other wholesales produce markets, like that of Paris-Rungis, which goal is not to sustainably deliver the city but to offer a complementary service to customers (mainly Ho.Re.Ca. establishments) that prefer to be delivered instead of traveling to buy themselves their required fresh food products. The system is operational and has important economic benefits, is based on a total supply at wholesalers located in Rungis FH, taking advantage of the synergies that this type of infrastructure can develop.

5. Conclusions

In this paper we have presented the concepts of food hub and last food mile, as well as an analysis framework to define the main characteristics of last food miles with and without urban consolidation-based food hubs. We compared a reference situation with the results of two UDCs (one being a food hub, the other not). We observe that food hubs, when used as UDCs, are more adapted to food distribution and present a high potential in terms of optimization. However, this notion is new and needs to be improved. Further analysis of environmental performance and comparison with other types of food hubs are needed to complete and expand this work.

6. References

Gonzalez-Feliu, J., Morana, J., "Are City Logistics Solutions Sustainable? The Cityporto case", *TeMA. Journal of Land Use, Mobility and Environment*, 3 (2), 2010, pp.55-64.

Morana, J., Gonzalez-Feliu, J., "Le transport vert de marchandises : l'expérience de la ville de Padoue en Italie", *Gestion : Revue Internationale de Gestion*, 36 (2), 2011, pp.16-24.

Morganti, E., *Urban food planning, city logistics and sustainability: the role of the wholesale produce market. The cases of Parma and Bologna food hubs*, PhD Thesis, 2011a, Alma Mater Studiorum, University of Bologna, Italy.

Morganti, E., "Urban food planning and transport sustainability: A case study in Parma, Italy". *Proceedings of European Association of Agricultural Economists*, EAAE 4th PhD Workshop, April 2011b.

Morganti, E., Gonzalez-Feliu, J., City logistics for perishable products. The case of the Parma Food Hub. Technical Report LET, 2014. Submitted to *Case Studies in Transport Policy*.

Morley, A., Morgan, S., Morgan, K., "Food hubs: The 'missing middle' of the local food infrastructure", Technical Report, 2009, BRASS Centre, Cardiff University.

Pirog, R. "Food miles: a simple metaphor to contrast local and global food systems. Hunger And Environmental Nutrition (HEN)", Dietetic Practice Group, American Dietetic Association, Summer 2004.

Pirog, R., Van Pelt, T., Enshayan, K., Cook, E., "Food, Fuel, and Freeways", Technical Report, 2001, Leopold Center for Sustainable Agriculture, Iowa State University, Ames.

Rosini, R., ed., *City Ports Project. Intermediary report*. Quaderni del servizio Pianificazione dei Trasporti e Logistica, Regione Emilia Romagna, 2011, Bologna, Italy.

Vaghi, C., Percoco, M., "City logistics in Italy: success factors and environmental performance". In Macharis, C., Melo, S. (eds.), *City distribution and urban freight transport. Multiple perspectives*, Emerald, Northampton, 2011, pp.151-175.

Supporting Decision for Road Crisis Management through an Agile and Collaborative Information System

Guillaume Macé-Ramète — Frédérick Bénaben — Matthieu Lauras
Jacques Lamothe

Centre Génie Industriel – Mines Albi – Université de Toulouse
Campus Jarlard, Route de Teillet, 81000 Albi, France
{guillaume.maceramete;benaben;lauras;lamothe}@mines-albi.fr

ABSTRACT. *During winter, road network can be hit by unusually weather conditions leading to a crisis situation. To solve this given situation, the crisis management unit has to ensure interoperability between all heterogeneous actors in order to give a response fitting with the current situation. To support the crisis management, an Information Decision Support System can be designed which has to ensure agility of the crisis response by detecting and anticipating future events. Given the different forecasts in terms of weather and traffic, the system might be able to anticipate the future situation in order to give a relevant and proactive response. This paper deals with the design of a system helping crisis management to understand the future situation given the on-going response and different predictions made. Methodology and technologies for developing such a system are exposed. This article is a result of a French funded project named SIMPeTra.*

KEYWORDS: *Agility, Road Crisis Management, Information Decision Support System.*

1. Introduction

In December 2010 and more recently in March 2013, the northwest of France (Britain and Normandy) was hit by exceptional winter weather conditions (heavy snow falls, icing rain, snowdrift). This situation was causing problems because of slick roads and as a consequence driving conditions were really bad all over the road network. In such circumstances, many road problems occurred (traffic disruptions, hundreds of kilometers of traffic jam, truck accident, etc.). In order to face this situation, the West CRICR (*Centre Régional d'Information et de Coordination Routière*, regional traffic coordination and information center) set up a crisis cell in charge of managing the road crisis situation. This cell has to: (i) make good decision to manage traffic (allow circulation, store trucks, etc.) (ii) ensure the coordination between the crisis actors (iii) give information and advices to road users.

In an experience feedback (Panhaleux, 2011) underlines dysfunctions in crisis management: (i) a lack of information for decision makers, (ii) a lack of coordination between heterogeneous actors (iii) and a lack of visibility on decisions taken. In order to overcome this statement the crisis cell should be supported by an Information Decision Support System which requirements are described in (Aligne, 2009): (i) gather information, (ii) analyse the current situation and (iii) support decision making. Another big challenge for such a system is to be agile. According to (Charles, 2010), agility is the ability of a system to detect evolutions and adapt his behaviour in an acceptable lead-time.

In road crisis situations, crisis management unit shall anticipate the future situation while taking a decision because of the latent period between the moment when they make the decision and the moment the decision is really effective on the field. This delay is due to administrative procedure (write a bylaw, validate it by the National Authority, etc.) that takes about two hours. In order to be efficient and to have a proactive behaviour facing the crisis situation, the targeted Information System needs to provide a "screenshot" of the situation considering the different predictions (weather and traffic forecasts).

Considering these statements, the main issue is *How to define an agile Information System supporting decision in a road crisis situation by anticipating future situation states?* In the remainder of this paper, we aim at providing a methodology to detect and anticipate the future crisis situation. Section 1 deals with a brief literature review, section II exposes the global mechanisms and Section III ends with a use case.

2. Literature Review

As defined by (Lagadec, 2006), a crisis can be considered as "a disordered state of a reference universe" and can be characterized by its problem, nature and release events. In order to be able to share information between all crisis stakeholders, the crisis cell shall have a good representation of the crisis situation. The description of this situation might be expressed in a common language that involves concepts understandable by all crisis actors. Thus, (Truptil, 2008) depicts a crisis metamodel to build ontologies for crisis management and (Liu, 2013) offers a state of the art of ontologies for crisis management. All these references reach the same goal to build models for crisis management unit. In a previous work, (Macé Ramète, 2012), we defined a road crisis metamodel aiming at provide a common base helping crisis management unit to build road crisis models.

We defined previously agility in crisis context as the ability of a system to detect an evolution in crisis situation and adapt his behaviour in a short lead-time. Thus, an efficient detection shall monitor the on-going process to know his relevance regarding the current situation. In (Barthe-Delanoë, 2013), a methodology is proposed in order to detect changes in a collaborative situation. This method compares the two following models during crisis response: the field model (representation of the on-going field situation updated by sensors, observations and reports) and the expected model (representation of a "should be" situation updated by activity status of the on-going process). The result of the comparison leads the crisis cell to choose to adapt the on-going process. A weakness of this mechanism is that it doesn't take into account the prediction of the future situation.

In order to "anticipate" the future, the crisis management unit needs to be aware of the future events going to occur. In the context of road crisis context, we only focus on weather forecasts and traffic forecasts. On the one hand, Meteo France (National Weather Service) is able to produce accurate weather forecasts within a two hours delay. These predictions are made through a specific Information System named OPTIMA. On the other hand in (Barcelo, 2010) depicts many traffic simulation models. According to this, we decided to focus on METANET simulation (Kotsialos, 2002) that deals with a macroscopic approach to model motorway traffic network. In (Farzaneh, 2007) an empirical study on traffic aims at showing the impact of bad weather conditions on traffic flows. We choose to couple this study with the different parameters of METANET model. The use of traffic and weather forecasts is helpful to design different scenario to foresee the future situation.

3. Scientific Proposition

In this section, we choose to go a step farther than the mechanism exposed in (Barthe-Delanoë, 2012) by introducing a "projected" model that is a projection of the current model (field model) in the future. Making this projection should help the crisis management unit to take decision anticipating what is going to occur. The main objective is to build a proactive system. The projection is made by (i) simulating the on-going process on the field model and (ii) taking into account the possible scenarios elaborated thanks to weather and traffic forecasts. Our method is based on four steps as described below.

3.1. First Step: Define a Reference Model

This step aims at defining a reference state. This model fits with the reference universe as described in (Lagadec, 2006). Thus, risks and consequences are considered "acceptable" according to the crisis management unit. The main objective of the crisis response is to target this "reference" model in order to start the recovery phase, it is the awaited situation after all processes responding to crisis situation have ended. This model is defined by crisis management during the preparedness phase.

3.2. Second Step: Definition of Scenario

Secondly, in order to make a projection of the crisis situation, the crisis cell has to define and choose a scenario fitting with expected forecasts (traffic and weather). This scenario also contains all process events (activity statuses, duration of activities, etc.). This scenario might be given by external systems helping crisis management such as forecasting weather or traffic simulation software. Thus the scenario is made of two parts, field events (weather, traffic) and process events (begin/start of activities).

3.3. Third Step: Making the Projection

The third step of our methodology consists in projecting the current field model according to the scenario defined before (step 2). The projection is done by unrolling the scenario like if it is the real behaviour of the system. Thus, the method to calculate the projected model is similar to the one developed in (Barthe-Delanoë, 2013). Indeed, the "field" part of the scenario acts like the sensors (to calculate field model) and the "process" part aims at calculating the "should be" system. It takes into account the on-going process activities to update and changes crisis problems. If an activity has been chosen for solving a risk, then the risk might disappear in the crisis model. At the end of the third step, we have the projected model taking into account (i) the forecasts (weather, traffic), (ii) the on-going response processes.

3.4. Fourth Step: Model Exploitation

Once the projected model is calculated, model exploitation should be done. The objective of this phase is to see if the projected model is acceptable through the point of view of the crisis management unit. In order to reach this goal, we use the comparison mechanism defined in (Barthe-Delanoë, 2013). But instead of making a comparison between field and expected models, the comparison is done between the projected model and the reference model.

If a divergence is detected, then the on-going process should be redesigned because it is no longer relevant to the crisis situation.

4. Conclusions

In this paper, we defined a new framework to detect future crisis evolutions based on forecasts of future events and on the monitoring of the on-going process. The main objective here is to detect if the on-going response is relevant to the current situation regarding the actual forecast. This proposal allows detecting potential gaps and adapting the current processes to fit better with the reality of the field. The comparison between "projected" and "reference" model aims at reaching this goal. Future works includes develop this method on a specific use case and implement it on a prototype for crisis cell.

5. References

Aligne F., "Which Information and Decision Support System for the Crisis Management", *Information Systems and Technology Panel (IST) Symposium, Bucharest*, 11-12 May 2009.

Barceló J., "Fundamentals of Traffic Simulation". *International Series in Operations Research & Management Science*, vol. 145, Springer, 2010.

Barthe-Delanoë A.-M., Truptil S., Bénaben F., Pingaud H., "Event-driven agility of interoperability during the Run-time of collaborative processes", *Decision Support Systems*, 2013.

Charles A., Lauras M., Van Wassenhove L., "A model to define and assess the agility of supply chains: building on humanitarian experience," *International Journal of Physical Distribution & Logistics Management*, vol. 40, no. 8/9, pp.722-741, September 2010.

Farzaneh Mohamadreza, Arafeh, Mazen, Hranac, Robert, *Empirical Studies on Traffic Flow in Inclement Weather.* Virginia Tech Transportation Institute, 2007.

Kotsialos A., Papageorgiou M., Diakaki C., Pavlis Y., "Traffic flow modeling of large-scale motorway networks using the macroscopic modeling tool METANET", *IEEE Transactions on Intelligent Transport Systems*, vol. 4, no. 4, pp.282-292, December 2002.

Lagadec P., *La Gestion des Crises, Outils de réflexion à l'usage des décideurs*, Paris, Ediscience International, 1992.

Liu S., Brewster C., Shaw D., Ontologies for Crisis Management: A Review of State of the Art in Ontology Design and Usability, in *Proceedings of the 10th International ISCRAM Conference* – Baden-Baden, Germany, May 2013.

Macé Ramète G., Lamothe J., Lauras M., Bénaben F., "A road crisis management metamodel for an information decision support system", in *6th IEEE International Conference on Digital Ecosystems Technologies (DEST)*, Campione d'Italia, Italy, June 2012.

Panhaleux J., David D., Labia P., Picquand J.-L., Rivière D., Terrié F., Leyrit C., "Retour d'expérience à la suite de l'épisode neigeux survenu le 8 décembre 2010 en Ile-de-France", Conseil général de l'Environnement et du développement durable, 2011.

Truptil S., Bénaben F., Couget P., Lauras M., Chapurlat V., Pingaud H., "Interoperability of Information Systems in Crisis Management: Crisis Modeling and Metamodeling", *I-ESA'08*, Berlin, 2008.

Workshop 6

Applications of Advanced Technologies in the Context of Disaster Relief and Crisis Management

Report

Aurélie Charles

Decision and Information Sciences for Production Systems
Lyon 2 University, France
a.charles@univ-lyon2.fr

The workshop focused on the application of advanced technologies in the context of disaster relief and crisis management. The aim of this workshop has been to underline the bottlenecks linked to ICT applications in this specific context and propose ways forward. We summarise the content of the presented papers and report the main questions brought up during the discussion in the workshop.

The first paper titled Enhancing the emergency response by using an event-driven system, by A.-M. Barthe summarizes the use-case of the European project, PLAY, dedicated to the construction of a platform, which collects information in real time (events) from many, heterogeneous, distributed event sources, process that events in a complex way, and, after discovering something relevant, forward such a situation (combination of events) to the parties interested in that issue. In this paper, the benefits of the use of Event-Driven techniques, such as Complex Event Processing, in crisis situations are shown by considering and applying these technologies on a nuclear use-case. This provided a good overview of what could be implemented on the field and the impact it would make on the response.

Discussions were mainly based on the follow up of the project and its application on real cases. Questions on how to implement such a system for the response to natural crisis were also raised. Indeed, implementing new IT systems is never easy, especially in uncertain environments.

The second paper titled Designing decision support systems for management organizations: requirements and issues, by A. Charles, provides a general overview of the specificities of this application sector. The presentation included also a proposal for a decision support system designed to facilitate critical logistics choices. This system ranks available possibilities based on their impact regarding key performance indicators such as quickness, cost and/or environmental impact.

Comments were made on the usefulness for researchers to understand this specific context and the work it represent to manage to gather this knowledge. The application has then been discussed. As the specifications of this proposal originated from a discussion at the French Red Cross, further questions aroused on the possibility to adapt the system for other organizations, and on the possibility to have them work together with similar IT systems.

The third paper titled Bridging the gap between developers, researchers and the reality of disaster: Experiences from a field trip to the Philippines following the 2013 Haiyan disaster, by T. Comes acknowledges the uncertainty and differences in understanding of researchers vs. practitioners, and compares this approach with other networks of remote collaboration. The presentation exposes the findings from a field trip to Philippines and shared conclusions and recommendations regarding the collaborations between researchers and practitioners in this specific context.

The discussion was focused on the research design used in this experiment. As this field trip will be followed by others, one being already planned with the United Nations, but with completely different settings (conflict instead of natural disaster, so remote work in a neighboring country instead of field presence, etc.)

Enhancing the Emergency Response Using an Event-Driven System

Anne-Marie Barthe-Delanoë — **Frédérick Bénaben** — **Matthieu Lauras** — **Sébastien Truptil**

University of Toulouse – Mines Albi
Campus Jarlard, Route de Teillet, 81000 Albi, France
anne-marie.barthe@mines-albi.fr

ABSTRACT. *This article aims at underlining the ability of an Event-Driven System to support the emergency response in context of crisis situations. The proposed approach consists on the one hand to model the business processes of the crisis response, and on the other hand to support the orchestration of these processes by using an Event-Driven System. The use of Event-Driven concepts can help the crisis management stakeholders in relieving them from non-value added tasks (by their automation) and in helping them to focus on the relevant information. Event-Driven techniques (such as Complex Event Processing) are very promising, even if very few research works consider them to improve emergency management. This paper tries to show their benefits by considering and applying these technologies on a nuclear use-case.*

KEYWORDS: *Emergency Management, Complex Event Processing, Decision Support System.*

1. Introduction

In a crisis situation, a lot of heterogeneous actors may be involved to solve or at least reduce it. The heterogeneity of services provided by these actors is probably the main cause of the difficulty to manage such a crisis situation. But there are many other difficulties to cope with. One of the most important challenges is to deal with the amount of data and information emitted by heterogeneous sources (stakeholders, sensors, devices, etc.) (De Maio et al., 2011). Usually, Emergency Management (EM) strategy is based on complex plans: they took into account various and numerous factors that may be complementary, contradictory or conflicting. The need for a tool that can support the decision-making in crisis situation seems to be obvious. This paper aims at describing the way Event-Driven techniques could be used to support EM. In section 2, a short state of the art of existing IT systems that are supposed to be relevant in our context are presented. Then, the proposed Event-Driven system and its interests are detailed and its use is illustrated by a Chemical,

Biological, Nuclear and Radiological (CBNR) use-case. The obtained results are discussed in the last section.

2. Background and Positioning

In a crisis context, decision-makers have to manage an exploding amount of data and information. The use of technological systems can help to manage them more efficiently. In the last years, some researchers have imagined to use Event-Driven Architecture (EDA) (Luckham, 2007) and Cloud-Computing to address this problem. According to (Etzion and Niblett, 2010), the elements that happened in the studied system and that embedded data can be considered and managed as events. Events can be collected in an event cloud. A Complex Event Processing (CEP) engine consumes and manages these events by filtering and applying business rules to detect relevant events or combination of events. The PRONTO project (Pottebaum et al., 2011) and the project described in (Yu and Cai, 2012) have tried to propose such a mechanism. But the first one is only a framework and does not constitute a concrete operational tool for EM practionners. The second one is limited by a high coupling between the CEP and the event sources. It is also focused on situational management and not on business process management. Based on this, our problem statement is the design of a new IT platform based on the EDA paradigm and in line with the results of (Pottebaum et al., 2011; Yu and Cai, 2012), providing a loose coupling and a concrete solution for emergency response.

3. PLAY Platform

The PLAY platform is a global (Internet-scale) structure to combine events from many sources with the goal of connecting and orchestrating services, devices and people. The platform has emerged as an event marketplace: it brings together the senders and receivers of events and provides numerous services on top of them. To that end PLAY combines various technologies to deal with delivery, processing and storage of events in real-time. We will briefly outline these technologies by introducing the main components that compose the platform (see Figure 1). The detail of the conceptual architecture of the PLAY platform is accessible to the reader on the dedicated website (http://play-project.eu).

The *Distributed Service Bus* (DSB) enables the Service-oriented Architecture (SOA) and EDA infrastructure to connect all the distributed components, devices and end user services (through the Information Systems of the stakeholders). The DSB aims at providing connectivity between services and event providers/consumers. Thus, distributed sources of events can be combined in the platform. The *Event Cloud* provides storage and forwarding of events. Interested parties can be notified of events according to content-based subscriptions. The Event Cloud is comprised of a peer-to-peer system of storage nodes organized in a controller area network (Filali et al., 2011).

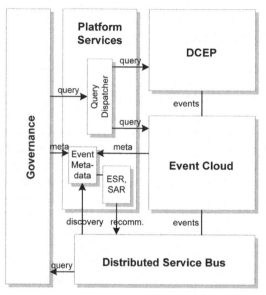

Figure 1. *The PLAY platform: its architectural components*

The *Distributed Complex Event Processing* (DCEP) component is dedicated to detect complex events and reasons over events in real-time. The CEP helps to deduce meaningful events from simpler events. The platform can detect such derived events, through its knowledge of all events and the application of event patterns to the input events, as described in (Etzion and Niblett, 2010). Finally, the *Service Adaptation Recommender* (SAR) suggests changes (adaptations) of services' configurations, composition or workflows, in order to overcome problems or achieve higher performance. Its objective is to support the decision by suggesting relevant adaptations, based on recognized situations. The decision-makers accept or reject the proposed alterations.

4. Use-Case

The use-case is based on a Chemical Biological Radiological and Nuclear (CBRN) crisis: a large quantity of radioactive substance is accidentally released in the atmosphere, due to a critical accident in a French nuclear plant. The use-case is based on French real emergency plans, processes and best practices. For test-run purposes, a sub-scenario was extracted from the original use-case (see http://www.play-project.eu

for more information on it), and cut into three major periods. In the 1st period, the representative of National Authority (Prefect) will use the PLAY platform to support the analysis of the huge amount of radioactivity and weather measures available. Based on this, he/she will be able to decide what perimeter has to be under-surveillance. He/she will be able to ask some advices through the platform to French Nuclear Expert Institution (IRSN) to support his/her decisions. This first part of the scenario is used to assess the scalability of the PLAY Platform and the ability to filter and produce added-value information for decision-makers. 2nd period begins when, on the basis of different measurements gathered, the PLAY platform will alert the Prefect that a confinement should be engaged. After a brief analysis of the situation, the Prefect will decide to activate the confinement plan. This decision will be sent to other crisis stakeholders via the PLAY system. Then, the representative of the Police will design the confinement plan and transmit it to other stakeholders through the platform. In this sub-scenario, only the "preventing entrances of new people in the concerned area" business process is managed. The representative of Office Infrastructure will design its own operational plan (circulation plan) based on the confinement plan established previously by the representative of the Police. When the circulation plan is ready, it is sent through the platform to the office infrastructure teams in order to be applied on the field. This second part of the scenario will be used to assess the capability of the PLAY Platform to manage coordination ("if task 1 is activated then task 2 should/must be activated") and propagation of structured data such as confinement plan here. During the 3rd period, the circulation plan implementation will be done on the field and tracked by the platform. But as for any real situations, different hazards will disturb the process execution. The PLAY system will detect that (i) some required resources will be insufficient to execute the plan, (ii) a task is too long regarding the standard and will activate an alert to decision-makers, (iii) the management of resources will suppose to manage inventory by checking all resources movements. This part of the scenario will be used to assess the capability to (i) track the execution of different tasks and consequently to detect potential problems, (ii) test its adaptation capabilities, and (iii) validate its data storage.

5. Results and Discussion

The execution of the CBRN use-case shows how the proposed system can support the management of information and decision in crisis management context. Five major benefits of the use of the PLAY platform to support the management of the crisis response and the decision making in such a context are:

– *Eliminating superfluous, inaccurate or irrelevant information.* The PLAY platform allows to drastically minimizing the amount of information exchanged between the stakeholders. During the first seven minutes of the use-case, within a classical configuration, the *Prefect* receives more than 200 raw measures of radiation and weather. With the PLAY platform, he/she can subscribe only to useful information for him/her. In our scenario, he/she has just received 1 report event every five minutes and 1 alert event when necessary (in that case at t_0+7 minutes). The platform is not only able to provide synthesis of measures (information aggregation), but it can also send message specifically on purpose.

– *Automating some actions or analysis based on pre-defined business rules.* CEP filters events but it can also reacts on specific incoming events, on the basis of pre-defined business rules. The use-case shows us that events like alert events can help to underline potential risks and allow anticipating incoming problems.

– *Reducing the time of data exchange between devices, stakeholders and decision-makers.* Connecting directly devices and actors from both crisis field and crisis cell allows the information to circulate almost instantaneously between the stakeholders. During the tests made within a distributed environment (more than hundred of kilometers between the systems), each event was distributed to all targeted actors *in less than 1 second*. Even if this feature is strongly dependent on the ability to maintain electronic networks operating, this is a good way to integrate all devices (stakeholders' and people personal's ones) in a context of crisis management.

– *Increasing the reliability of information.* SOA-based technologies allow a very loose coupling between the heterogeneous Information Systems, facilitating their integration and avoiding numerous information treatment or transformation. Risks of alteration and non-quality are reduced. This contribution has been used during the second stage of the test-run.

– *Improving the agility capabilities of the crisis cell.* The proposed platform helps the stakeholders to detect quicker evolutions and react in a finest way. This is defined as "agility" (Barthe-Delanoë et al., 2013). Our proposition brings solution to improve visibility, velocity and reactivity during the execution of the crisis response (demonstrated during the third period of the test-run).

Connecting efficiently the stakeholders with the PLAY platform, which is an Event-Driven system, contributes to (i) bridge the gap between information producers and information consumers in a loose coupled way, (ii) facilitating the information analysis and the decision-making whilst delivering quick response.

6. Conclusions

The PLAY platform presented in this article is an event management environment. Through this platform, the users can be dynamically connected to existing information systems, sensors or connected devices and persons. Considering (i) the heterogeneity of data sources, (ii) the high volume of heterogeneous information, (iii) the continuous changes in orchestration and in choreography of crisis response processes, and (iv) the high-pressure environment due to the context of the crisis situation, it is critical to select the right information, for the right person at the right time. The proposed event management can be used to deal with the amount and the heterogeneity of events in order to deduce the right information. It may be seen as a support to ensure the agility capabilities of the crisis cell decision-makers by relieving them from tasks that do not require human being skills. The PLAY platform was tested on simulated environments of crisis situation. Experiments on real or live use cases should be carried out to validate the platform in terms of relevancy and performance.

This research work has been funded by the European Commission under Seventh Framework Program (FP7) regarding the research project PLAY (*Pushing dynamic and ubiquitous interaction between services Leveraged in the Future Internet by ApplYing complex event processing*) (Grant FP7-258659). The authors would like to thank the project partners for their advice and comments regarding this work.

7. References

[1] Barthe-Delanoë, A.-M., Truptil, S., Bénaben, F., Pingaud, H. "Event-driven agility of interoperability during the Run-time of collaborative processes". 2013. Decision Support System.

[2] De Maio, C., Fenza, G., Gaeta, M., Loia, V., Orciuoli, F. "A knowledge-based framework for emergency DSS". *Knowl.-Based Syst.* 24, 2011, 1372-1379.

[3] Etzion, O., Niblett, P.. *Event Processing in Action*, 1st ed., Manning Publications Co., 2010 Greenwich, CT, USA.

[4] Filali, I., Pellegrino, L., Bongiovanni, F., Huet, F., Baude, F. "Modular P2P-Based Approach for RDF Data Storage and Retrieval". Presented at the *Advances in P2P Systems*, 2011.

[5] Luckham, D. SOA, EDA, BPM and CEP are all Complementary - Part Two, 2007.

[6] Pottebaum, J., Artikis, A., Marterer, R., Paliouras, G., Koch, R. "Event definition for the application of event processing to intelligent resource management", in: *Proceedings of the 8th International ISCRAM Conference*, 2011, Lisbon, Portugal.

[7] Yu, B., Cai, G. "Coordination of Emergency Response Operations via the Event-Based Awareness Mechanism", in: *Proceedings of the 9th International ISCRAM Conference*, 2012, Vancouver B.C., Canada.

Designing Decision Support Systems for Humanitarian Organisations

Requirements and Issues

K. Saksrisathaporn* — A. Charles* — A. Bouras *·**

Lyon 2 University, DISP, France

**Qatar University*

ABSTRACT. *The first step to ensure the success of applications in a specific field consists in producing a complete and representative model of the studied system. This alignment with reality is not easy to achieve though. This is particularly true in the humanitarian context, as in all new research areas, where researchers have difficulty identifying the right decision variables and parameters to be able to develop accurate and relevant models. At the same time, the uncertainty of the humanitarian operational environment does not facilitate data collection and analysis. This gap is true for many applications in the humanitarian sector, including research on ICT. This paper proposes an overview of the requirements and issues linked with the designing of decision support systems for humanitarian organisations.*

KEYWORDS: *Decision Support Systems, Humanitarian Response, ICT.*

1. Quick Review of Research Applications in the Context of Humanitarian Aid

The number of scientific articles dedicated to the study of Humanitarian Operations, either general or focused on a specific issue, was remarkably low ten years ago. This has changed recently with the publication of a substantial number of papers related to disaster management and the introduction of a dedicated journal (the Journal of Humanitarian Logistics and Supply Chain Management) in 2011. There were 120 publications registered in 2009 on this topic in the Science Direct database compared to only 20 publications in 1997 (Charles, 2010). About half of this research work uses quantitative techniques as optimisation decision-support systems. But due to the youth of this academic area, researchers are finding it difficult to develop accurate, and above all, reliable mathematical models to support their steps towards improvement. What is more, few of the current models consider the actual constraints in humanitarian operations and are thus feasible to introduce in the field (Kovács and Spens, 2011).

2. The Challenging Context of Humanitarian Aid

The humanitarian sector has been confronted with many changes over the last ten years. On the one hand, the global disaster profile is evolving toward more small- and medium-sized disasters, leading to more humanitarian operations all over the world. On the other hand, donors are pledging millions in donations in an economic context that imposes rationalisation (see Figure 1).

Disaster relief (also called emergency relief or humanitarian assistance) is therefore of vital interest for researchers, because it is confronted with many challenges, requiring innovative solutions. Much can be gained for researchers, but also for humanitarian agencies, who can seek advice on better ways of operating. This application to humanitarian aid is a challenging issue. Indeed, humanitarian organizations differ from private companies in many ways (Charles, 2010). Firstly, this sector is historically focused only on immediate response, in essence the day to day work needed to attend people affected by disasters, the beneficiaries. At the same time, such a focus has been criticised for fire-fighting and a lack of strategic thinking (Van Wassenhove, 2006). There is also a high turnover of staff, impeding strategic decision-making and reducing the possibilities to build knowledge on past experiences (Thomas and Kopcak, 2005). At the same time, decision-making needs to be quick, with high impact in terms of human live (Tomasini and Van Wassenhove, 2009; Charles *et al.*, 2010).

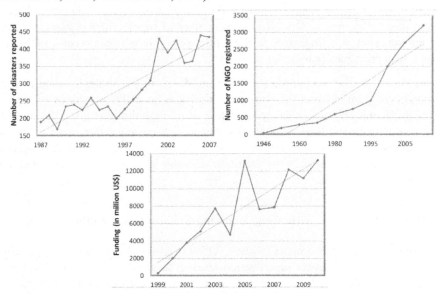

Figure 1. *Evolution of the numbers of disasters reported (Hoyois et al. 2007), of NGO registered (Durand et al. 2010), and of funding over the last years (www.ReliefWeb.int)*

Nevertheless, over the last fifteen years, a change towards recognition of the importance of supply chain management has been initiated by major organisations such as the IFRC (International Federation of the Red Cross and Red Crescent Societies) and WFP (World Food Program). "Other organizations in the sector are beginning to follow suit and raise the profile and professionalism of logisticians" (Van Wassenhove, 2006, p476). This has led to the definition of a clear "logistics strategy" for non-profit organisations.

3. The Lifecycle of Operations, a Call for Agile Systems

There has also been recognition that activities (or the lack of them) in the various phases of disaster relief impact on each other. For example, strategic prepositioning of items during the preparedness phase can reduce response times simultaneously with reductions in total costs (Charles et al., 2010). Different phases of disaster relief have also been depicted sequentially (Kovács and Spens, 2007) or in a cyclical fashion indicating the potential for learning loops (Safran, 2003; Pettit and Beresford, 2005). As for phases, a minimum distinction is made between preparedness and immediate response (Long, 1997; Van Wassenhove, 2006), to adding also mitigation and recovery (Altay and Green, 2006). In a similar vein, here we will refer to the phases of preparedness, immediate response, support, and dismantling (Charles and Lauras, 2011). The overall consensus is, though, that decisions taken in one phase of disaster relief impact on decisions in other phases – even though they may follow different principles of supply chain management, e.g. immediate relief adhering more to the agility principle whereas reconstruction can follow lean principles (Kovács et al., 2010).

In spite of the recognition of the need of more strategic supply chain management thinking and the impact of decisions in different phases of disaster relief impacting on each other, to date few or no organisations go as far as using optimisation-based decision-support systems nor is there any differentiation between the decision support needed for the various phases of disaster relief. Yet decision support systems should aim to facilitate decision-making during each phase of humanitarian operations.

4. Complex Situations, with Many Evolving Criteria to Take into Account

The use of decision support systems (DSS) is an important part of supply chain management. Almost every organization needs it to achieve an optimal level in its key performance indicators. This is true in both private and public sectors. Yet, quick and adequate decision making is sometimes difficult to achieve. Many criteria have to be taken into account. Cost efficiency, quickness and low environmental impact are often listed as key performance indicators for example (Davidson, 2006;

Beamon and Balcik, 2008, Pettit and Beresford, 2009; Huang *et al.*, 2011; Zhou *et al.*, 2011) Moreover, depending on the phase of operations (preparedness, immediate response, support, dismantling), priorities evolve (see Figure 2). For example, the speed of response is of prime importance at the beginning, especially following disasters such as earthquakes where it is hard to survive more than 5 days without aid. During this phase of immediate response, it is hard if not impossible to gather accurate data on the status of infrastructures, needs of beneficiaries, etc. This phase is also specific in terms of funding. With high media attention and specific appeal processes to accelerate the access to funds at the beginning of operations, operations efficiency is usually overlooked to give priority to aid effectiveness and reactivity. The situation is completely different after a few months or years. Funding usually becomes a real issue. One example is the situation in Haiti in 2012, two and a half year after the earthquake. According to the UN Office for the Coordination of Humanitarian Affairs, "as of 24 July, only US\$ 47 million was received against a total budget for the 2012 consolidated appeal (CAP) of US\$ 231 million." (OCHA, 2012). In other words, barely 20% of needs are covered for the latest phases of humanitarian operations in Haiti. By comparison, for the year 2010, 74% of the requirements were covered with more than 1.1 billion USD received (Financial tracking service, OCHA). In 2011, the percentage of the appeal covered was 55%.

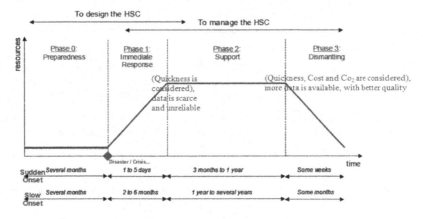

Figure 2. *Humanitarian operations lifecycle*
(modified from Pettit and Beresford, 2005 and Thomas, 2002)

Indeed, in the current situation, with humanitarian lacking the time and appropriate tools, it is difficult, if not impossible to apply those solutions. Humanitarian organizations, for example, have huge difficulties to build on past experiences, and often have to choose the first option they find because they need to take decisions quickly.

5. Conclusions

In the current situation, with humanitarian lacking the time and appropriate tools, it is difficult, if not impossible to collect data and devise new ways of operating. Focusing on ICT is one of the main ways to improve operations managements in this context. Yet, applications in this specific sector are not straightforward. First, a humanitarian response evolves over time. Available information and resources are constantly changing, in quantity as well as in quality. Priorities also evolve over time. Decisions are made mainly based on availability and quickness during the first two weeks, and become more and more cost oriented as the situation stabilizes. To insure its relevance for humanitarian operations, an ICT solution needs to address these challenges.

6. References

[1] Altay and Green, (2006), "OR/MS research in disaster operations management", *European Journal of Operational Research,* 175 (1), 475–493.

[2] Beamon and Balcik (2008), "Performance measurement in humanitarian relief chains". *International Journal of Public Sector Management* 21.1, pp.4–25.

[3] Charles, Lauras (2011) "An enterprise modelling approach for better optimisation modelling: application to the humanitarian relief chain coordination problem", *OR spectrum*, Vol. 33, No. 3, 815-841.

[4] Charles, Lauras and Van Wassenhove, (2010) "A model to assess the agility of supply chains: building on humanitarian experience" *International Journal of Physical Distribution and Logistics Management*, Vol. 40, No. 8/9, 2010, pp.722-741.

[5] Charles (2010) "Improving the design and management of agile supply chains: feedback and application in the context of humanitarian aid", PhD Thesis, Toulouse University.

[6] Davidson, (2006) "Key performance indicators in humanitarian logistics", MIT, Masters thesis.

[7] Durand et al. (2010), *Atlas de mondialisation : Comprendre l'espace mondial contemporain*, Les Presses de Sciences Po, fifth edition, 183p.

[8] Hoyois et al. (2007) Annual disaster statistical review: Numbers and trends 2006, http://www.emdat.be/publications

[9] Huang, Smilowitz, Balcik (2011) "Models for relief routing: Equity, efficiency and efficacy", *Transportation Research Part E: Logistics and Transportation Review*, Vol. 48, No. 1, pp.2-18

[10] Kovacs and Spens. (2007), "Humanitarian logistics in disaster relief operations" *International Journal of Physical Distribution & Logistics Management* 37.2 pp.99-114.

[11] Kovács, Matopoulos and Hayes. (2010), "A community-based approach to supply chain design", *International Journal of Logistics Research and Applications*, 13.5, pp.411-422.

[12] Kovács and Spens (2011) "Trends and developments in humanitarian logistics – a gap analysis". *International Journal of Physical Distribution and Logistics Management*, 41.1, pp.32-45.

[13] Long, D. (1997), "Logistics for disaster relief: engineering on the run", *IIE Solutions*, Vol. 29, No. 6, pp.26-9, 2012.

[14] OCHA (2012) financial tracking services, http://fts.unocha.org/reports/daily/ocha_R32 sum_A893___7_August_2012_(02_06).pdf.

[15] Pettit and Beresford. (2005) "Emergency relief logistics: an evaluation of military, non-military and composite response models". *International Journal of Logistics: Research & Applications* Vol. 8, pp.313-331.

[16] Pettit, Beresford, (2009) "Critical success factors in the context of humanitarian aid supply chains", *International Journal of Physical Distribution & Logistics Management*, 39.6, pp.450-468.

[17] Safran. (2003), "A strategic approach for disaster and emergency assistance". *5th Asian Disaster Reduction Center international meeting and the 2nd UN-ISDR Asian meeting* [online], 15–17 January 2003, Kobe, Japan. Available from: www.adb.org/Documents/ Policies?Disaster_Emergency/disaster_emergency.pdf.

[18] Thomas and Kopczak. (2005) "From logistics to supply chain management: the path forward in the humanitarian sector." Tech. rep. Fritz Institute, pp.1-15.

[19] Tomasini and Van Wassenhove (2009) *Humanitarian Logistics*. Palgrave Macmillan.

[20] Van Wassenhove. (2006) "Humanitarian aid logistics: supply chain management in high gear". *Journal of the Operational Research Society*, Vol. 57. pp.475-489.

[21] Zhou, Huang, Zhang (2011) "Identifying critical success factors in emergency management using a fuzzy DEMATEL method" *Safety Science*, Vol. 49, No. 2, February 2011, pp243-252.

From Global to Local Disaster Resilience

The Case of Typhoon Haiyan

T. Comes* — B. Van de Walle**

*Centre for Integrated Emergency Management
University of Agder, Norway*

**Tilburg University*
The Netherlands

ABSTRACT. *Resilience has been on the agenda of policy-making and research since the first Rio summit in 1992. Despite increased effort, public attention and an ever growing number of publications, since then, disasters associated with natural hazards alone have affected 4.4 billion people, caused US$ 2 trillion of damage and killed 1.3 million people. Clearly, there is a need to better understand the concept of disaster resilience, and to re-think risk management, sensemaking and decision support in the context of disasters. In this paper, we present our field research findings conducted in the aftermath of Typhoon Haiyan, which hit the Philippines in November 2013.*

KEYWORDS: *Disaster Resilience, Sensemaking and Decision Support, Humanitarian Information Management, Disaster Relief Supply Chain Management.*

1. Introduction

To understand the needs and requirements for sense making and decision support in practice, we explored the consequences of typhoon Haiyan on-site in December 2013 five weeks after the Hurricane had hit the Philippines. The response involved a large number of professionals and volunteers with very different background and skills – ranging from affected population, parents, trying to build up a living again, to highly professional responders setting up field hospitals and management structures and volunteers working remotely. Coordination structures between a large variety of international and national organizations, the government and the military were established at the national, provincial and local levels. These coordination efforts were accompanied by a significant information management effort, including the needs assessment of the affected population and monitoring and evaluation regarding the response and assistance provided.

To prepare for and respond to a disaster in such a complex and information-laden context requires a new understanding of *disaster resilience, relying on timely communication of relevant information.* In our presentation we will combine our findings from the field with on-going research on decision support and present our concept of resilience of in the context of globalised disaster response, including dynamic changes of the needs of population and responders.

2. Defining Disaster Resilience

As we cannot prevent hazards from happening, there is a shift in risk management: instead of reducing exposure or likelihood of a hazard event, decision-makers today more and more focus on improving resilience and/or reducing vulnerability (Birkmann, 2006; Kent, 2011). Although it is frequently used in different contexts, there is no generally accepted definition of resilience. Rather, the different concepts and methods to define and measure resilience reflect the diversity of fields, in which the term is used (Mitchell & Harris, 2012). In general, vulnerability can be understood as the characteristics of a system or asset that make it susceptible to the damaging effects of a hazard, whereas resilience refers to the coping capacity, including a dimension of learning (Johansson & Hassel, 2010; UN/ISDR, 2004). One of the most prominent aims of vulnerability assessments is improving preventative measures and allocating risk management resources in an efficient way, whereas resilience refers to the capacity to respond to change.

While for some authors, *resilience* is a factor that includes vulnerability (Klein, Nicholls, & Thomalla, 2003), we understand resilience as the ability of an actor, organization or system to cope with or adapt to stress (Pelling & High, 2005). In one of the earliest papers, Holling (1973) defined resilience as the ability of a system to absorb change while maintaining the same relations and characteristics. Today, this idea of maintaining or preserving structures has led to interpretations of resilience to reduce risk in the broad context of sustainable development (UN/ISDR, 2008). Initiatives such as the Rockefeller Resilient Cities Challenge or the Code4Resilience Program by the World Bank focus on programs that aim at improving resilience on a local (community or city) level closely related to sustainable development.

Instead of focussing on longer-term preparedness and development, this paper focuses on *disaster* resilience that we define the capacity to adequately respond to a hazard that creates a disruption in the processes and infrastructures that are vital for a society. Such *critical* infrastructures include services that are of immediate relevance for the physical health and well-being of the population, such as Water and Sanitation, Healthcare, or Food Supply (Rinaldi, 2004; Haemmerli & Renda, 2010) Others are related to the supply of vital goods, such as logistics, power supply, telecommunication, or banking. If some are all of these infrastructures are disrupted, the consequences of the disruptions propagate through the infrastructure network and neither the impact of nor the response to the failure can be limited to a sector or contained in a given region.

In disasters, the situation is even worse, since the initiating event – typically a natural or man-made hazard – creates in itself consequences that need to be dealt with. Harm to the population, environment and the wider socio-economic system needs to be alleviated while dealing with the disruptions. To organize the response in such settings, the UN coordinate the supply of aid by using clusters that represent key functions (Stumpenhorst, Stumpenhorst & Razum, 2011). Logistics, Emergency Telecommunication or Water and Sanitation are linked to widely recognized CIs. Other functions, such as Protection or Recovery are more generic, showing that the needs the notion of 'criticality' changes, i.e., what is perceived what a community or society perceives as vital is prone to shifts.

A typical example is the response to typhoon Haiyan, which made landfall in the Philippines on November 8, 2013. More than 14 million people were affected, and more than 4 million are still displaced. The UN organized the response into 11 clusters, and an international effort was made to save lives, provide protection, telecommunication, food, shelter and healthcare. This effort was supported by the work of remote volunteers, organized in networks such as the Humanitarian Open Street Map Team or the Standby Task Force.

3. Understanding the Dynamics of a Disaster

Communities or societies are complex systems and characterised by dynamic behaviour, non-linearity and emergence (Leichenko & O'Brien, 2002). A disaster is typically a shock that drastically change a system's behaviour. Therefore, we propose an approach that acknowledges that the dynamic nature of resilience, which will change with the phases of disaster management. Particularly in the early phases after an incident, information is scarce, uncertain and evolves dynamically. Starting from an information perspective, there are three types of information that need to be combined to assess resilience in the context of a disaster:

– *Structural information:* relatively stable or only slowly evolving information, e.g., topography of a region, meteorology.

– *Trends and developments:* information capturing meso-scale behaviour and predictable patterns such as economic growth, infrastructure capacity or migration.

– *Characteristic local information* capturing the direct and indirect impact of the hazard event.

To assess the consequences of the hazard event and to keep track of the needs and the impact of the response it is important to consider the temporal dimension. It is not sufficient to compare a sequence of snapshot assessments, and to derive adequate response. While it is important to analyse the needs and activities (for instance in terms of a 3W reporting – who does what and where?), we suggest embracing the fact that a crisis fundamentally changes the system, including technical components, preferences and critical needs. Response and recovery will naturally lead to a change of physical infrastructures and organizational processes and services within the wider socio-economic context. Therefore, we understand disaster resilience as a dynamic concept, closely linked to recovery processes and to the globalized response community. Understanding the dynamics requires focussing on relations and trends, patterns and risk drivers rather than getting situational updates and reports.

4. Challenges for Communication and Information Processing

Globalised communication enables information exchange between local communities and national governments, professional responders and volunteers, responders in the field and headquarters and donors. Each of these actors has different competences and skills, values, believes and aims. Equally different are the decisions that need to be made by each group, ranging from operational response to strategic positioning of an aid organization.

Due to this diversity, many responders and those who support response efforts describe the difficulties in pinpointing and finding information that may be useful for specific information needs. In part, this difficulty is linked to the lack of context and personal knowledge or experience with this very disaster that anyone working remotely will naturally have. Moreover, information is processed with different tools and accessed via different channels. While in headquarters and remote, access to electricity and computation resources are hardly limited, the situation in the field is very different. The massive destruction of infrastructure leads to communication that is geared towards high efficiency and low use of bandwidth or electricity. Satellite phones or walkie talkies and direct forms of communication are very frequent, down- and upload are brittle. Interoperability largely can be reduced to accessibility: can the information be obtained? And can it be interpreted and understood? The latter is most important in the communication with the local population.

The unguided and massive production of pieces of information happens largely spontaneously as an answer to a need that is perceived. Extrapolating individual needs (such as specific information about the population in a barangay, or about where to source a specific product, or request for information from a trusted source such as the local network) lead to a high degree of redundancy and a huge amount of information produced. On February 15, 2014, almost 12,000 information products about the response to Haiyan were available on reliefweb.info, and almost 1,500 maps had been produced.

Although confronted with this information overload in terms of snapshots and situation reports, which was unfiltered by limitations of bandwidth or accessibility when working remotely, a small group of researchers perceived a lack of knowledge about the reality of the strategic and operational decision-making in the response to Haiyan. The team came together under the umbrella of the Disaster Resilience Lab (DRL) with the aim to understand the needs for sensemaking and decision support in the field as well as commence an introductory understanding of how information products may be used by humanitarian practitioners in this context. Despite our common interest on how information is processed, communicated and shared, our backgrounds and research fields are very diverse – ranging from emergency medicine to supply chain management. These different lenses were not only the foci, via which we interpreted the information products when working remotely, but were also present in our intuitive understanding of the operations and the questions we asked in the field. In this sense, our research can be understood as an effort of co-construction and co-creation from both different scientific disciplines and via our engagement with practitioners.

In our presentation, we will discuss the design of our field research in the Philippines after Typhoon Haiyan, acknowledging the uncertainty and differences in understanding of researchers vs. practitioners, and reflect on the research and compare this approach with other networks of remote collaboration and provide an outlook on future research design in the field.

5. Acknowledgements

The authors thank the interviewees who devoted their valuable time in often difficult and trying conditions. This field research would not have been possible without the efforts of the Disaster Resilience Lab and its supporters.

6. References

[1] Birkmann, Joern. (2007). Risk and vulnerability indicators at different scales: Applicability, usefulness and policy implications. *Environmental Hazards*, 7(1), 20–31.

[2] Haemmerli, B. & Renda, A. (2010) *Protecting Critical Infrastructure in the EU*. Brussels: Centre for European Policy Studies.

[3] Holling C.S. 1973. Resilience and stability of ecological systems. *Ann. Rev. of Ecol. Systems*, 4(1), 1–23.

[4] Johansson, J., & Hassel, H. (2010). An approach for modelling interdependent infrastructures in the context of vulnerability analysis. Reliability Engineering & System Safety, 95(12), 1335–1344.

[5] Kent, R. (2011). *Disaster risk reduction and changing dimensions and dynamics of future crisis drivers*. Geneva, Switzerland.

[6] Klein, R. J. T., Nicholls, R. J., & Thomalla, F. (2003). Resilience to natural hazards: How useful is this concept? *Global Environmental Change Part B: Environmental Hazards*, *5*(1), 35–45.

[7] Leichenko, R. M., & O'Brien, K. L. (2002). The Dynamics of Rural Vulnerability to Global Change: The Case of southern Africa. *Mitigation and Adaptation Strategies for Global Change*, *7*(1), 1–18.

[8] Mitchell, T. & Harris, K. (2012). Resilience: A risk management approach. ODI Background Notes, London. Available online: http://www.odi.org.uk/sites/odi.org.uk/files/odi-assets/publications-opinion-files/7552.pdf.

[9] Stumpenhorst, M., Stumpenhorst, R., & Razum, O. (2011). The UN OCHA cluster approach: gaps between theory and practice. *Journal of Public Health,* 19(6), 587-592.

[10] UN-OCHA. (2013). *Philippines: Typhoon Haiyan Situation Report No. 19.* Manila/New York. Retrieved from http://reliefweb.int/report/philippines/philippines-typhoon-haiyan-situation-report-no-19-28-november-2013.

[11] UN/ISDR. (2008). *Indicators of progress: guidance on measuring the reduction of disaster risks and the implementation of the Hyogo Framework for Action.* Geneva, Switzerland: United Nations secretariat of the International Strategy for Disaster Reduction (UN/ISDR).

Workshop 8

Corporate Standardisation Management

Report

Kai Jakobs

RWTH Aachen University
ComSys
52074 Aachen, Germany
kai.jakobs@cs.rwth-aachen.de

The Workshop aimed to address the variety of aspects that relate to the management of standardisation. That is, looked at managerial issues of corporate standardisation as well as at standards management in the public sector. This included aspects like, for instance, organisational structures, intra-organisational processes, decision making, education and training, links to general management models etc. The main overall objective was to contribute to a development of best-practices in organisational standardisation management. The workshop comprised two sessions, one offering 'General Insights' and the other looking at 'Case Studies'.

The first paper, by Christian Sillaber, Michael Brunner and Ruth Breu of the University of Innsbruck, presented and discussed 'A framework for the management of intra-organizational security process standardization'. This framework supports the standardisation of collaborative security processes and the management of business security requirements, within and across organisational boundaries. While essentially representing a technical solution to a decidedly non-technical problem, the presentation and subsequent discussion also highlighted the need for adequate user training and education; after all, the human is the one most unpredictable? component in any information system.

The second paper also put emphasis on the human aspect. The paper 'Some Factors Influencing Corporate ICT Standardisation Management' by Kai Jakobs, RWTH Aachen University, presented a classification of corporate standardisation strategies to support the overall business strategy in a given sector. It also discussed the pillars of such a strategy. These included in-depth knowledge of the complex ICT standardisation landscape, the characteristics of the potentially relevant standards bodies, the links between them and how they could be exploited. Also, the need for well-trained staff was highlighted.

The paper by Gamze Canarslan, from the Turkish Standardization Institute, came to similar conclusion. Her paper on 'Human Resources Management Strategies in Public Sector Entities Engaging in Standards Developing Processes' highlighted the need for well-educated, well-trained and highly motivated employees to successfully represent the public sector in standards setting. Particular focus was on the necessary soft-skills and on the need for adequate motivational measures. The discussion showed that the problems are very similar, if not even identical, to those encountered in the private sector.

Amalia Foukaki, from Lund University presented an on-going case study on 'Standardization decision-making and best practices: The case of a large Swedish automotive company'. The company in question had made some bad experiences with inadequate standardisation management in the past and had been eager to not let this happen again. Obviously, the somewhat peculiar approach subsequently adopted works just fine for them. The discussion centred on the question why the company makes even most internal standards freely available (to contribute to a more homogenous standards environment across the industry) and why the internal approach to standardisation was purely reactive (to solve real-world internal problems).

'Standards roles in Hacklin's strategic model: The Space business ecosystem case' was the title of the paper by Karim Benmeziane, Bureau Normalisation de l'Aéronautique et de l'espace and Anne Mione, Montpellier 1 University. Hacklin identifies four basic corporate strategies to survive in converging technologies. Only one of these, the 'Technology Pioneer' is associated with standardisation. Using the case of satellite positioning systems and space launcher services, the paper aims to show that also two other identified strategies, the 'Ecosystem Aggregators' and the 'Business Remodelers' could strategically benefit from standards setting activities.

Finally, Tore Hoel of the Oslo and Akershus University College of Applied Sciences presented a paper entitled 'Lack of openness as a potential failure in standardisation management – lessons learnt from setbacks in European learning technology standardisation'. He discusses the case of the highly successful CEN Workshop on Learning Technologies and its eventual closure by CEN because of an alleged misconduct of the Workshop – it made its output publicly available. He also stressed the point that the implementation of standards should also be addressed by standards bodies. The discussion brought up the issue about some standards bodies' business models and the importance of generating income by selling standards.

Lack of Openness as a Potential Failure in Standardisation Management

Lessons Learnt from Setbacks in European Learning Technology Standardisation

Tore Hoel

Oslo and Akershus University College of Applied Sciences
Norway
tore.hoel@hioa.no

ABSTRACT. *Formal standards organisations (e.g., CEN and ISO) struggle to adapt to the work processes of the 21st century, especially within ICT standardisation where open innovation principles are promoted. European pre-standardisation activities in the field of learning technologies are now (beginning of 2014) put on hold due to resistance from CEN to allow for open processes and open distribution of documents free-of-charge. This paper analyse this case on the background of a holistic standards process and potential failure model. Openness is presented as a key factor in enabling pre-conceptualisation, scoping, negotiating, drafting, implementing and maintaining ICT standards. Insisting on a business model of selling standards documents could potentially hamper participation from research and restrict implementations and user engagement in a way that for this domain puts the whole standardisation system at risk.*

KEYWORDS: *Standardisation Management, ICT Standardisation, Open Innovation, European Standardisation Organisation CEN, Standardisation Failure, Open Document Policies.*

1. Introduction

"The policy officer [responsible for the implementation of the European Union Opening Up Education Action plan] made it clear that by open standards was meant free-of-charge specifications (which is clearly clashing with CEN's business model)" (CEN/CENELEC, 2013). This quote from a case document of CEN Technical Board shows that the main European standards organisation is finding itself at odds with a major European (and international) innovation policy trend, founded on openness (Bogers, 2011). It is not surprising that standardisation organisations, like other content industries, struggle to adjust to new publishing models. What is surprising, – in this case – is CEN's answer to the challenges: Instead of entering into a dialogue to learn about the new landscape with the rather limited community of learning technology stakeholders, the organisation just shuts down the main European focused learning technology standardisation operation and cancels projects.

Royalty-free standards are a recent phenomenon, dating from the late 1990s and early 2000s, and coinciding with the growth of the World Wide Web, the use of open source, and the democratisation of standards and participation in standardisation (Cargill, 2011). Free-of-charge standards for use by anyone for any purpose are not primarily a question of the cost of buying the standards documents. For some developer and implementer communities, "open and free" have become markers for a number of factors that at the end define the qualities of the normative consensus process they are looking for. If *not* open and free, – people, ideas, processes, timing, market positioning – all the pieces that make up the complex ecosystem of ICT standardisation may not be available. And, as there are alternative standard setting organisations out there, why go with the ones that are stuck with yesterday's models of standard setting as a business of selling physical documents?

This paper is sparked by the current challenges in European learning technology standardisation. The paper is experiential; with support of a case study, it relies on the author's observations over the last more than ten years in standardisation fora, most of this period in leadership positions as workshop chair or national delegate.

2. Related Work

Standardisation as a technical or economic phenomenon is analysed and praised for its contribution to innovation (Bogers, 2011; Ecke & Pinto, 2008; Blind, 2009). However, there are not many studies on why practical standardisation efforts fail, and what lessons could be learnt. This author has been concerned about quality issues of learning technology standardisation and has warned that this could impact the necessary legitimacy of the activity leading to lack of support to standardisation (Hollins & Hoel, 2010), ill scoped projects (Hoel & Mason, 2012), or meta design choices that produce standards that are too complex or too difficult to implement (Hoel & Hollins, 2011).

Based on models of Egyedi (2008) and Cargill (1995) and previous studies by the author the matrix of potential failure points, Table 1, can be constructed. One challenge of anticipatory standardisation is stakeholder engagement. To boost European industry, the European Commission has proposed to use standards as a way to leverage R&D results, which "inherently means 'early standardisation': standardisation takes place at a very early stage of technology development" (Ecke & Pinto, 2008). However, it is not self-evident that the R&D community wants to work with the particular standards community or standard setting organisation.

Stage	Failure modes
Pre-conceptualisation Idea phase: Input from Research & Practice	The standard fails to get started R & D community lacks motivation to interface with standardisation Requirement solicitation too weak to provide input from the market No prototype implementations available to demonstrate proposed concepts SSO without appeal to standardisation experts
Conceptualisation Scoping of New Work Item	The standard fails to get started; the standards group fails to achieve consensus, and deadlocks Inadequate scope (e.g., too wide) too weak guidance for drafting Non-representative expert group Work based on misfitting meta design strategies
Discussion Specification	The standard suffers from "feature creep", and misses the market opportunity. Time consuming specification process Diverting interests in the standards group prolongs drafting
Writing Specification	The standard suffers from "feature creep", and misses the market opportunity. The standard grows too complex and difficult to implement
Implementation	The standard is finished and the market ignores it. The standard is finished and implementations are incompatible. Too few implementations to feed maintenance and feedback loop The standard is accepted and is used to manage the market.
Input / Feedback / Maintenance	Users are not heard – requirements are not solicited SMEs do not relate to standards community – see no incentives to contribute to development or maintenance

Table 1. *Stages of standardisation and possibilities for failures*

3. The Case of CEN WS/LT

The CEN Workshop for Learning Technologies was officially launched in February 1999. As a Workshop under the CEN umbrella, WS/LT has published CEN Workshop Agreements, a kind of lightweight standards that reflect the consensus of the experts sitting around the table. The Workshop is open to all, without any prior endorsement from CEN Member Bodies. In 2007 CEN established a technical committee (TC 353), which has been working in close cooperation with the workshop, publishing some of its CWAs as European Norms.

In 2013, after the finalisation of one of the most successful projects in the history of the Workshop, in terms of stakeholder engagement in development, the CEN/CENELEC Management Centre (CCMC) put on the brakes. The CEN Standards Director and Program Manager were alarmed by the openness of the work procedures, e.g., by using a wiki for collaborative writing, commenting, and consultation outside the password protected wall of the standards setting body. The CCMC insisted on a work process restricted to the use of an e-mail reflector with a limited list of participants, and document exchange via a repository system. Minutes from the Workshop meetings and e-mail exchange between CCMC and the Workshop chairs show that it is the "sustainability of the standardisation system" that is as stake. In 2013 CEN also introduced a new partnership organisation fee of 500€ per year that will impact on the ability of CEN workshops and committees to solicit input from external organisations, e.g., EU projects.

4. Discussion

The long term effects could be a setback to the ability of standardisation to contribute to innovation within the educational market. The European Commission seems to put a lot of trust in standards being able to "level the playing field for all market players" within education, provided they "remain open" (EC, 2013). A response by CEN, only focussing on the threat to their business model, seems to ignore what drives the innovation cycle within learning, education and training (LET).

The learning technology standardisation ecosystem is fragile and needs to be carefully nurtured to prevent breakdowns. The closed model of formal standardisation has no appeal to the most innovative companies and research communities, and therefore, the most promising actors will not even enter *the pre-conceptualisation stage* of standardisation, let alone stay on through the more tedious phases of negotiations and drafting. And the standardisation bureaucrats cannot fill their place. In the last ten years, most of the contributions to European learning technology standardisation have come from experts engaged in European projects. The European Commission has committed the projects to liaise with standards organisation as a means of dissemination. When the experts are university employees devoted to open research and open access, IPR barriers as pay-per-copy represent a dead end at the very beginning of a development process. Furthermore, when the European Commission mandates open access to all results of projects, it is no longer a question of the opinion of the individual; it is a matter of EU policy (CEN/CENELEC, 2013). Even if the research communities are reluctant to contribute, if there is a need one could expect the market, i.e., the industries, vendors and SMEs, to solve the problem. However, the market for learning technologies is very fragmented with a mix of small enterprise players together with big institutional and even governmental actors – none of them seeing learning technology standardisation as their main field of interest. With a very rapid innovation cycle it is again the flow of ideas that is the challenge. Open innovation is an answer to this challenge, and the companies that manage to cope with the tension of knowledge sharing and protection are the winners (Bogers, 2011).

If projects pass the first failure point and enter *conceptualisation and drafting phase* the need for openness prevails. And this need is observed by formal standardisation as well. CEN and ISO adhere to the principles of transparency and an open and due process, and would not like to be described as not embracing the principle of openness. However, Krechmer (2005) has observed that different stakeholders in standardisation (creators, implementers, users) emphasise different aspects of openness. Open documents are not an important requirement for standards creators, who are more concerned about the formalities of the process, like open meetings, consensus, due process, and open IPR (lack of patents). On the other side, implementers and users have more practical interests, and access to documents and functional aspects of the specification are more in focus.

Also in the *consensus and drafting phases* of standardisation, openness is important. In the war stories of formal standardisation, 'the table' plays an important role. Who are sitting around the table, and what are the positions and how to they develop towards consensus? (Jakobs et al., 1998). The challenge of managing consensus processes with active back channels will vary from project to project, and there is no one size fits all. For the learning technology standardisation, however, it has been extremely important to solicit inputs and comments alongside the drafting. Waiting for a formal consultation after the first draft will not be productive.

5. Conclusions

The fragile standardisation ecosystem with different actors playing different roles in different phases of the standardisation cycle is prone to failures. When a project is initiated by university researchers, scoped and conceptualised by standardisation managers, drafted by standards experts, and implemented by SME entrepreneurs – and they all are partly different persons, coordination and knowledge exchange become imperative. This study shows that the European Standardisation Organisation is moving in the wrong direction by establishing barriers that are not easy to understand or accept by the stakeholder communities.

More research is needed to explore why a standard setting body like CEN feels that their business model is threatened by free-of-charge CWAs from a rather peripheral Workshop like CEN WS/LT. When a "substantial part of the standardisation work is financed by voluntary and gratuitous participation from businesses, through their participation in committees, financing of projects, etc.", and there is no market for these standards and no sale, one would think the "obligation to protect the [commercial] value of these Publications" should be irrelevant, and other values of the CEN system could come into play. CEN guidelines promotes the principle of "the widest possible dissemination and use of Publications throughout the world" (CEN/CENELEC, 2010).

6. References

Blind K. 'Standardisation: a catalyst for innovation'. Inaugural Addresses Research in Management Series; Erasmus School of Economics (ESE); 2009.

Bogers M. 'The open innovation paradox: knowledge sharing and protection in R&D collaborations'. *European Journal of Innovation Management*. 2011; 14(1): 93–117.

Cargill C.F. 'Why Standardization Efforts Fail'. *Journal of Electronic Publishing*. 15 August, 2011; 14(1).

Cargill, C.F. 'A Five-Segment Model for Standardization', in *Standards Policy for Information Infrastructure*, ed. Brian Kahin and Janet Abbate (Cambridge, Mass.: The MIT Press, 1995), 79–99.

CEN/CENELEC Guide 10. Guidelines for distribution and sales of CEN-CENELEC publications, 2nd edition; 2010.

CEN/CENELEC Management Centre. *Follow-up on CEN/WS on 'Learning technologies'*. BT N 9384. Issue date: 2013-11-13.

Ecke, P., Pinto, P. 'EU Study on the specific policy needs for ICT standardisation'. oa.uninova.pt; 2008.

Egyedi, T. M. 'An Implementation Perspective on Sources of Interoperability and Standards' Dynamics', in Egyedi, T. M., Blind, K. *The Dynamics of Standards*; (2008).

European Commission. 'Opening up Education: Innovative teaching and learning for all through new Technologies and Open Educational Resources'. COM(2013) 654 final; Brussels; 25.9.2013.

Hoel, T., Hollins, P.A. 'Standards for Learning, Education and Training – a proposal for an improved process', *ICALT* 2011.

Hoel, T., Mason, J. 'Deficiencies of scope statements in ITLET standardization'. In I G. Biswas et al. (eds.) (2012). *Proceedings of the 20th International Conference on Computers in Education*. Singapore: Asia-Pacific Society for Computers in Education.

Hollins, P.A., Hoel, T. 'Learning Technology Standards Adoption – Process Improvement and Output legitimacy', *ICALT* 2010.

Jakobs K, Procter R, Williams R. 'User participation in standards setting—the panacea?' *StandardView*. 1998; 6(2): 85–9.

Krechmer, K. 'Open standards requirements'. *International Journal of IT Standards and Standardization Research (IJITSR)*, 2005; 4(1), 43–61.

The Individual in Standard Setting

Selection, Training, Motivation in the Public Sector

G. Canarslan

Turkish Standardization Institute, OFİM,
Ostim Mah. 100. Yıl Bul. No: 99, Kat: 2 OSTİM, Ankara, Turkey
gcanarslan@tse.org.tr

ABSTRACT. *This paper seeks to analyze the effect of and correct of use of human resources strategies in the public sector for efforts in standard developing processes. The motivational background of public entities in engaging in standard developing processes has been summarized along with often encountered issues throughout the processes. This summary was done to be leveraged on to produce a practical approach to human resources management. Criteria for selection of personnel, training outline for the personnel engaging in standard developing activities have been emphasized. Last but not least, measures to keep the motivational factors high have been outlined.*
KEYWORDS: *Public Sector, Standard Development, Personnel, Selection, Training, Motivation.*

1. Human Resources Perspective in Standard Setting in Public Sector

Organizations participate in standard setting organizations (SSOs)' and standards development organizations (SDOs)' processes via their workforce. This article analyzes the effect of, and correct use of human resources managament strategies in the public sector in the standard setting processes. Joining an SSO/SDO imposes financial burden on the organization in terms of participation fees, personnel manhours and expenses. Additionally, public sector has important goals in joining SSO/SDO framework. For this investment to materialize as added value and for goals to be reached, it is required to construct effective, correct and to the point human resources management strategies. Such strategies include: the criteria for selection of the personnel to be employed in SSO/SDO activities, ideas for training procedures, and motivation enhancement methods.

2. Public Sector Goals in Joining SSOs/SDOs

Public entitites engage in SSO/SDO work for various reasons. Some of the most significant factors, both strategic and economic, are listed here below, in order to draw up a connection to possible the human resources management strategies to reach them. Public entities become part of SSOs/SDOs in order to gain easy and accurate access to the standards and the processes. With know-how becoming more and more important for each and every industry or service activity, public entities from different countries are becoming more active in standard making processes in order to influence an industry, the evolution of standards, a region, or simply to meet other interested players in a given niche. The public entity may aim to easily adapt the standards by an organization into their regional territory by joining that SSO/SDO. Full membership to CEN/CENELEC, for instance, has allowed TSE to publish EN standards as TS in shorter time periods. Another goal is to advance in technical know-how, which may then be shared with domestic stakeholders. Oftentimes the public entity becomes part of an SSO/SDO out of the pure necessity of introducing a new standard or family of standards. The efforts of Turkey in founding the SMIIC framework and consequent participation are a good example. Economic goals are not to be overlooked. The public entity may aim to manipulate import barriers in some contexts. The goal may be to make sure that domestic industry is being judged fairly, activities may be pursued so that methods out of reach of the domestic industry or services sector are not becoming compulsory immediately. Or, the aim may be to lobby for a certain method of a conational company's or R&D organization's transcendence over competing parties.

3. Issues Encountered on the Way to Active Participation in Standard Developing Processes

If a public entity fails to define key areas for active participation in standard making, the effects will not be significant. It might be better for Norway to 'spare' efforts in SMIIC standards making, given the lack of expertise in Islamic production practises and the relatively low request from the Norwegian citizens for SMIIC compliant products and services; however it would make more sense for the country to become actively involved in activities in offshore drilling standards or for sustainable ocean fishing. The next step is defining the goals to be achieved. By actively participating in standard making process, the public entity has the possibility to influence the timelines and application methods of standards in their country of origin. Additionally; the public entity has to have an accurate picture of the status quo of the country. The stakeholders include, but are not limited to, the following: the public sector, the private sector, universities, NGOs, trade associations. There might be conflicts of interest of between these stakeholders. The public sector may be looking forward to tighten the emission standards, but the private sector may not be ready for the correct and full application of the said standard. Understanding the origins of the disputes that can arise within cooperative standard setting is a crucial step in finding ways to resolve them (Layne-Farrar, 2010). Standard making is a long, gruesome process. It requires years of research, work, follow-up, participation to the events in order to influence the process in accordance with recognized goals. Sometimes the priority will be to create a single specification, sometimes the aim will be to create multiple related standards, in other cases the job will be maintaining a family of standards. Absenteeism is a problem that may be encountered so easily during standard developing processes.

4. Human Resources Perspective in Addressing these Issues

The public entity's standard developing team 'consists of "standardization talents", namely persons who master professional knowledge or expertise of standardization, are competent in domestic and international standardization activities, […], who mainly consist of standardization technicians, standardization researchers, and standardization administrative managers' (Wand & Zhao, 2013). Carefully designed human resources strategies are required for this team.

4.1. Selection

Derous and De Witte describe the Social Process model on Selection (SPS model) as having eight characteristics. They assume job applicants to value: (1) provision of general information on the job opening, (2) participation and control, (3) openness to assertiveness, (4) creation of transparency of testing, (5) provision of feedback, (6) guarantee of objectivity and standardization, (7) assurance of human treatment, and (8) respect for privacy and job relevance of information gathering (Derous & de Witte, 2011). The model may be a good start. Professional criteria for personnel selection must include requirements for knowledge in the field. The personnel would ideally be able to understand the position and the requests of the private sector. The experience requirement may be evaluated on a case by case basis. Economy knowledge may be required as well. Most bachelors' programmes offer basic micro and macro economy courses as must courses, course content or grade may be evaluated. Basic sustainability knowledge shall be required, or adequate training measures may be taken. The work environment is multinational, accordingly, language skills shall be imposed. Personal traits include: good negotiation skills, good communication skills, an open personality, being a good mediator and being fit for group work. Another key property is self-motivation. Standard developing positions are similar to research jobs: Goals are not always clear and obvious, deadlines are long. For such positions, self-motivated people are better matches. Furthermore, an analytical thinker with a mind-set that is flexible but straight forward at the same time would be ideal for: reaching conclusions, sensing where the standard developing efforts are leading, and bringing together facts and innovating actions.

4.2. *Human Resources Perspective in Addressing these Issues: Training*

The personnel need to be adequately trained. The training agenda may include, but in any case shall not be limited to the following. First of all, an extensive orientation program about the public sector is necessary. The non-profit organization framework and management not be clear to all employees, especially if they have no working experience or if they are coming from the private sector after many years of service. In order to eliminate future misunderstandings, all new personnel need to be adequately informed about how things work in the public sector. After that, an adequate orientation to the entity itself would be beneficial. Every public entity has a defined mission within the government or regional framework. This mission has to be communicated to the new personnel. Most technical personnel come across standards of some sort during their work, they may know how to read or to apply a technical standard, but most probably the functions and structure of the SSOs/SDOs or the life cycle of a standard are unbeknownst to them. Adequate education shall be provided. The employees shall be kept updated about the industry. Big players in the industry may be asked to provide training on how they conduct business. This may help to establish connections which may become helpful and key in following steps of the standard developing process. The personnel will need to work in a multi-national, multi-stakeholder environment, they should be provided with good communication skills and negotiation techniques.

4.3. *Human Resources Perspective in Addressing these Issues: Motivation*

In the article the importance of selecting self-motivated employees had been highlighted. The personnel needs to be strong willed and needs to be able to put up with the pressures which may arise from the negotiations within the standard developing framework. Influencing the direction in which a given standard or group of standards may evolve is not an easy work. To keep the self-motivation traits alive, the public entity should embrace a meritocratic career opportunities approach. Differences between the personnel participating in standard developing activities (performance, responsibility, experience differences) must correspond to differences in rewards (wages, career opportunities etc.) In addition, the personnel need to be recognized for the efforts they put in a certain area of work, addressed and praised openly. As long as self motivation is supported with extrinsic motivation, performance will be enhanced. The personnel would be motivated if his efforts are recognized and further career opportunities are offered to him. Training in the field, trainings which may come in handy during his work (business English, anyone?), team building sessions; as in any area of activity become good motivation tools and they would provide to be positive influence on the work. Sending staff to trainings not only helps increase their worth as personnel, but it also benefits the public entity in staying abreast of new techniques and technology. Locke's (1968) goal setting theory states that intentions play a significant part in behaviorial pattern. Intentions towards goals can be manipulated. In this paper we have defined certain goals of standard developing. From the personnel point of view, the goals need to be specific, difficult but yet achievable, measurable and shared (within the country, within the industy, within the public entity, etc.). The goals must be perceived as reachable. As an essential part of activities for motivating the personnel, an open doors policy regarding other stakeholders is important. A big part of the job in standard developing is streamlining and consolidating the needs of various stakeholders, and the employee will act confident knowing his employer is willing to communicate, cooperation also helps to publicly demonstrate commitment to markets and technologies. The public entity, needs to ambrace the whole life cycle of the standard and the process. The famous 'Plan, Do, Check, Act' of Deming takes a more complicated approach in standard developing. The IEEE states that the standard developing cycle is as follows : 'Initiating the Project, Mobilizing the Work Group, Drafting the Standard, Balloting the Standard, Gaining Final Approval, Maintaining the Standard' and on. The personnel may not be able to assist the whole process. The approach to work, the motivational measures, the goal setting shall be applied with this knowledge. Maintaining the standard and keeping the standard alive are important tasks. The motivational measures should be set up accordingly. If the public entity is announcing that they would be paying incentives to 5 most successful personnel, measuring the success with the number of amendments they get to succesfully ballot in a year, that would not be as big as an incentive, as most personnel would be able to work on a single amendment for longer time periods. Financial worries of the personnel need to be eliminated. During the meetings and the activities aimed at standard developing, the public entity should be able to provide their personnel with adequate lodging and travel expenses. When reimbursements are made, time frames need to be respected.

5. Conclusions

In this article components of an effective human resources management strategy for public entities seeking to actively work in standard developing processes have been analyzed. The reasons for participation and the problems encountered have been listed to come up with the correct personnel traits and to structure the components of an effective human resources management strategy. These components include professional and personal traits to be requested from the personnel during recruitment stage. These traits contain, but are not limited to, knowledge about the field, economy knowledge, language capabilities, experience in the private sector, communication style, analytical thinking abilities and so on.

Training necessities for the personnel have been determined as: public sector orientation, orientation to the specific public entity and the world of standards, and other training activities designed to keep the personnel up to date about the situation of the sector and the technical advances in the sector. Communication tools need to be provided as well. Ways to keep the motivation high were also loooked at. The personnel shall be given meritocratic career opportunities, trainings, and proper goal setting. In addition, the public entity has to support the personnel on many levels including having an open doors policy vis-a-vis other stakeholders, embracing the whole life cyle of the standard and the process and providing adequate financial support.

6. References

Derous E, De Witte K. 'Looking at selection from a social process perspective: Towards a social process model on personnel selection'. *European Journal of Work and Organizational Psychology*, 2001; vol. 10, No, 3, p. 319.

Layne-Farrar A., *Business Models and the Standard Setting Process*, The Pros&Cons of Standard Setting, Swedish Competition Authority, 2010.

Wang Y, Zhao W. China National Institution of Standardization. *Framework of Standardization Education System*. European Telecommunications Standards Institute. http://docbox.etsi.org/Workshop/2013/201306_ICES/Presentations/7-Papers%20and%20 posters/Zhou%20et%20al%20CNIS%20China%20Framework%20of%20Standardization %20Education%20System.pdf (accessed on 16 December 2013); 2-3.

A Framework for the Management of Intra-Organizational Security Process Standardization

C. Sillaber — M. Brunner — R. Breu

Technikerstraße 21a
6020 Innsbruck, Austria
christian.sillaber@uibk.ac.at
michael.brunner@uibk.ac.at
ruth.breu@uibk.ac.at

ABSTRACT. *The increasing need for service organizations to ensure compliance with various laws and regulations as well as different internal and external policies and security standards requires businesses to ensure a high level of standardization of their internal and external security processes in order to achieve efficiency and to avoid costs. As a direct result of different stakeholder needs, organizations are required to manage a balance between aligning security goals with organizational goals and ensuring efficient external compliance checks, often conducted through third party audits. To align with an associated strategy, we suggest an IT architecture with embedded workflows to manage this balance between the needs of security process standardization and managerial goals. A prototype and evaluation with encouraging results show the viability of the proposed architecture design for a security management system to standardize intra-organizational security processes.*

KEYWORDS: *Security Process Standardization, Collaborative Security Management.*

1. Introduction

As service organizations increasingly embrace new models of IT service orchestration to create new business models, information security management can no longer be an isolated task (Marinos et al., 2009). Internally, service organizations create and manage complex service orchestrations in order to provide value to their respective customers (Mohammed et al., 2010). From a security perspective, the increased complexity of intra-organizational processes leads to an increase in the number of security requirements on their actual business processes – referred to as Business Security Requirements – such organizations have to properly manage (Subashini et al., 2011; Susanto et al., 2011). This is required to ensure compliance with various laws and policies as well as contractual obligations to customers.

A branch of a large IT outsourcing organization (several billion dollar annual turnover; more than 70,000 employees; anonymous for confidentiality reasons) operates a cloud based streaming business that offers media content distribution for corporate customers. Due to the complex nature of their service landscape and the high number of different internal processes, services and components which are distributed around the world, managing the standardization of security processes is a difficult task. Efficient management of business security requirements in a standardized way is a requirement for day to day IT operations, a task that goes hand in hand with the documentation of said requirements for both internal and external use (Chakraborty et al., 2010). However, this call for standardization is often ignored, when it comes to the management of business security requirements which are more than often found in isolated silos of information such as unstructured, scattered documents, or only in the form of tacit knowledge spread across several security managers. This gap calls for experimentation to identify successful business security requirement management strategies, as efficient business security requirement management lowers cost for organizations and standardization promises to drastically decrease the workload on security managers (Mohammed et al., 2010; Thalmann et al., 2012). To address this deficiency and to provide a framework for the systematic management of business security requirements, we suggest an IT architecture enabling the standardization of business security processes in the context of the organization's service landscape.

The proposed architecture allows for the organization to standardize the collaborative security processes and management of business security requirements by systematically connecting each security process artifact to the organizational asset it protects. By providing different views on the security process and service landscape the proposed framework can satisfy the needs of both internal and external stakeholders. It allows the organization to quickly adapt to security requirement changes (top down; e.g., implementation of a new privacy law applicable to one branch) or changes resulting from changing strategic objectives (bottom up; e.g., a physical server is added to a server farm and compliance to a specific policy must be ensured) in a standardized manner. A prototype implementing the proposed architecture has been used in a near life assessment and user feedback data has been collected. We use the collected data to verify the functionality of the presented architecture in the context of the security process standardization. In this paper we show how the proposed architecture is able to create a potential benefit for the organization by improving security process management efficiency.

2. Background and Methodology

Due to the specific characteristics of complex inter-organizational IT service architectures and organizations being fully responsible for all parts of their IT during all life cycle stages (Bardhan et al., 2010), particular challenges have arisen with respect to security process management and compliance (Thalmann et al., 2012). It is increasingly important for businesses to provide evidence to customers that security requirements are addressed and continuously managed in a standardized manner, which is difficult in such complex arrangements (Jansen, 2011). Seeing the need to standardize the management of business security processes to fit internal and external stakeholder requirements, the question arises how IT systems can be aligned in support of this objective. This is especially important for IT service organizations as their organizational structure constitutes largely of IT systems by definition. It is obvious that developing an architecture enabling the collaborative management of business security requirements is a relevant task.

As we want to create an artifact, we follow the Design Science paradigm which describes an approach rooted in the engineering sciences. A common methodology in this area is suggested in (Hevner et al., 2004). Henver et al's (2004) fundamental principle of design-science research proposes that the knowledge and understanding of a design problem and its subsequent solution should be derived from the building and application of an artifact. Furthermore, they provide several guidelines which we follow in the construction of the proposed architecture: The introduction and the theoretical foundation in section 2 show the relevance of the problem of managing business security requirements in complex service provider landscapes. Our proposed architecture, the design artifact, addresses this problem and provides a solution in section 3 which is the result of the rigorous search for a solution to the identified problem of standardizing security management processes in complex service provider landscapes.

3. Architecture, Metamodel and Design Artifact

After giving a short introduction of the implementation context, we briefly present the architecture and the underlying metamodel. The goal of the proposed framework is to enable the standardized management of business security requirements in the specific context of the organization. *Security Requirements* are the central component of the proposed model. Each requirement can be composed of sub-requirements allowing to build an arbitrary dependency graph (cf. to the extended description of the metamodel in (Sillaber et al., 2013) for detailed information). In the proposed framework, any requirement may be derived from a *Source* being either a law, a policy or some other origin (e.g., a service level agreement with a business partner). Attribute-wise security requirements have a distinct title and hold the textual description of the security requirement The framework uses natural language descriptions for requirements as this is the most commonly used approach (e.g., most relevant standards are formulated in that manner) and does not require knowledge of specialized formal languages from participating stakeholders. Furthermore, every requirement is related to one or more *Stakeholders* holding various functions.

To express the behavior of requirements upon state-changes in a standardized manner, the framework manages distinct states and *Fulfillment Models*. We distinguish between fulfilled, partially fulfilled and non-fulfilled requirements. A fulfillment model defines when a requirement's state has to be set to one of these states if state propagation is enabled. For requirements without state propagation the state has to be managed manually by defined responsible stakeholders. For automated state propagation the Object Constraint Language (OCL) (Warmer et al., 2003) is utilized to define conditions for partial and total fulfillment. By utilizing OCL the framework provides support for very expressive user-defined fulfillment models further enhancing the versatility and support for various security management methodologies. The UML state machine diagram in Figure 1 displays the standardized operation-states together with all transitions in between them.

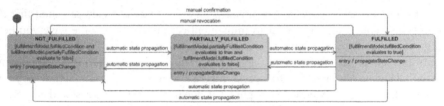

Figure 1. *Standardized states of operation*

Standardized Management of Confirmations and Revocations: It is of utter importance that everything concerning the fulfillment (or non-fulfillment) of security requirements is clearly traceable. Therefore, the framework provides two artifacts enriching the model: *Confirmation* and *Revocation* to explicitly express the standardized confirmation and revocation of requirements. A confirmation is always linked to a requirement, is issued by a stakeholder and has a date indicating how long this confirmation stays valid. Further every confirmation needs to provide a justification. If a user manually confirms a requirement he needs to state why he confirmed the requirement giving a justification for his claim. In case of state propagation, the justifications are automatically generated hinting on which event caused the fulfillment of the requirement. A revocation is always linked to the confirmation it revokes, stores the user issuing the revocation and also stores a justification (i.e., "paper trail").

4. Case Study

We present the results from the evaluation of our prototype based on the proposed IT architecture in this section. The evaluation is based on the introductory example of managing security requirements in a complex service provider landscape and consisted of two parts, an end-user training part and an assessment part held as a workshop at the premises of a large IT service provider together with security management stakeholders. For the full length version of the Case Study, please refer to (Demetz et al., 2013), as this section presents only the results relevant to the scope of this paper.

Standardization of Security Process Introduction: Using the prototype, the end-users had to first add a new PCI DSS requirement using the template system of the prototype. This took 4 minutes. Subsequently, all sub-requirements for PCI DSS were created automatically using the template system which took 2 minutes per sub-requirement, where the end-users stated that this "would save a couple of hours" for implementing all sub-requirements of PCI DSS compared to manually performing that task. According to the end-users the human resource consumption would be reduced because information is centralized with the prototype.

Organizational impact and behavioral change: One interviewee stated that the prototype would make it "easier to implement certain controls, otherwise you need to go through all the documents". One interviewee stated that "it's a good place to centralize all these requirements and keep track of them in terms of compliance again". Having an interface to access all data stored in a central repository, the service providers' dependence on physical documents which are stored in various locations across organizational boundaries could be reduced. Although the end-users recognized the benefits, they also expressed that the approach might not be valuable for every business process as "we don't need those many changes [in requirements] that often", and highlighted that for some business processes "the effort to make that functionality just to control the requirements" might be too high. However, the end-users highlighted the benefits of the prototype if changes in security requirements happen often.

5. Conclusions

In this paper, we presented a framework for organizational security process standardization. We introduced the core artifacts of the framework and summarized the encouraging results from a near life assessment. By enabling the standardized management of business security requirements in the context of complex service provider landscapes, the internal and external quality of business security requirements can potentially be increased compared to static, generalized approaches. The suggested approach enables efficient access to all information to external and internal stakeholders – as it is highly adaptable to specific needs. The usage context as presented in this paper is only one possible application from many.

6. Acknowledgements

This work was supported by the Austrian Federal Ministry of Economy, the Tyrolean business development and partially funded by the European Commission.

7. References

Bardhan, Indranil, Demirkan, Haluk, Kannan, P.K., Kauffman, Robert, Sougstad, Ryan. (2010). 'An interdisciplinary perspective on IT services management and service science'. *Journal of Management Information Systems*, 26(4), 13-64.

Chakraborty, Rajarshi, Ramireddy, Srilakshmi, Raghu, Rao, H Raghav. (2010). 'The information assurance practices of cloud computing vendors'. *IT professional*, 12(4), 29-37.

Demetz, Lukas, Maier, Ronald, Manhart, Markus, Plate, Henrik. (2013). D1.7 Final Project Evaluation: PoSecCo (project no. 257129).

Hevner, Alan R, March, Salvatore T, Park, Jinsoo, & Ram, Sudha. (2004). 'Design science in information systems research'. *Mis Quarterly*, 28(1), 75-105.

Jansen, Wayne A. (2011). 'Cloud hooks: Security and privacy issues in cloud computing'. Paper presented at the *44th HICSS*, 2011.

Marinos, Louis, Kirchner, Lutz, Junginger, Stefan. (2009). 'Integration of an IT-Risk Management/Risk Assessment Framework with Operational Processes'. Paper presented at the *Wirtschaftsinformatik* (1).

Mohammed, Ashraf Bany, Altmann, Jörn, Hwang, Junseok. (2010). *Cloud computing value chains: Understanding businesses and value creation in the cloud Economic models and algorithms for distributed systems* (pp. 187-208): Springer.

Sillaber, Christian, Brunner, Michael, Breu, Ruth. (2013). 'Towards an Architecture for Collaborative Cross-Organizational Security Requirements Management'. Paper presented at the *Business Information Systems - 16th International Conference, BIS 2013*, Poznan, Poland.

Thalmann, Stefan, Bachlechner, Daniel, Demetz, Lukas, Maier, Ronald. (2012). *Challenges in cross-organizational security management*. Paper presented at the *45th Hawaii International Conference on System Science (HICSS)*, 2012.

Warmer, Jos, & Kleppe, Anneke. (2003). *The object constraint language: getting your models ready for MDA*: Addison-Wesley Longman Publishing Co., Inc.

Standards Roles in Hacklin's Strategic Model

Cases in the Space Sector

Karim Benmeziane — Anne Mione

MRM (Montpellier Research in Management)
Espace Richter, Bâtiment B, Rue Vendémiaire, CS 19519
34960 Montpellier Cedex 2
benmeziane@bnae.asso.fr
anne.mione@ univ-montp1.fr

1. Introduction

Describing converging industries, Hacklin's et al. (2013) propose a taxonomy of strategic profiles that mentions the role of standards. They only consider driving standards as a technology pioneer's means to foster the diffusion on the market. We question this position and argue that standards play more diverse and subtle roles. Since Shapiro and Varian (1999), scholars have actually identified specific strategies directly or indirectly associated with standards in converging industries context. Gawer and Cusumano (2002) presented strategic drivers for obtaining platform leadership in environments characterized by technical modularity, Waguespack and Fleming (2009) showed how a start-up could implement standards to foster IPO[1] opportunities and Ballon (2008) demonstrated the interest of gathering ecosystem partners around the same business model being defined through standards. We particulartly investigate the mecanisms through which standards are strategized. We observe two segments of the space sector. Sticking to Hacklin's model, our results propose standards strategic principles to serve the different strategic profiles.

2. Hacklin et al. (2013)'s Strategic Profiles

This taxonomy describes four profiles: technology pionneer, market attacker, ecosystem aggregator and business remodeler, as mentioned in Table 1. Hacklin

---

1. Initial Public Offering.

and al. (2013) only mentions the use of standards in the technology pioneer profile. We argue that not only Technlogy Pionneers but also the others profiles may strategically use standards. We then describe their aim and strategic implementation.

Position in industry	Strategic profiles	Description
Entrants	Technology pionneer	They are early entrants using their technological advantage as a way to contribute to convergence.
	Market attacker	They try to tranform fragmentation of value chains into commercial and revenues opportunities.
Incumbents	Ecosystem agregator	They leverage their competencies and market experience to establish an innovation platform aimed at complementary products and services.
	Business remodeler	They redefine the core business model in well established networks.

Table 1. *Adapted from Hacklin et al. (2013)'s model*

3. Methodology

We choose satellite positioning systems and space launcher services as converging technological segments of the space sector. Our operationalization to identify the four different profiles was designed accordingly with Hacklin's profile description[2]. Eleven interviews were led with the major space actors (Arianespace, CNES, Astrium, Thales Alenia Space, etc.) to understand the market and non market strategic intentions of the firms.

4. Results: A Refined Approach on the Roles of Standards in Hacklin's Model

We could identify cases situations where the different profiles used standards.

---

2. The key element for each profile was: (1) Technological pioneer: introduction of a new to the market technological product; (2) Market attacker: a new offer to as segment already covered by competitors; (3) Ecosystem aggregator: the creation and commercialization of an innovative plateform enabling complementary products and services to operate; (4) Business Remodeler: a change in the business model modifying the relations to customers and the structure of cost raised by an innovation.

Strategic Profiles	Strategic Use of Standards
Technology Pioneer	In the mid-eighties, *Magellan* was the first to commercialize GPS receivers. These products were first intended for professionals use in the maritime sector. To expand its business, Magellan became involved in the NMEA[3]. As part of the development of NMEA 0813 standard, Magellan provided the test equipment so that it became the reference from which the positioning messages are encoded. *Thus, by participating to standardization activities led by downstream partners, Magellan fostered technology appropriation.*
Market Attacker	To attack a market, it is necessary to understand the customer needs. As a manager at *Thales Alenia Space* (TAS) states it *"We need to focus on the functional need and adapt our langage to show our added value"*. This testimony comes as the result of the involvement of TAS in the ITS[4] stakeholders' standardization actitivies. TAS aimed at pushing a certification scheme for evaluating the performance of positioning receivers based on standards controlled by TAS. Thus, *by participating to customer's standardization activities and by promoting standards which are "under control", TAS succeeded in attacking the positioning receivers market for road transport.*
Ecosystem Agregator	To help technically stabilizing the Ariane launcher, *Arianespace* encouraged their main suppliers in participating in ISO TC20 SC14[5]. In this context, Arianespace asked Snecma (the Ariane propulsion system supplier) for its participation in SC14. This way, Arianespace *enabled complementary products to operate by encouraging partners to take leadership in standardization activities for their products.*
Business Remodeler	When *Arianespace* orders a launcher such as Ariane to its contractor ADS[6] (ex-Astrium), it enforces the use of LS-SM[7] internal standards needed for the production of Ariane. When Ariane 5 was developed, this enforcement helped Arianespace to change its business model by creating a capacity to launch two satellites in-orbit simultaneously. This business model was new in 2000. In the meantime, Arianespace took the leadership for the development of several ISO standards[8] to define all the interfaces requirements between launchers and satellites. Thus, *to technically enable the creation of a new business model, Arianespace have enforced the evolution of internal standards for upstream partners and led the development of interface standards along with complementors.*

Table 2. *Strategic profiles and strategic uses of standards*

---

3. National Marine Electronics Association.
4. Intelligent Transport Systems.
5. International standard technical subcommittee developing standards for space systems.
6. Airbus Defense and Space.
7. Launcher System-Specifications of Management.
8. ISO 15863 in 1997, ISO 17401 in 1999, and ISO 14303 in 2001, all of these standards being interface standards.

Previous literature results emphasized on the firm leading capacity, either to search for first-mover advantages, to innovate, to control the customer base and block competitors from offering compatible products, or to strengthen complementaries (Shapiro and Varian, 1999). Our contribution refines these views by showing how the standardization activities can be managed differently in technology converging industries, for instance by offering other firms the leading capacity, supporting a corporate strategy of platform leadership (Gawer & Cusumano, 2002). Another result is that not only standardization can be used to develop nascent industries (Garud, 1994) – in other words, to establish the market rules – but it is also a tool to conduct disruptive strategies (Hamel, 1998) to technically enable new business models (Ballon 2008) and create alternative market rules.

5. Conclusions

We observed that, not only technology pioneers, but the three others profiles can use standards to implement strategies in a technology converging industry. Hacklin et al (2013)'s model finally constituted a fruitful matrix to shed light on these specific standards implementation strategies, notably to serve the ecosystem aggregator profile. Futher investigation is now required to explore in a more systematic way the relation between the profiles and strategies. From this, we expect a deeper knowledge of the strategic use of standards in the firms' strategies.

6. References

Akerlof. "The Market for 'Lemons'. Quality Uncertainty and the Market Mechanism", *Quarterly journal of Economics*, 78 (3), 1970, pp.488-500.

Ballon, "Standardization and Business Models for Platform Competition: The Case of Mobile Television", *International Journal of IT Standards and Standardization Research*, 7(1), 2008.

Blind, *The Economics of Standards – Theory, Evidence, Policy*, Edward Elgar, 2004.

David, "*Some New Standards for the Economics of Standardisation inthe Information Age*", in Dasgupta, P. and P. Stoneman (eds), *Economic Policy and Technological Performance*, Cambridge: Cambridge University Press, 1987.

David, Greenstein, "The Economics of Compatibility Standards: An Introduction to Recent Research", *Economic Innovation and New Technology*, 1, 1990.

De Vries, *Standardization. A Business Approach to the Role of National Standardization Organizations*, Boston: Kluwer Academic Publishers, 1999.

Eisenhardt, Kathleen, "Building theories from case study research", *Academy of Management Review*, 14(4), 1989, pp.532-550.

Garud, "Cooperative and competitive behaviors during the process of creative destruction". *Research Policy*. 23(4), 1994, pp.385-394.

Hacklin, Battistini, Von Krogh, "Strategic Choices in Converging Industries", *MIT Sloan Management Review*. 55(1), 2013, pp.65-73.

Hamel G., "The Challenge Today: Changing the Rules of the Game", *Business Strategy Review*, vol. 9, 1998, p.19.

Shapiro, C., Varian, H.R., "The art of standards wars", *California Management Review* 41, 1999, pp.8-32.

Van de Kaa, van den Ende, de Vries, van Heck, "Factors for winning interface format battles: A review and synthesis of literature", *Technology Forecasting & Social Change*, 78, 2011, pp.1397-1411.

Waguespack, D.M., Fleming, L., "Scanning the commons? Evidence on the benefits to startups participating in open standards development", *Management Science*, 55, 2011.

Standardization Management and Decision-Making

The Case of a Large Swedish Automotive Manufacturer

A. Foukaki

The Institute of Economic Research
School of Economics and Management
Lund University, PO Box 7080, SE-220 07 Lund, Sweden
Amalia.Foukaki@fek.lu.se

ABSTRACT. *This article examines the standardization management in a large Swedish automotive manufacturer, exploring which factors determine the standards-related decision-making within the company and subsequently its standardization strategy. Since the company has managed to lead the Swedish standardization ("first-mover"), as well as to actively participate in international standardization committees, and in fact illustrates an example of virtuous utilization of corporate standardization, a well-motivated and deep understanding of the case addresses managerial best-practices of intra-organizational information flows towards the enhancement of the company's competitiveness. The study is based on interviews with representatives of the standardization unit in the company, departing from its organizational structure and activities.*

KEYWORDS: *Corporate Standardization, Standardization Management, Decision-Making, Standardization Strategy, Competitive Advantages.*

1. Introduction

The immensely, to all of us, known PDF (Portable Document Format) consists today of an International Standard (ISO 32000-1:2008). The PDF technology entails an indicative example – but not the single one – of an innovative product that was spun into a standard instead of being patented. Perhaps the immediate question is how come the company reached such a decision. In the last decades, firms engage increasingly in standards creation and adoption, which rational firms shall only if the expected payoff is high enough to justify the commitment (Zhao et al., 2007). Though, the uniformity among competitors, that the use of common standards fetches, could be argued to impair differentiation and eliminate the space for strategic behavior. As long as standards bring uniformity and force homogeneity (Brunsson et al., 2012), they could be considered to hinder competitive advantages, which are highly connected to uniqueness in strategic management literature (Peteraf 1993; Barney 1991). Standards, which are universally accessible to a large number of potential adopters (Brunsson et al., 2012), are clearly not following the above idiosyncrasy. Moreover, Makadok (2010) examines the logic that regimes of rivalry restraint and competitive advantage are competing ones, meaning that firms ought to choose either one or the other. Standardization processes and adoption of common standards suggest a cooperative situation, thus it is implied that it makes no sense to be employed in parallel with efforts to obtain competitive advantages.

On the other hand, Schilling (1999) presents a line of argumentation that faces standards as means to actually gain competitive advantages, depending on how a firm employs them. Saltzman *et al.* (2008) argue that there can be several different combinations of rivalry and excludability (or availability) tactics. Contrary to conventional strategic wisdom, Schilling argues that standards' adoption and imitation comes with strategic associations, enhancing competitive advantages instead of eliminating them. Current research though does not offer further insights under what the premises a firm chooses either uniqueness or standard adoption. Additionally, standards adoption itself and contemporary standardization management remain unclear up to date. This report aims to shed light on the procedures related to standards adoption and firm standardization management, as well as the motives behind it, through the explorative case study.

2. Standards against Uniqueness?

2.1. *Organizational Structure*

The company will be anonymized and will be referred to as Company A. It is a large Swedish automotive manufacturer, employing today thousands of people, owning production facilities in many countries and reaching markets all over the world. Company A's standardization unit is organized within one of its 8 different organizations, but in fact supports all parts of the company related to production. In terms of size, the unit employs 12 persons, who though collaborate strongly with a vast number of people and teams all over the corporation, such as managers, experts, users and suppliers. They formulate several working groups, which undertake the various standardization projects, depending on the different teams' competence.

2.2. *Strategic Rationale towards a Standardization Unit*

The standardization unit has been part of Company A since 1944. The importance of being well informed about the status quo of the ongoing standardization was powerfully stressed at a time that the company neglected to do so, when new emissions regulation (Euro 4 legislation) triggered standardization work. Company A failed to follow up on the information about it and basically almost missed out the game! It was led close to an expensive re-design of its products due to overlooked critical developments. After all, the company managed to solve the situation, which though could have been fatal. Lesson learnt; it couldn't happen again. It became clear that it is necessary to safeguard the strategic areas by being informed and even involved. Nowadays, active involvement in standardization work is Company A's systemization to remain well informed about the state of the industry, as well as observe and understand competitors.

Furthermore, the wide application of standards within the company was the outcome of an intra-organizational experience of inefficiency due to the extensive use of non-standardized parts and tools. Without the establishment of standard parts, Company A faced and would continue facing terribly unproductive situations, easily pictured by considering the occasion of an organization using special screws for each of its different products. The described need for an efficient assortment limitation has not eroded with the passage of time; quite the opposite. Consequently, the standards' system and culture progressively developed within the company over the years, but the strategic rationale behind it has not really changed: it pertains as a way to monitor the development of the industry and to solve "in-house" efficiency problems.

2.3. The Function of the Standardization Unit and its Activities

In this section a detailed description of the standardization unit's function and activities will be offered, towards a deep understanding of the case. Departing from the question addressed, on how the decision-making around standard adoption is conducted, the finding was that actually there is barely such a decision-making in the company. There is no adoption concept in the sense of examining particular standards and decide whether they need to be adopted - at least when referring to production-related standards. On the contrary, the starting point of such a decision-making is always a request, raised openly by anyone in the organization, and addressed straight to the standardization unit. That request may be prompted due to any kind of malfunction in the production, or any need that might have emerged in the company. Thus, every technical standardization work in the company is merely triggered by a relevant need or request. Further, in addition to the possibility of a request raised by anyone in the company, an important pathway to identify an emerging need is early phase research within the company.

Following the above, the 1st actual decision point of the unit comes when examining whether the particular request shall be spun into a standardization project. Thus, the standard related decision-making already starts before the instigation of the actual standardization project ("pre-initiation-decision"). That, as well as the rest of the standardization process, are not determined by explicit factors but is based on the particular circumstances and experience, precisely as Saltzman *et al.* (2008) also support. To a large degree those are ad-hoc decisions, made by the various Technical Committees (TC), consisting of high-level managers. If the TC approves the initiation of a standardization project, then the most relevant experts are searched within the company in order to formulate a working group that will conduct the detailed, specialized work towards the creation of the standard. Content-wise, the experts conduct the real decision-making, while the standardization unit focuses on the management of the document.

Besides the experts, users' involvement is crucial and is stimulated all the way in the standard development. Principally, the users themselves initiate the standardization process through a request and remain involved in the creation process. Instead of a regular process where one gives input and develops and someone else is the end consumer: (*Initiator = Input ==> Output ==> User*), in standardization the consumers are the developers who contribute in the development of what they consume and could thus be characterized as "prosumers" (*User ==> Input ==> Corporate Standards + other stakeholders ==> User*). At the end of the standard's development process comes the 2nd decision point, when the standardization group decides that the draft of the standard is ready, and is sent out (to selected people within the company) for a feedback round. After the feedback is accounted and the draft is adjusted, the 3rd decision point designates the end of a regular standardization process, with the release of the standard.

Most of Company A's internally developed standards are externally visible (up to 90%). A remarkably smaller number (the rest 10%) are available only internally. Thus, Company A appears to have two distinct standardization strategies; its core one is to allow its standards be externally visible to everyone. Its second strategy, applied for a very small number of standards, is to keep them only internally visible. The latter one, involves standards addressed for intra-organizational application (activities that the company conducts internally), while the former concerns external activities, such as communication with suppliers and cooperation with others, even competitors, to facilitate an efficient coordination that shall benefit them all.

2.4. Why Then, Standardize Instead of Using Internal Unique Solutions?

In the previous section, the standardization management in Company A is presented, hinting that there could be considerable costs connected to the rather long and complex process of standards creation. Though, the company chooses not to protect the outcomes of the process (the internally developed standards), but to have them available to be used by free-riders (Weiss et al., 1996), them even being its competitors. The rationale for the above is that in fact, Company A perceives being benefited by the diffuse of its technical standards, since their wider establishment serves its purposes better. Standards are approached as the language of communication among different companies and hence the use of common standards facilitates it. For instance, the communication with the suppliers is much more efficient if Company A's requirements entail well-known standards, and of course the more diffused a standard is among competitors, the more well known it is to the suppliers as well, leading to higher volumes, lower prices and higher quality.

Subsequently, Company A is not hesitant to enhance the cooperation with its competitors, to the creation of mutually adopted standards. This does not necessarily limit the space for competitive advantages. To a certain degree, homogeneity is anyhow part of the business, and only particular traits suffice in providing differentiation. Indicatively, the competing automotive companies are mainly producing the engines and the cab, while being supported by the same bodybuilders for the rest of the truck. It would be simply too costly if each company were using merely special parts. Everything cannot be unique; heterogeneity needs to be the point of differentiation, not of dominance.

2.5. Why Then, Standardize Internally Instead of Using International Standards?

The company is attentive to utilizing already available international standards, but strictly under the premise that they are suitable for its demands. The focus is always the company needs, which Company A usually finds better covered by its internally developed standards. Often, the company's standards embrace a noticeably superior level of product quality, by setting higher requirements.

Furthermore, and perhaps even more essentially, in order to serve its purposes and needs to the uppermost, Company A aims at actively participating and leading the international standardization work, since first movers enjoy an opportunity to impact the international standards towards the company's benefit, signifying a concept of strategic intelligence – as Edler et al. (2012) describe it. By being active in internal standardization and then bring that knowledge in the scene of international work, the company is in a position to promote the specifications that suit its products and strategies best. Therefore, the company's standardization unit reflects that leading its field and being involved in the development of international standards serves its interests, and is thus willing to share relevant information, even with competitors, instead of protecting it.

3. Conclusions

Some tentative inferences can be drawn, but mainly in order to point the issues that cast further investigation. To start with, the logic behind the 90-10 percentages of available and protected company standards shall be scrutinized. An exploration of that distinction's criteria could further shed light on the company's standardization management. Also, an exploration of the company's distinctive strategic approaches in relation to the initiation of standardization processes (such as the re-active problem solving in contrast to the pro-active look out through early phase research) reveals interesting aspects of standardization handling and planning.

Furthermore, standards development driven by early phase research reveals impending linkages to innovation, and potentially innovation enhancement. The issue is definitely worth investigating, since standardization has conventionally considered a hindrance to innovation, but has also been signified as innovation catalyst (Blind 2013).

4. References

Barney, J., "Firm resources and sustained competitive advantage", *Journal of Management*, vol. 17, 1991, pp.99-120.

Blind, K., "The Impact of Standardization and Standards on Innovation", Report within the *MIoIR-NESTA Compendium of Evidence on Innovation Policy*. London/Manchester, 2013.

Brunsson, N., Rasche, A., Seidl, D., "The dynamics of standardization: Three perspectives on standards in organization studies", *Organization Studies*, vol. 33, 2012, pp.613-632.

Edler, J., Georghiou, L., Blind, K., Uyarra, E., "Evaluating the demand side: New challenges for evaluation", *Research Evaluation*, vol. 21 no. 1, 2012. pp.33-47.

Makadok, R., "The interaction effect of rivalry restraint and competitive advantage on profit: why the whole is less than the sum of the parts", *Management Science*, vol. 56 no. 2, 2010, pp.356-372.

Peteraf, M., "The cornerstones of competitive advantage: a resource-based view", *Strategic Management Journal*, vol. 14 no. 3, 1993, pp.179-191.

Saltzman, J., Chatterjee, S., Raman, M., "A framework for ICT standards creation: The case of ITU-T standard H. 350", *Information Systems*, vol. 33 no. 3, 2008, pp.285-299.

Schilling, M., "Winning the standards race: Building installed base and the availability of complementary goods", *European Management Journal*, vol. 17, 1999, pp.265-274.

Weiss, M., Toyokuku, R., "Free-ridership in the Standards-setting Process: the case of 10BaseT", *StandardView 4.4*, 1996, pp.205-212.

Zhao, K., Xia, M., Shaw, M.J., "An integrated model of consortium-based e-business standardization: Collaborative development and adoption with network externalities", *Journal of Management Information Systems*, vol. 23, 2007, pp.247-271.

Some Factors Influencing Corporate ICT Standardisation Management

Kai Jakobs

RWTH Aachen University
CoSc Dept., Informatik 4
kai.jakobs@comsys.rwth-aachen.de

ABSTRACT. *In the field of Information and Communication Technologies, standards are of overriding importance. Accordingly, much has been written about their economic impact. Yet, comparably little is known about how firms manage their standardisation activities. This paper develops a framework as a basis for both practitioners and researchers to get a better understanding of how to improve a firms' performance in ICT standardisation. To this end, I offer a closer look at the major types of actors – firms, standards bodies and individual standards setters and at the links and similarities that exist between a firm's strategic behaviour in a market and its approach to standardisation. These aspects are integrated to form a framework for future research and practical deployment.*

KEYWORDS: *Standardisation, Management, ICT.*

1. Introduction, Motivation and Background

Today, virtually all Information and Communication Technologies (ICT) are based on standards. Thus, standards now under development will be an integral part of future ICT systems, and will to no small extent define their functionality. In a way, this gives those who actively contribute to standardisation the opportunity to pro-actively shape these future systems; a tempting prospect for some. Aspects to be considered include, for example, the characteristics of potentially relevant Standards Setting Organisations (SSOs), the identities, capabilities and ideally strategies of potential adversaries and allies, and the needs and requirements of the different stakeholders and potential users. Internal factors include, among others, a clear alignment of standardisation activities with (sectoral) business strategies, an in-depth knowledge of the standardisation environment and an adequate management of all standardisation activities.

2. Aspects Influencing Standardisation

A standardisation process is subject to the influence of a number of different factors, particularly including a broad variety of stakeholders. In the following I will first have a brief look at the range of stakeholders that impact standards setting and the associated processes through which this influence is exerted.

3. The stakeholders

3.1. *Companies*

3.1.1. *Categorising Organisational Strategies*

A very popular categorisation of organisational strategies was introduced by Miles & Snow [1978]. Four types of organisations are identified:

– A Prospector is innovative and growth oriented, searches for new markets as well as for new products and services and is prepared to take risks. Its product/ service domain is rather broad and changes over time.

– The Analyser tries to strike a balance between the search for new product/ service opportunities and a stable set of offerings. That is, part of its domain is stable and part is in a state of flux.

– A Defender aims to maintain its current markets and its limited set of products and/or services to the satisfaction of its customers. It has only a moderate emphasis on innovation.

– The Reactor's strategy is inconsistent or ill defined; it is not really equipped to respond to environmental changes.

3.1.2. *Categorising Strategic Approaches to Standardisation*

Here, [Updegrove, 2006] and [Jakobs et al., 2010] also propose four categories:

– *Leader*: For companies in this category participation in a certain standards-setting activity is business critical. Leaders aim to control the strategy of an SSO or a Technical Committee rather than merely participate in the technical activities.

– *Contributor*: A Contributor company is an active participant in the standardisation process. Yet, it is less interested in (or lacks the resources for) influencing the strategic direction of an SSO.

– *Follower*: Organisations in this category want to enjoy full membership privileges and may occasionally want to influence the technical content of a standard (in addition to gathering intelligence). They are, however, not much interested to influence any strategic decisions.

– Spectator: A Spectator's main motivation for participation is intelligence gathering. Spectators do not actively contribute to the creation of the standard. Rather, they want to be informed about its technical nuts and bolts.

3.1.3. *Linking the Classifications*

A link between the two classifications introduced above, may easily be established (see Table 1). It should be noted that the type of a company (Prospector, Analyser, Defender, Reactor) may well change over time and/or differ between markets.

	Leader	Contributor	Follower	Spectator
Prospector	++	+	-	--
Analyser	+	++	-	--
Defender	--	+	++	-
Reactor	?	?	?	?

Table 1. *Linking Organisational Strategies and Approaches to Standardisation*
++ = most likely; + = may well be; - = rather unlikely; -- = most unlikely; ? = unclear

3.2. Standards Setting Organisations

A number of attributes can be used to describe SSOs. These attributes can be sub-divided into four categories (see also [Jakobs et al., 2010]).

3.2.1. *'General' Attributes*

These attributes serve to provide some high-level information about an SSO. Information on its internal structure and on the way it is governed will be especially important for those who would like to influence the strategy of an SSO. Its structure and governance have ramifications for the openness of an SSO. The same holds for its liaisons with peer organisations, which also are means of co-ordination. A good level of co-ordination reduces the risk of standardising on a technology that may eventually become incompatible with other relevant standards. Conversely, a 'monopoly' situation suggests a reasonably safe bet. Finally, the Intellectual Property Rights (IPR) policy has a significant impact on an SSO's attractiveness.

3.2.2. *'Membership' Attributes*

The overall number of members may be used as a rough indicator of the success of an SSO's output. A broad membership base may well imply valuable support for a standard. However, the prominence of members (in terms of e.g. market share) is rather more important. Active contributions by large and important companies will significantly improve a standard's chance to be successful in the market.

3.2.3. *'Standards Setting Process' Attributes*

An SSO's standards setting process is decisive for its ability to quickly adapt to a changing environment and to newly emerging requirements. Relevant aspects here include 'short time to market' and the ability to spot a window of opportunity and to deliver inside this window. Obviously, this depends very much on, for example, the level of consensus sought, the degree of openness of a standards setting process, its transparency and the observation of due process. In many cases, it will be necessary to balance the requirement for speed and the need for a broad consensus.

3.2.4. *'Output' Attributes*

The deliverables an SSO produces give an indication about its flexibility. For instance, full-blown formal standards indicate a more lengthy process, technical reports or similar types of deliverables suggest a faster, more adaptable process with a lower level of consensus. A standard that is maintained over time also says something about the SSO's willingness to adapt its deliverables to changing environments. A mechanism to ensure consistency of a standard is also important.

3.2.5. *Different Stakeholders' Perspectives*

Different stakeholders will assign different levels of importance to the attributes outlined above. For example, from a large user company's[1] perspective the standard should adequately reflect user requirements and enjoy the support of many/all relevant major vendors. Ideally, no royalties should be associated with it. On the other end of the spectrum holders of a strong relevant patent portfolio may well aim to make as much money as possible out of their IPR. To that end, they will primarily aim to assume a leadership position; a less democratic, hierarchical structure and processes will allow them to exert the desired influence.

The above, though over-simplifying, highlights why different stakeholders will look for different characteristics in an SSO, depending on their respective strategy.

3.3. *Individual Standards Setters*

A standard is the result of the efforts of the members of an SSO's working group. Consequently, these individuals' motivations, attitudes and views are very likely to have an influence on the outcome of the standards setting process. In fact, the influence a strong-minded individual standards setter may have on the final outcome of the process should not be underestimated.

In the field of ICT the WGs are almost exclusively populated by engineers. One should, therefore, assume 'technical quality' to be the most important individual

---

1. Think of it here as e.g. a large petro-chemical company.

success factor for a proposal to become the new standard. Yet, there is strong evidence that speaking out at meetings for or against a proposal is more important (see e.g. [Jakobs et al., 2010]). To be able to do so successfully a sustained participation by the same capable representatives is the most promising approach. Over time, such individuals will have established extensive personal networks with their peers; they will have amassed a wealth of social capital [Dokko & Rosenkopf, 2010]. This will make it much easier to solve any identified in a more informal way.

Individuals act according to the role each of them assumes. These roles may be categorised along two dimensions. The first might be referred to as 'Task'. Such a Task may, for example, be to contribute fine-grained technical details ('Architect'), just observe ('Bystander'), guide the whole process ('Facilitator') or indeed try and thwart it ('Obstructionist'; see e.g. [Spring et al., 1995]. The second dimension could be called 'Representation'. According to [Jakobs et al., 2001], WG members may see themselves as e.g. 'Company Representative', 'User Advocate' or 'Techie' (i.e. focus on technically clean and advanced solutions).

4. Putting it All Together

Thus far, the paper looked at the actors 'SSOs', 'Companies' and 'Individuals' separately. Obviously, though, they are closely intertwined. Moreover, other influencing factors may be identified (see e.g. [Brons, 2007] for a more in-depth discussion.). Plus, of course, a standard is not an end in itself. Rather, it needs to be diffused and, ultimately, adopted in order to be of any relevance for the market and, not least, its developers. Figure 1 puts it all in pictorial form.

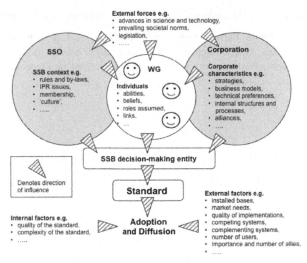

Figure 1. *Some factors that influence standards development*

Stakeholders that want to excel in ICT standards setting need to be aware that all aspects discussed above need to be taken into account; their respective relevance will vary between categories. Followers and Contributors need to make sure that they have good technical proposals to be defended by equally good representatives. Leaders, on the other hand, will need to focus more on strategic aspects. In any case, representatives at all levels need to be well informed about their employer's strategic and tactical goals in the field. Obviously, this implies that the employer is very clear about his goals.

5. References

Brons, T.F. (2007): *Effective participation in formal standardization: A multinational perspective. Rotterdam*, The Netherlands: Rotterdam School of Management.

Dokko, G.; Rosenkopf, L. (2010): "Social Capital for Hire? Mobility of Technical Professionals and Firm Influence in Wireless Standards Committees". *Organization Science*, vol. 21, no. 3.

Jakobs, K.; Lemstra, W.; Hayes, V.; Tuch, B.; Links, C. (2010a): "Creating a Wireless LAN Standard: IEEE 802.11". In: Lemstra, W.; Groenewegen, J.; Hayes, V. (eds.): *The Innovation Journey of WiFi*. Cambridge University Press.

Jakobs, K.; Procter, R.; Williams, R. (2001): "The Making of Standards". *IEEE Communications Magazine*, vol. 39, no. 4.

Michael B. Spring, M.B.; Grisham, C.; O'Donnell, J.; Skogseid, I.; Snow, A.; Tarr, G.; Wang, P. (1995): "Improving the Standardization Process". In: Kahin, B.; Abbate, J. (eds.): *Standards Policy for Information Infrastructure*. MIT Press.

Miles, R.E.; Snow, C.C. (1978): *Organizational Strategy, Structure, and Process*. McGraw-Hill.

Updegrove, A. (2006): Participating In Standard Setting Organizations: Value Propositions, Roles And Strategies. *The Essential Guide to Standards*, Chapter 2. http://www.consortiuminfo.org/essentialguide/participating1.php (accessed 8 May 2013).

Workshop 9

Standardisation Developments
for Enterprise Interoperability
and the Manufacturing Service Domain

Report

Martin Zelm* — David Chen**

* INTEROP-VLab, Belgium
martin.zelm@t-online.de

** IMS, University of Bordeaux
351, Cours de la libération, 33405 Talence, France
david.chen@ims-bordeaux.fr

The goal of Workshop 9 of the I-ESA 2014 has been to share, exchange and disseminate new knowledge on standardisation developments in the manufacturing service domain based on performed in the MSEE project and on topics related to Enterprise Interoperability, from the research aspect as well as from a practitioners view. We summarise the content of the presented papers and report the issues brought up during the discussion in the workshop and add comments generated in the peer reviews of the papers.

The first paper titled Towards Standardisation in Manufacturing Service Engineering of Ecosystem by M. Zelm presents pre-standardisation work in the MSEE project on product related services which are key elements of manufacturing engineering in ecosystem. A proposal has been started in CEN TC310/WG1 for a Service Modelling Language (SML) that is built on existing modeling business process modeling languages which need to be mapped in both directions on one-another .

One comment was about how to enrich the information model of the construct relationships precising terms is-a or has-a. How will the mapping between the several standards and languages to compose the constructs be expressed and realized. More work is proposed on an illustrative example of SML, to prove the usefulness in practical terms in addition to the two pilots started. Further to work out the benefits and what is changing in the two SMEs involved in the pilots.

This second paper titled Framework for Manufacturing Servitization – Potentials for standardization by D. Chen elaborates a framework to support manufacturing companies to access their strategy and objective for a servitization project. The three dimensional framework structures existing concepts and knowledge on manufacturing servitization. The framework will help end users to define the migration path in their servitization project.

From the discussion on the value of the framework showed in the illustrative examples that enterprises gain an improved understanding of the their capabilities needed for instance in enterprise changes, reorganisations or mergers. A standard could be developed on the framework basis acting as a wrapper for the SML.

The third paper titled How can existing standards support Service Life Cycle Management by M. Freitag presents an overview of existing standards that can support Service Lifecycle Management (SLM). First, a common approach for a framework of Service Lifecycle Management is provided. Second, an overview about existing standards in the service domain is given, and – third – it is shown, how existing standards can support which phases of the Service Lifecycle Management.

In the discussion, a standardisation action was proposed to write a common vocabulary comparing the terms used in the identified existing LCM standards. In addition, it was proposed to structure all objects into (user) views for easier handling of models. More work was suggested on how the existing standards can support service lifecycle management

The focus of the fourth paper titled An approach to Interoperability testing to speed up the adoption of standards, by A. Brutti is on the interoperability testing of software implementations based on standard specification of business documents. The aim is to present an approach to prepare and set up interoperability tests to verify the data communication based on (XML) standards, checking semantic correctness and supporting users in the verification and test of their implementation. In fact conformance testing could not find all errors and interoperability testing are needed to reduce interoperability problems.

The use cases of this work have been business documents for eProcurement, developed in the PEPPOL project.

An illustrative use case showed that a difference in the notation of data formats (year/month/day) may not be detected in conformance testing. Problems like this happen when the constraints supported by XML Schema are not effectively used; for example, when the xsd:string data type is used for date elements instead of xsd:Date data type (that states that the date must be in the form "YYYY-MM-DD"). It would be interesting to further explore situations where two systems are partly interoperable and to understand the sharing of semantically correct information.

The fifth paper titled A common vocabulary to express standardization features: towards the interoperability of industrial data standards by A.F. Cutting-Decelle elaborates on knowledge about standardization and standards can be expressed through a set of well-defined concepts as for instance described in the ISO/IEC Guide 2 providing different categories of standards. It is attempted to develop a vocabulary of standards and standardization, written as an ontology which to date, comprises 125 classes, 44 object properties (used for specifying axioms) and 4 datatype properties, with the goal to obtain a common vocabulary to communicate and to achieve semantic interoperability. Definitions of relationships and constraints between the terms and concepts are critical.

Questions discussed: How can the number of multiple interpretations among standards be reduced. How generic should a reference ontology for Manufacturing be. Which are the best tools to build the ontology and enable maintenance and amendments? Describe the procedure adopted, even if it is still in progress. Interest was expressed to clarify if the ontology has been validated in a standards committee, process or standard.

This sixth paper titled An Info*Engine based architecture to support interoperability with Windchill system by M. Dhuieb deals with the complex issue of interoperability methods and technologies especially in PLM field using Windchill as PLM software. A new interoperability framework is proposed as a Webservice based solution using the capacities embedded in the Windchill Info*Engine mechanisms and J2EE application technology.

A number of questions was brought up which need further work: What are the benefits and limitations for the user? To what extend the proposed architecture and approach can be generalized and extended to other kinds of software systems? Which particular interoperability problems (semantic, syntax, etc.) does the proposal aim to tackle? What kinds of interoperability tests have been performed on the proposed framework?

Towards Standardisation in Manufacturing Service Engineering of Ecosystem

Martin Zelm — Guy Doumeingts

c/o INTEROP VLab, Belgium
martin.zelm@t-online.de
guy.doumeingts@interop-vlab.eu

ABSTRACT: Product related services are key elements of manufacturing engineering in ecosystem and become highly important in the virtual factory of the future. This short paper presents opportunities for new standards anticipated in the European Integrated Project - Manufacturing SErvice Engineering (MSEE). The MSEE project developed the Service Modelling Language (SML) that is built on existing modeling business process modeling languages and will be embedded in the Model Driven Service Engineering Architecture (MDSEA) adapted from MDA/MDI. We also discuss the standardization process of a Service Modelling Language in CEN TC 310 and report on dissemination activities via workshops and use cases.

KEYWORDS: Manufacturing Service Engineering, Standardisation process, Service Modelling Language.

1. Introduction

To keep up with their competitors, enterprises have to continuously improve their operation focusing on innovation, with regard to product, process and organization and to reduce tasks that do not provide added value. In this process manufacturing enterprises are becoming more and more committed to product related services that support the need for growing quality requirements [1].

Standardisation will provide a basis of common understanding for effective system interoperation. However, standards should complement the development of technical specifications beginning during the research activities in order to ease the implementation of new products and services [2]. But standardisation is built on consensus among all stakeholder e.g. research, industrial vendors, end users and public authorities, which is difficult to achieve during the development phase and often handicapped by budget constraints.

The FP7 Integrated Project MSEE (Manufacturing Service Ecosystem) [3] aims to create new Industrial Models for the Virtual Factory. MSEE envisions new methodologies in management and in business infrastructure within the Future Internet that will enable self-organization in distributed ecosystem. The components of such ecosystem are merged dynamically and delivered as services along the global value chain. The build up of an ecosystem includes major tasks as design and implementation of new services, maturity assessment of enterprise services and validation of business requirements using ICT tools.

The goal of the standardisation in MSEE is to promote the transfer of research results into new standards and to support academia, researchers and industry via dissemination activities and use cases with industrial pilots.

The paper first presents the state of the art of standards for enterprise services, then discusses the selecting Service Modelling Language (SML) for standardization and reports on dissemination activities. In the conclusion section, we discuss further work and issues in the standardization of SML

2. State of the Art in Standardization

Standards Development Organizations (SDO) as ISO, IEC, and industry consortia like W3C, OMG and OASIS that have been active to standardize aspects of services as for example service functionalities, service behaviour or quality of services, both on the user level or on the ICT system level. The major service related standards are:

Service Oriented Architecture (SOA) defines a reference framework of services for business functionalities that are built as software components. Major language standards in the framework are 'Unified Service Delivery Language (USDL) [4] developed in the OMG, and Web Service Description Language (WSDL) developed in W3C. Digital Business Ecosystem (DBE) [5], is an open source, distributed software reference platform. A well accepted standard in Product Lifecycle Management (PLM) is ISO 10303 'Automation systems and integration – Product data representation and exchange'. DIN [6] has published a number of user oriented standards for the service economy in Publicly Available Specifications (PAS). Standardisation of Service Quality and Service Processes has been addressed in ISO/IEC 20000.

Complementary to the work of SDOs, numerous initiatives mostly from academia have developed innovative proposals for service specifications like ontologies and formal languages. Recent research initiatives about the Future Internet, services and standardization aspects are for instance: The FI-WARE [7] project is introducing an innovative infrastructure for creation and delivery of services. The European Research Cluster on the Internet of Things (IERC) [8] aims to build a broad consensus in realizing IoT-based capabilities in Europe. The FInES (Future Internet Enterprise Systems) Cluster [9] of relevant European projects is addressing new concepts of enterprise in the Future Internet. In the frame of FInES, a Standardisation Taskforce [10] has produced a report with recommendations for standardisation in Enterprise Modelling, in Ontologies and in Cloud Computing.

3. Opportunities for Standardisation in MSEE

Three proposals for potential standards have been identified via a questionnaire executed among the MSEE project partners. The proposed candidates are: Service Modelling Language, Service Lifecycle Management and Reference Ontology for Assets. These candidates are briefly described:

1. *Service Modelling Language* (SML): There is no international language standard for the modelling of a service system. As elaborated by Chen 2013 [11], most of existing enterprise languages can be reused to model part of a service system. However, concepts of those modelling techniques need to be integrated to cover all the modelling requirements of service system engineering. An SML standard can provide a common base for modelling of product related services.

2. *Service Lifecycle Management* (SLM): A standard for Service Life Cycle Management, could for instance address categories, types or methods within the proposed SLM Framework (Freitag, Hirsch, 2012 [12]). The benefit for the practitioner is that Service oriented enterprises could collaborate seamlessly by sharing interoperating services. An SLM standard would enable common solutions for Service Lifecycle control.

3. *Reference Ontology for Assets*: Formal semantics are considered to be key drivers for standardization. Ontology elements can be used to capture, structure, and elaborate both explicit and implicit knowledge in a given domain. The resulting ontologies can support, bridge and align design, engineering, and operation of products and services. (Freitag, HirschC[13])

Table 1 shows the standardisation proposals and directly related standards or specifications. From the number of standards related to SML, it becomes obvious that multiple mappings among these standards will be required.

MSEE Standardisation proposal	Related standards
Service Modelling Language	CEN/ISO 19440, BPMN, VDML, USDL, WSDL, MDA/MDA, IEEE 31320-1, ISO 15745, CEN/ISO 11354
Service Lifecycle Management	DIN Tech Report 95, DIN PAS 1076 , QLMC[14]
Reference Ontology for Assets	Formal Manufacturing Reference Ontology [15], OWL [16]

Table 1. *MSEE standardisation proposals and related standards*

In the present environment of the MSEE project, SML is more advanced compared to the other two proposals with regard to documentation and potential use in standardization bodies.

4. SML and the Standardisation Process

According to the work of Chen, 2012 [17] and Chen 2014 [18], the proposed Service Modelling Language (SML) allows to be integrated and to interoperate with heterogeneous modelling languages through its meta-models and templates. Furthermore, some language elements identified in the proposed SML are already standards or technical specifications: e.g. CEN/ISO 19440 to model process, resource and organisation, IDEF0 (Integrated DEFinition) to model functions, BPMN to model process and CEN TS 14818 – GRAI Grid (Graph with Model and Activities Interrelated) to model decision structure.

SML defined as text, template, and graphical representation, allows us to map those standards together with other existing languages as Value Driven Modelling Language (VDML) [19]. Until now, the SML language constructs have been completely defined as part of XXX at the Business Service Modelling (BSM) level.

Following the SML proposal, a New Work Item (NWI) titled 'Constructs for Service Modelling' has been proposed to the committee CEN TC310/WG1. This Working Group has been selected because the members have many years of experience developing standards in the domain of System Automation, Enterprise Architectures and Modelling. The purpose of the NWI is to specify normative requirements for servitization support e.g. service design and operation in the manufacturing domain. At present, the draft NWI has been distributed to collect comments.

5. Industrial Pilots and Dissemination

The MSEE project has developed industrial pilots with the goal to prove the business benefit of the ecosystem concept and demonstrate the functionality of the ecosystem ICT infrastructure. The results of the pilots are very important to reach consensus on the standard proposal.

Two of these pilots employ the Service Modelling Language in use cases at SME companies BIVOLINO (a scenario 'Garments Manufacturing Services Ecosystem') and INDESIT (a scenario 'White Goods Manufacturing Ecosystem'). Both scenarios employ the language for the flexible modelling and configuration of service oriented business processes and of the related decision making processes.

To disseminate standardisation results from the MSEE project, a workshop [20] with six papers has been held at IFIP Working Conference IWEI 2013. Further, a dissemination meeting [21] was held to present SLM Toolbox and to receive feedbacks from external potential users about the toolbox, standardisation aspects and service applications.

6. Conclusions

The creation of standards during the project development phase bears several risks. Standard proposals of competing initiatives may exist and the range of information to be shared in the standard or diverging interpretations of the content may make the consensus building among the partners in the working group difficult.

Further work on Service Modelling Language is following a schedule using the CEN standardisation process. However, this process can only be completed as a European Norm (EN) if three country organisations approve the New Work Item (NWI). If for any reason, the approval cannot be obtained, the fallback solution will be to publish a Technical Specification of the NWI.

Acknowledgement: The paper is based on work performed in the project *MSEE - Manufacturing SErvice Ecosystem*. MSEE is an Integrated Project funded by the European Commission within the ICT Work Programme under the European Community's 7th Framework Programme (FoF-ICT-2011.7.3).

7. References

[1] Thoben, K.-D., Jagdev, H., Eschenbächer, J. (2001) "Extended Products: evolving traditional product concepts". In *Proceedings of the 7th International Conference on Concurrent Enterprising*, Bremen, Germany, June 2001.

[2] The Rolling plan for ICT Standardisation, http://ec.europa.eu/digital-agenda/en/rolling-plan-ict-standardisation.

[3] MSEE www.msee-ip.eu/.

[4] Unified Service Description Language (USDL), W3C USDL Incubator Group, (2011), available from http://www.w3.org/2005/Incubator/usdl/.

[5] http://www.digital-ecosystem.org/.

[6] http://www.DIN.de.

[7] http://www.fi-ware.eu.

[8] http://www.internet-of-things-research.eu/.

[9] http://www.fines-cluster.eu/jm/.

[10] Pattenden, S., Young, R, Zelm, M. *Standardisation Task Force Report to Future Internet Enterprise Systems FInES*, (2012).

[11] Chen D. "Service Modelling Language and potentials for a new standard", *IWEI 2013 Workshop*, ISTE/Wiley.

[12] Freitag, M, Kremer, D, Hirsch, M, Zelm, M: "An approach to standardize Service Lifecycle Management", *IWEI 2013 Workshop*, ISTE/Wiley.

[13] M. Freitag, M. Hirsch, Neuhüttler, J.: "How can existing Standards support Service Life Cycle management", *I-ESA 2014*, Workshop#9. ISTE/Wiley.

[14] Unified Product Life Cycle Management - the QLM Working Group (2012) of the OpenGroup, available from https://collaboration.opengroup.org/qlm.

[15] Usman, Z, Young, RIM, Chungoora, N, Palmer, C, Case, K, Harding, J.A. "Towards a formal manufacturing reference ontology", *International Journal of Production Research* (2013).

[16] OWL Web Ontology Language (OWL). World Wide Web Consortium, available from http://www.w3.org//2004/OWL.

[17] D. Chen: "Service Modelling Language and potentials for a new standard", *IWEI 2013 Workshop*, ISTE/Wiley.

[18] D. Chen: "Framework for Manufacturing Servitization - Potentials for standardization", *I-ESA 2014, Workshop#9*, ISTE/Wiley.

[19] A. A. Berre at al: "Open Business Model, Process and Service Realisation with VDML and Service ML", *Proceedings of the SOEA4EE*, 2013.

[20] http://www.utwente.nl/ewi/is/events/IWEI2013/workshops.html.

[21] http://interop-vlab.eu/news/workshop-on-service-modelling-and-standardisation-october-10th-2013-brussels-be.

Framework for Manufacturing Servitization

Potentials for Standardization

David Chen* — Sergio Gusmeroli**

University of Bordeaux - IMS
351 cours de la libération, 33405 Talence cedex, France
david.chen@ims-bordeaux.fr

*** TXT e-solutions*
Via Frigia, 27, 20126 Milano, Italy
sergio.gusmeroli@txt.it

ABSTRACT. *This paper presents a framework to support manufacturing companies accessing and determining its strategy and objective for a servitization project. The framework is elaborated within the frame of a FP7 European Integrated Project 'MSEE'. Basic concepts and notions relating to the servitization will be first introduced. Then various dimensions that constitute the framework will be detailed. The three dimensional framework will be presented and examples to illustrate the framework will be given. Finally potentials for a possible standardization will be discussed. Conclusions are given in the end of the paper.*

KEYWORDS: *Service, Framework, Servitization, Standardization.*

1. Introduction

It is generally considered that European manufacturing enterprise will progressively migrate from traditional product-centric business to product-based service-oriented virtual enterprise and ecosystems [1]. This is a long and complex process that needs to be carefully assessed, prepared and planned. In particular, it would be necessary, for a company that decides to pursuit this servitization project, to know clearly where it is (the current position) and where to go (the target position) so that strengths, weaknesses and needed investments can be identified. It is also necessary for a company to know all the steps, options and strategies in a servitization project. The framework for manufacturing servitization was elaborated for those purposes under the frame of FP7 MSEE European IP project. The project will provide a set of models, methods and tools to support the manufacturing servitization project from traditional product based enterprise to service oriented virtual enterprises and ecosystems.

2. Basic Concepts and Definitions

A framework is a conceptual model which does not provide any operational solutions. It is an organizing mechanism to categorize and structure concepts, issues and concerns in a given domain or on a particular subject of interest. A framework is usually defined by several independent axes or dimensions.

Generally speaking, a service can be seen as a provider/client interaction that creates and captures value (IBM). A manufacturing service is defined as an optimal combination of products and services to generate more income and better satisfaction for customers.

Servitization is a migration process wherein product companies embrace a service orientation and / or develop more and better services, with the aim to offer total client solutions.

The framework for manufacturing servitization presented in this paper is based on the concept of 'Extended Product' (EP). This concept is explained by Thoben [4]. An extended product is seen as an integrated offer of a physical product "extended" by services aiming at the provision of a customer oriented solution (see figure 1 [4]).

The Extended Product concept can be illustrated in a model consisting of three layers, the kernel as a representation of the core functionalities of a product (core product or product in a narrow sense), the middle layer representing the overall product (packaging) and the outer shell describing the intangible parts of the offer (services) [4].

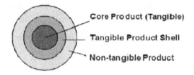

Figure 1. *Extended Product concept (Thoben, et al. 2001)*

3. Main Dimensions of the Framework

Three different framework dimensions are envisioned.

3.1. *Dimension 'Extended Product'*

This dimension aims at defining the steps of evolution from a simple physical product to virtual intangible service. The process from a traditional manufactured product to an extended product including service is described by Thoben [4]. Figure

2 illustrates this migration process from the tangible product to the intangible services around the product and finally the service as product. It shows our view is clearly focused on extending a formerly tangible product to an intangible one.

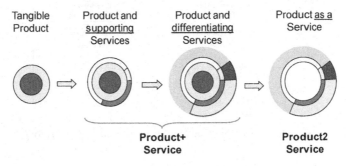

Figure 2. *Extended Product dimension*

As an example take the airplane engine company. Traditionally the company manufactures engines (this is the tangible product at the starting point). Than the company provides some supporting services such as maintenance for example (selling engines + maintenance); this is step 2. An engine manufacturer may also provide some other services which are not directly related to the physical product like financing (Product + differentiating services). Finally the company will not sell the physical product but only offer service and selling flying hours (immaterial good): this is step 4.

3.2. Dimension 'Servitization'

The servitization (SV) dimension concepts are based on the work of Service Typology by Variety and Contact Intensity done by Meiren [2]. They differentiate services with the help of the two characteristics "variety" and "contact intensity" of services. As result there are four different classes of service types (see figure 3). "Customer-focused services" such as training exhibit high contact intensity between service provider and customer, however, they are narrow in their variety. "Knowledge-focused services" as consulting are also very contact intensive, yet their complexity or variety is much higher. "Flexibility-focused services", for example the repair of a machine, exhibit a wide variety (e. g. variety of problems to be solved by repair services), and are rather limited with regard to contact intensity. Process-focused services such as transportation do not have a lot of varieties and are not very contact intensive [2] [3].

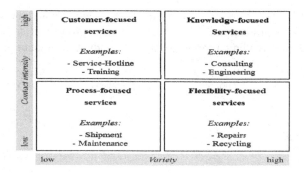

Figure 3. *Service Typology by Variety and Contact Intensity [2]*

3.3. Dimension 'Service Innovation'

The dimension 'Service Innovation' (SI) aims at identifying basic types of manufacturing value creation organizations from the single traditional simple enterprises to more complex innovation ecosystems. Four steps of evolution have been defined as shown figure 4.

Step 1 corresponds to an initial case (a simple traditional manufacturing company). Step 2 is a supply chain which can be seen as a system of product manufacturer, raw material and components suppliers as well as customers, which transform natural resources, raw materials, and components into a finished product that is delivered to the end customer. Step 3 is a value network which is a set of organizations and/or individuals which interact with each other to create values that benefit the entire group. Step 4 is an innovation ecosystem considered as a complex structure formed by the interaction of the participating community within an environment. The community consists of industry companies, start-ups, universities and research centers, collaboration institutions, technical and business services. The environment is composed from core markets where the community coexists and adjacent markets from which know-how is shared.

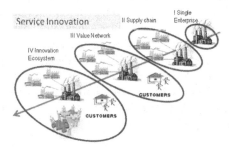

Figure 4. *Service Innovation from single company to ecosystem*

3.4. *Framework for Manufacturing Servitization*

Putting together the three dimensions presented in the above sections, the resulting framework for servitization is shown figure 5. The intersection of the three axes identifies a given situation for a company (from a business point of view). For example the initial case (EP=Product only, SI=Single enterprise, SV=Process oriented) corresponds to a traditional product manufacturing firm with only defined product shipping and delivery process. On the other side, the most evolved situation of servitization is for example a service innovation consultant company (EP=Service as product, SI=Innovation ecosystem, SV=knowledge oriented).

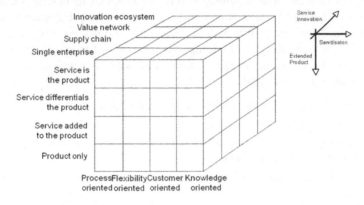

Figure 5. *Framework for Manufacturing Servitization*

Let us take a concrete example. A washing machine manufacturer wishes to move towards more services in order to better sell the product and gain competitiveness in the market. The company has already implemented after-sale service to maintain and repair their washing machines. It desires to develop more differentiating services e.g. to add some sensors to the washing machines so that users of those machines can be alerted if they don't use the machine correctly, be advised on how to save detergents and be informed on new product/service and so on. These initial and target servitization situations can be identified in the framework (see table below).

AS-IS situation			TO-BE situation		
EP	SI	SV	EP	SI	SV
II- Service added to the Product	Supply chain	Customer oriented	III- Services differentiate product	Value network	Customer oriented

It is to note that in the MSEE project, a methodology for manufacturing servitization has also been elaborated. The proposed framework is used as one asset at an early stage in a structured approach of the methodology [5].

4. Potentials for a Possible Standardization

Manufacturing servitization is still a new enterprise innovation domain where only very few standards are available. As a starting point in a servitization project, the standard framework proposed in this paper will help companies to better identify and reach possible target servitization levels, be aware of its current situation and help to know all possible choices and options. Not all enterprises need to reach the highest servitization level: this will depend on the business objective and the strategy of each company. Submitting the proposed framework to a relevant standardisation body would trigger a new work item for which the underlying standardization activities might be:

– Identifying and defining relevant concepts and vocabularies related to manufacturing servitization;

– categorizing and structuring those concepts, issues and concerns for a better clarity and rigor for use in industries;

– facilitating the communication between actors and stakeholders in a servitization project;

– favouring the development of models, methods and tools under a standard framework for industry adoption.

5. Conclusions

This paper has presented a framework for manufacturing servitization that was elaborated in FP7 IP project MSEE. This framework categorizes and structures some existing relevant concepts and knowledge on manufacturing servitization. The added value of the framework is a better organisation of dispersed and fragmented knowledge in one unique and consistent structure. From the end users point of view, the framework will help them best defining the migration path in their servitization project. Consequently there is a good potential to develop a standard on the basis of the proposed framework.

6. Acknowledgements

The authors of the paper wish to thank and acknowledge all partners of the MSEE project consortium for their contribution to this project.

7. References

[1] MSEE, "Manufacturing SErvice Ecosystem", Annex I – "Description of Work", *MSEE consortium*, 2011-04-29.

[2] Fähnrich, K.; Meiren, T. (2007). "Service Engineering: State of the Art and Future Trends". In *Advances in Services Innovations*, pp.3-16.

[3] MSEE D14.1, "Integrated Service Life Cycle Model, MSEE Integrated Project deliverable D14.1", Owner: Mike Freitag (Fraunhofer IAO), October 24, 2012.

[4] Thoben, K.-D., Jagdev, H., Eschenbächer, J. (2001) "Extended Products: evolving traditional product concepts". In *Proceedings of the 7th International Conference on Concurrent Enterprising*, Bremen, Germany, June 2001.

[5] Chen David, "A Methodology for Developing Service in Virtual Manufacturing Environment", *The 19th IFAC World Congress*, Cape Town, South Africa, 24-29 August 2014.

How Can Existing Standards Support Service Life Cycle Management

Mike Freitag* — Manuel Hirsch**— Jens Neuhüttler*

Fraunhofer IAO
Nobelstr.12, 70569 Stuttgart, Germany
Mike.Freitag@iao.fraunhofer.de
Jens.Neuhüttler@iao.fraunhofer.de

***Centre for Management Research, DITF Denkendorf**
Koerschtalstr. 26, 73770 Denkendorf
Manuel.Hirsch@DITF-MR-Denkendorf.de

ABSTRACT. *Servitization is a grand challenge for all manufacturing companies to extend their business. As main result this paper presents an overview of existing standards that can support a Service Lifecycle Management. As a first step a common approach for a framework of Service Lifecycle Management is presented. In the second step an overview about existing standards in the service domain is given, and in the final third step it is shown, how existing standards can support which phases of the Service Lifecycle Management.*

KEYWORDS: *Service Innovation, Life Cycle, Manufacturing Ecosystem, Service Science, Service Management, Service Engineering, Servitization, Standards.*

1. Introduction

Servitization for manufacturing companies becomes more important in order to find new business and new customers (Spath et al. 2010; Freitag, Ganz 2011). Traditional product-centric sectors evolve step by step to more service-centric companies because this way is a grand challenge for every company, but not only for a company but also for their products, services and employees. This evolutionary process is often referred to as the servitization process for non-tertiary sectors (Spath et al. 2010). However, the servitization process is not just a change in the business model: it involves all the aspects of the enterprise, which therefore needs methodological and technical support concerning an integrated development and management of service offerings (Freitag, Ganz 2011; Spath, Ganz 2011). And not every method or every standard can be developed from scratch. That's why it is important to use existing standards and methods to speed up this servitization process.

The objective of this paper is to present an overview of existing standards that can support Service Lifecycle Management.

The paper is structured in following main chapters:

– an approach for Service Lifecycle Management;

– an overview about existing standards in the service domain; and

– an overview of phases of the Service Lifecycle Management that can use existing standards.

2. An Approach to Standardize Service Life Cycle Management

Service Lifecycle Management can follow different approaches (Freitag et. al 2013). A good overview is given by Freitag and Stadler (2013a) depicting the *Service Lifecycle Management* framework which consists of the three axes "Phases of Service Life Cycle Management", "Role Model for Service Life Cycle Management" and "Methods and Tools for Service Life Cycle Management". In this article only the first axis "Phases of a Service Lifecycle Management" is elaborated in detail.

Figure 1 gives an overview of the architecture of the Service Lifecycle Management Framework. The three main phases of Service Lifecycle Management "service ideation", "service engineering" and "service operations management" consist of various subphases.

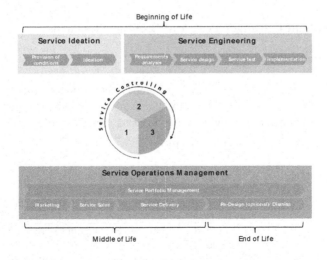

Figure 1. *Framework of a Service Life Cycle Management (Freitag, Stadler 2013)*

Service Ideation: Service ideation is a hardly describable phase at the beginning of the Service Lifecycle Management. Mainly this phase consists of two pillars, provision of conditions and ideation. These *idea providing* influences may be changing customer needs, new emerging technologies, transformations of the company environment, and other causes or drivers of change. For service ideation they serve as triggers or stimuli. When a collection of service ideas is handed over to the first phase of service engineering, "idea management", a structured collection and subsequent evaluation of the service ideas is generated.

Service Engineering: The service engineering process is a waterfall model for the development of new services. In this framework the phase "Service Engineering" consists of four phases: Requirements Analysis, Service Design, Service Test and Service Implementation. In the *requirements analysis* the internal and external requirements are collected. The second phase of the service development process is called *service design*, in which the new service is defined and described. In the third phase the service should be *tested* by customers or by using a simulation tool or at least by a checklist. The *implementation* of the service also includes the operative realization of the described services concepts. Furthermore, the involved employees need to be trained as planned.

Service Operations Management: The first phase is to do acquisitions of customers respectively service projects. After the acquisitions phase, the service needs to be delivered to the customers. This happens within "Service Delivery". The support activities for Service Operations Management are also important, for instances to manage the service portfolio and to control the service operations.

3. Overview about Existing Service and Ontology Standards

3.1. *Service Standards*

In Germany there is a long history to standardise products and since 15 years also to standards service, mainly from the German standardisation organisation DIN. An overview about existing standards can be found at www.nadl.din.de.

Phase	Norm (PAS or SPEC)
Ideation	
Service Engineering	DIN Fachbericht 95 (Technical Report 95) Service Engineering Entwicklungsbegleitende Normung (EBN) für Dienstleistungen (Standard for Service Engineering)
	DIN PAS 1076: Aufbau, Erweiterung und Verbesserung des internationalen Dienstleistungsgeschäfts (Reference Process in International Service Business)
Service Operations	DIN SPEC 77224 "Achieving customer satisfaction through Service Excellence"

Table 1. *Overview about standards in the service domain*

To develop new services and to adapt to customer requirements, market conditions and economic conditions, new development concepts are required. The systematic definition of this development process, briefly called "service engineering", is the core of the DIN Technical Report 95. It summarizes the latest research on this topic from the perspective of Standardization in the R&D Phase' (EBN).

The DIN PAS 1076 is standardised document about establishing, expanding, and improving international services. PAS 1076 is based on the methodology of Service Engineering written in DIN technical report 95.

The DIN SPEC 77224 is a specification, which is dedicated to highly relevant and complex issue of creating and promoting service excellence. This creates a guideline to handle the Service Lifecycle Management in a good way.

3.2. Ontology-Driven Standards Supporting Service Lifecycle Management

Standardization of services is a challenging task that can benefit from recent developments within the field of applied formal semantics, namely ontologies.

Notion	Standards and/or standardisation attempts
Service Catalogues and Offers	Well established open standard Unified Service Description Language (USDL) for automation in service offer retrieval and bundling
	„Standards zu Servicekatalogen in der Leistungsbeziehung zwischen Service Provider und Dienstleistungsempfänger" Catalogues of exchange between Service Provider and Service Consumer. Initiative of DIN NADL, NA 159
Services	Attempt for standardization of Management Consultancy Services (NADL, NA 159 BR-01 SO) as well as the already established standard for management-related information services (ISO/IEC 10165)
	IT-Service Definition in ISO/IEC 20000 about Service Quality and Processes. Web-Service Description Language (WSDL) of "Norm 225 BiPRO" for web-service orchestration and communication. Human-machine-interaction DIN EN ISO 9241-210:2011-01
	Collaborative production and manufacturing related standards not yet applicable.
Process	Well established ISO 18629, Process Specification Language (PSL) allows for representing arbitrary (business) processes and workflows
	Process management standard DIN/ISO 9001-2000 and project management standard DIN 69901 are also applicable for the service design and operation phases.
Manufacturing	DIN ISO 37500 Outsourcing and DIN ISO 9000 ff. on quality related aspects in production and manufacturing industry, both also covering semantic glossaries
	Formal Manufacturing Reference Ontology in (Usman, 2013) and the MSEE project[1]
Collaboration and Innovation	Very early attempt to provide comprehensive collaboration support by means of the Collaborative Innovation Ontology (CIO) in (Hirsch, 2012)
	Standardisation attempts for innovation management, IPR and service/product design (CEN/TC 389, 00389001-7 of NADL, NA 159)

Table 2. *Overview on service-related Ontology standards*

1. In-/Tangible Asset Ontology deriving from EU-Project MSEE on Manufacturing ServicE Ecosystems, http://www.msee-ip.eu

Formal semantics can be used to capture, structure, and further elaborate explicit as well as implicit knowledge all along the Service Life Cycle Management process – also covering e. g. the notion of Servitization within the manufacturing domain (Freitag et al. 2013b). The following table provides a summary of state-of-the-art service-related standards that are based or driven by formal semantics.

4. Conclusions

As the overview shows there are some standards that can be used to support Service Lifecycle Management. In some areas, standards can help to establish a systematic Service Lifecycle Management in companies. But there are still a lot of open points that must be discussed and elaborated.

Acknowledgement: The paper is mainly based on the initial work performed in the project MSEE - Manufacturing SErvice Ecosystem. MSEE is an Integrated Project funded by the European Commission within the ICT Work Programme under the European Community's 7th Framework Programme (FoF-ICT-2011.7.3).

5. References

Freitag, M., Ganz, W., "InnoScore® service. Evaluating innovation for product-related services", *Service Research & Innovation Institute (Hrsg): Annual SRII global conference (SRII)*, 2011. March 29, 2011 - April 2, 2011, San Jose, California, USA; proceedings, IEEE, Piscataway, NJ, 214–221.

Freitag, M.; Kremer, D.; Hirsch, M.; Zelm, M.: "An Approach to standardize a Service Life Cycle Management", in *Proceedings of International IFIP Working Conference on Enterprise Interoperability (IWEI)*, Workshop on Standardisation for interoperability in the service oriented enterprise, Enschede (The Netherlands), 2013.

Freitag, M.; Stadler, S.: "Requirements for a Service Lifecycle Management", In: *European Association for Research on Services -RESER-: Finding growth through service activities in barren times: XXIII International RESER Conference*; September 19-21, 2013, Aix en Provence.

Hirsch, M., *Smart Services for Knowledge Integration - Ontologiebasierte Dienste zur Unterstützung der kollaborativen Wissensarbeit in Innovationsnetzwerken*, Düsseldorf: VDI-Verlag (Fortschritt-Berichte VDI), 2012.

Spath, D., Fähnrich, K.-P., Freitag, M., Meyer, K., *Service Engineering internationaler Dienstleistungen*, Stuttgart, Fraunhofer Verlag, 2010.

Spath, D., Ganz, W., *Taking the Pulse of Economic Development. Service Trends*, München, Hanser, 2011.

Usman, Z, Young, RIM, Chungoora, N, Palmer, C, Case, K, Harding, JA (2013) "Towards a formal manufacturing reference ontology", *International Journal of Production Research*.

An Approach to Interoperability Testing to Speed up the Adoption of Standards

Arianna Brutti — Piero De Sabbata — Nicola Gessa

ENEA X-LAB
Via Martiri di Monte Sole, 4, 40129, Bologna, Italy
arianna.brutti@enea.it
piero.desabbata@enea.it
nicola.gessa@enea.it

ABSTRACT. *Interoperability among eBusiness application is becoming nowadays more and more important. Adoption of common communication standards could be a solution, but this requires some improvements in their definition and management. In this paper we focus on the testing of a software implementation based on standard specification. Our aim is to present the approach we follow to prepare and set up interoperability tests to verify the data communication based on standards, to support the users in the verification and test of their implementation, and to ease the adoption of the standard. The use cases of this work have been business documents for eProcurement, in the context of PEPPOL project.*

KEYWORDS: *Standard Life Cycle, B2B, Interoperability, Testing.*

1. Introduction

The pervading diffusion of eBusiness applications require more and more interoperability capabilities of the software, especially when operating on Internet. Comparing the eBusiness domain with other contexts, for example in respect of the telecommunication domain, some aspects appear to be different: the domain is wider and its boundaries not completely defined, the systems and the applications are continuously evolving, customization for specific needs are often unavoidable, the semantics more difficult to be tested.

As a consequence of this, interoperability testing has recently received an increasing attention, and testing is now a crucial and unavoidable phase in the life cycle of interoperable system development, whether the development is based on standard specifications or not. In this paper we face the problem of supporting and strengthen the adoption of eBusiness standards, defining a way to perform interoperability test on software implementations based on standard specifications.

2. The Role of Interoperability Testing

Speaking about implementations based on standards, testing may consist of either Conformance Testing (to prove conformance towards the specifications) or Interoperability Testing (to check the capability of different implementations to interoperate) (Bergengruen et al. 2010). Our focus points on the latter one.

The objectives of Interoperability Testing might be different:

– in some cases, for example telecommunication, the aim is validating the standard in order to discover weaknesses in the specifications themselves;

– on other cases, for example in the eBusiness field, the objective is assuring that implementations of an existing standard can interoperate.

A crucial point in these cases is achieving Interoperability without losing Conformance: for example, a study on an ETSI Plugtest (ETSI TR 2010) observed about 90% positive results regarding Interoperability between the Systems Under Test (SUTs) and, in parallel, only 60% positive results regarding Conformance.

Recent initiatives, like GITB (Global Interoperability Test Bed) and CEN WS BII on public eProcurement (CEN CWA 16073) with its pilot PEPPOL, pointed out some trends on eBusiness testing:

– use, as much as possible, of automated test (Ivezic et al. 2010) to avoid the unsustainable costs of manual testing (and test designing);

– tests should become reusable and independent, as far as possible, from the testing tools and the SUTs (Bausà et al. 2012);

– there is an increasing need for tests based on Use Profiles that customize standards specifications for concrete applicative scenarios (Brutti et al. 2011).

Examining the role of Interoperability Testing from the point of view of the Standards Life Cycle, in (Brutti et al., 2012) an Efficiency indicator for standard specifications is proposed, defined as the ratio between efforts spent for Interoperability Testing and effort for Interoperability Assessment:

– *Interoperability Testing* involves both solution providers and users and aims to test, before the real business use, if the systems are really interoperable.

– *Interoperability Assessment* is performed upon real systems and real business transactions; it is very sensitive for users because any problem might have relevant economic consequences.

The rationale of such indicator is that the higher efficiency is achieved when problems are removed earlier, before the deployment and use of systems implementing the standards. This paper focuses on Interoperability Testing with the aim to improve the Efficiency of the whole life cycle and reduce the efforts and costs required by the testing activities.

3. Interoperability Test Set-Up

In the standards life-cycle designed in (Brutti et al., 2012) the "Implementation" phase of a standard-based system for data-exchange and business transaction is composed of various, different steps that lead to the real adoption and use of the implemented system.

More in particular, after the "Product Development" (that results in software components used for the communication), two critical steps are those related with testing activities; these steps are fundamental in order to find implementation errors, misleading interpretations of the specification, interoperability issues.

In the "Implementation" phase, the first testing activity is the verification of the conformance to the protocol/standard identified for the communication. Conformance testing tools must then be available to the users in order to perform this stage. This activity aims to certify the technical interoperability of the system and it is mainly related with the standard specifications and with constraints defined in a use profile.

Since we are speaking on XML-based eBusiness standard, conformance testing can be (relatively) easily performed really starting from the specifications that are typically written using schema languages (like XML Schema or Schematron). In this case conformance validation merely consists in the validation of the XML instance against the XML Schema and/or Schematron files provided by the standard.

Once conformance is attested, the following phase regards the interoperability testing. Interoperability testing is strictly related with the correct use and interpretation of the specification and aims to finally achieve the upper levels of interoperability between two systems: semantic and organizational interoperability.

In supporting the adoption of the PEPPOL project specifications we started facing the problem of interoperability testing, and thus we considered the two aspects of this activity:

a) testing the semantic correctness of the exchanged standard documents;

b) testing the correct use of the documents in relation to the business processes.

In order to perform such activities, standard specifications are no more enough: what is needed is to define and prepare test specifications, deriving them from the standard; and since we want to provide software tools to support semantic testing, we need to formalise them in a machine readable language.

Considering the first aspect (a), it is worth to note that, differently from conformance validation, semantic validation is more difficult to test, since requires performing the verification on the content and meaning of the exchanged document.

More, semantic testing in many cases must be designed and tailored for each specific System Under Test (SUT), since the semantic verification strongly depends from the correct usage and connection with their Database and ERP, that provide the data to exchange. Another relevant point in testing the interoperability is that this requires, in some manner, the involvement of two or more partners.

We experimented the need for semantic test by monitoring some of the first conformance tests: some documents resulted valid, while presenting clear problems related to the use and comprehension of the document elements. In our approach we decided to verify the interoperability of an implementation, using a simulation performed with a software validator. In other words, the users can check the documents produced by a system loading and validating them into a software that contains rules that check the correct usage of the document structure.

We defined two different sets of rules, the first set to test the semantic interoperability of the document (a), the second to verify the correct usage in the process (b). Both the types of rules were written using the Schematron validation language. We want to remark that these rules no more regard the structure of the document, but its content. This leads us to build some sample checks to verify the interoperability of the implemented software.

The test set-up changes in case of testing rules (a) or (b). For type (a), it is composed of the following steps (one test case for example is related with the Invoicing process):

1. Identification of the data set for the test: first of all we identify a specific set of data of an invoice on which to build the test. Such set of data are not general, but strictly related with a specific simulation of a transaction for the SUT.

2. Building of a correct XML document instance for the invoice. This step at the moment is performed manually.

3. Automatic generation, from the XML instance (of step 2), of the all Schematron rules for interoperability check. These rules are thus based on the content of the correct version of the invoice (that is built manually).

4. Loading of the rules on a software system for validation. Now the design of the test is completed, and it is possible to verify the interoperability of the system.

5. Automatic generation from the enterprise software system (that implements the standard) of the XML instance related with the data set (invoice) of step 1.

6. Interoperability test on the invoice generated automatically, with the validator software that plays the role of a sparring partner in the simulation. For example, we identify in the Invoice document the following set of data:

Invoice number	22/2013
Invoice issuing date	2013-12-04
The date applicable VAT	2013-11-20

This set requires the following - correct - implementation:

```
<cbc:ID>22/2013</cbc:ID>
<cbc:IssueDate>2013-12-04</cbc:IssueDate>
<cbc:TaxPointDate>2013-11-20</cbc:TaxPointDate>
```

Nevertheless, with simple conformity rules, like the following

```
<assert test="(cbc:IssueDate)" flag="fatal">An invoice MUST have...</assert>
<assert test="(cbc:ID)" flag="fatal">An invoice MUST have...</assert>
```

it is not possible to check the correctness of the implementation; we need more stringent rules to verify the semantic interoperability, like the following ones:

```
<assert test="(cbc:IssueDate) and (cbc:IssueDate = '2013-12-04'" flag="fatal">The invoice MUST
have the date of issue and it MUST be '2013-12-04'.</assert>
<assert test="(cbc:ID) and (cbc:ID = '22/2013')" flag="fatal">...</assert>
<assert test="(cbc:TaxPointDate) and (cbc:TaxPointDate = '2013-11-20')" flag= "fatal" >....</assert>
```

The approach to verify the correct implementation of the rules of type (b) (correctness of business process implementation) is different:

– the rules are not related to a specific data set, but have been defined from the process design. So in this case the test is not strictly related with a specific partner, but it is more generic;

– the validation does not concern a single document, but at least a couple of document that must be compared in order to evaluate the coherence of the some internal data.

In this case then the validation process is:

1. definition with Schematron of (general) business process validation rules, and set-up with them of the validation tools;

2. loading on the validator of the set of document instances (generated by the partner) for the validation.

This set of interoperability tests allows us finding and correct many interoperability errors, and to do this in a protected way, outside the real transactions. For sure we still need further interoperability tests also with the real business partner, before to definitely adopt the communication systems, but this approach minimizes the effort for debug correction during the test in scenarios with real application.

4. Conclusions

This paper attempts to define an approach for interoperability testing that could be sustainable in terms of time and costs, and having a positive impact on the process of adoption of standards. We summarize an evaluation of this work in:

– weakness: the interoperability testing artifacts are developed manually and are specific for the SUT;

– strength: the validation tool automatizes the execution of the tests, allows to quickly discover interoperability problems and to reduce the effort in the testing

Future developments are collecting experiences from a more extensive campaign of testing, in order to analyse and understand the main interoperability issues that arise in standard adoption, and to improve and automate the process of test design, delivery, execution and evaluation, also in case of *ad hoc* test for specific System Under Test (SUT).

5. References

Bausà O., Legner C., "Global eBusiness Interoperability Test Beds (GITB) Facilitating Large Scale Projects in Europe", in *Standards improving Enterprise Interoperability benefits for a service oriented Future Internet, Workshop at I-ESA 2012*, Valencia, March 21, 2012.

Bergengruen O., Fischer F., Namli T., Rings T., Schulz S., Serazio L., Vassiliou-Gioles T., "Ensuring Interoperability with Automated Interoperability Testing", *ETSI White Paper*, European Telecommunications Standards Institute (ETSI), Sophia-Antipolis, 2010.

Brutti A., De Sabbata P., Ciaccio G., Frascella A., Novelli C., "A model to analyse critical factors in B2B interoperability standards life cycle", in *Enterprise interoperability, I-ESA 2012*, Valencia, 2012.

Brutti A., De Sabbata P., Frascella A., Novelli C., Gessa N., "Standard for eBusiness in SMEs networks: the increasing role of customization rules and conformance testing tools to achieve interoperability", in *Enterprise Interoperability, proceedings of the Workshops of the Third International IFIP Working Conference IWEI 2011*, ISTE/John Wiley and Sons, 2011.

CWA 16073, CEN Workshop Agreement from CEN Workshop on "Business Interoperability Interfaces for Public procurement in Europe (CENBII)", Brussels, 2010, www.cen.eu/cwa/bii/specs/

ETSI Technical Report TR 102 789 v1.1.1, 2010-01, "Methods for Testing and Specification (MTS); Automated Interoperability Testing;" *Summary of ETSI experiences about using automated interoperability testing tools*, ETSI, 2010.

Ivezic N., Woo J., Cho H., "Towards Test Framework for Efficient and Reusable Global e-Business Test Beds", in *Enterprise Interoperability IV: Making the Internet of the Future for the enterprise*.

A Common Vocabulary to Express Standardization Features

Towards the Interoperability of Industrial Data Standards

A.-F. Cutting-Decelle* — G.-I. Magnan** — C. Mouton*** — R.I.M. Young****

* École Centrale de Lille
Cité Scientifique, F-59651Villeneuve d'Ascq
University of Geneva, ICLE
CH 1227 Carouge and CODATA France, F-75016 Paris, France
afcd@ec-lille.fr

** Transportation Energy and Communication Department, AFNOR Group
F-93571 La Plaine Saint-Denis, France

*** EDF, Nuclear Engineering Branch, Nuclear PLM Project
F-92120 Montrouge, France

**** Loughborough University-Wolfson School of Mechanical & Manufacturing
Engineering, Loughborough, Leicestershire, UK

ABSTRACT. Knowledge about standardization and standards can be expressed through a set of well-defined concepts described in several Guides and Directives, written by both ISO and IEC. Those documents provide very precise definitions and guidance for the main concepts dealing with standards but also with the standardization process and the different phases of the standardization project. Based on the existence of those regulatory documents, and given the crucial aspects of interoperability problems met in manufacturing and the importance of the role played by standards, it was tempting to see to what extent a vocabulary of standards and standardization, written as an ontology, would help.

KEYWORDS: Standards, Industrial Data, Standardization, Interoperability, Ontologies.

1. Introduction

Knowledge about standardization and standards, at the international level, is represented through a set of well-defined concepts provided in several Guides and Directives, written by both ISO and IEC. Those documents, updated on regular bases, give very precise definitions and guidance for all the concepts dealing with standards but also with the standardization process and the project as a whole.

In manufacturing, particularly, one of the best way to effective systems interoperation is probably through the use of standards, as these should provide a shared basis upon which all the parties involved can develop a common understanding. However the use of current standards has critical shortcomings where multiple interpretations of a standard are possible and where multiple standards are needed to cover the range of information to be shared. Typically interoperability between existing standards themselves is not achieved and hence they cannot be expected, in their current form, to support the information sharing requirements of complex multi-system networks (Young et al., 2013). It should be noted that a number of attempts to improve cooperation among standards have been attempted and failed – given the importance of effective industrial data sharing, solutions must continue to be sought.

The proposal here targets a fundamentally important concept: if you are going to be able to communicate then you must necessarily have a common vocabulary to support it. Based on the existence of those regulatory documents, the aim of the work presented in this paper is to propose an ontology of standardization concepts.

The need for formal representations to achieve semantic interoperability is well understood and a lot of work has been done in this domain. Given the page limits it is impossible to reference all the works of relevance to this research, for a more detailed background analysis, see for example Chungoora et al., 2011. The FP7 FLEXINET project N. 688627 (FLEXINET, 2013) is one of a number of projects following this approach and pursuing a formal definition of manufacturing concepts. Situated at the junction between standardization and manufacturing knowledge based approaches (Chungoora et al., 2012, Imran et al., 2012), this paper explores the application of formal representation techniques to the standardisation domain itself.

2. The Standardization Context

ISO (the International Organization for Standardization) is a worldwide federation of national standards bodies (ISO member bodies). The work of preparing International Standards is normally carried out through ISO technical committees. ISO collaborates closely with the International Electrotechnical Commission (IEC) on all matters of electrotechnical standardization. (ISO) Most of the Technical committees (TC) are subdivided into sub-committees (SC), whose role is to refine the standardization activity of the corresponding TC, focusing on specific aspects of the domain covered by the TC. Among the existing TCs (more than 280 active TCs), ISO TC 184 (Automation systems and integration) is one of the biggest in terms of number of standards (754 published ISO standards), with 19 participating countries and 22 observing countries. The scope of ISO TC 184 is standardization in the field of automation systems and their integration for design, sourcing, manufacturing and delivery, support, maintenance and disposal of products and their associated services. Areas of standardization include information systems, robotics for fixed and mobile robots in industrial and specific non-industrial environments, automation and control software and integration technologies. ISO TC 184 is composed of 4 active SCs and one Advisory Group (AG). (ISO TC 184)

Among the standards developed by SC4, let us mention: ISO 8000 data quality, ISO 10303 STEP (STandard for the Exchange of Product model data), ISO 13584 P-LIB (Part Library), ISO 15531 MANDATE (MANufacturing DATa Exchange), ISO 15926 Oil and Gas, ISO 16739 IFC (Industry Foundation Classes) and ISO 18629 PSL (Process Specification Language). (ISO TC 184/SC4)

3. Standardization and Standards: Main Concepts and Definitions

At the international level, standardization and standards are concepts well-defined through several guides, written by both ISO and IEC, which are, for the most commonly used:

– ISO/IEC Guide, Standardization and related activities – General vocabulary (Eighth edition, 2004); (ISO/IEC Guide 2, 2004);

– ISO/IEC Directives, Parts 1 and 2 and the Consolidated ISO supplement, 2013. (ISO/IEC Dir, Part 1, 2012, Part 2, 2011, Consolidated ISO supplement, 2013).

Those documents, particularly the ISO/IEC Guide, provide very precise definitions for all the terms related to standards and to the standardization process, among which: (ISO/IEC Guide 2:2004)

– *standard*: document established by consensus and approved by a recognized body, that provides, for common and repeated use, rules, guidelines or characteristics for activities or their results, aimed at the achievement of the optimum degree of order in a given context;

– *standardization*: refers to the activity of establishing, with regard to actual or potential problems, provisions for common and repeated use, aimed at the achievement of the optimum degree of order in a given context.

Terms defined in the ISO/IEC Guide 2 are organized into categories, among which: standardization, aims of standardization, normative documents (for the different types of standards), bodies responsible for standards and regulations, types of standards. According to the ISO/IEC Guide 2, the terms expressing more specific concepts may generally be constructed by a combination of terms representing more general concepts. The latter terms thus form "building blocks", and the selection of terms and the construction of definitions within this Guide have been based on this approach in cases where equivalent English, French and Russian (official languages of ISO/IEC documents) combined terms contain the same "building blocks".

4. Fundamental Concepts of the Vocabulary

The work done within the framework of the FLEXINET project is committed to the use of formal representation techniques (such as CL, or OWL) although here we provide a visual graphical representation in UML for ease of understanding. Key-concepts of the standardization ontology are represented using UML class diagrams, as a first model of a "lightweight" ontology of standards. Main key-concepts are: SB_organizational_structure, standard, standardization_actor, standardization_work_organization, standard_document_stage, standard_document_type. Figures 1 to 3 below show some examples of the diagrams.

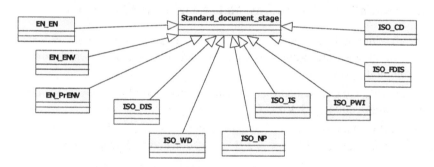

Figure 1. *A UML model of the Standard_document_stage concept*

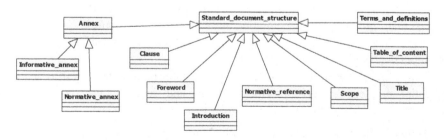

Figure 2. *A UML model of the Standard_document_structure concept*

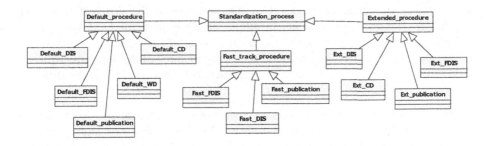

Figure 3. *A UML model of the Standardization_process concept*

The work of most research is targeted at the formal semantic definition of "terms and definitions" as illustrated in figure 2. However, for cross-standard interoperability to be achieved it is essential that the same rigour is applied to the normative references shown in the same figure. FLEXINET aims to support this approach through the provision of standard reference ontologies. However, it is also critical to understand and define the relationships and constraints between the various standardisation processes illustrated in figure 3 if a fully comprehensive view of interoperability potential is to be realised (Chungoora et al., 2011).

5. Discussion: On-Going Issues and Perspectives

To date, the ontology comprises 125 classes, 44 object properties (used for specifying axioms) and 4 datatype properties. The development of the ontology is being done on a manual basis, through the analysis of ISO Directives and based on the authors' skill and experience as either members of SDOs or experts in standardization. This ontology is intended to be used as a common vocabulary applicable to the representation of whatever kind of standardization document, or activity, in order to make the information contained widely shareable and interoperable. The criteria used for structuring the ontology have been to keep as far as possible the duality of the standardization concept: both a method (the standardization process) and a result (the standard being developed). Given the complexity of the standardization world, and in order be as complete as possible with respect to the regulatory documents, the writing process of the set of axioms is still in progress.

Given the commitment of the authors in the standardization activities of the ISO TC 184 committee, the ontology is validated as and when appropriate.

This work on defining a standardization ontology looks very promising as a route to providing a basis for improved interoperability across standards (Pattenden et al., 2012), by reducing the level of interpretation of the different normative documents. However, there is much still to be done, particularly in the way of understanding and interpreting the technical content of the standards: work is ongoing at the ISO TC 184 level to build up a "Big Picture" of the standards (Michel, 2005), thus enabling a roadmap of the technical concepts handled in the different documents.

This work on a common vocabulary to express standardization aspects can be considered as one of the fundamental "bricks" of the problem of interoperability across manufacturing systems, but also as a part of domain of knowledge of the Manufacturing Intelligence approach, as dealt with by Hastilow (Hastilow, 2013). As such, it will provide an input to the Task 8 (standardization) of the WP8 (Dissemination, Exploitation and standardization) workpackage of the FLEXINET project.

6. Acknowledgements

The work presented in this paper is done within the framework of the FLEXINET project N. 688627, funded under the Seventh Framework Programme FP7-2013-NMP-ICT-FOF (RTD), "Intelligent Systems Configuration Services for Flexible Dynamic Global Production Networks (FLEXINET)".

AF Cutting-Decelle, C Mouton and R Young are members of ISO TC 184, experts for SC4, GI Magnan is, as AFNOR representative, secretary of ISO TC 184.

7. References

Chungoora, N., Cutting-Decelle, A.-F., Young, R.I.M., Gunendran, G., Usman, Z., Harding, J.A. & Case K. (2011). "Towards the ontology-based consolidation of production-centric standards", *International Journal of Production Research*.

Chungoora, N., Gunendran, G., Young, R. I. M., Usman, Z., Anjum, N., Palmer, C., Harding, J.A., Case K. and Cutting-Decelle A.-F. (2012). "Extending product lifecycle management for manufacturing knowledge sharing". *Proc IMechE* Part B: J Engineering Manufacture 226(12) 2047–2063.

Hastilow, N. (2013). "An Ontological Approach to Manufacturing Systems Interoperability in Dynamic Change Environments". PhD thesis in preparation. School of Mechanical and Manufacturing Engineering, Loughborough University, UK.

http://www.flexinet-fof.eu/Pages/FLEXINETProjectOverview.aspx (accessed February 2014).

Imran M., and Young R., Usman Z. (2012). "Formal assembly reference ontology for assembly systems compatibility assessment". *Advances in Manufacturing Technology XXVI Tenth International Conference on Manufacturing Research* Edited by T. S. Baines, B. Clegg and D. K. Harrison. Pp.146-151.

ISO TC 184/SC4: http://isotc.iso.org/livelink/livelink/open/tc184sc4 (accessed February 2014).

ISO/IEC Directives, Part 1, *Consolidated ISO Supplement – Procedures specific to ISO*, 4th Edition, 201.3

ISO/IEC Directives, Part 1, *Procedures for the technical work*, 9th Edition, 2012.

ISO/IEC Directives, Part 2, *Rules for the structure and drafting of international standards*, 6th Edition, 2011.

ISO/IEC Guide 2, *Standardization and related activities – General vocabulary*, 8th Edition, 2004.

ISO:http://www.iso.org/iso/home/standards_development/list_of_iso_technical_committees/iso_technical_committee.htm?commid=54110 (accessed February 2014).

Michel, J.J., 2005. Terminology extracted from some manufacturing and modelling related standards. CEN/TC 310 N1119R2.

Pattenden, S., Young, R., and Zelm, M. *Standardisation Task Force Report to Future Internet Enterprise Systems* (2012).

Young, R.I.M., Hastilow, N., Imran, M., Chungoora, N., Usman, Z. and Cutting-Decelle, A.F., "Reference ontologies for manufacturing", *IWEI workhop*, 2013.

An Info*Engine-Based Architecture to Support Interoperability with Windchill System

Mohamed Anis Dhuieb* — Farouk Belkadi* — Florent Laroche*
Alain Bernard*

* LUNAM Université
Institut de Recherche en Communications et Cybernétique de Nantes
École centrale de Nantes, 1 rue de la Noë, 44300 Nantes
Mohamed-anis.dhuieb@irccyn.ec-nantes.fr

ABSTRACT. This paper deals with the complex issue of interoperability methods and technologies especially in PLM field. Windchill is one of the most popular PLM software proposing robust solutions to support communication with external information systems. The purpose of this paper is to prospect the interoperability mechanisms offered by PTC editor as a solution to interoperability issue. A new interoperability framework is proposed as a Webservice based solution using the capacities embedded in the Windchill Info*Engine mechanisms and J2EE application technology.

KEYWORDS: Interoperability, PLM, Windchill, Webservices, Info*Engine.

1. Introduction

According to (Srinivansan, 2011), the scope and definition of PLM are expanding and maturing to meet the demands of an increasingly complex network of industrial partners spread globally and bound together by common business objectives. These partners have to collaborate by sharing and exchanging products and processes information, and integrate their engineering and business decision support systems. For this need, each partner needs to develop the capacity of their information systems to communicate easily with the other partners systems. In this context, interoperability becomes an important challenge for the ICT scientific and industrial community (Stanescu, 2009). Another definition is given by The United States Department of Defense, which proposes an extension of the interoperability concept to the ability to exchange services between various systems and organizations. Generally, three scopes of interoperability are distinguished with different terms and definitions. For instance: the Conceptual interoperability that concerns the definition of concepts and semantic supporting the communication between data and knowledge models; the Organizational interoperability, which focus on the connection between processes and the Technical interoperability that deals with technological issues to support data exchange between software applications (Ruggaber, 2005) (Bellatreche et al., 2006).

This work deals with the last category of interoperability and aims to investigate the advantages given by the PTC Info*Engine framework for communication with PLM (Product Lifecycle Management) system. PLM is a collaborative backbone allowing people throughout extended enterprises to work together more efficiently (Choi et al., 2002). The Enterprise Information System (EIS) results from the integration between Enterprise Resource Planning (ERP), Product Data Management (PDM) and other related systems such as Computer-Aided Design (CAD) and Customer Relationship Management (CRM). Due to the collaborative character and the main role consisting of data exchange throughout heterogeneous information systems, PLM is one of major field in which interoperability have an important contribution (Song et al., 2006).

First, we present a state of the art about the current technical developments used to support communication between ICT systems. Then, we present a new architecture based on Info*Engine integration engine and Webservice technology and proposed as a solution to support automatic import/export operations in the case of Windchill system. The following section presents an overview about the problematic of interoperability. A focus is made on the recent developments concerning the technical interoperability. The third section presents a description of the different interoperability mechanisms offered by Windchill that is one of most popular PLM systems, developed by PTC Company. The fourth section presents the proposed technical architecture and the developed interface to ensure the automatic communication with Windchill server.

2. Literature Survey about Interoperability

In addition to the term definition, another important characteristic of the interoperability concept concerns the variety of classification according to the interoperability goal, the type of interoperable items or also the nature of methods and technologies that are used for the interoperability strategy.

In practice, three major approaches are currently used to support the data exchange between Computer Aided applications (CAx). The first category uses a standard based mechanism to guarantee the semantic translation between heterogeneous models. Several standards are used in the literature such as the project ATHENA, in which Process standards (ISO15288, CMII) and product standards (STEP: STandard for the Exchange of Product model data. Ex: AP214, 233, 209, 239) have been studied. IGES (Initial Graphics Exchange Specifications) and DXF (Drawing Exchange Format) standards are also used to manage the geometric data of the product. The second category uses the ontology and the Semantic Web technologies to achieve the data mapping between heterogeneous software. Several studies implementing different approaches to product design have been conducted on Ontology, as standard for data exchange between design and other engineering activities in collaborative tasks. The last category use dynamic interfaces, based on API Standards (Application Program Interface), to guarantee the communication between software. In this kind of interoperability mechanism, software integration is fulfilled through the web services technologies to support the distribution of heterogeneous information between members of a project team. "OMG PDM Enablers" based on middleware technologies and "PLM Services" are Web technologies developed to support communication between PLM systems.

Owing to the recent facilities offered by the World-Wide Web technologies, Web Based Modeling and Simulation has been proposed to support the modelling and simulation tasks in a PLM context. The use of this concept is facilitated by the MDE (Model Driven Engineering) technology dedicated to the formulation, the formalization and the automation of the development process.

3. Info*Engine-Based Framework for Interoperability

Windchill integration with other enterprise's applications requires the use of low-level APIs and complex application adapters. Supporting new integration scenarios is a labor task and requires strong development skills. For this need, Windchill Info*Engine server provides mechanisms for retrieving and manipulating the data that users or custom applications want to view or receive from the PLM server. The next section presents the technical architecture of the proposed interoperability framework base on Info*Engine mechanisms.

3.1. Technical Architecture

As it is shown in Figure 1, the proposed architecture is based on Info*Engine Java 2 Enterprise Edition (J2EE) connector, that is an implementation of J2EE Connector Architecture (JCA). JCA was designed to supply standard implementation for interaction between J2EE application servers and enterprise information systems (EIS). The Info*Engine J2EE connector uses SOAP protocol to allow communication between Info*Engine and the two modules of the interoperability application. For instance, J2EE application server and associated client application are developed as an integrated solution for the interoperability purpose.

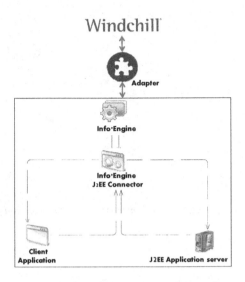

Figure 1. *The Info*Engine based architecture*

The client application is deployed on Oracle 11g application server. Using the client application, the user can perform different interoperability actions like creating/deleting an object in the Windchill server or even adding a link between a part and a document. The J2EE application server supports the interpretation and execution of actions prescribed by the client application. Otherwise, Info*Engine is directly interfaced with Windchill application by means of the Native Adapters component. The implementation of the proposed solution is achieved by a set of interactions between the different components of Info*Engine framework and the interoperability client application. As it is shown in figure 1, the client application communicates directly with the Info*Engine SOAP Servlet that catch and process SOAP requests and send the required information to the client application. For this need, the SOAP servlet invokes tasks execution on the SAK (Service Access Kit), which is an API facilitating the development of Java applications, including JSP pages, using Info*Engine functions and features. During task execution, SAK interacts with the naming service in order to instantiate required services. With the Naming Service, SAK can identify in the LDAP directory all network addresses and configuration properties. In the meantime, the client application has a direct connection to the SAK and the naming services to extract the services parameters and code interpretation respectively, which are required for the definition of the Webservice request.

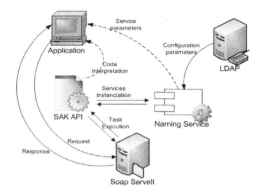

Figure 2. *Internal and external interactions in the proposed framework*

3.2. *Demonstrator*

Based on the technical architecture presented above, we developed a Webservice based application. Figure 3 illustrates the interactions schema between the user, the interoperability client application and Windchill, throughout the Info*Engine framework.

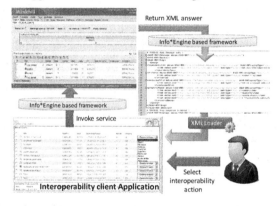

Figure 3. *Webservice-based application*

After the user identification by entering his Windchill login and password, the client application receives from Windchill a list of different objects that are associated to the user role in the database. At the right of the interface, a set of authorized actions are proposed to the user to perform on the Windchill server throughout the Info*Engine based framework. For instance, the user can obtain more details about the selected object, check out, modify or delete this object or also, creates link with other Windchill objects.

When the user validates his/her action, the client application invoke the corresponding service(s) on the Info*Engine framework according to the general interaction schema presented in Figure 3. Then, the Windchill send the answer in a predefined XML file to the Info*Engine framework.

4. Conclusions

This framework is a first step for the development of an integrated connector for Windchill server. The main utility of this connector is to handle process and product knowledge to be integrated in a virtual decision support system. Using this framework, the user can benefit from relating an external application with Windchill allowing the application to create and manipulate parts and documents in Windchill. Further work will aim at the definition of robust loader tool to support the interpretation of Windchill responses in a knowledge management perspective. The first results of the interoperability tests performed on the proposed framework illustrate a high level of reactivity to different requests. The main advantages of the proposed architecture is that it offer a large possibilities to pilot the communication with Windchill system through an external third-party application while ensuring a coherence with internal mechanisms of Windchill, since it exploits directly the internal components of Windchill.

5. References

Bellatreche, L., Xuan, D.N., Pierra, G., & Dehainsala, H. (2006). "Contribution of Ontology-based Data Modeling to Automatic Integration of Electronic Catalogues within Engineering Databases", *Computers in Industry* Vol. 57, No. 8-9, pp.711-724.

Choi, G.H., Mun, D., Han, S. (2002). "Exchange of CAD Part Models Based on the Macro-Parametric Approach", *International Journal of CAD/CAM* Vol. 2, No. 1, pp.13-21.

DoD, United States Department of Defence, Joint Publication 1-02, "Department of Defence Dictionary of Military and Associated Terms", 12 April 2001; p.270.

Ruggaber R., (2005), "ATHENA: Advanced Technologies for Interoperability of Heterogeneous Enterprise Networks and their Application", *International Conference on Interoperability of Enterprise Software and Applications*, Geneva, Switzerland.

Song H., Roucoules L., Eynard B., Lafon P., (2006). "Interoperability between Cooperative Design Modeller and a CAD System: Software Integration versus Data Exchange", *International Journal for Manufacturing Science & Production*, Vol. 7, No. 2, pp.139-149.

Srinivasan, V. (2011). "An integration framework for product lifecycle management". *Computer-aided design*, 43(5), 464-478.

Stanescu A.M., Dumitrache., Caramihai S.I., Moisescu M.A., Sacala I.S. (2009), "The Grand Unification: Emerging Sciences to Support Interoperability Based Complex Adaptive Systems in Intelligent Manufacturing", *8ème Congrès international de Génie Industriel*.

Doctoral Symposium

Report

B. Archimède* — J. Lamothe**

* INP-ENIT, University of Toulouse
47 avenue d'Azereix, BP1629, 65016 Tarbes cedex, France
bernard.archimede @ enit.fr

** Mines Albi, University of Toulouse
Campus Jarlard, Route de Teillet, 81000 Albi, France
jacques.lamothe@mines-albi.fr

The goal of the Doctoral Symposium of the I-ESA'2014 is to propose to PhD students in any area of enterprise interoperability an opportunity to submit an article and present their research works in an international conference and interactively discuss their research issues with senior researchers. We summarise the content of the presented papers and report the issues brought up during the discussion in the workshop and add comments generated in the peer reviews of the papers.

1. Build Enterprise Relationship Network to Support Collaborative Business, L. Wang

In this paper, authors propose a new definition of enterprise relationship network (ERN), which consists of four graphs, the enterprise relationship graph (ENTG), the employee relationship graph (EMPG), the product relationship graph (PROG), and the three-level hypergraph (TLHG), gives differences with other social networks and propose some first analysis views.

The authors have built a big data set inspired from a real case. The distance between the real case and the data set should be evaluated. The experimental part should be oriented on the specific characteristics of the model that permit developing interesting views.

2. Analysing Internet of Things to Feed Internet of Knowledge: Support Decision Making in Crisis Context, A. Sirko

This paper presents some ambitious objectives on a research project aiming to collect information about the world through the Internet of Things in crisis context. It tries to highlight the main issues of such a project and then offer some short definitions of required concepts.

In crisis context social network produce high volumes of low credibility data. Nevertheless value added information can be extracted when crossing all these data. The proposed model should be more detailed on this point.

A use case could be of high added value to validate the propositions.

3. *On the interoperability in marine pollution disaster Management, V. Nicolescu.*

Marine pollution disasters in offshore platforms require international collaborations. This paper presents an approach to integrate sensor networks and a proposed common framework model for multiple-countries disaster monitoring devices, which require the collaboration of several management organisations resulting in heterogeneous systems.

4. *A framework for characterizing collaborative networks of organisations, A. Montarnal*

This paper describes a new framework to characterize collaborative networks of organisations oriented towards three axes of study including the concepts of sharing between the partners, of network governance and of perspective of collaboration. On similar frameworks, recent results have been developed in European FP7 projects that should be integrated in the literature review.

Build Enterprise Relationship Network to Support Collaborative Business

Liqiang Wang — Shijun Liu — Lei Wu— Li Pan — Xiangxu Meng

School of Computer Science and Technology
Shandong University, Jinan 250101, P.R.China
Shandong Province Key Laboratory of Software Engineering
Jinan 250101, P.R.China
wanglq1989@163.com
lsj@sdu.edu.cn
i_lily@sdu.edu.cn
panli@sdu.edu.cn
mxx@sdu.edu.cn

ABSTRACT: Collaborative business among enterprises is based on a symbiotic relationship, where each company has a product or service that will help the other, when they trade or share these items, both companies benefit. Enterprise relationship network (ERN) can be used to support the business collaboration by maximize current and future opportunities and facilitate network-enabled processes, leading to value co-creation. The main technical difficulty is in the expression of ERN which combined by many forms of relations that address specific organizational constituencies and product structure. We proposed a new definition of ERN and gave the analysis of its characteristics. The ERN model in this paper consists of four graphs, the enterprise relationship graph (ENTG), the employee relationship graph (EMPG), the product relationship graph (PROG), and the three-level hypergraph (TLHG). The comprehensive utilization of these graphs can string the main objectives in the business together, such as enterprise, business, employee and product. ERN can be used in supporting business analysis, applications, employee collaborations and other commercial appreciation services. We introduced a case study on SDCMSP and some relationship visualization results at last.

KEYWORDS: Enterprise Relationship Network; Enterprise Social Network; Enterprise Relationship Management; Business Collaboration; Social Network.

1. Introduction

Collaborative business is a concept where companies share information with each other in order to create stronger operations. The collaboration functions as a symbiotic relationship, where each company has a product or service that will help the other, when they trade or share these items, both companies benefit.

Social networks (Wikipedia 2013) have got tremendous development and popularity in the past few years, and it has changed the way of people's communication and information research to a large extent. There are some distinctions of ERN compared to existing social networks, such as social network, Enterprise 2.0 and enterprise social network. The core factor of social network is people, and the social relationships are often not related to business. Enterprise 2.0 is the use of emergent social software platforms within companies, or between companies and their partners or customers. It aims to help employees, customers and suppliers collaborate, share and organize information via Web 2.0 technologies (Capuano, N. et al., 2010). Enterprise social network (ESN) emerged and grew quickly, some software based on ESN has come out, e.g., Salesforce's Chatter, Microsoft's Yammer and IBM Connections. This software provides convenience for collaboration and communication among employees. But in these applications ESN is confined to communication among people ignoring the business.

For the similarity to social network, it's reasonable to organize the enterprises with a network based on business relationships, we name it as 'Enterprise Relationship Network'. The main purpose of ERN is to support collaborative business as well as to discover valuable information from enterprise relationships. And we propose a new ERN model to build the network with the enterprise as the core entity and the business between enterprises as the principal line.

The remainder of this paper is organized as follows. In section 2, we introduce the related work mainly about the theory and analysis of social network. The definition and modeling of ERN is provided in section 3. Our ERN model is applied to support collaborative business which is discussed in the section 4. In section 5, we present a case study and relationship visualization works. Finally the conclusion and future work are given in section 6.

2. Related Work

To build a stable and reasonable social network, there are some points should be considered. (Holroyd, P. 1983) examined the general characteristics of networks and the factors which influence their stability. (Junhua Ding et al., 2011) extended a high level Petri nets with channels for formally modeling social networks.

Some methods are useful to build an employee social network. (DiMicco, J.M. et al., 2009) designed a social network site to support employees within an enterprise in communicating with each other through personal and professional sharing. (Jin Cao et al., 2013) combined the organization graph and the social interaction graph to analyze and model user interaction in enterprise social networks. (Kohout, J. et al.,

2013) introduced an algorithm for social network graphs clustering, which can be applied in ERN. (Dong Liu et al., 2013) used an expert finding model to carry on the influence analysis. (Bennett, S. 2012) gave the benefits of communicating and collaborating in a real-time enterprise social network.

Social network analysis (SNA) has been a hot topic and provided many algorithms for us to apply in ERN. (Jamali, M. et al., 2006) presented a state of the art survey of the works done on social network analysis ranging from pure mathematical analyses in graphs to analyzing the social networks in semantic Web.

3. Enterprise Relationship Network Definition

Definition 1 (ERN): enterprise relationship network.   An ERN is a social structure made up of a set of entities and a set of the relationships ties between these entities. We propose a hypergraph-based hierarchical model to support ERN.

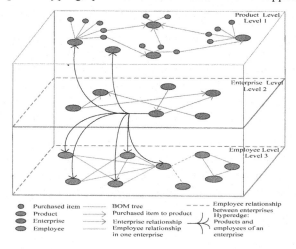

Figure 1. *Hypergraph-based Hierarchical ERN Model*

Definition 2 (ENTG): enterprise graph. ENTG = (ENT, E). ENTG is a directed enterprise graph. ENT is the enterprise node collection of the graph. E is the edge collection. A directed edge in E is a relationship from an enterprise to its partner.

Definition 3 (EMPG): employee graph. EMPG = (EMP, E). EMPG is an undirected employee social graph. EMP is the employee node collection of the graph. E is the edge collection. An undirected edge in E is a social relationship between two employees.

Definition 4 (PROG): product graph. PROG = (PRO, PUR, F, E). PROG is a combination of BOM (Bill of Material) trees and a directed graph. PRO is the product collection and PUR is the purchased item collection. F is a forest of BOM trees. E is the edge collection. A directed edge in E means that the source of a purchased item is a product from another enterprise.

Definition 5 (TLHG): the three-level hypergraph. TLHG = (ENT, EMP, PRO, H). TLHG is a directed hypergraph. H is the hyperedge collection. A directed hyperedge in H is from an enterprise to a collection composed of subsets of ENT, EMP and PRO. A hyperedge in TLHG means that an enterprise has some employees in EMP and products in PRO.

Definition 6 (BUS): business. BUS = (ENTG, EMPG, PROG, TLHG, B). BUS is a group of edges of the four graphs with some parameters. B is the business collection. A business in B is an edge collection composed of subsets of E(ENTG), E(EMPG), E(PROG) and E(TLHG). Though BUS may be an incomplete business process, it can link all the factors in part of the business process, through which we could describe the business clearly.

4. Supporting Collaborative Business

We can get a lot of valuable information and applications on the base of ERN, which are extremely promising in the enterprise management and industrial innovation. We can do more deeply work in the following directions to support collaborative business.

Business Analyzing. The information in ERN provides the original data for analyzing the business of one or some enterprises, e.g., we could find out all the suppliers of an enterprise through the supply relationships. Then the sub-tier suppliers are easy to get after one more traversal.

Application based on ERN. Many applications are developed to manage the business relationships such as Customer Relationship Management (CRM) and Supplier Relationship Management (SRM). ERN is good at collecting and describing business relationships so that it's more effective and simple to develop such applications. An important part of ERN is employee social network, which makes it possible to collaborate with colleagues in one enterprise and employees in other enterprises with restrictions to guarantee security and privacy.

Recommendation. Recommendation is always a commercial appreciation service for its effect of advertisement. In ERN we can master the information of every enterprise, product and business process, which can be used to run analysis algorithms to recommend enterprise, product or service to target enterprises.

Data Mining. We can analyze the ERN data in a way similar to SNA and big data analysis to get more valuable information. SNA and big data analysis have been widely studied and become more mature gradually.

5. Case Study

5.1. *Generating Dataset*

In this section, we introduce a case study based on Shandong Cloud Manufacturing Service Platform (SDCMSP). We made a dataset trying to simulate the real situation. In this dataset, we just consider one kind of relationship, the supply-purchase relationship. We simulated one thousand enterprise entities, based on which we made 5009 business relationships, 14438 products and 52013 purchased items.

5.2. *Relationship Virtualization*

Relationship visualization becomes quite necessary for people to understand and deeply analyze the data in ERN. We carried out some primary data visualization work. Figure 2 is the picture of relationships from suppliers to purchasers. The grey disks are enterprises and the directed edges are relationships from suppliers to purchasers. The ten core red enterprises are extremely obvious to find. Figure 3 is links between purchased items of a purchaser and products of its suppliers, which helps to understand the source of the parts of an enterprise's products. The biggest red disk is the purchaser. The smaller red disks are the suppliers. The upper green disks are the products of the purchaser for producing and selling. The lower green disks are the products of the suppliers. The black disks are the purchased items of the purchaser. And the purple edges are the links. The red path goes through products and purchased items from an enterprise to another.

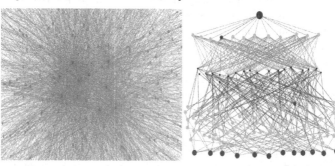

Figure 2. *Enterprise graph*   **Figure 3.** *Product graph*

6. Conclusions

In this paper we proposed a new definition of enterprise relationship network and gave the analysis of the characteristics and differences with other social networks. Then we built a model to explain the ERN like other social networks, but our model is composed by ENTG, EMPG, PROG and TLHG. ERN has broad application prospects to support collaborative business. Furthermore, we introduced a case study on SDCMSP with a simulated dataset. We achieved some relationship visualization and social analytics results based on this dataset.

Our plans for future work include to continue investigating the analytics and visualization technologies on ERN and to develop suitable means for enterprises to leverage to get advantages over the competitors. Moreover, with the increasing amount of enterprises involved in ERN and more applications based on ERN being developed, the problems of security and privacy are unavoidable, which will be a valuable topic.

7. References

Bennett, S., "The benefits of communicating and collaborating in a real-time enterprise social network," *Professional Communication Conference (IPCC), 2012 IEEE International*, pp.1-4, 8-10 October 2012.

Capuano, N.; Gaeta, M.; Orciuoli, F.; Ritrovato, P., "Semantic Web Fostering Enterprise 2.0," *Complex, Intelligent and Software Intensive Systems (CISIS), 2010 International Conference on*, pp.1087-1092, 15-18 February 2010.

DiMicco, J.M.; Geyer, W.; Millen, D.R.; Dugan, C.; Brownholtz, B., "People Sensemaking and Relationship Building on an Enterprise Social Network Site," *System Sciences, 2009. HICSS '09. 42nd Hawaii International Conference on*, pp.1-10, 5-8 January 2009.

Dong Liu; Li Wang; Jianhua Zheng; Ke Ning; Liang-Jie Zhang, "Influence Analysis Based Expert Finding Model and Its Applications in Enterprise Social Network," *Services Computing (SCC), 2013 IEEE International Conference on*, pp.368-375, June 28, 2013-July 3, 2013.

Holroyd, P., "Applications of network theory to social systems," *Physical Science, Measurement and Instrumentation, Management and Education - Reviews, IEE Proceedings A*, vol.130, no.5, pp.273-280, July 1983.

Jamali, M.; Abolhassani, H., "Different Aspects of Social Network Analysis," *Web Intelligence, 2006. WI 2006. IEEE/WIC/ACM International Conference on*, pp.66-72, 18-22 December 2006.

Jin Cao; Hongyu Gao; Li, L.E.; Friedman, B., "Enterprise social network analysis and modeling: A tale of two graphs," *INFOCOM, 2013 Proceedings IEEE*, pp.2382-2390, 14-19 April 2013.

Junhua Ding; Cruz, I.; ChengCheng Li, "A formal model for building a social network," *Service Operations, Logistics, and Informatics (SOLI), 2011 IEEE International Conference on*, pp.237-242, 10-12 July 2011.

Kohout, J.; Neruda, R., "Two-Phase Genetic Algorithm for Social Network Graphs Clustering," *Advanced Information Networking and Applications Workshops (WAINA), 2013 27th International Conference on*, pp.197-202, 25-28 March 2013.

Wikipedia. 2013. Social Network. http://en.wikipedia.org/wiki/Social_Network.

Analysing Internet of Things to Feed Internet of Knowledge

Support Decision-Making in Crisis Context

Alexandre Sirko — Sébastien Truptil — Anne-Marie Barthe-Delanoë
Frédérick Bénaben

Université de Toulouse, Mines ALBI
Campus Jarlard, 81000 Albi, France
Alexandre.sirko@mines-albi.fr
Sebastien.truptil@mines-albi.fr
Anne-marie.barthe@mines-albi.fr
Frederick.benaben@mines-albi.fr

ABSTRACT. *This article aims at presenting ambitious objectives of information collection in crisis context. Among these objectives, there is (i) the gathering of the most diverse possible data, (ii) the semantization of these data into information, (iii) the trust establishment upon these information and their sources, and (iv) the interpretation and aggregation. These objectives are all rolled into only one tool, able to adapt itself dynamically over runtime. The tool developed into these research works would enable to automatically and continuously model a subset of the world as it is evolving in order to monitor some crisis risks and during a crisis follow the main indicators that represent this crisis.*

KEYWORDS: *Trust Establishment, Complex Event Processing, Open Data, Big Data and Data Mining.*

1. Introduction

Swiftness to analyze a crisis is a key point in order to solve or at least reduce such a situation. A simple decision can completely change a crisis. If, in critical situations, it takes too long to decide to evacuate people, it can have very serious consequences.

This is why the collection of data and their interpretations into understandable information or indicators is so critical. Being able to observe the world directly as it is and not being dependent of information that is coming from the operation areas of crisis should be a real asset in crisis management.

The research subject aims to link two actors:

– those who generate data or spend time to gather data;

– those who use these data to make decisions.

The goal is to develop a bridge between the Internet of Things (IoT) (Atzori et al., 2010) and Internet of Knowledge (IoK). By aggregating data, it is possible to generate and so to monitor some complex indicators. But this project is not built in order to just make a statistical analysis of available data. The collection and semantization of data are tasks of equal importance in future research works.

The number of sensors that surround us is continuously growing. In addition, recent policies of public data are turning more and more towards "Open Data" (for example: "data.gouv.fr" is a platform for diffusion of public data, it is a mission under the authority of the Prime Minister of France). Finally, individuals generate more and more information, primarily via social networks. These three elements allow us affirming that there is a mass of data available. Such data need to be found, understood (or interpreted) and used.

2. Main Issues

A major problem in the extraction of data is linked to the heterogeneity of formats, providers, sources etc. The heterogeneity of data format implies two main issues and the very first of these issues lies in extracting data. There are already many techniques available to extract data from different data structure, andeach method has their advantages and weaknesses. And each of these methods is usually dedicated to a specific kind of data. The main methods are: languages for wrapper development, HTML-aware tools, NLP-based tools or ontology-based tools (Laender et al., 2002). The second issue is related to the use of data from different sources. It is impossible to ensure on a semantic point of view that data are equivalent, but in addition, it is also difficult to have confidence in these data.

The last idea highlights the problematic of trust. In any information system, the trust is really important because the system relies on information. In the most common systems, information is reliable because it comes from stakeholders. In this research project, data sources and interpretation rules evolve dynamically during the runtime. It is why it is imperative to evaluate the "trust level" of anything inputted into the system (data, data sources, interpretation rules, etc.). The idea hidden behind the concept of "trust level" refers to the trust establishment (Abdul-Rahman and Hailes, 1997).

The tool has to be designed to be flexible(IEEE, 1990); in fact, it is impossible to guess all sources and all behaviours that may exist during the design in order to take them into account during the runtime. The tool must be able to accept that resources evolve over time (adding new data sources, questioning trust on related data, writing new aggregation rules, etc.).

Interpretation of the data is a delicate point of this research project. This step aims to aggregate data with low added values into information with higher added values. These information with higher added values can be, for example, some indicators to monitor a critical crisis point of view. Aggregating data is somewhat similar to the Complex Event Processing (CEP - Etzion and Niblett, 2010). It is important to let the possibility to create new rules of aggregation while the tool is in use to allow the consideration of new way of interpreting data (to respect flexibility aspect). But it is also primordial to have a time reliable process.

Lately, innovations have shown us that information technology evolves really quickly, so quickly that it is impossible to build a tool that will be used without making continuous updates. Therefore, the whole project has to be design asanarchitecture with some pre-existing tools that can be modified, exchanged or completed by users.

3. Our Proposal within Four Components

In order to build the bridge between IoT and IoK, we suggest a 3-step method: (i) extracting raw data through Internet, (ii) reconciliating and validating these data with the aim of consolidating the usable set of data and, finally, (iii) transforming, associating, aggregating data within the goal of building knowledge.

But these only 3 steps don't take into account any concept of continuous improvement. In this research project, continuous improvement is mainly build with trust establishment ideas. It is why a fourth component is required; this component should be dedicated to monitor the 3 previously described steps, allowing them to evolve through the runtime.

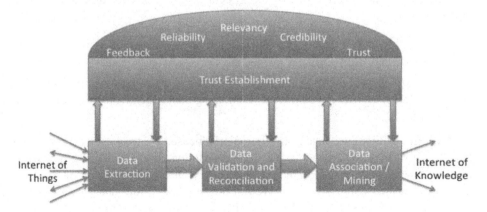

Figure 1. *From the Data of Things to the Data of Knowledge*

Data extraction: This is the first component directly in relation with the rest of the world. Accordingly to this, the data extraction is the component that will be in charge of format heterogeneity issues. Therefore, this component should be in charge of extracting data from heterogeneous sources with different formats, different units and on different subjects. From the extracted data, it should encapsulate all these information in a chosen format to send it to the next component.

Note that, in Figure 1, some of the input arrows of "Data Extraction" block are oriented outwardly. This choice was made to symbolize the fact that some data may be listened (listening emitted events) while other data must be extracted from where there are stored (the Open Data portals have to be queried).

Data validation and reconciliation: The main goal of this component is to transform characterized data (coming from the previous component) into information with a higher level of credibility (explained later). This step is primarily thought for consolidating the set of usable data.

For example, if several data on temperatures are received at the same time and if there are coming from the same place with equivalent values then it this component should emit information of temperature on this area and referring to this period. The value of the temperature should be a weighted average of previous values and weightings could depend on the different trust level.

Data association/mining: This component generates high added value information. It uses consolidated sets of data (generated by the previous step).

To generate these high added values, data must be transformed, associated, compared, aggregated, etc. Each of these manipulation should be described in a specific place, allowing the rest of the system to reuse, modify of evaluate these manipulation.

Many really interesting features can correspond to these requirements in the field of CEP (Etzion and Niblett, 2010).

Trust establishment: This component, the main on, allows to improvement the whole process by monitoring and comparing data behaviour through each component.

Majority of literature made on this topic is focused on trust establishment in a peer-to-peer network context(Marti and Garcia-Molina, 2005). This kind of analysis aims in highlighting trustable node in the network; in addition, they know the type and the format of data circulating through the network. In our analysis, we would like to analyse the credibility of manipulated data and the credibility of how there are manipulated.

In our proposal, we introduce some vocabulary to specify and detail the idea of mixing concept of trust and semantization of heterogeneous data:

– *Trust:* it refers to authors and/or providers of data, it expresses if information sources can be trusted. The whole process described above depends on data sources; therefore the main vulnerability of this system is the quality of inputted information.

– *Credibility:* it is the character of something that can be believed; therefore, it represents the possibility to trust one single data.

– *Relevancy:* it refers to a certain usage of a data on a specific topic. A relevant data is appropriate to be used in a particular calculation. It is possible to split the relevancy into two different aspects: semantic and technical. For example: to calculate an temperature average on certain area, it is necessary to use values that represent the idea of temperature (semantic aspect) and these values must be made approximately in the specified area (technical aspect).

– *Reliability:* it refers to the possibility, in some situation, to have errors in calculations or in extraction of data. Taking into account the reliability of data sources allows taking into account the risks to generate and propagate errors.

– *Feedback:* it is the first true concept allowing the continuous improvement. By inputting past and true information in the system, the feedback process could update the 4 previous concepts. The feedback is a tool dedicated to re-evaluate trust, credibility, relevancy and reliability.

4. Conclusions

This article presents some ambitious objectives on a research project aiming to collect information about the world through the Internet of Things. It tries to highlight the main issues of such a project and then offer some short definitions of required concepts.

This is a presentation on an early research project, this means that definitions given above need to be completed and developed. In addition, a Use Case could give a better idea to how the described concepts should work together.

But the ambitious goals involve having ambitious perspectives. How might look like the crisis detection if it were possible to have a tool, in real time, monitoring key factors of the crisis? What look like a crisis if at any time we could have a fair idea of what is happening? It is why a clear definition of KPI that could be monitored thanks to the data gathering and aggregating is also a strong perspective as a future work.

5. References

Abdul-Rahman, A., Hailes, S., 1997. "A Distributed Trust Model". Presented at the *Proceedings of the 1997 workshop on New security paradigms*, pp.48-60.

Atzori, L., Iera, A., Morabito, G., 2010. "The Internet of Things: A survey". *Comput. Netw.* pp.2787-2805.

data.gouv.fr [WWW Document], n.d. URL http://www.data.gouv.fr/fr (accessed 1.27.14).

Etzion, O., Niblett, P., 2010. *Event Processing in Action 1st*. Manning Publications Co. Greenwich, CT, USA.

IEEE, 1990. *IEEE Standard Glossary of Software Engineering Terminology*.

Laender, A.H.F., Ribeiro-Neto, B.A., da Silva, A.S., Teixeira, J.S., 2002. "A Brief Survey of Web Data Extraction Tools". *ACM SIGMOD Rec.* 84–93.

Marti, S., Garcia-Molina, H., 2005. "Taxonomy of trust: Categorizing P2P reputation systems". *Comput. Netw.*

On the Interoperability in Marine Pollution Disaster Management

Virginia Nicolescu* — Mitrut Caraivan** — Gheorghe Solomon***
Victor Ciupina**

* Romanian Maritime Training Center CERONAV, Constanța, Romania
69A Pescarilor Street, 900581 Constanța, Romania
virginianicolescu@ceronav.ro

** Ovidius University of Constanța, Romania
124 Mamaia Blvd., 900527 Constanța, Romania
caraivanmitrut@gmail.com
vciupina@univ-ovidius.ro

*** Politehnica University of Bucharest, Romania
313 Splaiul Independentei, 900527 Constanța, Romania
ghe.solomon@gmail.com

ABSTRACT. The frequency of maritime disasters and also their effects during the last years draws considerable attention from decision makers in communities and governments. Disaster management requires the collaboration of several management organizations resulting heterogeneous systems. Interoperability of these systems is fundamental in order to assure effective collaboration between different organizations. This paper proposes to improve a reference model of interoperability in the case of a marine pollution disaster management system using Enterprise Architecture Principles.

KEYWORDS: Interoperability, Disaster Management, Enterprise Architecture.

1. Introduction

The natural disaster following the explosion of BP Deepwater Horizon offshore oil-drilling rig in the Gulf of Mexico has raised questions more than ever about the safety of mankind's offshore oil-quests. For three months in 2010 almost 5 million barrels of crude oil formed the largest accidental marine oil spill in the history of petroleum industry. The frequency of maritime disasters and their effects appear to have dramatically increased during the last century (Eshghi et al., 2008). This fact along with the more and more often necessity of underwater instrumentation systems in offshore oil-drilling industry, nearby well-heads and well control operations issued the idea of deploying multi-purpose underwater sensor networks along-side with oil companies' offshore operations.

2. Interoperability Frameworks

Interoperability plays a pivotal role in enabling collaboration among disaster management organizations in order to reduce the effects of disasters and the loss of property and human life (Kapucu et al., 2010). Research efforts in the exploration of offshore resources have increased during the last decades, thus contributing to greater global interest in the area of underwater technologies. Underwater sensor networks are going to become in the nearby future the background infrastructure for applications which will enable geological prospection, pollution monitoring and oceanographic data collection. Furthermore, these data collection networks could in fact improve offshore exploration control by replacing on-site instrumentation data systems used today in the oil-industry system nearby well heads or in well control operations. Therefore, our study is trying to show the collateral benefits of deploying such underwater sensor networks by addressing state-of-the-art ideas and enterprise architecture principles compliance for possible interoperability of different applications such as military surveillance of coastal areas and disaster prevention systems using the same underwater sensors hardware (Caraivan et al., 2013). All of the above in order to justify the biggest challenge of development: the cost of implementation.

Gottschalk (2009) defines interoperability as an "ability of diverse systems and organizations to work together". An interoperability framework is a set of concepts, standards and guidelines that are helpful for different systems to interact with each other. Disaster management requires multiple agencies to work together, and information needs to change rapidly as the disaster event evolves. There are several interoperability frameworks, although most only differ in their terminologies, assigning different names to the same concepts. The European Interoperability Framework (EIF) was designed to guide e-government services development to ensure interoperability among governments throughout Europe (EIF, 2004). Loos et al. (2011) propose an interoperability framework based on three interoperability concepts: Business, Process and Information Systems. The last refers to the conditions of the successful exchange of information between entities which include the compatibility of applications, data representation semantics and hardware infrastructure. Software communication protocols are the next step of our study for underwater sensor network data transmission to onshore facilities, which is likely to include secure data transmission over TCP/IP satellite communication, where available.

Another interoperability framework was defined by Chen D., 2006, having three dimensions: barriers to interoperability, enterprise levels and interoperability approaches. The barriers refer to the packaging and transmission mechanisms for data, as well as semantics (the ability of two parties to agree on the meaning of data). Different approaches can be used: a common format which all parties shall agree upon (integrated approach), a Meta-model format at a Meta level which allows the mapping of all under-level models (unified approach) or a federated-approach, which doesn't have a common model, but the parties must share their ontologies in order for all other to understand the meaning of the data.

3. Underwater Sensor Networks around Offshore Structures

While offshore constructions' number grows, we should be able to implement auxiliary systems that allow us to better understand and protect the ocean surface we are building on. These devices can also be used as a very diverse sensor-based solution for biological wide-area map tracking, pollution monitoring and seismic investigations.

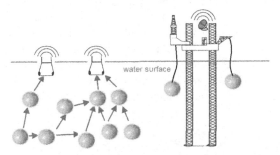

Figure 1. *Underwater sensor network deployment around jack-up rig*

Our approach will be a hybrid system, like the one in Figure 1 that will incorporate both tethered sensors and wireless acoustic, where absolutely no other solution can be implemented. Although, there are no routinely operational underwater sensor networks, their development is imminent (Heidemann et al., 2012). Both the vehicle technology and the sensor technology are mature enough nowadays to motivate the idea of underwater sensor networks. We are using PerrySlingsby Triton XLS and XLR models for the ROV, which are available in the Black Sea area. While having in mind the desire for deploying such networks on a large scale, we can only think for a test bed and beforehand any real-life situation, we are validating our models through simulation scenarios (Figure 2), using a VMAX-PerrySlingsby Remote Operated Vehicle Simulator (Caraivan et al., 2013).

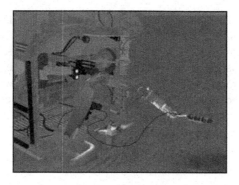

Figure 2. *Triton XLX in Remote Operated Vehicle (ROV) simulation scenario*

Also, we developed a common standard easy-to-use device framework for all multi-purpose underwater sensors, which is modular in order to accommodate various sensors for future use. Marine operations and stranded locations make this modular approach best-suited for application development, providing the maintenance characteristics needed for prolonged use. The buoyancy capabilities and pressure dissipation characteristics needed for a stand-alone device launched at sea leaded to an almost spherical model. The sensors devices modelled in 3D have drawers that allow different electronic component modules to be fitted inside modular layers. On the same modular approach we designed a pollution detection sensor model fitted with an aperture membrane, as it can be seen in Figure 3.

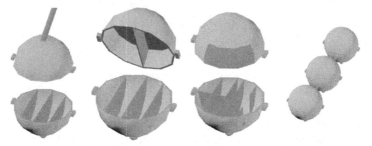

Figure 3. *Sensor devices modelled in 3D based upon common modular framework*

4. Enterprise Architecture Principles

Enterprise Architecture Frameworks usually aim at providing a complete set of tools, methods and models to be used and provide logical structure, as well as ways to manage complexity. The Enterprise Architecture Principles as a fundamental part of the Enterprise Architecture Framework are derived from industry best practice and constitute a basic reference point for every IT project. The principles are mapped to the architectural layers of Business, Application and Technology or cross-cutting concerns such as Security, Environment and "The Internet of Things" concept. In the following, we will try to document how the implementation of an underwater sensor network in the Black Sea area can comply with most of these strategies:

– *Business Architecture and Processes: Innovation for competitive advantage and productivity* is a goal that can be accomplished by the development of the common modular framework for all underwater sensors deployable by ROV means. *Business Priority* and *Benefit Optimisation* in regards of *Partnership* is achieved by using the same network node for more than one application, which can be essential for cost-wise analysis and moreover, this modular compatibility can improve the financial desirability of any future projects.

– *Information/Data Architecture: Business Authority* ensure there is a designated business owner for the information. Integrity is improved and maintenance is simplified. *Ensure Data Integrity* and *Data Classification* should be done by software encryption, as different classes of data need to be managed, stored and protected accordingly.

– *Security:* Security should not be compromised by the release of network diagrams, nor system specifications. Geological prospections of marine areas are of highly strategic importance to a national level, therefore data should be organized and managed to maximise and also protect its value.

– *Application Architecture:* modular components that implement services induce resilience and flexibility, performance and scalability are improved by minimising interdependencies, all covered by our common modular framework.

– *Service-Oriented Architecture (SOA): Design for Reuse and Interoperability, Keep Error Conditions Private* limits the direct impact of errors and decouples the service consumers, thus avoiding the *cascading errors* syndrome. Also, each sensor can *Address a Distinct Problem,* which ensures that the services are self-contained and independent to the whole network.

– *Environmental/Green IT:* Ensure infrastructure is sized appropriately to meet the non-functional requirements and allow for predictable growth. We can think at browser-based applications which are easier to deploy and manage. Thin client reduces the need for client-side hardware resources. Also, efficient use of hardware resources is needed in order to reduce energy consumption. When tethering is possible, our Safe-Nets can use external power supply coming from offshore structures.

– *Technology: Adopt and Enforce Standards* it's a must. We must formally adopt technical standards and any non-compliance needs to be justified and explained. Standardisation helps achieve economies of scale, reduces complexity and improves flexibility.

5. Conclusions

This paper presents an approach to integrate underwater sensor networks and a proposed common framework model for multi-purpose disaster monitoring devices. We have expanded our previous studies and linked to the higher level of disaster management and systems interoperability point of view. We consider that a Meta-level common format model approach according to Chen's interoperability framework is best suited for our needs, as different disaster management systems in Romania use data links far apart from each other. One of the first integration approaches of all systems was in fact a pre-requisite of European integration process prior to year 2007 when the Special Telecommunications Services implemented 112 unique emergency number services. This Meta-level common format model of interpreting data, including our underwater sensor networks, should be explained in disaster management joint exercises events. Seismic monitoring centre located on the Black Sea coast line could be also included in the loop. Last, but not least, the collaborative network for disaster management has to be implemented to all levels in disaster management-related agencies by Government by precise laws.

6. References

Caraivan M.C., Dache V., Sgarciu V., "Common Framework Model for Multi-purpose Underwater Data Collection Devices Deployed with Remotely Operated Vehicles", *7th IEEE International Conference on Intelligent Data Acquisition and Advanced Computing Systems: Technology and Applications*, IDAACS'2013 Berlin, Germany, September 2013.

Chen, D., "Framework for enterprise interoperability", *IFAC Ei2N Workshop on Interoperability for Enterprise Software and Applications*, pp.77-88, 2006.

EIF, "European interoperability framework for panEuropean egovernment services", *IDA working document*, version 2, 2004.

Eshghi, K., Larson, R.C., "Disasters: lessons from the past 105 years", *Disaster prevention and management*, vol. 17, pp.62-82, 2008.

Gottschalk, P., "Maturity levels for interoperability in digital government", *Government Information Quarterly*, vol. 26, pp.75-81, 2009.

Heidemann, J., Stojanovic, M., Zorzi, M., "Underwater sensor networks: applications, advances and challenges", *Philosophical Transactions of The Royal Society A*, pp.158-175, Royal Society Publishing, London, 2012.

Kapucu, N., Arslan, T., Demiroz, F., "Collaborative emergency management and national emergency management network", *Disaster Prevention And Management*, vol. 19, pp.452-468, 2010.

Loos, P., Werth, D., Balzert, S., Burkhart, T., Kamper, S., *Handbook of research in enterprise systems*, book in response to Kumar, S., Esteves, J. and Bendoly, E., *Handbook of research in enterprise systems*, 2011.

A Framework for Characterizing Collaborative Networks of Organizations

A. Montarnal* — X. Fernandez* — J. Lamothe* — F. Galasso*
C. Thierry** — F. Bénaben* — M. Lauras*

*Mines Albi, University of Toulouse
Campus Jarlard, Route de Teillet, 81000 Albi, France
{aurelie.montarnal, xenia.fernandez, jacques.lamothe, francois.galasso,
frederick.benaben, matthieu.lauras}@mines-albi.fr

**IRIT/ADRIA, University of Toulouse 2 Le Mirail
5, allée Machado, 31058 Toulouse, France

ABSTRACT. *In recent decades the exchanges between organizations have evolved with the emergence of new information technologies. Informatization has allowed fast and reliable data exchange and thus closer relationships between organizations. In this paper a new framework is proposed to characterize these collaborative networks of organizations oriented towards three axes of study including the concepts of sharing between the partners, of governance and of perspective of the collaboration. This paper explores the different types of collaborative networks that are commonly used.*

KEYWORDS: *Collaboration, Networks of Organizations, Virtual Enterprise, Framework.*

1. Introduction

Since the 70's Collaborative Networks of Organizations (CNO) have been evolving from workshops to inter organizational relationships (Camarinha-Matos and Afsarmanesh, 2005). This growth has largely been supported by the massive utilization of Electronic Data Interchange (EDI) these last decades. This paper focuses on the different types of networks of organization which are commonly used in order to provide a large vision of their characteristics and usage contexts. Based on a literature review oriented on three axes of study, a new framework is proposed for characterizing these collaborative networks according to the degree of sharing between the partners, the topology and the perspective of the network.

2. Characterization of Collaborative Networks of Organizations

2.1. *Three Axes of Study*

In (Camarinha-Matos et al., 1998), Camarinha-Matos characterizes a CNO through 4 terms:

– *duration*: long or short term;

– *geometry*: internal behaviour, exclusivity or many alliances for a partner and fixed (e.g., little variation among the partners) or dynamic structure;

– *visibility*: which partners can be seen by another partner;

– *coordination*: which structure is used between the partners.

Based on these characteristics, this paper proposes a new framework which aims to describe CNO through three axes oriented towards the management of the network and the reasons of its creations: (i) the intensity or degree of sharing between the partners, (ii) the network management topology, and (iii) the perspective of the CNO.

2.1.1. *Degree of Sharing*

The degree of sharing in a CNO is what the partners decide to have in common when working together. In the literature different words can characterize this degree (see Figure 1):

– *Communication*: (Touzi, 2007) defines communication as a data exchange.

– *Coordination*: (Camarinha-Matos et al., 2009) describes a coordinate network in which activities are executed in predefined order to reach a specific goal. In the same vision, (Dameron, 2003) refers to coordination as a way 'to order parts according to a logical plan'. The author insists on the fact that the coordination is static and does not take place as an action. Finally (Touzi, 2007) writes that it is 'sharing and synchronizing tasks'.

– *Cooperation*: (Camarinha-Matos et al., 2009) mentions an autonomous work from each partner of the CNO that have their own objectives, with a leading entity, but also a sharing of the resources, in order to create a final product or service.

– *Collaboration*: it is hardly distinguishable from cooperation and authors have generally different point of view. On the one hand (Touzi, 2007) does not make any difference between the two terms, and already evokes a sharing of the objectives between the participants of the cooperation. On the other hand, (Camarinha-Matos et al., 2009) makes a clear difference and the objectives are only shared in a collaboration. (Rose, 2004) argues that tasks are independent in a cooperation, and coordination is used to gather them into a final result. (Dillenbourg, 1996) considers that collaboration comes along with the permanent interaction between partners, but is not totally independent of cooperation in the sense that two partners working with the same resources will instinctively distribute sub tasks in order to work more effectively.

– *Fusion*: as (Touzi, 2007) mentions the term of integration, (Bénaben, 2012) evokes the fusion as 'the affiliation of the partners to the same entity'. Including the previous levels, it also adds a common structure and leads to the term of interoperability, that means help interactions in the CNO. (Konstantas, 2006) says that interoperability is the "capacity of different systems to interact with each other without having to implement specific efforts".

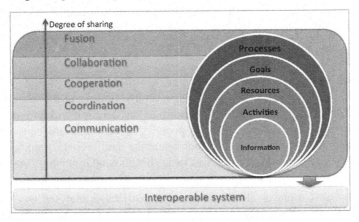

Figure 1. *Overview of the different degrees of sharing, inspired by (Bénaben, 2012)*

2.1.2. Network Management Topology

With the evolution of such communities of organizations comes the necessity of the management of the network. This part of the paper focuses on giving a relevant and the most exhaustive possible list concerning the topologies of management of CNOs in the literature, from strong hierarchical to democratic networks. Here an organization is considered as a node and a network as a graph.

Stadtler (Stadtler, 2005) depicts the famous House of Supply Chain Management (SCM) whose roof relies on two pillars "integration decision" and "coordination decision". The first one consists of the choice of the structure given to the CN that allows organizations working together (e.g., which partners and relationships between them). The second one focuses on the flows within the CNO (e.g. information, materials, etc.). Based on these two pillars, the topology axe is particularly interesting since it presents a decision regarding the management of the network. The Table 1 details the main characteristics concerning the CNO topologies.

	P2P	Chain-like	Star-like	Grid-like
One to all interaction	Yes	No	No	No
All at equals level	Yes	Yes	No	No
Integration decision	None	None	To the facilitators	To the facilitators
Coordination decision	None	Partially to all	To the facilitators	Of a group: to the facilitator Inter-groups: to all of the facilitators

Table 1. *Summary of the main characteristics for each topology*

– *Peer-to-peer*: Each node can interact with the others without any hierarchy. The power of decision is equally shared between the nodes and there is no particular forms of "integration decision" or "coordination decision" in the network and responsibilities are distributed. Peer-to-peer (P2P) networks are considered to be rare because they often emerge spontaneously and do not require a global management : each node knows its own tasks to achieve (Goranson, 1999; Karvonen et al., 2005; Katzy et al., 2005).

– *Chain-like*: Croom et al. (Croom et al., 2000) have analysed the literature on supply chain: the chain-like topology can be associated to the supply chain management. Its definition could be the following: a coordinated system in which partners are ordered depending on information, service or materials transfers, to the end customer (e.g., to achieve a specific final goal) (Ellram, 1991; Kopczak, 1997; Lee and Billington, 1993; Tan, 2001). Consequently the "coordination decision" process exists to define the order of organizations appearance during the collaboration but no organization takes the decision: coordinated parts are managed by each organization for its own needs and finally constitute a global chronological chain of tasks.

– *Star-like*: An organization is in the centre of the collaboration and sets the exchange standards and rules to comply. This topology is rather used in a fixed structure with long term customer/supplier relationships where the collaborative project require a strong "coordination decision". Interactions are exclusively established between the supervisor and the partners. Both "integration decision" and "coordination decision" are managed by the central entity.

– *Grid-like*: Zhu (Zhu, 2006) defines this topology as follows: each node can interact with its neighbour nodes, moreover nodes are gathered into groups that are supervised by a facilitator and a node can only be part of one group. If a node needs to interact with another node that is not its neighbour, it should pass through its facilitator. For each group the facilitator makes the "coordination decisions", it is up to all the facilitators to take "integration decisions" and global "coordination decisions".

2.1.3. *Perspective of the Network*

When choosing the type of CNO it is obviously important to know its perspective. This characteristic depends on the duration and the goal of the CNO and can be divided into three levels:

– *One project goal*: (Camarinha-Matos et al., 1998) depicts short-term alliances established for a project. They are organizations "made for single business opportunity" and "dissolved at the end of such process". In (Camarinha-Matos and Afsarmanesh, 2008) Camarinha and Afsarmanesh mention the term 'Grasping-opportunity driven CNOs', which correspond to a collaborative system as an answer to a specific and unique business opportunity. The network is designed once for the entire project life.

– *Program goal*: The same authors in (Camarinha-Matos and Afsarmanesh, 2008) use 'Goal-oriented networks' to describe a mid-term CNO where partners have precise and clearly defined roles. The CNO is dedicated to the program which can be product or project oriented. The program life consists of a repeated loop of a pre-established project structure with a known end.

– *Program flow*: (Camarinha-Matos and Afsarmanesh, 2008) depicts long-term agreements on a set of potential partners, that can be quickly configured as soon as a new type of opportunity emerge. It results in a series of projects or programs, each adapted to a type of opportunity.

3. Conclusions

A new framework for characterizing inter-organizational relationships has been proposed through three dimensions, based on a literature review.

After having characterized the work between organizations, it would be very interesting to study each organization behaviour and contributions within the network. Concretely one of the main issues when creating a collaborative network is the selection of the partners. This step is divided into two parts: (1) How to describe the advantages and disadvantages of an organization within a network? (2) How to evaluate the global performance of the network, which means of the set of chosen partners?

4. References

Bénaben, F., Conception de Systèmes d'Information de Médiation pour la prise en charge de l'Intéropérabilité dans les Collaborations d'Organisations, 2012.

Camarinha-Matos, L.M., Afsarmanesh, H., "Collaborative networks: A new scientific discipline". *J. Intell. Manuf.* 16, 2005, pp.439-452.

Camarinha-Matos, L.M., Afsarmanesh, H., "Classes of Collaborative Networks", in: Putnik, G.D., Cunha, M.M. (eds.), *Encyclopedia of Networked and Virtual Oragnization.* Hershey, New York, 2008, pp.193-198.

Camarinha-Matos, L.M., Afsarmanesh, H., Galeano, N., Molina, A., "Collaborative networked organizations – Concepts and practice in manufacturing enterprises". *Comput. Ind. Eng.* 57, 2009, pp.46-60.

Camarinha-Matos, L.M., Afsarmanesh, H., Garita, C., Lima, C., "Towards an architecture for virtual enterprises". *J. Intell. Manuf.* 9, 1998, pp.189-199.

Croom, S., Romano, P., Giannakis, M., "Supply chain management: an analytical framework for critical literature review". *Eur. J. Purch. Supply Manag.* 6, 2000, pp.67-83.

Dameron, S., Structuration de la coopération au sein d'équipes projet, 2003.

Dillenbourg, P., "Some technical implications of distributed cognition on the design on interactive learning environments". *J. Artif. Intell. Educ.* 7, 1996, pp.161-180.

Ellram, L.M., "Supply-Chain Management: The Industrial Organisation Perspective". *Int. J. Phys. Distrib. Logist. Manag.* 21, 1991, pp.13-22.

Goranson, H.T., *The Agile Virtual Enterprise: Cases, Metrics, Tools.* Greenwood Publishing Group, 1999.

Karvonen, I., Salkari, I., Ollus, M., "Characterizing Virtual Organizations and Their Management", in: Camarinha-Matos, L.M., Afsarmanesh, H., Ortiz, A. (eds.), *Collaborative Networks and Their Breeding Environments, IFIP – The International Federation for Information Processing.* Springer US, 2005, pp.193-204.

Katzy, B., Zhang, C., Löh, H., "Reference Models for Virtual Organisations", in: Camarinha-Matos, L.M., Afsarmanesh, H., Ollus, M. (eds.), *Virtual Organizations.* Springer US, 2005, pp.45-58.

Konstantas, D., *Interoperability of Enterprise Software and Applications.* Springer, 2006.

Kopczak, L.R., "Logistics Partnerships and Supply Chain Restructuring: Survey Results from the U.S. Computer Industry". *Prod. Oper. Manag.* 6, 1997, pp.226-247.

Lee, H.L., Billington, C., "Material Management in Decentralized Supply Chains". *Oper. Res.* 41, 1993, pp.835-847.

Rose, B., "Proposition d'un référentiel support à la conception collaborative: CO\$^2\$MED (COllaborative COnflict Management in Engineering Design), Prototype logiciel dans le cadre du projet IPPOP". Université Henri Poincaré-Nancy I, 2004.

Stadtler, H., *Supply chain management and advanced planning: concepts, models, software and case studies; with 56 tables.* Springer, Berlin; Heidelberg [u.a.], 2005.

Tan, K.C., "A framework of supply chain management literature". *Eur. J. Purch. Supply Manag.* 7, 2001, pp.39-48.

Touzi, J., Aide à la conception de Système d'Information Collaboratif, support de l'interopérabilité des entreprises, 2007.

Zhu, Q., "Topologies of agents interactions in knowledge intensive multi-agent systems for networked information services". *Adv. Eng. Inform.* 20, 2006, pp.31-45.

Index of Authors

CPSIA information can be obtained at www.ICGtesting.com
Printed in the USA
BVOW09*0331171214

379730BV00002B/4/P

9 781848 217997